Villa-Lobos and Modernism

Villa-Lobos and Modernism
The Apotheosis of Cannibal Music

Ricardo Averbach

LEXINGTON BOOKS
Lanham • Boulder • New York • London

Published by Lexington Books
An imprint of The Rowman & Littlefield Publishing Group, Inc.
4501 Forbes Boulevard, Suite 200, Lanham, Maryland 20706
www.rowman.com

86-90 Paul Street, London EC2A 4NE

Copyright © 2022 by The Rowman & Littlefield Publishing Group, Inc.

© 2022 Succession H. Matisse / Artists Rights Society (ARS), New York

All rights reserved. No part of this book may be reproduced in any form or by any electronic or mechanical means, including information storage and retrieval systems, without written permission from the publisher, except by a reviewer who may quote passages in a review.

British Library Cataloguing in Publication Information Available

Library of Congress Cataloging-in-Publication Data

Names: Averbach, Ricardo, author.
Title: Villa-Lobos and modernism : the apotheosis of cannibal music / Ricardo Averbach.
Description: Lanham : Lexington Books, 2022. | Includes bibliographical references and index.
Identifiers: LCCN 2022015425 (print) | LCCN 2022015426 (ebook) | ISBN 9781666911350 (cloth) | ISBN 9781666911374 (pbk.) | ISBN 9781666911367 (ebook)
Subjects: LCSH: Villa-Lobos, Heitor—Criticism and interpretation. | Music—Brazil—20th century—History and criticism. | Modernism (Music)—Brazil.
Classification: LCC ML410.V76 A94 2022 (print) | LCC ML410.V76 (ebook) | DDC 780.981—dc23/eng/20220331
LC record available at https://lccn.loc.gov/2022015425
LC ebook record available at https://lccn.loc.gov/2022015426

*To Fernando, my father,
the last of the Mohicans*

Contents

	Acknowledgments	ix
	Preface	xi
Chapter 1	The Anthropophagic Aesthetic	1
Chapter 2	Villa-Lobos, The "Cannibal Who Wore Tails"	37
Chapter 3	The Sad Clowns of Carnival: Polichinelo and Petrushka	69
Chapter 4	Taking Flight with Two Ballet Birds: Uirapuru and Firebird	85
Chapter 5	Dissecting Uirapuru	103
Chapter 6	Breaking Treaties: *Amazonas* and *Le Sacre du Printemps*	141
Chapter 7	Diving into the *Amazonas*	163
Chapter 8	Toward a New Assessment of Villa-Lobos	205
Chapter 9	Villa-Lobos, The Surrealist	239
Appendix 1	The Anthropophagous Manifesto: An Annotated Translation	289
Appendix 2	Glossary of Musical Terminology	343

Bibliography	349
Index	369
About the Author	377

Acknowledgments

Writing a book of this nature has been a major challenge, as I ventured for the first time in such type of endeavor. As foremost a performer, I thought many times about Brahms's statement when attempting to write his first symphony—referring to Beethoven, he said: "You don't know what it means to the likes of us when we hear his footsteps behind us." In the same way, I tried to follow on the footsteps of remarkable texts about Villa-Lobos written before this manuscript.

I have received support from many scholars and intellectuals for the formulation of the theories developed, and it would be difficult to list all them. Yet, it is important to mention the guidance given by my colleague Thomas George Caracas Garcia, and the discussions with Gênese Andrade, Kenneth David Jackson, Antoine Chareyre, Paulo de Tarso Salles, Maria Alice Volpe, Augusto Massi, and Anderson Freitas. Miami University allowed me one semester of research leave, and I would like to recognize the grants received from the College of Creative Arts and the Office for the Advancement of Research & Scholarship, my participation in a scholarly publishing workshop through the Humanities Center, and the support of the Miami University Libraries.

Among the wide bibliography researched, two sources deserve special mention: the outstanding study about Villa-Lobos's compositional process conducted by Paulo de Tarso Salles, who graciously allowed me to quote some of his musical examples, and the dissertation about the Anthropophagous Manifesto by Ana Beatriz Azevedo. The Villa-Lobos Museum in Rio de

Janeiro and Pedro Belchior were essential in providing numerous research resources, while Raphael Pinheiro and the Academia Brasileira de Letras provided materials about the Brazilian poet Manuel Bandeira.

I am indebted to the publishers who allowed me to quote musical examples, particularly Universal Editions (Vienna) and Hal Leonard/Europe, as well as the Academia Brasileira de Música, responsible for the rights over Villa-Lobos music. The photographers Gordon Heard and Dianes Marcelino allowed me to reprint their photographs, while the Museu de la Música de Barcelona provided the photograph of the violinophone. Raphael Dias's talent is displayed in the cover of the book. Tarcilinha do Amaral allowed me to reproduce the beautiful painting *Abaporu*, by her aunt Tarsila do Amaral.

The text benefited from editing insights by Kelly Waldrop, Gene McGarry, and William McKenna. Max Liber produced a number of musical examples using music notation software. My gratitude goes to Courtney Morales and Lexington Books for their support and commitment to this publication. My wife, Silvia, as always, stood by my side, giving me valuable insights about the text, and my son Peter produced some of the illustrations. Together with my other son, Andrew, they witnessed numerous periods of intense concentration in detriment of everything else.

Preface

This book started from a curious observation. When I conducted the world premiere recording of *Amazonas* by Villa-Lobos over thirty years ago, it was paired with *Uirapuru*, which made perfect sense, since the two compositions have similar instrumentation and were considered "sister compositions written as a pair," according to Lisa Peppercorn. Not having any interpretation that could serve as reference, I was concerned about the responsibility of such a recording, so I tried to learn as much as possible about the two compositions through the literature available, such as the Peppercorn studies, since she was one of the first Villa-Lobos scholars of international reputation.

As a doctoral student, I was under Stravinsky's spell, involved in a performance of Petrushka, and knowing that the early ballet trilogy by Stravinsky were the most influential compositions that propelled twentieth-century music into modernism. Considering that *Uirapuru* and *Amazonas* were also ballets, apparently written in 1917—a little after the tour of the Ballets Russes to Brazil—I made a connection: *Uirapuru*, the story of a magic bird, and *Amazonas*, a composition that "broke composition treaties," must have been the Brazilian response to *Firebird* and *Rite of Spring*. As to *Petroushka*, a composition initially thought for the piano, it had to be connected with *Polichinelo*, from 1918. And according to Lisa Peppercorn, the young composer played cello in the orchestra that accompanied the Ballets Russes! I was excited to observe that while there were articles indicating that Stravinsky influenced Villa-Lobos, nobody made this connection explicit . . .

However, my subsequent findings demonstrated that the progression of developments was different, and that previous scholarship on Villa-Lobos led to a distorted view about his accomplishments, which remain inaccurate in most circles. Despite having left Brazil many years ago, his music remained what connects me most with my country, in spite of the distance. It gave me the desire to leave something that reflects my love for music and the way I think about it; after all, when writing about a composer we admire and love, we are infusing the writing with our own autobiography.

I learned that Villa-Lobos was much more than a composer who employed folklore to write nationalistic music. This connection with folklore obscures the fact that he went beyond, and became a precursor in creating a bridge between classical and Brazilian popular music, and not only folk music, thus anticipating what many composers are trying to achieve today. His other accomplishments also deserve to be disclosed and his music to be more widely performed.

In order to come up with some of the controversial ideas described in the text, I used a holistic analytical approach to supplement the traditional tools. While I think that such an approach is important no matter the style of music studied, it is essential when addressing modernism. That was a time when artists were exploring the sinesthesic relation of the senses in the entanglement of the arts, while scientists were in search for unified theories. The combination of insights from anthropology, sociology, philosophy, mathematics, and other fields allowed for the emergence of original ideas in terms of musical form as a flexible process for the manipulation of time, the use of the Fibonacci series for aesthetic purposes, a conceptualization of the arrow of time as it functions in music, as well as an original approach to musical spacetime.

Most of the past studies about Villa-Lobos used a Eurocentric approach, and only recently Brazilian musicologists started to focus on the anthropophagic nature of his style, producing a new evaluation and understanding of his musical contributions. The starting point for a new study of Villa-Lobos requires a substantial comprehension of the meaning of cultural cannibalism. Incidentally, "cannibalism" should not be confused with "anthropophagy," and Oswald de Andrade established a marked difference between the two terms.[1] However, for the purposes of this study, the two terms are used interchangeably.

In addition to the notion of sealed identities, anthropophagy broke with the notion of evolution and progress originating from a deterministic and linear idea of time, which normally produces the hierarchical assimilation of the subaltern and the repression of its values. The overvaluation of a hierarchy associated with technical prowess and the notion of civilization imposes on peripheral civilizations a view that they are eternally backward and do not have the possibility of being original. It was against this position that anthropophagy reacted, proposing a new understanding of the movement of history, a movement that crosses the evolutionary flow and returns to the beginning, to the "matriarchy of Pindorama," mentioned in the Anthropophagous Manifesto.

Anthropophagy became a central reference in cultural studies that refer to Latin America and the Caribbean, particularly within literature, and now, music. It became the foundation for academic debates on hybridity and postcolonialism. This approach took the present study to unexpected directions, such as the conclusion that Villa-Lobos's modernist style is essentially surrealist, something that might be challenged by musicologists. Others will contest the position that the dating of Villa-Lobos's compositions is not particularly relevant in an aesthetic that advocates for the abrogation of time.

In parallel with outstanding artistic achievements, major composers presented human flaws. I don't consider necessary to address such less-than-positive aspects of Villa-Lobos's trajectory in a text that has the goal to rescue his most important contributions. His collaboration with the Vargas dictatorship, his messianic and conservative view of the role of music education, and his characterization as "unreliable narrator" about his life and work are of no interest to me, except for the picturesque aspects that make him a typical personality of that time in history. He became a mythological figure who embodies the Brazilian spirit, full of contradictions, and whose life turned into a carnival song.[2] Life would be too boring without people like him.

Since a large number of bibliographical sources were in other languages, most of the translations in this manuscript are mine, except when noted. They were done in a way so as to convey as close as possible the meaning of the original text, without necessarily adhering closely to a literal translation. Tables, musical examples, and figures created by others received their proper attribution.

As a performer for several decades, I am sensitive to the issue of copyrights. The renowned Brazilian intellectual Millôr Fernandes would tell the story of an occasion when he was present at a party given by a military general. Upon learning of Millôr's presence, the general approached him and asked: "So, you are the famous humorist Millôr Fernandes? Tell me a joke!" Millôr replied: "Only if you fire a cannon for me!"

In the same way that copyrights need to be respected, the principle of "fair use" was created to promote the advance of knowledge and freedom of expression by permitting the unlicensed use of copyright-protected works in certain circumstances. *Every effort has been made to trace copyright holders and to obtain their permission for the use of copyright material.* This became my full-time job for an extensive period of time close to the end of the publication process. In the same way that copyrights should be respected, serious scholarly efforts done with integrity should also be recognized, and publishers should not impose unreasonable barriers to a scholarly publication.

One aspect that was not developed in this text is the Afro-Brazilian contribution to Villa-Lobos's music. This is something important, that would deserve a separate study dealing exclusively with this aspect of his output, its originality, and its relationship with modernity. The richness of the Brazilian composer's life and the legacy of his art remain an inexhaustible source of inspiration for scholars and interpreters, reflected in the inner contradictions of his wisdom: "Artists live with God—but give their little finger to the devil. I sleep with the angels and dream of the devil."[3]

Notes

1. Anthropophagy is a ritual of incorporation of alterities through exocannibalism, while cannibalism is the eating of human flesh by hunger, without being associated with a ritual.

2. In fact, Villa-Lobos's life is the subject of not one, but two glorious *samba-enredos* (samba-plots) of top samba schools in the carnival of Rio de Janeiro: Mangueira (*Exaltação a Villa-Lobos*, 1966) and Mocidade Independente (*Villa-Lobos e a Apoteose Brasileira*, 1999). In 2009 the samba school Pimpolhos da Grande Rio created a third samba-enredo, with the title *Carnaval das Crianças Brasileiras de Heitor Villa-Lobos*.

3. Villa-Lobos quote taken from Ralph Gustafson, "Villa-Lobos and the Man-Eating Flower: A Memoir," 1.

CHAPTER ONE

The Anthropophagic Aesthetic

Je est un autre. —Arthur Rimbaud[1]

The beginning of the twentieth century brought radical changes in human thought, reflected in a European aesthetic that valued, above all else, new discoveries and the search for artistic originality. Ezra Pound's dictum "Make it new" became the motto of modernism, an artistic movement that reshaped the vision of the entire century.

This new vision promoted a reconciliation of the arts and sciences, both of which sought within their respective parameters a deeper investigation of the nature of reality. Advances in science led to a break with the past as classical physics was replaced by new concepts, including the theory of relativity and quantum mechanics. The arts likewise experienced a rupture of tradition as classical art was challenged by multiple new aesthetics.

These multiple aesthetics were the product of a concurrent evolution in all fields of knowledge that incorporated the great technological and scientific advances of the period and generated a profound impact on the way in which Western civilization came to perceive the manifestation of "artistic truth" and authenticity of expression. As humans are highly visual beings, visual artists played a fundamental role in evoking visionary images that corresponded to revolutionary discoveries in the field of science since the end of the nineteenth century. This is how the great artistic styles of that period emerged—impressionism, expressionism, Fauvism, Dadaism, primitivism, surrealism, cubism, neoclassicism, and several others. As a result, modernism in Europe was characterized by a multiplicity of cultural trends that rejected Enlightenment thinking in the face of the emergence of a fully industrialized world.

Conscious of their unique situation, Brazilian intellectuals saw themselves as "*mestizos*," artists who were inventing new forms of expression in a postcolonial era that emerged in the wake of the horrors of the First World War. Their attitude of renewal drove their search for the roots of a nationalist art that would combine the cultures of the Portuguese colonizers, native indigenous Brazilians, and African slaves.

Standing on the periphery of the multiple modernist manifestations in Europe, the Brazilian Anthropophagy movement did not deny European values in its search for an original nationalist form of expression. Instead, Cultural Cannibalism embodied a newly generated idea of hybridism, carrying a flag that migrated from the aesthetic to the sociopolitical realm. Contemporary theories such as the concept of "cultural hybridism" developed by Néstor García Canclini contributed as effective analytical instruments for explaining the process of the modernization of Latin America.[2] Therefore, the validation of cultural anthropophagy as a legitimate aesthetic posture is essential for an evaluation of the contributions of Brazilian art toward modernism. While European modernism fragmented into multiple manifestations such as primitivism, futurism, cubism, surrealism, and others, Cannibalism became the driving force that united the diverse array of artistic manifestations in Brazil of the modern era: "Cannibalism alone unites us. Socially. Economically. Philosophically."[3] Without such awareness, Brazilian art would be in danger of being considered purely derivative, or it would remain the victim of a more serious type of prejudice directed against a culture excluded from the Western European canon. Once Anthropophagy is recognized as a self-conscious cultural manifestation, a reevaluation of Heitor Villa-Lobos's contributions becomes necessary, providing a new, compelling assessment of his legacy as a composer.

The Advent of Brazilian Modernism

The first relevant modern aesthetic to migrate to Brazil was futurism. Brazilian modernism lacked the rich tradition of European culture, so at least in its initial phase, it made sense for the movement to turn to the future to justify its existence, rather than focusing on a reaction to the past. In 1912, the poet Oswald de Andrade and the painter Anita Malfatti became acquainted with the Futurist Manifesto and its author, Filippo Tomasso Marinetti, in Paris and sympathized with the fresh commitment of literature to the new technical civilization that celebrated speed, machinery, violence, youth, and industry.[4] As a writer, Oswald de Andrade, who would become the father of Anthropophagy, identified with the ideal of combating academicism, marked by a rupture with decadent literary styles such as parnassianism and symbolism, in an attempt to create a new language free of syntax, punctuation, and meter that was geared toward free expression.

The first signs of modernism in the plastic arts in Brazil appeared in 1917. In a solo exhibit, the painter Anita Malfatti introduced European and North American modern influences into her expressionist style. According to the Grove online, "her formal innovations, including Cubist planar distortions, a vibrant high-color palette, and forceful drawing, were deemed unintelligible"[5] and were a source of controversy among those adhering to the more traditionalist academic tastes of the time. But it was the Modern Art Week of 1922 that marked the true advent of modernism in Brazil. As the nation was celebrating the centennial of its independence from Portuguese colonizers, the Modern Art Week brought together Brazilian artists from multiple fields who created some of the most avant-garde works ever seen in the country.

The events took place in the Municipal Theater in São Paulo and included plastic arts exhibits, lectures, concerts, and poetry readings. Among the initiators and organizers were the painters Emiliano Di Cavalcanti and Anita Malfatti, plus the poets Oswald de Andrade and Mario de Andrade (although the two shared the same surname, they were not related). Prior to 1922, São Paulo had been a prosperous city but relatively unimportant in cultural terms. In previous decades, it had been growing economically due to the coffee boom and the influx of immigrants to the city. The economic conditions and increase in population spurred the modernization of the city, as reflected in developments in architecture, public transport, and the technological progress associated with industrialization. This climate generated an enthusiasm for progress and for all things new, and cosmopolitan intellectual groups that opposed cultural elites created the conditions for the Modern Art Week.

At that time, Brazilian artists were visiting Europe and exploring artistic trends from abroad, most notably Paris, gaining experience that they incorporated into their own uniquely Brazilian works upon their return. Scholars tend to detect particularly the influence of futurism, Dadaism, and surrealism in the Brazilian artistic production of this period, in works characterized by boldness and exaggeration associated with an anarchic nature.[6]

The Modern Art Week made São Paulo a new center for the arts, as opposed to the more traditional and conservative Rio de Janeiro, capital of the country and site of the Academia Brasileira de Letras (Brazilian Academy of

Letters), inspired by the Académie Française. The young modernists of São Paulo adopted an experimentalism that rejected the strict conservatism of the Academy, invoking a heightened consciousness of the social problems and political currents within Brazil. The tension between São Paulo, the economic center of the country, and Rio de Janeiro, the "marvelous city" that maintained the glamour of the past long after it lost its status as the country's capital, still exists today.

The only member of the Brazilian Academy of Letters to participate in the Modern Art Week was Graça Aranha, who opened the event with a conference titled "The Aesthetic Emotion in Modern Art." As a result, he was ostracized by his academic colleagues. Besides representatives from the plastic arts and literature, the Modern Art Week included musicians, among whom Villa-Lobos was the most prominent representative—another visitor from Rio de Janeiro, like Graça Aranha himself. This demonstrates the importance of Villa-Lobos within the framework of conceptualization of modernism in the country; after all, he participated as a composer since the early manifestations of the movement.

After the Modern Art Week, the preoccupation of the younger generation with its revolt against the artistic past gave way to an intense debate within the movement over the meaning of the modernist ideology.[7] The aesthetic focus of this ideology was concentrated on the relationship between painting and literature, while music was sidelined because it was associated with greater abstraction. The importance of Villa-Lobos's participation in the Modern Art Week is that it made him better known outside of Rio de Janeiro and among major music critics, particularly Oscar Guanabarino, who criticized the modernism of the carioca composer for displaying "a reprehensible departure from the principle of beauty in music."[8]

The debate, which continued for the next eight years, drew participants from all over Brazil, each of them pretending to lead the movement toward a meaningful artistic orientation and to supply it with a definition of the true national themes. The most significant moment in the debate was the confrontation between two groups, the *anthropophagi*, or "cannibals," and the *verdeamarelos*.[9]

Verdeamarelismo is usually translated as "The Green-Yellow Movement," after the two prominent colors in the Brazilian flag. The group was founded by Menotti del Picchia, Cassiano Ricardo, and Plínio Salgado in 1926, and their main characteristic was a rejection of foreign influences in their desire to affirm a "purely Brazilian" form of art. In 1927, new orientations led to the conversion of the *verdemarelismo* into the Grupo da Anta (the Tapir Group), symbolized by the figure of the tapir, a creature that "makes its way through the forest" looking neither to left nor right, a custom that the Tupi-Guarani Amerindian culture interprets as "the absence of prejudice." The movement thus made it clear that the type of nationalism it advocated was subjective, sentimental, and religious.

The *verdeamarelists* proposed a "return to the past," considered as the depository of the true traditions of the country. They perceived in the peaceful nature of the masses the soul of nationality, to be guided by the country's political-intellectual elites. They defended national borders against foreign cultural influences, and their discourse was characterized by *ufanismo*—a boastful nationalism that combines a patriotic exaltation of the country with hostility toward foreign origins and influences.

The second school of thought to emerge from the Modern Art Week was the Anthropophagic movement, the product of the interaction of the so-called Group of Five, a party of influential painters and writers associated with Brazilian modernism that included Anita Malfatti, Tarsila do Amaral,[10] Menotti Del Picchia,[11] Oswald de Andrade, and Mario de Andrade. While Malfatti and Amaral were painters, their three male counterparts were poets and writers. The members of the Group of Five worked together from approximately 1922 until 1929, a collaborative interval during their respective careers.

According to Oswald de Andrade, the discovery of primitivism was the foremost achievement of the Modern Art Week.[12] It marked the origin of the path of evolution that culminated in the Anthropophagic movement. In 1923, one year after the Modern Art Week, both Oswald de Andrade and Villa-Lobos were in Paris, and their distance from their homeland allowed them to develop a greater awareness of "brazilianness," a phenomenon that impregnated the works of most modern artists of the time who were under the spell of the Modern Art Week. A number of authors agree that many artists, such as Oswald de Andrade, Tarsila do Amaral, and Villa-Lobos, "rediscovered" Brazil through their trips abroad, complemented by their travels inside the country that allowed them to get a more direct contact with folk culture.[13] Upon returning to Brazil in 1924, Oswald de Andrade formulated the *Manifesto da Poesia Pau-Brasil* (Manifesto of Brazilwood Poetry),[14] a statement based on a critical review of the past and written in the same year as Breton's First Surrealist Manifesto. It called for a renewal of language, making it less erudite and more colloquial, more primitive. Oswald advocated for a poetry that was naïve, original, and spontaneous, in the sense that it was not contaminated by preestablished rules for thinking and making art. In the Brazilwood Manifesto, he encouraged Brazilians to direct their efforts toward the reality of the country, in an attempt to create, from the inside out, a new nationalistic view that would replace the stereotyped and prejudiced opinion of Brazilian art as inferior.

In the Brazilwood Manifesto, Oswald de Andrade declared that the original task of the modernist movement had been accomplished. The attack on the older generation succeeded in setting right the imperial clock of the national literature. This stage having been achieved, the problem became a different one: to become regional and pure in its era. "Modernism thus would remain an art movement tuned to the sensibilities of the twentieth century, but at the same time it would have to be on the lookout for new national values."[15]

The values that Oswald de Andrade had in mind were those he considered in opposition to the conventional European cultural heritage. The manifesto put it this way, in its aphoristic style:

> The carnival in Rio is the religious event of our race. Brazilwood. Wagner submerges in front of the human lines of Botafogo.
> The savage is ours. The rich ethnic formation. The abundance of plants. The mineral ore. The cooking. The *vatapá*, the gold and the dance.
> All the history of the penetration and the commercial history of America. Brazilwood.
> Against the calamity of the first arriving white who diplomatically dominated the savages of the jungle. Citing Virgil to the Tupiniquins. The *bacharel*.[16]

In this Manifesto, Oswald de Andrade promoted a shift toward the themes of cultural primitivism. He believed that the first moment of contact between the Portuguese adventurers and the Amerindian was a golden age, when the *bandeirantes*[17] brought the traits of the loose European morality of their civilization in the formation of a new Brazilian society. It was from this society that an authentic Brazilian culture originated, a culture that was an alternative to the superficial imitation of the values of the colonizer. However, when the cultivated European came—the one who began citing Virgil to the Amerindian—Brazil was transformed into a "country of anonymous sorrows. Of anonymous doctors. A society of erudite castaways."[18] Thus the book of poems *Pau Brasil* that followed the publication of the manifesto addressed in the beginning the vitality of the early colonizers of Brazil, but the initial enthusiasm cooled down and changed into a tone of irony as he moved closer to the modern period in the poetic description of Brazilian history.

Throughout this process, Oswald de Andrade promoted a "rediscovery" of Brazil, symbolized by his invocation of the tree that gave its name to the country as the organic centerpiece of his manifesto.[19] By exploring the historical and cultural contrasts to which the population was subjected, he attempted to synthesize the erudite and popular sides of culture, the modern and archaic forms of nationalist expression, and a vision of primitivism as imagination and freedom of spirit, culminating in an artistic and cultural renovation based on the primitive roots of the Brazilian people. His poetry humorously decomposed the cultural framework of Brazilian society in order to foster a return to native originality and to refashion it into the ingredient of a national art for export.[20]

In contraposition, *verdeamarelismo* was founded in 1926 by Menotti del Picchia, Cassiano Ricardo, and Plínio Salgado, who challenged the ideas of *Pau Brasil* in an attempt to assume the ideological leadership of the modernist movement in the country. Initially, they called for the integration of nationalism and art through literary bravado and an intimidating attitude. They did not subscribe to Oswald's primitivist orientation, replacing it with a different exaltation of *brazilianism*, one responsible for a new Brazilian race that included the Negro, the Amerindian, the *mameluco*,[21] the Lusitanian, and the immigrants. Their principal line of attack was to accuse Oswald's group of continuing to import avant-garde ideas from Europe.

The emergence of new ideas within the *verdeamarelismo* group led its members to reform as the Grupo da Anta (Tapir Group). The *anta*, or tapir—the totem worshiped by the Tupi Amerindians—was chosen as a symbol for the spiritual independence of Brazil, as suggested by Plínio Salgado as early as March 1927. Ideologically, the Tapir Group did not view nationalism as a matter of adopting Amerindian beliefs, but merely as a symbolic reassertion of Brazilian freedom from Europe by proclaiming Amerindian descent. Since the Amerindian called himself "son of the tapir," the Tapir Group would be breaking with any compromises that linked Brazilians to European prejudices. What made the *anta* a significant turning point in the development of *verdeamarelismo* was Salgado's intention of using the term as a new banner, signaling the shift of his group to the realm of political and social action.

One year later, in 1928, Oswald de Andrade published the Cannibal Manifesto, explaining that "Anthropophagy comes as an immediate successor to Verdeamarelismo and Anta." The manifesto appeared in the newly created *Revista de Antropofagia*, a small eight-page pamphlet, which was published monthly and ran for ten issues between May 1928 and February 1929. In explaining the concept of cannibalism, Oswald clarified that anthropophagy was not a campaign of hate, but rather the admission of the superior qualities of your opponent. Cannibalism was to be understood as a symbolic human act aimed at making the opponents' virtues one's own. Earlier Brazilian generations had not been ready for such a reaction. But now, because of the recent change in the social climate, the opportunity presented itself. That is when the artist steps in: "We, the artists—sensitive seismographs of the psychic change of direction of the masses—we the hyper-aesthetic avant-garde understand it. And we are trying to set it right."[22] Although Oswald de Andrade still left a lot of questions unanswered, he at least promised that Anthropophagy would set an example for the masses.

The Anthropophagy movement was conceived as a platform around which all modernist artists could gather, including the *verdeamarelistas*. In fact, Oswald cited the names of Plínio Salgado, Menotti del Picchia, and Cassiano Ricardo, along with Mario de Andrade and Guilherme de Almeida, as among the founding members of the new group. Out of the three *verdeamarelistas* whom he mentioned, Salgado actually contributed articles on the Tupi Amerindian to the first two issues of the magazine. However, this unity was fragile and only temporary.

The *Revista de Antropofagia*, like most of the modernist magazines, lasted for a short period of time, to which Oswald referred as the "primeira dentição" (first dentition), keeping the humorous tone of anthropophagy as a digestive act. In 1929 he inaugurated the "second dentition" in the form of a weekly page in a São Paulo newspaper. Tarsila do Amaral and Di Cavalcanti contributed illustrations for the articles. The "second dentition" included fifteen issues, and its main message was a call for complete moral liberation, including sexual freedom and liberty of thought. The moral radicalism of the second phase of anthropophagy was complemented by political messages against totalitarian regimes that served as incubators of subversive activities and revolutionary ideas. While conceived initially as a platform welcoming all modernist artists, in this second phase anthropophagy positioned itself diametrically opposite *verdeamarelismo* by pointing out the reactionary nature of the latter.

The economic depression in late 1929 and a major political revolution the following year brought to an end the confrontation between anthropophagy and *verdeamarelismo*. Oswald de Andrade and other anthropophagites moved toward Marxism and joined the Communist Party in 1931. Plínio Salgado migrated to Italian fascism, becoming the leader of a movement called Integralism. While the 1930s witnessed a disillusioned Oswald de Andrade proclaiming his wish to become a foot soldier in the proletarian revolution and denouncing earlier times when he had played the role of clown to the bourgeoisie, the perspective of time allows us to declare today that the Anthropophagy movement had a greater reach and a more forward-looking program than any other in the construction of modernism in Brazil.[23] Throughout the period described, Villa-Lobos, being a musician from Rio de Janeiro, stayed aside from the polemic confrontation between anthropophagy and verdeamarelismo, and only much later have his works been viewed as associated with an anthropophagic aesthetic.

Cultural Cannibalism

While futurism left its mark in the form and literary style of the Anthropophagous Manifesto,[24] its contents were ideologically closer to the surrealism of André Breton, for example in the juxtaposition of elements that apparently had no connections among themselves. The writing style itself recalled the mechanical writing advocated by the surrealists. For De Andrade, "Brazil's greatest strength rested in its ability to 'cannibalize' other cultures by incorporating them, re-appropriating them, and regurgitating them as an entirely new and unique creation."[25] In his manifesto, De Andrade metaphorically cannibalizes figures from fields as diverse as psychology (Freud), literature (Shakespeare), and Portuguese colonialism (Dom João VI). Cultural cannibalism became the Brazilian method of appropriating and transforming cultural models, a form of avant-garde experimentalism, a process where artists consumed select foreign influences and assimilated them within the syncretic and heterogeneous Brazilian culture made up of Portuguese colonizers, native indigenous Brazilians, and African slaves.[26]

In Europe, a number of "isms" characterized the multiple ways artists from all fields sought to express the far-reaching transformations in Western society that came with the rapid growth of cities, the progress of modern industrial societies, and the reaction against Enlightenment thinking and the horrors of the First World War. In Brazil, artists had to find a way to integrate multiple influences—internal and external—in the search for an "authentic" style that would express the Brazilian soul in that particular moment of heightened nationalist awareness. Like most of the European artistic movements of the time, Anthropophagy became a conscious aesthetic movement that brought together the Brazilian artists who already worked within the modernist spirit. Assuming a position of lucidity, they created their own "ism": Cultural Cannibalism, a system or process that provided a sense of cohesion to the pronounced, disparate influences and mosaic-like raw materials that constituted Brazilian art.

> In its original meaning anthropophagy signifies the sacrificial practices common to tribal societies—some of them found in Brazil's indigenous societies, for example—consisting of the ingestion of the flesh of enemies taken prisoner in combat, with the aim of absorbing their strength and powers. The term

was used metaphorically . . . [to express an attitude of] critical assimilation of foreign cultural values [in combination with] internal cultural elements suppressed by the process of colonization.[27]

Notions of cannibalism in Brazil dated since the beginning of the sixteenth century, and the most famous reports include the voyage of the German sailor Hans Staden (published in 1557),[28] the French travelers André Thevet (published in 1557 or 1558) and Jean de Léry (published in 1578),[29] and the writings of the Jesuit missionaries in charge of catechizing the Amerindians. According to Oswald de Andrade, "the (Amer)indian didn't devour due to gluttony, but as a symbolic and magical act, upon which lies his whole understanding about life and man."[30] From this perspective, cultural anthropophagy became a way to inspire a revolt against colonialism without denying the positive qualities of the colonizer. By appropriating these qualities while destroying everything else, and at the same time incorporating the richness of the native culture of Brazil elevated from its perceived inferior condition, the movement aimed to produce a new and modern art, one that would be hybrid and original and that could be exported back to the colonizer, promoting an inversion of values whereby the European colonizer would consume Brazilian art.

The Anthropophagy movement should be viewed as a violent reaction against colonialism. Oswald de Andrade considered catechism the greatest of evils imposed by Europeans over the native Brazilians, the system that brought the repressive political-religious colonial apparatus under which the modern Brazilian civilization was formed—the patriarchal society with its moral standards of conduct, its messianic hopes, and the rhetoric of its intellectuality, which bowed to European aesthetics, stripping the Amerindian from his natural condition. Against the violence imposed by the colonizer, the author advocated for an equally violent reaction, one that would rehabilitate the warrior, avenger, and cannibal Amerindian in the guise of the Brazilian modern artist.

The cannibal's violent reaction would redeem the frustrations of the colonized, his inferiority complex, not by a complete denial of European influence, but by an assimilation of the enemy's qualities through cannibalism. In the process of devouring history, there would be an exchange of roles, an inversion of hierarchies, and a projection of the future when the "technicized barbarian" would come to exist, leading civilization to experience a new golden age.[31] This golden age would not be a retroactive return to the Amerindian past, but a cyclical revival of the same condition, according to the

Nietzschean idea of "eternal return." The golden age had already occurred in the distant past of the country, and its remnants were still present.

> Oswald's was not a plea for ethnic sympathies and Christian compassion. He invoked indigenous values like leisure, fraternity, abundance, sexual freedom, and Edenic life as a revolutionary program for a technified world. He would restore instinct and enchantment to an industrial age.[32]

Oswald de Andrade's conception of anthropophagy is closely associated with the idea of a utopia. For Oswald, the encounter with the primitive world, with the natural man, was the generator of all utopias: "I have the impression that the encounter of the naked humanity of discovery [i.e., the discovery of Brazil and America, which confronted the European with the naked savage] greatly influenced the general movement of the ideas of that historical moment. Knowing that on the other side of the earth there had been a man without sin or redemption, without theology nor hell, would not only produce utopian dreams, but a general upheaval in European consciousness and culture."[33] Besides a reversal of hierarchies, Oswaldian thought brought about a reversal of history ("We already had communism. We already had the surrealist language") and geography ("We made Christ to be born in Bahia"). His ideas are permanently permeated by the sign of a utopian-revolutionary dialectic between a past not only pre-capitalist, but pre-patriarchal, and a future not only socialist, but "matriarchal," a utopia that he defined as "the social phenomenon that makes society move forward . . . at the bottom of each Utopia there is not only a dream, there is also a protest."[34]

Like other artistic movements that preceded it, the Anthropophagy movement was inspired by the visual arts, specifically by the painting *Abaporu* (1928) by Tarsila do Amaral (1886–1973), whose title means "Anthropophagous" in the Tupi-Guarani language of the Brazilian indigenous inhabitants. Considered one of the leading Latin American modernist artists, Tarsila do Amaral was Oswald de Andrade's wife and is regarded as the painter who best reflected the Brazilian aspirations for nationalistic expression in a modern style.[35]

Abaporu depicts a sensual cannibal thinker, a naked savage with a voluminous body and a minuscule head in the same position as the famous 1882 sculpture *Le Penseur* by Auguste Rodin.

> With its diminutive head, the image subverts Rodin's emphasis on intellectual contemplation, however. By drastically distorting the figure's anatomical proportions, Amaral makes the foot as the focal point of the composition instead.

As if performing an exaggerated exercise in illusionistic foreshortening, Amaral painted the foot and hand closest to the bottom edge of the canvas much larger than the head and arm near the top of the frame. Instead of creating the illusion of deep space, Amaral offers a disconcerting effect. Since she rendered the figure in profile, parallel to the picture plane, the viewer expects the upper and lower body to be rendered in similar proportion. Reducing the size of the head and upper torso creates the illusion that the figure is of great size and that the viewer is looking up at it from below. In other words, we are compelled to enter the picture at the base, at ground level.[36]

Figure 1.1. The painting *Abaporu* (1928) by Tarsila do Amaral. It is considered the most valuable painting ever made by a Brazilian artist.
Museum of Latin American Art of Buenos Aires.

As primitivism became one of the most important driving forces of modernism in Europe, the Brazilian cannibal, represented by the Amerindian Tupi[37] people, served as an emblem of the Brazilian artist, a cannibal who devours foreign influences to produce works that promote a critical synthesis between the primitive and the civilized, the modern European and the historic local. "Tupi or not tupi, that is the question" became the motto of the anthropophagous movement. The wordplay reflects the dilemma between returning to the roots of the native Amerindian aesthetic or embracing the Western European aesthetic of the colonizers. It expresses the permanence of the ambivalent relationship of modernism with the "primitive," the desire to reconcile perceived opposites such as the primitive and the civilized, the body and the mind, the national and the foreign, the native and the cosmopolitan, the original and the derivative. In short, in the fight against postcolonial cultural domination, cultural cannibalism would still allow the Brazilian modern artist to absorb relevant elements from the foreign culture, as long as the cannibal artist would also incorporate the national culture,[38] to generate a product of quality not inferior to, but at least on par with the European.

Cultural anthropophagy in Brazil went beyond the creation of a national culture based on the incorporation of folk models into a Western European language. It was a conscious aesthetic procedure based on the "devouring" of imported and local cultures, allowing for the creation of an autonomous Brazilian art. At the same time, cultural anthropophagy was not a negation of European influences in search of a national identity, nor a glorification of native, indigenous, or African values. The movement wanted to assimilate the totality of the cultural reality of the country in order to generate a process of radical transformation. Instead of rejecting European culture, De Andrade championed the "absorption of the sacred enemy. To transform him into a totem."[39] In the course of cannibalizing Western culture, Brazilians adapted its strengths and incorporated them into the native self in a process of fusion, appropriation, and hybridism.

This is what allowed Brazilian modernism to reconcile an admiration of futurism with a strong primitivist orientation, producing what Oswald de Andrade called "technological barbarism." While primitivism was manifested in Western Europe by artists turning to civilizations of Africa and Oceania in search of a new conceptualization of reality, Brazilian artists turned to their backyard—the country's interior—to produce a new art that was at the same time modern, nationalistic, and universal.[40] Brazilian cultural anthropophagy uses primitivism as a way to relate African and indigenous cultures in direct dialogue with Western European culture. In this way, Brazilian primitivism was unique, as observed by Antônio Cândido:

> In Brazil, primitive cultures are mixed with everyday life or are still living reminiscences of a recent past. The terrible darings of a Picasso, a Brancusi, a Max Jacob, a Tristan Tzara were, deep down, more coherent with our cultural heritage than with theirs. Our habit of black fetishism, dolls, ex-votos, [and] folk poetry predisposed us to accept and assimilate artistic processes that in Europe represented a profound rupture with the social environment and spiritual traditions.[41]

Through the ritual of devouring foreign features, primitivists overcame the perceived limitations of Brazil's original culture, considered to be of inferior quality, and locked in a struggle to find its own identity while paralyzed by the imposition of the culture of the European colonizers. It became necessary to assimilate the qualities of the "enemy," the colonizers and imperialists, so as not to produce a derivative product. Rather, anthropophagy became a ritual that transformed the negative dimensions of colonialism and imperialism into something positive; the devouring of foreign influences, juxtaposed with native primitivism, turned into a strategy for cultural emancipation. Through anthropophagy, opposites were diluted: the national and the foreign, the primitive and the modern, the barbarian and the civilized, the derivative and the original. "The Oswaldian intention is clear: to digest the information coming from outside and regurgitate a new, finished product that is original, innovative and Brazilian."[42] In a reverse process, the resultant artworks were expected to influence European models.

Considering the comprehensive character of the anthropophagic style, its resulting aesthetic is often seen as the product of a culture recreated independently, an aesthetic that produced works of art impregnated with dense, profound, and hybrid multicultural characteristics.[43]

> This posture [. . .] allowed him [Oswald de Andrade] to assimilate the foreign experience under the Brazilian species and reinvent it in our terms, including unavoidable local features in the final product, which produced an autonomous character and gave it, at least in principle, the possibility to start functioning in turn as an export product when confronted with the international market.[44]

Brazilian modernism suffered from the same condition present in all South American countries, the need to find a national cultural identity, which frequently led to nationalist ideologies for the creation of an art unsullied by foreign elements. This is a result of the historic condition of these countries, which were economically dominated, first through colonization, and later through the influence of the United States, considered a more advanced country due to its technological prowess. Composers such as Villa-Lobos approached this challenge by turning to national sources—Brazilian folklore and popular music—as the music materials to be incorporated in their compositions, something that most of the European composers also practiced when transposing the cultural identities of their countries into their music. This produced a traditional view that considers Villa-Lobos's music the Brazilian equivalent to European Romanticism brought into the exotic tropical environment of a peripheral culture. However, this view ignores the incorporation of the anthropophagic aesthetics, which allowed Villa-Lobos to develop a highly original and "modern" conception of music, which will be the object of study of the subsequent chapters.

Anthropophagy and Primitivism

The European notion of primitivism is associated with the search for a natural state, the *modus vivendi* of one's ancestors, or the uncontaminated way of life of other non-civilized peoples that do not share the European heritage. In pursuit of the most distant origins of expression, primitivists went beyond the traditional beginnings associated with a Greco-Roman heritage. And while European primitivism is a response to the anxieties generated by the development of technology, it also became linked to the process of colonization during the age of discovery.

Considering that the discovery of primitivism was the greatest achievement of the Modern Art Week of 1922, one should add that this particular primitivism was nationalist, therefore distinct from the primitivism associated with European modernism, which explored mainly the features of the peoples of Africa and Oceania. European primitivism was essentially a *white* and *male* quest for an elusive ideal associated with civilizations that were geographically or chronologically distant, and through their differences constituted alternatives to modern civilization.[45] Brazilian primitivism, on the other hand, is anticolonial and matriarchal-oriented, in the sense that it advocates for the abolition of the main values of the colonizer: the institution of property, the deceitfulness of monogamy, the organization of society into classes, and the sovereignty of the state. The Brazilian primitive was not the "ultimate other," but instead assumed the features of the artists themselves, since through the Anthropophagy movement they were able to identify directly with the Amerindian who lived concomitantly with them. Therefore, the individual pursuit of "alterity" is one of the main characteristics that differentiates European from Latin American primitivism.

One of the major impulses of European primitivism was a "return to first principles through the discovery of some elemental and vitalizing energy observable in preindustrial societies, and particularly in peasant, tribal, and folk repertoires."[46] In other words, it stemmed from man's urge to confront the origins of Western civilization in the search for universal frames of reference that went beyond the traditional Greco-Roman foundations—a desire to return to the historically earliest times in search of fundamental perspectives regarding a new worldview. In the words of Edward Said, "The beginning as primordial asceticism has an obsessive persistence in the mind. . . . Formally, the mind wants to conceive a point in either time or space that marks the beginning of all things."[47]

The problematic of European primitivism is complex, encompassing multiple strands, mainly orientalism, blackness, Native Indianism, and the naiveté associated with the world of the child. The complexity resides in the fact that these strands are interrelated, creating perceived paradoxical associations. Already in the nineteenth century one can observe a tendency among certain European artists to conceive that in the Orient lies "the profound origins of the human race."[48] In contrast, during the 1920s, artists such as Jean Cocteau posited that *art nègre*, rather than a fundamental new impulse, was simply an assimilation to a slightly earlier and contemporary taste for *Japonisme*. Fusion between orientalism and primitivism happened to such an extent that it prompted speculation that even *Scheherazade* was a sort of *art nègre*,[49] and that the costumes and choreography of Stravinsky's *Rite of Spring*, which were associated with prehistoric Russia, were actually redolent of Native American or Caribbean civilizations.[50]

What may appear as a mélange of interpretations was actually the result of an attempt to provide a new orientation and promote fresh perspectives among impulses that are apparently dissimilar. The modernist pursuit of the primitive was not the type of escape from the present found in Romantic exoticism, nor a journey toward the unknown, but an attempt to uncover a new radical vision that was fleeting, due to the multiplicity of viewpoints about elemental origins, and at the same time rigid in its reliance upon mythologies. Underneath the mélange of viewpoints—orientalism, blackness, or Native Indianism—rests the inexorable dichotomy of impulses that accompany most ages: the exotic and the localized, male and female, black and white, local and cosmopolitan, imperialist and native, the noble and the savage, the old and the new, the high and the low. These dichotomies represent the big picture that illuminates the human dilemma of all cultural manifestations, and is naturally intensively explored in the Anthropophagous Manifesto.

As a parenthesis, one should note that for the European, the Orient included India, and this applied particularly to the Spanish and Portuguese navigators who were looking for a sea route in order to better promote the commercialization of Indian commodities. Their concomitant arrival in America led them to denominate as "Indians" the inhabitants of the New World—whom we conveniently denominate as "Amerindians" to avoid confusion—something that already approximates the European view that conjoins primitivism with orientalism.

In the pursuit of the most ancient origins of expression prior to the advent of Western culture, *art nègre* and native indigenous roots emerged as the most promising sources of primitivism: *art nègre*, because it laid no claim to either a European or Oriental lineage, and indigenous lineage because the native could be considered the "ultimate other"—unlike the Asian and the African, "he had been ignored by both the ancient Greco-Roman world and by the Bible."[51] Within this perspective, the Amerindian has been identified as the most exalted species of ancient barbarian. While in the nineteenth century, exoticism initially promoted the noble savage's display of purity, innocence, and natural goodness, the problematic evolved into the postcolonial mentality of Cultural Anthropophagy's identification with the barbarian violence of the cannibal, who possessed a pre-logical mind not corrupted by the catechism of the colonizer and committed the ultimate form of barbarism: the eating of human flesh.

In Brazil, where the modernists were involved in affirming Brazilian identity in the face of an imposed culture, they were not interested in a deeper anthropological interaction with the Amerindians who coexisted with them in historical time. They did not launch a fight for human rights and social justice, but instead used representations of the Amerindian as ways to elucidate elements of themselves in the present. Postcolonial critics have charged that this posture led Brazilian modernists to maintain the Romantic European stance of considering the Amerindian as an exotic alterity of purely ethnic interest: the fact that they live in the same country would not redeem them from treating the Amerindian as the ethnic other. What the critics failed to recognize is that the artistic experience is an authentic venture: In "rediscovering" Brazil and identifying with the Amerindian, the anthropophagous modernists discovered the Amerindians within themselves, turning their aesthetic into a genuine experience.[52] In doing so, Anthropophagy became a duality of sameness and difference mediated by reciprocity.

The brief picture given above would not be complete without the inclusion of a third orientation, which had a lasting impact on the primitivism both of Europe and Latin America. In Western Europe, the third impulse came from surrealism, which plunged into the subconscious as the source of the primary impulse of creation. In Latin America, surrealism assumed the form of a mythologic rite, which in the case of Brazil corresponded to what the European considered the supreme taboo: the anthropophagic ritual. Instead of reaching out to distant shores or primeval origins, Brazilian primitivism explored the mechanisms through which modern society and everyday life were contemporary with ancient rituals. In both European and Latin American counterparts, surrealism became an offshoot of the discoveries of relativism in science and the arts, representing the downfall of the authority of "first times," as time dilation produced the collapse of past and future into the everlasting now.

Criticism of the Anthropophagic Movement

The Anthropophagy movement is considered today a central frame of reference in cultural studies of Latin American and the Caribbean, functioning as a foundation for academic debates on hybridity and colonialism. Yet, due to being on the periphery of Western European cultural movements; due to its violent revolutionary character, which incorporates humor as an instrument of aggressive attack; due to its aphoristic formulation; and due to the amplitude of its reach, which was not limited only to aesthetic aspects, but also included sociological and political aspects, Cultural Anthropophagy continues to be misinterpreted.

The earliest critique of Anthropophagy cited its connection with other avant-garde movements in Europe and contended that the Brazilian movement derived from foreign models. For example, opponents asked whether the Oswaldian Anthropophagy was an imitation of the cannibalism of Picabia or a continuation of the surrealism of Breton. Brazilian scholars such as Benedito Nunes are clear on this point: "Brazilian primitivism does not reissue any of its species [the multiple foreign influences], but absorbs them all, while absorbing at the same time the popular, ethnographic and folk dimensions of Brazilian primitivism."[53] In Antônio Cândido's view, Anthropophagy is a product of the dialectic between the local and the universal, where the Oswaldian view is a new paradigm: "Its way of acting is the devouring not only of foreign techniques and information, but, above all, the rediscovery of all conceptions: the Amerindian (ancestral and modern), the national and the American. In studying these complex relationships with an open mind, he [Oswald de Andrade] incorporates and simultaneously creates a Brazilian 'tradition'—Anthropophagy."[54] According to Carlos Jáuregui, "the metaphor of cannibalism has been not just a paradigm of otherness but also a trope of self-recognition, a model for the incorporation of difference, and a central concept in the definition of Latin American identities."[55] This criticism was also firmly countered by Mário de Andrade and Oswald de Andrade.

Another criticism that comes to mind is the use of anthropophagy as a justification for a form of masked plagiarism, a justification for "borrowing foreign elements" under the guise of creating something apparently new. However, the hybrid character of the anthropophagic product is not analogous to standard practices of emulating, borrowing, and paraphrasing original sources, because the process is substantially more profound and complex. It is exactly its hybridism that brings universality to the anthropophagic product. As Edward Said asserted:

> By linking works to each other we bring them out of the neglect and secondariness to which for all kinds of political and ideological reasons they had previously been condemned. . . . Worldliness is therefore the restoration to such works and interpretations of their place in a global setting, a restoration that can only be accomplished by an appreciation not of some tiny, defensively constituted corner of the world, but of the large, many-windowed house of human culture as a whole.[56]

Some question whether Anthropophagy can be considered a unified movement at all. Scholars such as Carlos Jáuregui, for example, do not consider the Anthropophagy movement to be an academic movement, or a theory of identity formation through consumption, or a social emancipation program. They consider it a heterogeneous and often contradictory aesthetic venture.[57] Antônio Cândido indicated in 1970, "It is difficult to say what exactly anthropophagy is, since Oswald never formulated it, although he left enough elements to see some virtual principles under the aphorisms."[58] In both views, Anthropophagy is an ill-defined movement, with a malleable and constantly transformed meaning. The present study demonstrates that Oswald de Andrade's position about cultural anthropophagy has remained consistent and matured in the 1940s and 1950s, though, as the subsequent section will show, the malleability of the concept allowed it to be reframed as a postmodern phenomenon.

A more valid form of criticism points out Anthropophagy's exclusive reliance on the Amerindian perspective, while completely neglecting the pervasive influence of the African influence brought by the negro slaves. For the anthropophagites, Amerindianism was a means of explaining Brazil's racial miscegenation that elided the Afro-Brazilian contribution to the formation of the nation. Authors such as Doris Sommer draw attention to the fact that in (Amer)Indianist literature, the main protagonists were practically decimated in the formation of the nation, while African slaves—important participants in miscegenation in Brazil—were practically ignored.[59] The same omission happens in the Anthropophagous Manifesto, although Brazilian modern art certainly reserved a place of honor for the African slaves in the anthropophagic banquet.

One of the most common forms of misinterpretation rests in the narrow view of Anthropophagy as an exclusively postcolonial phenomenon. This led some scholars to understand the term *cannibal* to signify any resistance to enslavement, which, while true to a great extent, fails to encompass all the prospective reach of the movement. An important line of criticism proposes to identify "the central contradiction of the Modernist movement: it strives to define a Brazilian identity by incorporating popular speech and indigenous myths, but also seeks to create a cosmopolitan literature for international export. Modernism, in turn, exemplifies the more general paradox of the inherent ambiguity of the colonial and postcolonial situations overall."[60]

Brazilian modernism could not affirm national independence because it reproduces the relationship between the colonizer and the colonized. In other words, this criticism brings up the problem of colonialism and self-representation: Brazilian primitivism in the form of Anthropophagy is criticized for not being genuine. The argument is that most of the Brazilian artists "rediscovered Brazil" in their trips abroad, or through their incursions toward the interior of the country, when they became acquainted with a reality that was not part of their intellectual upbringing.

Villa-Lobos has been one of the targets of this criticism. During his stays in Paris in the 1920s, he benefited from the creation of a mythical image, where he was seen as a combination of the image of the noble primitive savage and the adventurous explorer. As a reincarnation of the noble savage, he embodied—falsely—the image of the Amerindian portrayed in his music. In the Parisian social circles, he was perceived as displaying the typical attributes of the noble savage: naivety, spontaneity, sincerity, and naturalness. And as an adventurous explorer, he embodied—also falsely—the image of the ethnomusicologist who researched the folklore of his country through scientific expeditions. However, this does not necessarily mean that he was an imposter, as his detractors have suggested. As the saying goes, "the wise traveler travels only with imagination."[61] As explained by Anaïs Fléchet, behind the two paradoxical mythical figures of the savage and adventurer, "il est à la fois celui qui découvre et celui que est découvert, celui que revèle et celui qui est révélé"[62] (he is both the one who discovers and the one who is discovered, the one who reveals and the one who is revealed).

Critics question what authorizes a certain individual to represent a group, when even the representation of that individual's own ethnic or national group merits critical examination. This led to the conclusion that the Brazilian modernists continued to look at themselves through "imperial eyes": By representing the Amerindian as themselves, they were in reality continuing to look at the Amerindian as "the Other." Consequently, Anthropophagy would have remained a paradoxical movement: striving to be cosmopolitan while simultaneously seeking to affirm Brazilian national identity, and ultimately embodying the inherent dilemma of aesthetic self-representation in postcolonial Latin America.[63]

The problem with the criticism above is the type of binary thinking that attempts to explain the world from the point of view of Western hegemonic culture. According to the hybrid cultures model developed by Néstor Canclini to explain Latin American modernism, the notion of hybridization goes beyond the dimension of dualistic relationships, such as those between the popular and the cultured; the ludic and the rational; the mythical and the technological; the traditional and the modern; and others.[64] Based on the principle of interculturality and the coexistence of transhistorical temporalities, hybridization denies the binary simplification between pairs of conceptual opposition as model for explaining reality and social dynamics in favor of a perspective that recognizes in the fusion of apparently disparate elements the very essence of this dynamics. The binary posture would block the thinking of the subaltern culture, which is peripheral, preventing the emergence of the heterogeneity of the "Other."[65] The consequence is that the "Other" ends up being constituted as a shadow of itself, where the subordinate culture cannot "speak" but "is spoken" through the voice of the central culture, and thus cannot express the reality of a way of life that occurs in non-European or non-Anglo-American socio-geographical spaces.

However, the plurality of world cultures, and the multiple ways of interaction between them, allows us to conclude that all postcolonial theories that view cross-cultural appropriation as potential exploitation lose validity. The identification of the Brazilian modernist artist with the Amerindian is not purely rhetorical. All art carries an autobiographical impulse, and the identification with the native in the case of the anthropophagite artist sprang from an authentic need to search for the roots of a nationalist culture. In this regard, we can evoke Stockhausen's assertion regarding music:

> If a European is moved by a piece of Indian music, he discovers the Indian within himself. If a Japanese is touched by some European music, he finds within himself a European from the period when this music was born out of the inner pressures of an absolutely specific historical moment.[66]

The artist cannot be penalized for considering valid a crossover between cultures that attempts to dissolve the boundaries between them. As stated by Glenn Watkins, "the current drive to reevaluate Western European history and the willingness of some Americans to flagellate themselves for their genetic connections to Europe and its colonializing attitudes has now led to a joyless discrediting in some quarters of all art and music potentially reflective of such encounters."[67] Anthropophagy emerges as a metaphor of the affirmation of life, not a contradictory venture, but a conflagration of lucidity through the possibility of adopting a more open point of view, in fact, multiple points of view, and not only the one of the colonizer.

Ultimately, the claim of the cannibal artists to primitivism remains their highest achievement, which stands at the heart of the greatest critical assaults against them. In contrast to works such as *Le Sacre du Printemps*, where the authors were attempting to approach mythical scenes from Pagan Russia, or Milhaud's *Creation du Monde*, where the composer went in search of African roots during the chaos that precedes creation, the anthropophagites were not looking to model themselves on the Brazilian Amerindians of yesteryear. They were not pretending to be impersonators in the most general sense of the word. They were originals, cannibals of the modern age. While they may have learned modern techniques and styles from the Europeans, when they were composing, painting, or writing, they were not "importers" or "emulators." They were part of the cultural heritage of their nation. Certainly, for marketing purposes, they may have exploited the idea of the exotic to satisfy the appetite of the Parisian public, as Villa-Lobos did, but at heart they were the genuine article, and their claim to cultural authenticity is the source of their power.

Legacy of the Anthropophagic Movement

As arguably "the most original metacultural reflection produced in Latin America to date," according to Viveiros de Castro,[68] the legacy of the Anthropophagy movement cannot be underestimated. After the Wall Street crash of 1929, followed by the Brazilian Revolution of 1930 that ended Brazil's Old Republic and ultimately installed Getulio Vargas's dictatorial regime, Oswald de Andrade demonstrated discontent with Anthropophagy and disowned his artistic productions up to that moment. He migrated toward the political militancy of his communist ideals, only to return in the mid-1940s with a renewed and more profound philosophical approach to Anthropophagy, geared toward shores that went beyond the aesthetic flag that gave rise to the movement.

Yet Anthropophagy proceeded during the 1930s. Raul Bopp's *Cobra Norato* was published in 1931; Oswald's *Serafim Ponte Grande* was published in 1933. Claude Lévi-Strauss completed his major ethnographic study of Brazilian Amerindians during the period between 1935 and 1939, producing influential materials for the future development of Anthropophagy, mainly in the form of an anthropological study, but his work was also significant for the advance of cultural cannibalism.

In the following decade, Oswald de Andrade returned to Anthropophagy and produced several texts in dialogue with thinkers such as Heidegger, Kierkegaard, Marx, Nietzsche, and Freud, formulating Anthropophagy as a philosophy, and ultimately concluding that it is a venture yet to be fully realized. In 1950 he completed his philosophical treatise, "The Crisis of Messianic Philosophy," and revisited modernist anthropophagy in various monographs in which he imagined the "synthesis" of natural and civilized men in a techno-industrial utopia where machines and technological advances would liberate humanity for creative leisure, love, and happiness, and where metaphysical fears, authoritarian patriarchy, and the state would be replaced with the Pindorama matriarchy.[69] While the beginning of the movement in the 1920s involved a number of collaborators in the *Revista de Antropofagia*, this later theoretico-philosophical enterprise became a solitary venture for him, and his academic style sharply differed from the anarchic discursive nature of the original Anthropophagous Manifesto.

Later in the 1950s, Lévi-Strauss published "The Structural Study of Myth" (1955), *Tristes Tropiques* (published in France in 1955 and in Brazil in 1957), and *Anthropologie Structurale* (1958). In the middle of the 1950s, a group of poets from São Paulo who called themselves Noigandres developed a new aesthetic for so-called concrete poetry,[70] which was highly influenced by Anthropophagy as well as avant-garde movements from Europe. The group included mainly the brothers Haroldo and Augusto de Campos plus Décio Pignatari. The main aesthetic practice of this branch of Brazilian poetry is the composition of the object-poem, in which traditional verse is abolished in favor of a construction that explores sound, visual, and semantic resources while making use of the typographic space and geometric arrangement of words on the page. These concretist poets became some of the most arduous defenders of the Anthropophagy movement.

All of the above developments culminated in the explosion of a new vision of anthropophagy that occurred in the 1960s, with the advent of Tropicália, an original Brazilian aesthetic movement that promoted a complete revitalization of the aesthetic movement postulated by the Anthropophagic Manifesto.

Tropicália, the Second Anthropophagic Movement

Tropicalism, or Tropicália, was a short-lived Brazilian cultural movement of 1968–1969 that nevertheless had great reach and profoundly marked various forms of artistic expression, especially music, but also cinema, theater, poetry, and the plastic arts. Despite the political persecution and censorship promoted by the government during the military dictatorship of the time, the Tropicália movement did not fail to hold important political debates and produce critical readings of Brazilian realities through its multiple forms of expression, as artists used the artifice of allegory as a tool to fight censorship.

The movement attempted to reinterpret Brazil—to rediscover the country, recovering its forgotten values and national symbols and resurfacing unimaginable heroes and neglected themes. The new political and aesthetic discussions generated debates and artistic approaches that renewed the ideals postulated during the Modern Art Week in 1922. At the same time, artists promoted an updating of ideas by incorporating foreign elements in the context of the recent dynamics of the cultural industry, and they anthropophagically exported a "genuinely Brazilian" brand, reproducing the initial proposal of the Anthropophagic Movement of the 1920s.

Characteristics of Tropicália include the proliferation of collages that combine the most disparate and contradictory images without transition between them; a violence aesthetically translated into abrupt contrasts; expression characterized by excess and a parodic language; and the transgressions of limits associated with syncretic and dissonant images. Within the strategy of abrupt montage, the tropicalist artists practiced the juxtaposition of a combination of the most archaic and precarious elements—called the "relics of Brazil" by Gilberto Gil—with hypermodernized elements originated from the technological development.

The movement started with Hélio Oiticica's installation created in 1967 named *Tropicália*, which reflected the spirit of rupture in the arts of the time. The installation, a geometric labyrinth or "penetrable" made with precarious materials that housed sand, plants, gravel, and a parrot, simultaneously recalled the constructivism of the international avant-gardes—with their pure colors and geometric structures—and the poor architecture of the Brazilian *favelas* (slums), especially Mangueira, where Oiticica moved, worked, and took much of his artistic inspiration from. At the end of the installation tour, a television turned on represented both the technological advances and the mass culture that television had come to embody. The phrase "Purity is a myth," which could be read as an inscription appearing on the inside of a penetrable, perfectly synthesized the aesthetic project that would define Tropicalism.

One of the most characteristic features of tropicalist music was the use of the electric guitar, which members of the traditional Brazilian popular music scene resisted as a foreign symbol, an instrument that to some extent would tarnish the originality of Brazilian musical tradition. Among the Tropicália artists, however, the use of amplified instruments and the inclusion of external influences took place in an anthropophagic, critical way, putting Brazilian culture and its references in perspective within the debate on cultural identity, which included the incorporation of the internal influence of Bossa Nova.

For the anthropophagic tropicalist artists, Carmen Miranda became the symbol, the muse that inspired the movement. After all, the artist—who was originally Portuguese and not Brazilian—was the emblem of the anthropophagous technicized barbarian of cinema, who migrated from the Brazilian jungle and ended up as an export product for Hollywood. If the motto of the original Anthropophagy movement was the aphorism "Tupi or not Tupi," the new motto became "It Is Forbidden to Forbid" (*É proibido proibir*), the title of a controversial protest song by Caetano Veloso during the military dictatorship. The song was violently booed by the audience of the Third International Festival of Song, held in Brazil in 1968.[71]

Despite Tropicália's allegorical resources and its great impact on Brazilian music, after a crackdown by the repressive military dictatorship, political persecution intensified in the country, and the climate of tension increased. Some of the main tropicalist artists, including Caetano Veloso, were arrested and later exiled, putting an end to the movement's effervescence. Scholars such as Ismael Xavier consider that Tropicália marked the final stage of modernism in the country, standing at the "threshold of the 'postmodern condition' in Brazil."[72] Despite its internal conflicts and controversies, Tropicália remained an incorporative project, which, unlike avant-garde purism, tended toward the creative incorporation of differences, always with a critical spirit. After a two-year residency in the United States, Hélio Oiticica returned to Brazil in 1972, and retook *antropofagia* by translating to English the original Anthropophagous Manifesto. In the same year, Caetano Veloso and Gilberto Gil returned from exile, and for several scholars this marks the end of the movement. "Tropicalism would end as it had begun: as a desire to inscribe Brazilian culture on the international horizon that would become manifest in an act of interpretive invention designed to rethink and reformulate Brazilian culture in its totality."[73]

In parallel with Tropicália, Lévi-Strauss continued his production of seminal anthropological works, particularly with *Le Totemisme aujourd'hui* and *La Pensée Sauvage* (1962), and *Le Cru et le cuit* (1964), of particular importance for the exploration of the homology between music and myth. In 1967, more than a decade after Oswald's death, with the staging of his play *O Rei da Vela* under the direction of Zé Celso Martinez Correa, Oswald de Andrade "became a new fashion, he caught on fire. Father of tropicalism, inspirer of Caetano [Veloso], example for literary critics, object of study of doctoral dissertations, unconditional hero of the discontented youth, model for beginning writers, favorite author of amateur theater groups. Oswald was suddenly elevated to the level of myth," stated Marília de Andrade, his daughter.[74] The above demonstrates that since its inception, the concept of Cultural Cannibalism has been frequently revisited in the artistic panorama of Brazil. The strategy of anthropophagy remained a central source of reference for the subsequent generations of artists and is manifested until our days, "although these generations cannot be characterized as a common cultural avant-garde movement, as occurred in the case of modernism and tropicalism."[75]

Anthropophagy as a Postmodern Phenomenon

The initial conceptualization of the Anthropophagy movement already included multiple ramifications for the social, political, and economic realms. The revival of Cultural Cannibalism as a postmodern phenomenon sparked the interest of numerous scholars and triggered a natural migration of the concept of consumption to multiple fields of knowledge. According to Jáuregui, "In the 1970s and 1980s the highly influential works of Augusto and Haroldo de Campos in the *Revista* and Andrade's poetry framed the contemporary reception of anthropophagy as a poetic and theoretical proposal equivalent to *transculturation and cultural appropriation* (a modernist antecedent of cultural studies paradoxically anchored in the fine-arts and literary realms)."[76] Anthropophagy became a recurring topic of interest in postmodern studies.

The significance of the anthropophagic program lies in its association of mythical and critical thought. Sebastião Vargas Netto posited:

> It is as a modern myth . . . that we must understand both the technicized matriarchy and the anthropophagic culture, inserted in a utopian horizon and endowed with a sense of universal worldview, not only from a historical perspective, but also from a psychological, existential and aesthetic perspective. The power of the symbol-myth-utopia of the technicized matriarchy and

the Oswaldian anthropophagic culture has the potential to anticipate and prefigure a wide range of sociological, artistic and philosophical proposals and formulations, all with a libertarian basis.[77]

Scholars noticed that since its beginnings, the aesthetic program of Brazilian modernism had included above all a political connotation, as it had an anarchist bias that was nevertheless divorced from the anarchist tradition. By the end of modernism, the movement became above all a political ontology, since in conceiving the undertaking, Oswald de Andrade ended up calling into question the entire political, legal, and economic structure of the West.[78] As a result, anthropophagy has infiltrated many contemporary fields: organizational studies, postcolonial studies, social theory, and other topics, such as environmental education, so important for understanding contemporary challenges related to climate change. According to Kenneth David Jackson,

> The Cannibal Manifesto's very ambivalence, idiosyncrasy, elasticity, and ambiguous language—in 52 aphorisms—have rendered it adaptable to a number of contemporary theoretical and ideological positions, from transculturalism and hybridity to Orientalism, subaltern studies, and even to the internet, described by Patrick Tonks as a "cannibal network."[79]

These aspects are beyond the scope of the current study. However, they open the door for a revision of postcolonial aesthetic theory from an anthropophagic perspective. In addressing the central aspect of the permeability between the original and the hybrid product—its "copy"—the radicalization of this perspective can lead to the argument that Anthropophagy transcends the Brazilian peripheral environment and becomes universal.[80] According to João Cezar de Castro Rocha, Anthropophagy is converted into "the promise of a theoretical imagination of alterity, through the creative appropriation of the contribution of the other." In other words, the relationship between America and Europe, the colony and the metropolis, which historically fueled Anthropophagy, disappears in favor of the elaboration of an abstract philosophy of alterity of alleged universal value.[81] Under this perspective, the anthropophagic process can apply to any system that places hegemony on one side and subalternity on the other in a globalized world.

While the equivalence of transculturation and anthropophagy might seem a big stretch of imagination, numerous scholarly articles keep appearing connecting the two concepts. The central tenets of the Anthropophagy movement laid out a new perspective for the relationship between the local and the universal in a process of de-hierarchization that makes it possible for peripheral countries to enjoy effective expression. Anthropophagy, like most processes of hybridization, produces the rupture of borders and demarcations, where cultural meanings are dissociated from their place of origin. In the arts, the new definitions of quotation, reference, rereading, and copying appear without the "guilt" of submissive appropriation to a given originality, but as an intercultural "devouring." This "transcultural devouring" consists of the critical absorption of alterity, based on the concept of intertextuality, which annihilates the idea that a work can be considered "original," because the intertextual relationship can illuminate both texts, the original and the derivative.[82] The derived "text" constitutes a novel product that has its own cultural identity and, even if related to the original "text," deconstructs or reconstructs the same in search for new meanings under the translocal standpoint of the artist who, in an act of admiration or revenge, devours the original. The relationship between the original and the copy has been the subject of study in Silviano Santiago's literary criticism, where he explains that in Latin America, the copy stands as part of the matrix of the creative process. Translation, pastiche, and parody are anthropophagic devices of creation that generate a "place between" (*entre-lugar*) of dogged resistance, an "intermediary place between code and aggression, disobedience and revolt."[83]

If Anthropophagy is seen as a critical, dialogical form of intertextual rewriting and as a transcultural movement, originality emerges as something that is nothing more than a matter of rearranging the original, enabling the global to become local and the local to become global. The boundary between the local and the universal disappears, and anthropophagy becomes an aesthetic-procedural concept that seeks to understand cross-cultural relations between different peoples and nations; such "transcultural devouring" establishes a reciprocity: "I devour you to make you part of me, and vice versa."[84] In this perspective, the process of transculturation produces an "infinite sequence of transfigurations [of the initial product], with no beginning or end, no first or second, worse or better."[85]

Transculturation in Latin American literature produces a positive and effective linguistic contamination, according to Silviano Santiago: "The notion of unity is overturned, contaminated in favor of a subtle and complex mix between the European element and the autochthonous element—a kind of progressive infiltration effected by savage thinking [*pensamento selvagem*], that is, the opening of the only possible path to decolonization."[86] All such positions promote the anthropophagic reading of the postmodern phenomena.[87]

Cultural Cannibalism changed the former Eurocentric colonialist connotation of "acculturation" into a more diffuse conception of transculturation, signifying the "complete cycle of positive processes set in motion by culture contact."[88] This development yielded a process in which the roles of fusion, transformation, and hybridism proposed by Cultural Cannibalism emerge as contemporary approaches, while notions of hegemony begin to fade, and the natural permeability among cultures is increasingly recognized. Within this context, the postmodern artist has to adapt to a new reality: Sensitive to being politically correct about other cultures, the artist seeks to eliminate any possible taint of colonialism, while the differentiation between the original and the copy is redefined to include all kinds of artistic or intellectual appropriation.

Yet, our times carry the scars of the exploitation to which subaltern cultures have been submitted. Concerns about imperialism and racial superiority provoke conflicting reactions, where the invalidation of the Western canon in favor of the anti-erudite is frequently advocated in the name of the Third World and human rights. The digital age has failed to live up to its promise of connecting and uniting the world. Instead, it witnesses the prevalence of ethnic conflicts that generate worldwide migrations and may lead to a postcolonial project that would "provincialize Europe."[89] The obsession with expressing respect for other cultures and redeeming the errors of the past in some American countries risks reducing the tradition of Western culture to a footnote. Unfortunately, the laudable intent to promote diversity and inclusion as a tool for social justice and civil rights activism has called tradition into question, leading some quarters to advocate against the veneration of artistic masterpieces and their authors, while promoting the cancelation of even the most arduous defenders of humanistic ideals, such as Beethoven. Or the fashionable attempts to suppress studies related to European repertoires in favor of other topics.

The perceived failure to deal with issues of diversity and inclusion is to a great extent the result of a tendency to treat each culture in isolation, rather than as part of a reciprocal mosaic. In this sense, Anthropophagy presents itself as a more honest proposal. Rather than subtracting the hegemonic culture, it assimilates that culture, yielding to the appeal of considering cultures in concert rather than through their discrete histories and contributions. Diversity is celebrated by addition, not subtraction or substitution.

Ironically, the Eurocentric scholarship that ignored Anthropophagy witnessed the decline of all the seminal modernist movements that shaped Western civilization—impressionism, expressionism, futurism, neoclassicism, surrealism, and many others—only to realize that Cultural Cannibalism survived them all and is very much alive. Today, it is Cultural Cannibalism that influences cultural exchanges under the new guise of transculturation, a movement that has become an export aesthetic, as Oswald de Andrade intended a century ago.

Notes

1. Arthur Rimbaud, "Lettre à Paul Demeny, 15 mai 1871," in Rimbaud: Oeuvres Complètes, 343.

2. See Néstor García Canclini, "Hybrid Cultures: Strategies for Entering and Leaving Modernity."

3. Anthropophagous Manifesto, aphorism 1. See Appendix I.

4. Although a translation of the Futurist Manifesto was published in 1909 in a newspaper in northeast Brazil, it escaped the notice of literary circles in the center of southern Brazil, which ignored productions outside their sphere.

5. Susan Fisher Sterling, "Malfatti, Anita," in The Grove Dictionary of Art Online (New York: Oxford University Press, 2000), https://doi-org.proxy.lib.miamioh.edu/10.1093/gao/9781884446054.article.T2021799.

6. See, for example, Benedito Nunes, "Antropofagia E Vanguarda," 317.

7. For a summary of the various modernist ideological points of view during the 1920s, see Wilson Martins, O Modernismo (1916–1945), especially pp. 88–116, and Mario da Silva Brito, "A revolução modernista," in A Literatura no Brasil, ed. Afrâneo Coutinho, vol. V, 20–37.

8. See Tiago de Oliveira Pinto, "Art Is Universal," 106.

9. The quest for modernism and the search for a Brazilian identity obviously was not a premise exclusive to Modern Art Week and the movements it spawned. In addition to the two movements mentioned above, other relevant schools of thought appeared, such as the "Metaphysic Nationalism" of Graça Aranha and the Nationalist Regionalism of Gilberto Freyre and José Lins do Rego, a peripheral movement in Recife, capital of Pernambuco state.

10. Although a member of the Group of Five, Tarsila do Amaral was away in Paris during the Modern Art Week. However, she returned to São Paulo a few months later and became an active member of the group. She married Oswald de Andrade in 1926 and had a pivotal role among the anthropophagites, becoming arguably the most renowned representative of the plastic arts in Brazilian modernism.

11. While Menotti del Picchia was a member of the Group of Five, he should be placed among the reactionary members of the Tapir Group, and not among the anthropophagites. His simultaneous position as a member of the Group of Five and one of the founders of *verdeamarelismo* is a reflection of his own contradictions concerning religion, modernity, and political conservatism.

12. "Native primitivism was our only discovery in 1922," stated the author. Oswald de Andrade, "O caminho percorrido," 96.

13. See, for example: Paulo Renato Guérios, "Heitor Villa-Lobos and the Parisian art scene" concerning the "discovery of Brazil" by Villa-Lobos, and "Oswald Viajante" by Antônio Cândido [Antônio Cândido, "Oswald Viajante," in *Vários Escritos* (São Paulo: Duas Cidades, 1970)].

14. *Pau-Brasil* or *paubrasilia*, a Brazilian timber tree commonly known as Pernambuco wood or brazilwood, is the national tree of Brazil and gave the country its name.

15. Ilan Rachum, "Antrofopagia Against Verdamarelo," 68.

16. The manifesto was republished in abridged form and with slight alterations in Oswald de Andrade's book of poetry *Pau Brasil*, published in 1925 in Paris. The passages cited are drawn from the two separate versions of the manifesto, and were translated by Ilan Rachum.

17. *Bandeirantes* (translated literally as "flag-carriers") were slavers, explorers, adventurers, and fortune hunters in early colonial Brazil. They were largely responsible for Brazil's great expansion westward, far beyond the Tordesillas Line of 1494, by which Pope Alexander VI divided the new continent into a western, Castilian section, and an eastern, Portuguese section.

18. Oswald de Andrade, "Obras Completas," 76.

19. One of the criticisms of Oswald de Andrade's perspective is the argument that he had to go abroad in order to "rediscover" Brazil, and therefore his aesthetic was not genuine or authentic. Villa-Lobos often frequented the same circles that Oswald de Andrade and Tarsila do Amaral did in Paris, and therefore attracted the same kind of criticism. The current study will advocate that the anthropophagic aesthetic turns this type of criticism into a meaningless venture.

20. See Benedito Nunes, "A Antropofagia ao alcance de todos," in *A Utopia Antropofágica*, 12. https://monoskop.org/images/a/ae/Oswald_de_Andrade_A_utopia_antropof%C3%A1gica_1990.pdf.

21. *Mameluco* is the ethnic product of the miscegenation of the white with the Amerindian.

22. Oswald de Andrade, *Os Dentes do Dragão*, 45.

23. See Haroldo de Campos, "Uma Poética de Radicalidade," 51.

24. Marinetti actually came to Brazil in 1926, therefore before the publication of the Anthropophagous Manifesto. While he enjoyed success in Rio de Janeiro, he was booed in São Paulo or received with indifference by the modernists in the city. Oswald de Andrade was not present—he was abroad. By the time Marinetti returned to Brazil in 1936, his movement had lost its initial impact.

25. Rachel Newman, "Primitivism and Identity in Latin America, 20."

26. While Cultural Cannibalism is presented in this text as the primary aesthetic movement that characterized modernism in Brazil, in the original "Anthropophogous Manifesto," it was postulated as the driving force for the development of all cultures and societies: "The world's single law. Disguised expression of all individualism, of all collectivisms. Of all religions. Of all peace treaties." See Oswald de Andrade, "Cannibalist Manifesto." Translated by Leslie Bary, in *Latin American Literary Review*, 38.

27. Ana de Oliveira, "Tropicalia: Ruidos Pulsativos. Geléia Geral." Accessed July 29, 2017. http://tropicalia.com.br/en/ruidos-pulsativos/geleia-geral/antropofagia, para. 1.

28. Hans Staden was a soldier who served as a gunner for the Portuguese colonizers in Brazil and was captured by the Tupinambá Amerindian tribe in 1550. The Tupinambás were allies of the French invaders of Brazil, and therefore hostile to the Portuguese. As a prisoner of the Tupinambás, Hans Staden witnessed rituals of

cannibalism practiced by the Amerindians, which he later recounted after his escape in a book that became an international bestseller and was translated in several languages (*Hans Staden's True Story and Description of a Country of Wild, Naked, Grim, Man-eating People in the New World, America*). A version in English can be found as Hans Staden, *Hans Staden's True History: An Account of Cannibal Captivity in Brazil*, transl. Neil L. Whitehead and Michael Harbsmeier (Durham: Duke University Press, 2008). The Brazilian modernists got acquainted with the story through two publications by their contemporary colleague Monteiro Lobato, who published one version of the narrative in 1925 and another in the form of a children's book in 1927.

29. The chronicles by Jean de Léry have been particularly influential. Jean de Léry, *Histoire d'un voyage faict en la terre du Brésil: autrement dite Amérique* (1585). http://gallica.bnf.fr/ark:/12148/bpt6k54640v. A modern English version is available as Jean de Léry, *History of a Voyage to the Land of Brazil*, transl. Janet Whatley (Berkeley: University of California Press, 1992).

30. Aracy Amaral, "Oswald de Andrade and Brazilian Modernism," 160.

31. The so-called myth of the golden age appeared in Greek mythology and describes the decline of the state of the golden race of humanity in five stages: golden, silver, bronze, heroic, and the current Iron Age. Therefore, "golden age" refers to a period of primordial peace, harmony, stability, and prosperity. During the age of gold, people did not have to work to feed themselves, for the earth provided food in abundance. European pastoral tradition appropriated the idea of the Golden Age by depicting nymphs and shepherds living an idyllic life of rustic innocence and peace in Arcadia.

32. Richard M. Morse, "Triangulating Two Cubists," 180. Accessed April 1, 2020. www.jstor.org/stable/20119418.

33. Oswald de Andrade, "A marcha das utopias," 165.

34. Oswald de Andrade, *Ponta de Lança*, 195.

35. Edward Lucie-Smith, *Latin American Art of the 20th Century*, 42.

36. Michele Greet, "Devouring Surrealism," 12.

37. The Tupi people (spelled "tupy" in older Portuguese orthography) were one of the most numerous of Brazil's indigenous peoples before colonization. They inhabited almost all of Brazil's coast when the Portuguese arrived in 1500. Their population was estimated at one million people, nearly equal to the population of Portugal at the time. They were divided into tribes, each tribe numbering from 300 to 2,000 people, and while there was not a unified Tupi identity, they all spoke a common language. Sometimes those tribes were in conflict with each other.

Tupi is also a shorthand for the more generic term "Tupi-Guarani people," which combines numerous tribes that spoke the most widely distributed subfamily of the Tupian languages of South America.

38. According to Adriano Netto, some articles in the *Revista de Antropofagia* establish that the incorporation of the national culture would occur through a process of sanitation: "In anthropophagy by hygiene, the target of devouring would no longer be the foreigner, but the local Brazilian. In this case, one would not eat out of a desire for assimilation, but for the elimination of what corrupts the country's

environmental integrity. In such endocannibalism, one eats the weak, those who deteriorate the health of the national body. It is, therefore, a therapeutic mechanism for Brazilian art." See Adriano Bitarães Netto, *Antropofagia oswaldiana: um receituário estético científico*, 125.

39. See aphorisms 18 and 36 in Appendix I.

40. As Oswald de Andrade stated: "The primitivism that in France appeared as exoticism was for us, in Brazil, genuine primitivism." Testimony to Péricles da Silva Ramos, published in Correio Paulistano on June 26, 1949. In Oswald de Andrade, *Os Dentes do Dragão*, 148.

41. Antônio Cândido, *Literatura e Sociedade*, 128.

42. Ana de Oliveira, "Tropicalia," para. 3.

43. The self-consciousness of this process is already felt in Villa-Lobos's posture during his first trip to Paris in 1923, right after the famous "Week of Modern Art" in São Paulo. Boasting and full of self-esteem, he was already affirming that the purpose of his trip was to showcase his works, rather than to learn. In an article from 1924 for the journal *Ariel*, the poet Manuel Bandeira wrote: "Villa-Lobos just returned from Paris. One would expect that whoever arrives from Paris, would arrive full of Paris. However, Villa-Lobos returned from there full of Villa-Lobos." See Manuel Bandeira, "Villa-Lobos," *Ariel* 2, no. 13, 475.

44. Haroldo de Campos, "Uma poética da radicalidade," 35–36.

45. See Abigail Solomon-Godeau, "Going Native: Paul Gauguin and the Invention of Primitivist Modernism," 314.

46. Glenn Watkins, *Pyramids at the Louvre*, 63.

47. Edward Said, *Beginnings: Intention and Method*, 40–41.

48. For example, in Goethe's *West-östlicher Divan* (West-Eastern Diwan) poems, the author reflects an increasing European awareness of the 'East' as the origin of Western civilization (the biblically informed culture). He saw in the East the origin of the world religions, the so-called cradle of civilization, in contraposition to the established view that the cradle of Western civilization rests in the Greco-Roman tradition. See Jeffrey Einboden, *The Genesis of Westliterature: Goethe's West-östlicher Divan and Kerygmatic Pluralism*.

49. Both the statement by Cocteau and the one concerning Scheherazade appear in Glenn Watkins, *Pyramids at the Louvre*, 67.

50. In a review of the dress rehearsal of the *Rite of Spring*, on May 30, 1913, the critic Adolphe Boschot wrote: "They want to show us the dances of prehistoric Russia: so they present us, to make primitive, dances of savages, of the Caribees and the Kanaks." See Thomas Forrest Kelly, *First Nights: Five Musical Premieres*, New Haven and London: Yale University Press, p. 305. The sentiment was echoed by another critic, Maurice Touchard, who asked, "Why were these prehistoric men dressed as Indians?" A translation of his review appears in Truman Campbell Bullard, "The First Performance of Igor Stravinsky's *Sacre du Printemps*," vol. 2, 196.

51. See Carla Baptista de Freitas, *Antropofagia Ritual e Identidade Cultural nas Sociedades Ameríndias*, 24: "The Portuguese [the colonizer] is defined . . . by traits such

as belonging to the Western world, having a Greek-Latin-based tradition and Judeo Christian [religion], while the 'Other,' the Indian, is characterized in the first place by the absence of precisely these traits."

52. This will be further developed in the subsequent section.
53. Benedito Nunes, *Oswald Canibal* (São Paulo: Ed Perspectiva, 1979), 24.
54. Beatriz Azevedo, "Antropofagia: Palimpsesto Selvagem," 59.
55. Carlos Jáuregui, "Anthropophagy," 22.
56. Edward Said, "The Politics of Knowledge," 28.
57. Carlos Jáugueri, "Anthropophagy," 22.
58. Antônio Cândido, *Vários Escritos*, 84–85.
59. Doris Sommer, *Foundational Fictions*, 150–64.
60. Kimberly S. López, "Modernismo and the Ambivalence," 25.
61. This quote is taken from Somerset Maugham's short story "Honolulu," which is part of the book *The Trembling of a Leaf: Little Stories of the South Sea Islands*.
62. Anaïs Fléchet, *Villa-Lobos à Paris*, 77.
63. In 1928 Mário de Andrade stated that the Brazilian modernists were a group "isolated and shielded in their own convictions . . . [they were] the only sector of the nation that makes the national artistic problem a case of almost exclusive preoccupation. In spite of this, it does not represent anything of Brazilian reality. It is outside of our social rhythm, outside of our economic inconstancy, outside of Brazilian preoccupation" (quoted in Aracy Amaral, *Textos do Trópico de Capricórnio*, 124). Such a statement needs to be evaluated with perspective. Mário de Andrade was a writer, and since 75 percent of the Brazilian population was illiterate at around 1920, how could the modernists not be isolated? As Néstor Canclini states, "artists 'addicted' to European models are not mere imitators of imported aesthetics; nor can they be accused of denationalizing their own culture. Nor, in the long run, do these minorities always end up being insignificant, as they were assumed to be in their texts." See Néstor Canclini, *Hybrid Cultures*, 51.
64. See Néstor García Canclini, *Hybrid Cultures*, chapter 5.
65. This topic is compellingly raised in the classic essay "Can the subaltern speak?" See Gayatri Chakravorty Spivak, "Can the Subaltern Speak?" in *Marxism and the Interpretation of Culture*, ed. Cary Nelson and Lawrence Grossberg (Basingstoke: Macmillan, 1988), 271–313.
66. Karlheinz Stockhausen, "Beyond Global Village Polyphony," 24.
67. Watkins, *Pyramids at the Louvre*, 460.
68. Viveiros de Castro, Eduardo. "Temos que criar um outro conceito de criação (2007)," 168.
69. *Pindorama* means "Land of Palms" in the Tupi language. It was the way the Amerindians referred to Brazil.
70. One of the aphorisms of the Anthropophagous Manifesto states: "we [the cannibals] are concretists." See Appendix I.
71. The song was based on the famous phrase that appeared on graffiti-painted walls in Paris in 1968. The public was shocked by the futuristic clothes of the per-

formers, the histrionic gestures of Caetano Veloso, and the aggressive sound of the guitars of the Mutantes, the band that accompanied the song. The audience threw eggs and tomatoes on stage, participating in the "happening" that Caetano Veloso intended to make out of his participation, which culminated in a famous speech that began with the question: "But is this the youth that wants to take power?" According to Caetano, all of the above was part of the music's staging. The singer-songwriter even asked on stage for the song to be disqualified from the competition, but his request was not granted and the song proceeded to the next phase.

72. Ismail Xavier, *Allegories of Underdevelopment*, 29.
73. Carlos Basualdo, "Tropicália," 24.
74. Marília de Andrade, "Oswald e Maria Antonieta," 75.
75. Irina Hiebert Grun, "A Recepção da Antropofagia na Arte Brasileira Contemporânea," 27. The author cites as examples the contemporary works of artists such as Adriana Varejão (b. 1964), Ernesto Neto (b. 1964), and Ricardo Basbaum (b. 1961), which expand the notion of anthropophagy until our days.
76. Carlos Jáuregui, "Antropofagia," 27. The italics are used for emphasis.
77. Sebastião Leal Fereira Vargas Netto, "Antropofagia Cultural," 295–96.
78. Eduardo Sterzi, "Uma Ontologia Política Chamada Antropofagia," interview by Ricardo Machado, *Revista do Instituto Humanitas Usininos*, 543 edition, October 21, 2019 http://www.ihuonline.unisinos.br/artigo/7687-uma-ontologia-politica-chamada-antropofagia.
79. Kenneth David Jackson, *Cannibal Angels*, 16.
80. See Lourdes L K A Alves, "A Assimilação ou A Transgressão," 127–45. The author proposes Anthropophagy as the basis for the process of transculturation of Latin American literature.
81. João Cezar de Castro Rocha, "Uma teoria de exportação?," 648.
82. Oswald de Andrade played with this idea, writing on the back of the title page of the first edition of his novel *Serafim Ponte Grande* that he granted the "right to be translated, reproduced and deformed in all languages."
83. Silviano Santiago, "O Entre-Lugar," 11–28.
84. For a more detailed explanation, see Marcel Álvaro de Amorim, "From adaptation to transconstruction." Another interesting application appears in Renato Sztutman, "The Re(turn) of the Anthropophagites," 214–15.
85. Roberto Schwarz, "Nacional por Subtração," 35.
86. Silviano Santiago, "O Entre-Lugar," 15.
87. For example, when Frederic Jameson posits that in postmodern art, citations or quotes are no longer considered to be momentary references, but rather genuine incorporation of substance, he is essentially promoting an anthropophagic reading of postmodernism. Fredric Jameson, *Postmodernism*, 2–3.
88. Margaret J. Kartomi. "The Processes and Results of Musical Culture Contact," 233.
89. Eduardo Restrepo, "Antropologia y Colonialidad," 293.

CHAPTER TWO

Villa-Lobos, The "Cannibal Who Wore Tails"

> *Many composers of our time aim to be modern, without having the gift of originality. And they don't understand that every original artist is modern by default.* —Heitor Villa-Lobos

Considered by many to be the best-known and most significant Latin American composer to date,[1] Heitor Villa-Lobos (1887–1959) was the most important and most active representative of the Brazilian modernist movement in music during the 1920s. In Brazil, modernism had to navigate between the need to accommodate avant-garde ideas brought from Europe and the internal demand for an art that was essentially nationalist, a result of the climate of patriotic exaltation that had characterized the republic of Brazil since the overthrow of the monarchy a little before the turn of the century.

The intersection of nationalism and modernism in the twentieth century constitutes a central musicological problem for the assessment of the intrinsic value of a number of composers, such as Sibelius, Bartok, Stravinsky, and Villa-Lobos. The main challenge rests in the aesthetic belief that works of truly great composers transcend national boundaries based on their originality and universal character. The writer and musicologist Alejo Carpentier described the challenge as follows:

> Our composer [Villa-Lobos] knows anxieties and dilemmas that never bothered the European composer. The desire to "find the universal within the details of the local," as expressed by Unamuno, keeps him on a tightrope at the border between the local and the universal. On one side are the rhythms

of the native land, full of raw lyricism waiting to be channeled. On the other, remain the eternal questions concerning expressivity and *métier* [associated with] . . . pure music.²

One of the typical characteristics of modernism is a tendency toward abstractionism, while nationalism in music frequently incorporates folk elements that bring extra-musical, concrete associations to artworks. In an era that praised originality and new discoveries over everything else, musicologists tended to place a much higher artistic value on works that stood on their own intrinsic value, a characteristic more typically associated with absolute music. This is likely what led Stravinsky to deny folk influences in *The Rite of Spring*; it also explains why Bartok's more abstract compositions, such as his *Music for Percussion, Strings and Celesta* or his *Concerto for Orchestra*, earned more praise than his folk-oriented works.

The problem escalates when one examines the music of Villa-Lobos: Since his output is intrinsically connected with Brazil, the musicological need for classification and categorization destined him to be kept at the periphery, among Latin-American composers, and not among the great composer-innovators of the twentieth century. This is compounded by another challenge: a failure to recognize the anthropophagic style of the composer. When musicologists find in Villa-Lobos's works elements present in the works of other composers, they tend to attribute them to foreign influences or a derivative style, manifesting an implicit form of prejudice directed against a composer coming from the tropics.

Since Anthropophagy is an aesthetic posture defined by the appropriation of external materials in a process of cannibalism, it is necessary to immediately differentiate it from other procedures for borrowing foreign materials—methods that cross historical periods and multiple traditions. It is no longer acceptable to sustain traditional Eurocentric colonialist views that understand Brazilian modernism as an adoption or adaptation of materials and procedures from Western European origins into Brazilian folk sources. The Anthropophagic method, when applied to music, needs to be discerned from all the traditional forms of borrowing from existing music, such as musical quotation, variation, paraphrase, stylistic allusion, collage, emulation, and many others.³ Essentially, it redefines the meaning of artistic and intellectual appropriation, into something much more profound: It is a concept that defies the notion of hegemony, to allow a more natural permeability among different cultures through a process of transculturation.

One century after the emergence of Anthropophagy, we can establish a parallel between its methods and the development of collage, a primary characteristic of the postmodern era that was already anticipated in modernism. "Collage" became the word of the day to express the process of fusion and transformation typical of more recent art, and is characterized by the juxtaposition of opposing impulses: the local and the cosmopolitan, the high and the low, the black and the white, and so on.[4] During the modern era, the hybridization characteristic of Anthropophagy served to empower the colonized against his inferiority complex, while at the same time conjoining the influence of the foreign with the beauty of the local—explained in Oswald de Andrade's manifesto as the "transformation of tabu into totem." In the postmodern era, collage emerged from the fascination of the artist both with the intangible idea of global fraternity and with the diversity and richness of local traditions, in a process that is analogous to Anthropophagy. Collage asserted itself through a pluralism that appealed to artists due to the fascination with cultural outreach as well as the seductiveness of appropriation as a creative stimulus. The pluralism that we find in the art of today is a manifestation of the prophetic ideas of Oswald de Andrade. Indeed, one could trace the lineage of collage back to the Anthropophagic movement instead of linking it to the individual movements that constituted the modern era; after all, Anthropophagy embraced them all while subjecting them to a process of fusion. In doing so, Anthropophagy itself metaphorically became the export product originally envisioned by the father of the movement.

Villa-Lobos: Tupi or Not Tupi?

A problem that arises in the musicological study of Villa-Lobos within the Anthropophagic movement is that, in addition to Oswald de Andrade, there is also another great influencer of ideas who shares the same surname: Mário de Andrade, a major exponent of Brazilian modernism in literature, who was not related to Oswald. Besides the same last name, there are several points of intersection between Oswald and Mário de Andrade. The latter has been traditionally ranked higher than the former by a number of scholars, who consider him the most outstanding representative of modernism in Brazil.[5] While Oswald wrote the two important manifestos discussed previously (the Brazilwood Manifesto and the Cannibal Manifesto), Mário authored *Paulicéia Desvairada* (literally "Frantic São Paulo," often translated as "Hallucinated City"), which is considered the first literary modernist text published in Brazil. He read several poems from this publication during Modern Art Week in 1922. The book's cover illustration was produced by another great modernist, the painter Di Cavalcanti, placing him and Mário in parallel with the painter Tarsila do Amaral and Oswald de Andrade, who married in 1926. Mário de Andrade wrote an introduction for *Pauliceia Desvairada*, which he called "Extremely Interesting Preface," advocating for the use of free verse in an irreverent and combative tone. This essay also became a sort of manifesto, a seminal work in the definition of modernism in Brazil, though with the perspective of time, it did not achieve the same reach and status as the Cannibal Manifesto, also referred to as the Cannibalist or Anthropophagous Manifesto.

Mário de Andrade belonged to the Group of Five mentioned in the previous chapter, and therefore was strongly connected with the development of the Anthropophagic movement. His magnum opus was the novel *Macunaíma* (1928), another founding text of Brazilian modernism, published in the same year as the Cannibal Manifesto and recognized as a vital enactment of the ideas of the manifesto. Writing in a style that later became known as "magical realism," the author includes images and representations of true cannibalism in the text. As Kimberle López writes, however,

> The anthropophagic consumption of the Other in Andrade's rhapsody goes far beyond the simple representation of cannibalistic acts: in a more general sense, the entire project is anthropophagic in that it consumes materials from a broad range of sources and incorporates them in a de-hierarchized whole, without categorically excluding any discourse, including that of the colonizer. Significantly, *Macunaima* shares with Oswald de Andrade's Pau-Brasil and Anthropophagic movements the central paradox of Latin American modernism: an attempt to create an independent literature for export, while still adhering to aesthetic norms established by the European colonizer.[6]

To further complicate matters, Mário de Andrade was a musicologist of great erudition, lucidity, and knowledge, who interacted substantially with Villa-Lobos and greatly influenced the musical evolution of modernism in Brazil for decades. Despite being best known as a poet and novelist, Mário de Andrade was trained as a musician; he became a pioneer ethnomusicologist of international stature and held the Chair of History of Music and Aesthetics at the Conservatório Dramático e Musical of São Paulo.

Recent studies[7] demonstrate that Mário de Andrade's musical background strongly influenced his writing style, which clearly presents multiple musical characteristics. For example, his poem "As Enfibraturas do Ipiranga" (The Enfibratures of the Ipiranga) from *Pauliceia Desvairada* borrows from the structure of the oratorio;[8] *Macunaima* was conceived as a novel with a rhapsodic structure; and his poems in the book *Clã do Jaboti* (The Tortoise Clan) frequently transpose into literature generic characteristics from Brazilian popular music, such as the modinha, samba, côco, and others. In his literary works, Mário de Andrade attempts to structure poems as musical genres, as if they were written to be performed musically, while on other occasions he displays a concern with the musicality of words, inherited from symbolist aesthetics. The entanglement between music and literature proposed by Mário de Andrade is a ramification of a syncretic process characteristic of the turn of the century, when artists were trying to show the correspondences among the human senses and scientists started their quest for a unified theory of the universe.

All these features contributed to place Mário de Andrade as the epitome of the modernist Brazilian artist, while at the same time establishing his influential stature. At least during the first stage of national modernism, from the Week of Modern Art until the first phase of the *Revista de Antropofagia*, the writer of *Macunaíma* is considered a pioneer anthropophagite who produced original works from the fusion of national and foreign influences. Even more, he transcended this type of Anthropophagy by incorporating musical cannibalism into literature as the product of entanglement between the two arts.

It is not surprising that the overwhelming literature on Villa-Lobos during the twentieth century tends to view him through the lens of the authoritative musicological ideas of Mário de Andrade. According to him, the creation of a musical idiom simultaneously Brazilian and modern should go through three stages: a) faithful adoption of a folk melody whereby the composer, in his arrangement of the same, keeps his individuality at a low profile; b) adoption of a folk melody as basic material to be worked on by the composer, in the process of which he places greater emphasis on his own individual musical voices; c) the highest artistic level at which it is possible to compose music that is truly nationalistic in spirit without the need of a faithful adoption of a folk melody.[9] While this seems to summarize Villa-Lobos's composition strategies at one point or another, Mário de Andrade did not detect the anthropophagic style of the composer as the method of incorporating nationalism without the need of a faithful adoption of folk melodies.

In fact, it was Mário de Andrade who helped perpetuate the myth of Villa-Lobos as an intuitive musician who lacked a refined composition technique and therefore produced works of uneven quality, frequently committing gross mistakes due to lack of theoretical knowledge. The statements below, extracted from a letter from 1933, demonstrate this position:

> The ignorant, uncultured Villa, with a very deficient knowledge of musical facts, had always displayed composition technique. His works were quite uneven: when large, they almost invariably displayed awkward forms, especially

irritating lengths, and puerile clumsiness. But Villa had inventiveness. Not knowing orchestration, he created admirable instrumentations. Not knowing what the human voice is, he leaves behind an impressive array of vocal effects. While ignorant in terms of harmony, to the point that he couldn't define what a false relationship was, he harmonized with an exactness of character, as if a product of a fatal necessity, yes, a fatal necessity . . . completely incapable of discerning musical facts (mainly because his vanity led him to produce *creatio ex nihilo*), ignorant to the extreme as to a critical understanding of Brazilian music, his work became an incomparably rich repository of the facts, the constancies, the subtleties, and the musical originalities of Brazil.[10]

While praising the composer's aptitude for the exploration of timbres and melodies, Mário de Andrade was particularly critical of Villa-Lobos's capacity to produce coherent larger compositions, but he concluded that this "deficiency" did not prevent the composer to display the force of his creative genius in smaller compositions due to his inventiveness and originality. During the 1930s, Mário de Andrade completely despised what he considered the composer's attitude of prostituting his art by writing politically engaged compositions connected with the fascist dictatorial government of the country. He condemned such posture as an attempt to obtain self-serving benefits, combined with a criticism of the morality of the composer's attempt to please all tastes in search for applause. The excerpt below constitutes a good example of Mário de Andrade's position:

> What hinders V. Lobos is the fantastic lack of intellectual organization. His head is full of poorly digested teachings, with huge failures in instruction which, despite his musicality, prevent him from displaying a secure aesthetic vision of the moment or of the work itself. He is undeniably the most brilliant of our musicians, the one with the highest and most original inventiveness, the one with the most free and audacious sense of Brazilianness, but in general his merit comes down to this inventiveness. The longueurs, the lack of synthesis and sobriety, the inability to sacrifice, mainly in the larger compositions, make his output irregular and sometimes painful. While the touch of genius is felt inside, it is terrible when one can observe more the defects than the qualities attributed to the genius. However, in the smaller pieces, where these deficiencies of the musical genius cannot be seen, Villa-Lobos has given us the most perfect masterpieces.[11]

Ultimately, Mário de Andrade limited himself to a perception of Villa-Lobos based on his personal nationalistic/modernist view, which did *not* incorporate an Anthropophagic approach.[12] His nationalism implied a conservative aesthetic for the affirmation of a "national identity," which contrasted with Oswald de Andrade's anthropophagy. The latter presupposed a radical devouring of the other (or the multiple others), and therefore the anthropophagic alterity was contrary to any form of "unique identity." For the anthropophagites, "purity is a myth,"[13] so they didn't look for the nationalist purity preconized by Mário de Andrade, who nevertheless had the power of his scholarship securing his authority:

> Anthropophagy was poorly received for several reasons. First, because Oswald de Andrade was a Frenchified dandy (paradox is part of the theory . . .) who had no academic credentials. He didn't do field work like Mário de Andrade, for example. Mário de Andrade collected popular music, songs, went after myths, invented a whole look about Brazil. But Oswald had superior rhetorical firepower; his inconsequence was visionary. . . . He had an incomparable punch. If Mário was the great cataloger of diversity, Oswald was the great theorist of multiplicity—something very different.[14]

Mário de Andrade believed that Brazilian modernism should be found in the updating of the folk traditions to the present, because according to him, folk tradition was mobile and had this ability to update itself, and in doing so, it carried the national identity over time. The inclusion of folklore in music should take place within a language still attached to the universal tonal system developed by classical-romantic or impressionist composers, which corresponds to a traditionalist vision more in line with the practice of nineteenth-century composers.[15] For the popular tradition to be incorporated in artistic works, a meticulous scholar study would be necessary, in contraposition with a more intuitive sort of incorporation. This is one of the points that distanced him the most from the anthropophagic vision, since, according to him, Oswald de Andrade's work would be incapable of synthesizing opposites, which for Mário would be the true mark of "Brazilianness." Furthermore, he found the ironic and satirical joy employed by Oswald to portray reality to be corrosive, also preventing him to construct a modern Brazilian culture.[16]

Mário de Andrade's evaluation was authoritative and influential due to his intellectual stature and knowledge, but he created a paradoxical image of Villa-Lobos that was propagated through practically all subsequent studies: that of the ignorant but intuitive talent capable of overcoming his deficiencies due to his genius. Many of Mário de Andrade's evaluations of the composer were written after he finally broke with the Anthropophagic movement. Despite collaborating with it during the first phase of the journal *Revista de Antropofagia*, later on he did not hide his objections to some of the more radical tenets of the movement. By 1929, the rupture between Oswald and Mário de Andrade was official, and the *Revista de Antropofagia* began to attack the author of *Macunaíma* both personally and aesthetically.[17]

As a consequence, references to the Anthropophagic style of Villa-Lobos in most of the existing literature have been marginal until a reevaluation of the composer began to take shape in Brazil, mainly during this century. Today, Brazilian musicologists conspicuously define Villa-Lobos's style as anthropophagic, and more detailed analyses of his works have started to appear.[18] One of the main contributions of the present study is to shift the frame of reference for the study of Villa-Lobos's aesthetics from Mário de Andrade's perspective to the most radical tenets of Anthropophagy as preached by Oswald de Andrade, who was not a musician.[19] Yet, the poet was an intellectual who displayed affinity with music as attested by the artistic circles he frequented in Paris. In his memoirs about Paris, he remembers learning of Satie, Stravinsky, Cocteau (the literary spokesman for the group of composers known as "*Les Six*"), and others; he called his book of poems *Pau Brasil* a "*cancioneiro*," or songbook, recalling the tradition of fourteenth-century Iberian troubadour poets; the Anthropophagic Manifesto has been considered a "poetic score";[20] and Oswald de Andrade even wrote "Cântico dos Cânticos for flute and piano" (1945), which is actually a poem dedicated to his future wife, Maria Antonieta d'Alkmin, and not a musical composition.

Until recently, little has been written about the relationship between Oswald de Andrade and Villa-Lobos beyond their simultaneous participation during the Modern Art Week of 1922 and their encounters in Paris. Parallels exist between the aesthetics of Tarsila do Amaral's paintings and the music that Villa-Lobos wrote at the time. Despite producing several portraits, including those of Oswald and Mário de Andrade plus a number of self-portraits, Tarsila did not produce a portrait of Villa-Lobos. This is significant because portraiture in the modern era was one of the most distinctive features of the modernist circle of artists in Brazil, a focus centered on images and portraits of themselves or of the country:

> In the same way that the modernists constantly improvise on topics related to their circle and times, they likewise create and exchange likenesses and portraits of themselves as a main focus of their works, whether in literature, visual arts, or music. . . . In music, Villa-Lobos specializes in compositions designed as portraits of Brazil that highlight its folk music, popular instruments, and indigenous chants.[21]

In 1925 Oswald de Andrade dedicated a poem to Villa-Lobos, which can be viewed as a poetic portrait of the Brazilian composer created by the father of *Antropofagia*. The poem was published in the literary magazine

Novíssima,[22] founded by Cassiano Ricardo, one of the members of the *Verde-amarelismo* movement. Its writing style is such that it could perfectly have been included in the renowned poetry book *Pau Brasil* (Brazilwood) that Oswald de Andrade published that same year in Paris, with the help of Blaise Cendrars. It can be compared with the poem *Atelier* (Art Studio), dedicated to Tarsila do Amaral, which appears in the section titled "*Postes da Light*" in that publication.[23] In this poem titled *O Artista* (The Artist), the poet uses his synthetic aphoristic language and critical wit to capture the essence of the composer with the utmost economy of words. The symbolic images, which are almost impossible to translate, have an ambiguity that makes one wonder if the humorous caricature features the composer in a positive or negative light—or if the poem is just a joke between friends.

O artista	The artist
Cabeleira *de chantage*	Long hair for blackmail
Celebridade por hora e por táxi	Celebrity by the hour and by taxi
Parlapatatão	Big talker
Bombardino de barbeiro	Barber's euphonium
Desafinação	Off key
No teu fundo fundo	Deep, deep inside
A maroteira dos primeiros mestiços	The sly mother of the first mestizos
Repousa como um índio	He reposes like an Indian
Sob a árvore nacional da confiança	Under the tree of confidence
Pires técnico	Technical foundation
Da paulificação	of São Paulo modernization[24]

That same year, Villa-Lobos wrote his *Choros No. 3 "Picapau"* (Woodpecker), a short composition under four minutes long, which is one of his few works that makes explicit use of documented Amerindian music. He dedicated the composition to Oswald de Andrade and Tarsila do Amaral. The exchange of dedications reinforces the connection between the Brazilian poet and the composer.

It remains to clarify that the process of cultural cannibalization in music is not viewed today as something that started with Villa-Lobos. Richard Greenan states that "Brazilian popular music [which Villa-Lobos thoroughly explored in his compositions] is the product of centuries of cultural melding."[25] The process would have started in the seventeenth century with the cannibalization of the *lundu* dance originated from the Kongo-Angola region, followed by the introduction of the *modinha* of Italian origin in the eighteenth century, and then the introduction of European rhythms such as the polka and the waltz, which were incorporated into the popular musical idiom in the country. These found their way into the *choro*, an instrumental genre that combined these European dances such as polkas and waltzes with an Afro-Brazilian syncopation, a genre that was embraced by Villa-Lobos, who took it to the next level and brought it to the concert hall. Even the Brazilian authenticity of samba as a purely Brazilian genre is contested as being an "invention designed to mask Brazil's history of cultural cross-pollination and foster political and cultural stability in a time of turbulence and change."[26] Therefore, Villa-Lobos's Anthropophagy would be another manifestation of cultural cannibalism within the overall context of cultural hybridization typical of Brazilian music since its formation.

The "Cannibal Who Wore Tails"[27]

The Oswaldian notion of Anthropophagy, or cultural cannibalism, outlined the way in which Brazilian artists in the first half of the twentieth century were able to create a national cultural identity while at the same time aligning themselves with the avant-garde, modernist manifestations in Europe. Applying this perspective to Villa-Lobos may help to rid him of the stigma closely associated with the category of exotic nationalist composers,[28] an association he strongly rejected. While commenting on the *Choros*, a series of original compositions in a traditional musical genre of Brazil, Villa-Lobos stated: "I am not a folklorist. Folklore does not occupy my mind. My music is just as I feel it. I don't hunt for themes with a view to using them. I write compositions with the spirit from which one makes one's music. I abandon myself completely to my temperament."[29]

It was common for composers in the nineteenth and early twentieth centuries who used national folklore in their music—either through direct quotations or through the emulation of folk-style music—to be labeled nationalists. However, a number of these composers transcended the nationalistic features of their music and, through innovative approaches, created works of universal appeal.[30] Bartok and Stravinsky (at least during the early stages of his career) immediately come to mind as examples. In the case of Villa-Lobos, Gerard Béhague concluded that nationalism was part of the eclecticism of the composer—his urge to express the diversity of a colossal country while at the same time unifying the national culture. In other words, nationalism was a result of the composer's "need to be nonexclusive and comprehensive concurrently in the attempt to disclose the various cultural vibrations of Brazil. . . . At the center of this disposition is obviously the changing perception of the concept 'national culture.'"[31]

Similarly to Villa-Lobos, Stravinsky attempted to deny folk influence in his music, particularly in *The Rite of Spring*, which became the most emblematic composition of the modern era.[32] However, scholars have identified more than a dozen folk references from published folk-song anthologies in this ballet. In a lecture given at Harvard in 1943, Bela Bartok clearly outlined the strong connections linking Stravinsky's *Sacre* to the folk music of Russia, describing the relationship between the revolutionary findings of Stravinsky and the characteristics of the music of rural Russia. Bartok stated: "Even the origin of the rough-grained, brittle and jerky musical structure backed by ostinatos, which is so completely different from any structural proceeding of the past, may be sought in the short-breathed Russian peasant motives."[33] Taruskin asserts that precisely the most novel aspects of Stravinsky's music, its form and rhythm, were those most heavily indebted to folklore.[34]

Villa-Lobos and Stravinsky were both concerned about how being labeled as nationalist or folklorist composers would impede recognition of the originality of their musical contributions. But they both made contradictory statements on this issue. Stravinsky told Robert Craft that he "was bored with folk music and even more so with the question of its connections with his work."[35] Yet in later years he expressed how his Russian background had always been inherent to the inner, latent nature of his music, even when it was not noticeable at first glance.[36] Likewise, as a pioneer of the Anthropophagy movement, Villa-Lobos did not attempt to hide his use of folklore, which he regarded as part of the process of creating music of universal character. Paradoxically, he regarded the music of J. S. Bach as the prime example of a source of universal folklore.[37] At the same time, the European public's appreciation for the exotic, particularly for an artist coming from Brazil, led Villa-Lobos to fuel interest in his music by exaggerating his association with nationalism. When touring Europe he said, "I don't use folklore. I am the folklore."[38]

Ultimately, Villa-Lobos became a victim of his own strategy to achieve greater recognition. By the end of his life, it was too late to claim that "universal" composers such as Mozart and Beethoven also used folklore in their music. The stigma of the nationalist, exotic composer was already ingrained in the appreciation of his work. Villa-Lobos would state:

> I was born in Brazil, was educated in Brazil and live for Brazil. Since, however, art is universal, I have at my disposal universal ideas that stretch beyond that part which concerns my native country alone. For this reason, even those of my compositions that reveal the typical character of my country are also representative in a universal sense.[39]

Ironically, it was Stravinsky who quoted published folk songs in his early ballets yet became recognized as a great pioneer of modern music. Villa-Lobos, who did not quote folk songs[40] in his early ballets, has still not been recognized as a universal, modernist pioneer.

The apparent exoticism of Villa-Lobos's music led audiences to wrongly think that his music was the embodiment of the Brazilian nation in the form of sound. In fact, this was a typical case in which life and art complemented each other. The public and critics thought his music evoked the rustling of wild forests, the rhythm of Amerindian dances combined with the captivating and strange poetry of their melodies, as well as an exuberant nature, prodigal in fruits, flowers, and dazzling birds, which captured the soul of the country in its most intimate essence. The composer's buoyant personality matched the sonorous richness of the music. He was viewed as the incarnation of a radical alterity, the "ultimate Other," representative of the Amerindian primitives and the rich and immense nature that he represented in his music. He was considered a "racial composer," possessed by the soul of Brazil. In several compositions, the public and critics identified the characteristics of a Dionysian fury and violence generated by a vital energy capable of producing a sonorous cataclysm, elements that were much in vogue in Paris during the 1920s modernism.[41]

However, this exoticism is deceptive. Instead of being shaped by Brazil, Villa-Lobos's music shaped and created a new vision of Brazil.[42] In an essay published on the website of the Orquestra Sinfônica do Estado de São Paulo, Leopoldo Waizbort states that Villa-Lobos's music "imagined a nation and set it to music, as well as imagining it as contradictory and complex."[43] In other words, the composer did not build his individual style upon the national style of the country; rather, his individual style shaped the national style of Brazil. Villa-Lobos's compositions created and revealed a new musical identity for the nation in the form of an export product that was the pure embodiment of the Anthropophagic process asserted by Oswald de Andrade.

The Early Life of Villa-Lobos: A Brief Historical Background

Villa-Lobos's biography is clouded by numerous uncertainties that are a result of the manipulation of facts, in great part encouraged by the composer himself, in an attempt to create the image of a bright and energetic artist whose prolific output was the embodiment of the diversity and magnitude of the country he represented. One of the main challenges comes from the composer's practice of backdating a number of his compositions to suggest they were written earlier than they actually were. While this practice has been explained as an attempt to forge the image of an original creator whose messianic discoveries left a lasting impact on music history, it deserves to be examined more closely in relation to the aesthetics of the time.

The composer's travels and his assimilation of original folk music present additional challenges. This includes his fictional participation in scientific expeditions, such as the Roosevelt-Rondon expedition to the Amazon basin in 1913–1914. While an accurate account of the composer's travels would certainly clarify many aspects of the life of someone whose music has been so closely associated with the folk materials of his homeland, detailed evidence is lacking. In any case, it is known that Villa-Lobos's study of national folklore was not as systematic as the one undertaken by his contemporary Bela Bartok, for example. Yet numerous biographies have documented that Villa-Lobos did travel extensively throughout Brazil during his youth and had the opportunity to assimilate a great deal of folk music from different parts of the country. On certain occasions, this assimilation happened even without the need to travel. The Brazilian sociologist and anthropologist Leopoldo Waizbort argues that by surrounding himself with indigenous artifacts while listening to the original phonograms brought by Roquette-Pinto from the expedition to the Amazon basin, Villa-Lobos was indeed transported from the National Museum into the hidden, virgin, and wild region where the phonograms were collected. In those phonograms the primitive and the modern intertwined, creating and determining each other, enabling an almost genuine experience.[44]

Villa-Lobos's tendencies to obscure his biography by backdating his compositions and misrepresenting the extent of his travels in Brazil evoke two of the most central characteristics of the Anthropophagic movement, namely, the reframing of the concepts of time and space, which some scholars have defined as "the untimely and the deterritorialized," using insights from the philosophers Giles Deleuze and Félix Guattari.[45] While already addressed in chapter 1, this concept is discussed in more detail the last chapter of this book, where the manipulation of time and space is framed as a result of the interaction between surrealism and Anthropophagy.

Villa-Lobos (1887–1959) was born just before slavery was abolished (1888) and Brazil became a republic (1889), so he grew up during a period of heightened nationalist awareness. He lived in the capital of the recently created republic and was only twelve years old when his father died, leading to financial challenges for his family. It was under the supervision of his father that Villa-Lobos developed an early, severe, and disciplined education in music, learning clarinet and cello and developing an acute ability to "identify genre, style, character and origin of compositions, in addition to recognizing quickly the name of a note, of sounds or noises."[46]

Villa-Lobos was still an adolescent when he started attending the *chorões*, groups of public employees who developed a new, Brazilian, popular music genre. This genre, called *choro*, represented a fusion of European dances, such as waltzes and polkas, with African rhythms, resulting in a new, essentially Brazilian genre that preceded the samba.[47] There is some contention among ethnomusicologists regarding the classification of the *choro* as urban folklore or popular music, but it remains a fact that in Rio de Janeiro, the capital of the nation, multiple influential musical genres developed, including the *maxixe*, the Brazilian tango, the *modinha*, the *choro*, and the samba. A self-taught guitar player, Villa-Lobos became a virtuoso performer and a *chorão* himself.[48]

Villa-Lobos's contact with genuine folk music happened a little later, during the early 1900s, when he began traveling around the country, initially to the northeast region of Brazil. His acquaintance with folk, urban, and classical Western music happened in an unsystematic way. Contrary to the experiences of most of his contemporaries, he did not undergo formal training, except for a brief incursion into the conservatory in Rio de Janeiro. Stravinsky started studying with Rimsky-Korsakov when he was twenty-three years old. Villa-Lobos started studying in the conservatory when he was twenty-two years old but abandoned his studies after a few months.

At the beginning of the twentieth century, two events had an important bearing on the further development of Villa-Lobos's music. The first one was the Roosevelt-Rondon scientific expedition to the Amazon in 1913–1914. The expedition sparked an Amerindian fever in Brazil, as the participants' tales of adventure spread around the country and they returned as heroes. This interest in the native, indigenous culture became the Brazilian response to the primitivist fever in Europe. The expedition brought back phonograms, which Villa-Lobos listened to numerous times and harmonized,[49] according to Beatriz Roquete Pinto Boiunga, daughter of the prominent Brazilian anthropologist Edgard Roquette-Pinto.

The second event was the advent of the First World War. It was due to the war that Diaghilev's Ballets Russes ended up going to Brazil in 1913 and 1917. These tours were of great importance because the Ballets Russes was one of the most significant cultural manifestations at the beginning of the twentieth century, leaving an astonishing legacy in music, dance, and art that revolutionized Western culture. The company's influence continues to be felt today, and by traveling to Brazil during its golden period, it helped to disseminate in South America the most avant-garde art of the time. The Ballets Russes performed a wide repertoire in Rio de Janeiro for about two weeks during each visit, but despite speculations to the contrary, according to Jane Pritchard, the company's repertoire did not include any ballets by Stravinsky (see Table 2.1).[50]

Table 2.1. Repertoire performed by the Ballets Russes in their two tours of Brazil

	Date	Repertoire
1st Tour: 1913 Performances at the Municipal Theater of Rio de Janeiro	10/19	Le Pavillon d'Armide, Les Sylphides, Le Spectre de la rose, Prince Igor
	10/20	Le Pavillon d'Armide, Les Sylphides, Le Spectre de la rose, Prince Igor
	10/21	Le Carnaval, Les Sylphides, L'Oiseau et le Prince, Prince Igor
	10/22	Le Lac des cygnes, Cléopâtre
	10/24	Le Lac des cygnes, Cléopâtre
	10/25	Les Sylphnides, Thamar, Schéhérazade
	10/26	Thamar, Le Carnaval, Cléopâtre
	10/27	Le Lac des Cygnes, Schéhérazade
	10/29	Giselle, Cléopâtre
	10/30	Thamar, L'Après-midi d'un Faune, Prince Igor, Le Dieu bleu
	10/31	Thamar, Le Spectre de la rose, L'Après-midi d'un Faune, Cléopâtre
	11/01	Le Carnaval, Les Sylphides, La Tragédie de Salomé
2nd Tour: 1917 Performances at the Municipal Theater of Rio de Janeiro	08/14	Les Sylphides, Le Carnaval, Prince Igor, Schéhérazade
	08/16	Le Carnaval, Sadko, Prince Igor, Cléopâtre
	08/17	Sadko, Les Sylphides, Prince Igor, Cléopâtre
	08/18	Cléopâtre, Le Spectre de la rose, Midnight Sun, Les Sylphides
	08/19	Sadko, Le Spectre de la rose, Midnight Sun, Schéhérazade
	08/20	Sadko, Enchanted Princess, Les Papillons, Schéhérazade
	08/22	Les Papillons, The Good-Humoured Ladies, Las Meninas, Thamar
	08/23	Thamar, Le Spectre de la rose, Le Carnaval, The Good-Humoured Ladies
	08/24	Thamar, L'Après-midi d'un Faune, Contes Russes, Les Sylphides
	08/25	Les Sylphides, Contes Russes, Las Meninas, Midnight Sun
	08/26	Thamar, The Good-Humoured Ladies, Le Carnaval, Prince Igor

(continued)

Table 2.1. *Continued*

2nd Tour: 1917 Performances at the Municipal Theater of São Paulo	Date	Repertoire
	08/28	Les Sylphides, Le Carnaval, Prince Igor, Schéhérazade
	08/30	Sadko, Les Papillons, Midnight Sun, The Good-Humoured Ladies
	09/01	Thamar, L'Après-midi d'un Faune, The Good-Humoured Ladies, Les Sylphides
	09/02	Le Carnaval, Las Meninas, Le Spectre de la rose, Cléopâtre
	09/03	Le Carnaval, Thamar, Prince Igor

Consequently, the multiple claims that Villa-Lobos heard and studied with fascination Stravinsky's works during this period are unsubstantiated,[51] and they erroneously minimize the originality of the Brazilian composer's contributions.

In 1917, Villa-Lobos met the composer Darius Milhaud (1892–1974), secretary to the French poet and dramatist Paul Claudel (1868–1955), who was working at the time as a diplomat in Rio de Janeiro.[52] There is substantial evidence indicating that the relationship between Villa-Lobos and Milhaud was superficial during the French composer's residence in Rio de Janeiro, which lasted less than two years.[53] The fact that a version for piano four hands of Stravinsky's *The Rite of Spring* received a private performance in 1918 attended by Claudel, and possibly Milhaud, does not imply that Villa-Lobos had contact with this work. The first orchestra performance of *Petrushka* in Brazil happened in 1935, while both *The Firebird* and *The Rite of Spring* were performed in Brazil for the first time after the Second World War.[54]

Villa-Lobos's first contact with the early works of Stravinsky is, therefore, a matter of controversy. His initial encounter with *The Rite of Spring* seems to have happened in 1923 during his sojourn in Paris; Villa-Lobos stated that it had been "the greatest musical experience of [my] life."[55] Conversely, Stravinsky, in one of the many demeaning statements against his peers that he made in his later years, said: "Why is it that whenever I hear a piece of music I don't like, it's always by Villa Lobos?"[56]

While the two tours of Diaghilev's Ballets Russes to Brazil were motivated by the war in Europe, repercussions of the war in Brazil created the conditions for Villa-Lobos to present the first public concert of his music in 1915, generating controversy over its quality. From that moment onward, Villa-Lobos began to present his compositions to Rio de Janeiro audiences in chamber music recitals. Symphonic compositions were included for the first time at the fifth recital of his works, which happened in 1918, five years after the premiere of *The Rite of Spring*. It was difficult for the composer to organize a symphonic concert given the large number of musicians necessary to perform his orchestral music.

There are curious parallels between the careers of Stravinsky and Villa-Lobos, who was five years younger than the Russian composer (and six years younger than Bartok; see Figure 2.1). By the time the Ballets Russes were debuting in Paris and Stravinsky was asked to write the *Firebird* by Diaghilev, Villa-Lobos was a teenager who had given up musical studies at the conservatory and was eagerly absorbing multiple musical experiences in his travels in Brazil. An amusing anecdote tells how upon returning from one of those trips in 1912, the composer was surprised to learn that his mother, who had not heard from him for about two years, considered him dead and intended to organize a mass on behalf of his soul.[57]

By the time of the premiere of Stravinsky's *The Rite of Spring* in 1913, Villa-Lobos was twenty-six years old. Approximately six months later, he married the pianist Lucília Guimarães and began to enjoy a period of greater stability that allowed him to dedicate a substantial amount of time to writing music. Considering the five-year age difference between Villa-Lobos and Stravinsky, it is a curious coincidence that the first public performance of Villa's works happened on November 13, 1915, when he was twenty-eight years old, the same age as Stravinsky when his first ballet, *Firebird*, premiered.

   Igor Stravinsky (1882-1971)      Heitor Villa-Lobos (1887-1959)

1910: Firebird

1911: Petrushka

1913: Rite of Spring

1916: Weariness at Dawn (Tédio de Alvorada)
       Myremis (lost)
       [also The Golden Centaur (lost)]
       Symphony No. 1

1917: Uirapuru
       Amazonas
       [also Saci Pererê, Lobisomen and Yara (all lost)]
       Symphony No. 2

1918: Polichinelo (A Prole do Bebê, Suite No. 1)
       End of World War I
       1st public performance of orchestral works

Figure 2.1. Parallels between the trajectories of Stravinsky and Villa-Lobos (born five years apart) in the beginning of their musical careers.

Villa-Lobos's compositions from 1916 reveal a strong European influence.[58] For example, in that year he wrote *O Naufrágio dos Kleônikos* (*The Shipwreck of Kleonikos*), a tone poem/ballet based on a Greek mythological theme that can be linked to works such as Ravel's *Daphnis et Chloe* or Debussy's *Prelude to the Afternoon of a Faun*, as well as compositions by Saint-Saens. The same is probably true of Villa-Lobos's *Golden Centaur*, whose music materials are lost. His two early symphonies were written in the style of Vincent d'Indy.

The compositions that were *allegedly* written in 1917 apparently reveal a breakthrough, a rupture with the past.[59] *Uirapuru* is a reworking of *Weariness at Dawn*, while *Amazonas* is a reworking of *Myremis*. This is the moment, musicologists have suggested, when Villa-Lobos found his nationalistic language, starting with the choice of subject for his compositions. Most of the orchestral works listed in the third edition of the official catalog of the Villa-Lobos Museum (1989) bear titles based on Brazilian folk legends and Brazilian mythology.

Unfortunately, the materials of compositions, such as *Saci Pererê* (a famous Brazilian folk character of [Amer]Indian origin from southern Brazil, later shaped by African influence); *Lobisomen* (the Brazilian version of the werewolf, a legend of European origin brought to Brazil by the Portuguese); and *Yara* (the Brazilian indigenous version of a mermaid who lives in the rivers of the northern region of Brazil), are lost.

Two tone-poems/ballets, *Uirapuru* and *Amazonas*, plus the "Polichinelo" movement from Villa-Lobos's *Prole do Bebe Suite No. 1* for piano from 1918, form the core of the present study. While the *Prole do Bebe Suite No. 1* is definitely a composition from the 1910s, doubts about the precise dates of several works from the same period, which include *Uirapuru* and *Amazonas*, led to questions concerning the sudden irruption of a nationalistic style in Villa-Lobos during the last years of the decade. For musicologists such as Paulo Guérios, the nationalist turn in Villa-Lobos's music occurred a little later, during the composer's stay in Paris in the 1920s.[60] According to Guérios, the predominant aesthetics in the music of the composer up to that point had developed mainly under the influence of Wagner and of the French impressionism represented by Debussy. However, by the time Villa-Lobos arrived in Paris in 1923, that aesthetic was considered outdated, thanks to the emergence of new ideas represented in works such as Stravinsky's *Rite of Spring* and Erik Satie's *Parade*. In the French context, in order for foreign music to be considered modern and fashionable, it had to incorporate elements of popular music from the country of origin, liberated from the aesthetic influences of Western European tradition. Villa-Lobos's contact with this artistic environment in Paris would have contributed to his conversion into a quintessential nationalist composer.

Such a phenomenon is not isolated. Numerous Latin American artists traveled to Europe during this period, particularly to important cultural centers such as Paris and Barcelona, in search of technical improvement, aesthetic updating, and an expansion of their cultural horizons, as well as greater recognition abroad. Many of these artists were impressed by the interest of the French in their native cultures, which contrasted with the disdain shown by the economic and cultural elites of their home countries. Among them are artists as distinguished as Guatemalan writer Miguel Angel Asturias, who won the 1967 Nobel Prize for Literature, and the celebrated Mexican muralist Diego Rivera.[61]

In Villa-Lobos's case, the incorporation of nationalist elements into his music does not seem to have been as sudden a shift as some musicologists such as Guérios suggest, but the outcome of a process that started during the 1910s, continued during the composer's participation in the modernist movement in Brazil, and established itself with greater intensity during his stay in France. While nationalist elements were already present in compositions that Villa-Lobos definitely wrote before his first sojourn in Paris,[62] such as the *Suite Popular Brasileira* (1908–1912), the *Danças Características Africanas* (1914–1916), *Lenda do Caboclo* (1920), and *Choros No. 1* (1920), it is possible that the Amerindian element of *Amazonas* and *Uirapuru* found its way into his music during his stay in Paris.[63] The cult of primitivism present in French literary circles drew the attention of Brazilian writers such as Oswald de Andrade to the "national primitive reality" of Brazil, and the same phenomenon appeared in the visual arts with Tarsila do Amaral, and in music with Villa-Lobos.

The musicological problem is that the received view of Villa-Lobos's originality rests essentially on the presence of nationalist elements in his music, for in the early twentieth century such borrowings were particularly praised as a characteristic of "modernity." The foregrounding of Villa-Lobos's nationalism, however, overshadowed the aesthetic updating integral to Villa-Lobos's compositional style, which incorporated original techniques discussed in this book, and which constitutes his important and original contribution to the development of modernism.

Villa-Lobos Reconsidered

The universal appeal of Villa-Lobos's music is due mainly to two characteristics. In the first place, he transcended the "exotic" quality of the folk material by presenting it in a dazzling and highly imaginative aural landscape. As Béhague puts it, "Villa-Lobos's nationalism was multifaceted and nonexclusive, since his nationalist concerns and treatment tended to be integrated with his numerous stylistic experiments, resulting in a complex and varied musical language."[64]

Villa-Lobos used not only folk melodies, but also melodies from Brazilian popular music. Sometimes it is difficult to separate those two categories, because the popular music of the time in Rio de Janeiro is occasionally classified as urban folklore. This study relies on the distinction drawn by Oneyda Alvarenga, a disciple of Mário de Andrade, who was the most prominent intellectual among the folklore scholars in Brazil during the first half of the twentieth century:

> Folk music, which is used anonymously and collectively by the uncultivated classes of civilized nations, comes from the anonymous and collective creation by the same uncultivated classes, or comes from the adoption and accommodation of popular or cultivated works that have lost the vital use of the means from which they originated. Popular music, which is composed by a known author, is diffused among and used by, to a greater or lesser extent, all the layers of a collective society.[65]

If Villa-Lobos's use of themes from folk and popular music suggests a Romantic posture, his treatment of them was anti-Romantic, as it employed a more contemporary language. This treatment reveals an attempt to rupture the barriers between high and low art, merging the sophistication of European art music with the spontaneity of national popular culture.[66] This, in fact, is one of the aspects that makes Villa-Lobos's music so contemporary. This rupture is an anthropophagic device that connects Cultural Cannibalism with the postmodern movement:

> Recent calls for parity between "high" and "low" in all the arts reflect a further dimension of the contemporary infatuation with cultural criss-cross. A great deal of the Postmodernist argument has centered on the destruction of traditional differentiations between categories: high and low, artist and critic, signified and signifier.[67]

The second characteristic of Villa-Lobos's music that accounts for its universal appeal is the originality of his composition method, which he developed independently of any school or movement, a circumstance that sets him apart from other major composers of the time. Beneath what may initially be perceived as naiveté, lack of technique, and an arbitrary compositional method lies a deliberate process of structuring that displays remarkable erudition. This becomes particularly evident when one studies Villa-Lobos's compositions from the point of view of Cultural Anthropophagy. In this sense, the comparison of three of his emblematic works with the early ballets of Stravinsky is particularly useful, since Stravinsky's ballets are considered works that propelled both ballet and music into the modern age.

As noted above, the parallels in the trajectories of the early careers of Villa-Lobos and Stravinsky are remarkable. The years 1916–1918 in the career of Villa-Lobos can be compared with Stravinsky's first period of success in 1909–1913, when he wrote his early breakthrough scores for Diaghilev's Ballets Russes: *Firebird*, *Petrushka*, and *The Rite of Spring* (Figure 2.1). Stravinsky was twenty-eight years old when he received his first commission, about the same age as Villa-Lobos when he started composing the orchestral compositions that initially won him fame. But the chronological analogies belie the difference in orientation between the two composers. Stravinsky had studied under Rimsky-Korsakov, the dean of the renowned St. Petersburg Conservatory that today bears his name, and was circulating in Paris, the cultural capital of the world, working with the most renowned artists of the time. Villa-Lobos, on the other hand, received little formal training. "One foot in the academy and you are changed for the worst!" he would say. This attitude is in line with the Cannibal Manifesto, which positions itself "down with the urban sclerosis. Down with the Conservatories and speculative tedium."[68]

As explained previously, there is great controversy about the dating of Villa-Lobos's compositions due to the composer's habit of backdating a number of his works. Rather than formulating a critical speculation about the composer's motives for this manipulation of time, this study approaches the problem via the cannibalist aesthetic, demonstrating that the chronological dimension of composition is greatly weakened when analyzing artworks whose governing aesthetic advocates the abrogation of time.

So far, most of Western musicology has failed to address the real nature of Brazilian modern artistic production and has instead reduced it to a facet of Western colonial modernity, which relegates its contributions to a condition of peripheral Occidentalism. This approach continues to perpetuate myths of civilization and progress as a dialogue between a Eurocentric view and a colonial reaction. However, Brazilian Anthropophagy by definition denies the type of categorization of which Villa-Lobos was a victim, when he was labeled an exotic, folklorist composer. The Anthropophagous Manifesto states: "It was because we never had grammars or collections of old vegetables. And we never knew what urban, suburban, frontier and continental were."[69] On one hand, this statement praises as more authentic the real coexistence with nature of the indigenous population of Brazil in comparison with the sterile categorizations promoted by the civilized European society. But indirectly, one can interpret the text as praising the type of intuitive discoveries of a composer like Villa-Lobos, who had to rely more on his personal instincts than the study of grammars, treatises, or a more systematic education. Frivolous matters such as the categorization or labeling of plants are trivial when brought to a context of someone who is living alongside those plants, and there conducting one's own existence.

This book hopes to elucidate the problems mentioned above in the chapter by selecting and analyzing three emblematic compositions by Villa-Lobos that are particularly suitable for the study of his Anthropophagic style. Not only will the investigation of these works examine the compositional process of a great creator, but it will also effectively establish his contributions to modernism by comparing these works with the trilogy of Stravinsky's early ballets, which, according to several musicologists, "put him on the international map and propelled both ballet and music into the modern age."[70]

Through cannibalism, Villa-Lobos's music absorbed the influence not only of Stravinsky, but also of Bach, Wagner, Debussy, and a number of other French composers. The process of appropriation or emulation was very different for each one of these influences. While numerous studies about the Brazilian composer attempt to pinpoint the multiple foreign stimuli to which he reacted, most of them fail to access the real nature of those influences because of the lack of a greater understanding of the process of appropriation linked with cannibalism. As Ralph Waldo Emerson stated: "We are as much informed of a writer's genius by what he selects as by what he originates. We read the quotation with his eyes, and find a new and fervent sense; as a passage from one of the poets, well recited, borrows new interest from the rendering. As the journals say, 'the italics are ours.'"[71]

In the case of Stravinsky, Glenn Watkins describes how the process of appropriation of external materials was integral to his compositional style:

> Pierre Boulez has correctly pointed to Stravinsky's love for manipulating musical objects, a delight in taking things apart and putting them together again in a different fashion, thereby giving them 'significance.' For Stravinsky the invocation of a known and one's expectations regarding it became the starting point of the creative process. In this gloss of pre-existent material, however, Stravinsky was obliged to define his own voice with increasing precision. A personal style was thus coined not so much through the appropriation of

ingredients from a particular historical or cultural model as through their fracture and purposeful reassemblage: criticism of received materials becomes the modus operandi for the creative act.[72]

Stravinsky is credited with having stated that "a good composer does not imitate; he steals."[73] Villa-Lobos always insisted on his complete independence from the influence of other composers, and his declaration that "as soon as I feel myself being influenced, I jump out of it" is viewed with irony and a great dose of mistrust.[74] Unfortunately, due to a preoccupation with the identification of external influences, most studies fail to acknowledge the true originality of some of his important compositions, which the current study attempts to rescue. After all, despite his lack of formal training and his avoidance of other composers' influence, Villa-Lobos found another way to master the art of the modern composers from the time: He ate them.[75]

The process will be clarified by addressing the practice of Cultural Cannibalism through a detailed analysis of three compositions by the Brazilian composer, which appear in the official catalog of the Villa-Lobos Museum[76] as follows:

> *Amazonas*: Symphonic poem and Brazilian (Amer)Indian ballet, written in Rio de Janeiro in 1917, orchestra version published and premiered in 1929, and piano version published in 1953 by Éditions Max Eschig.
>
> *Uirapuru*: Symphonic poem and ballet, written in Rio de Janeiro in 1917 with the subtitle "The Enchanted Bird," premiered in Buenos Aires in 1935, and published by Associated Music Publishers. The piece is dedicated to Serge Lifar, former principal dancer of the Ballets Russes.
>
> *Polichinelo*: Seventh movement of *A Prole do Bebe* (*The Baby's Family*) Suite No. 1, written in Rio de Janeiro in 1918 with the subtitle "The Dolls," and first published by Arthur Napoleon Publishers in Brazil. The suite is dedicated to Lucília Villa-Lobos, wife of the composer.

References to Villa-Lobos's ingestion of the work of his contemporaries should not be confused with his use of cannibal-related stories for self-promotion. For example, in December 1927, the Parisian newspaper *L'Intransigeant* described how Villa-Lobos had been taken prisoner by cannibals during a trip to the region close to Paraguay. According to the tale, he was tied to a tree as the (Amer)Indians rejoiced in his capture; they dedicated three days to ritual celebrations in preparation for killing and eating him, before his narrow escape and miraculous rescue. The story was entitled, "L'aventure d'un Compositeur: Musique Cannibale" (The Adventures of a Composer: Cannibal Music).[77]

Looking beyond the fantastic tales of actual cannibalism that fueled Villa-Lobos's fame, this book will examine the issue of musical cannibalism with a focus on the relationship between the early ballets of Stravinsky and the three selected key works that Villa-Lobos composed allegedly between the years 1916 and 1918. These are works of unprecedented originality that allowed him to find his personal style, characterized by a symbiosis of primitive elements drawn from native Brazilian legends and sounds, combined and assimilated with European elements in a very personal way. The result is an individual and unique soundscape of nationalistic, yet universal, character completely in line with the Anthropophagous Manifesto published by Oswald de Andrade a decade later.

Notes

1. Béhague stated that Villa-Lobos was "the single most significant creative figure in twentieth-century Brazilian art music." See Gerard Béhague, "Villa-Lobos, Heitor," in *The New Grove Dictionary of Music and Musicians*, eds. Stanley Sadie and John Tyrrell 26: 613 (London: Macmillan, 2001). Vasco Mariz wrote that "Heitor Villa-Lobos is undoubtedly one of the twentieth century's foremost composers." Vasco Mariz, foreword to *Heitor Villa-Lobos: The Search for Brazil's Musical Soul*, by Gerard Béhague (Austin: Institute of Latin American Studies, 1994).

2. Alejo Carpentier, "Uma Força Musical da América," 37–38. Miguel de Unamuno was a prominent Spanish intellectual.

3. For a discussion of musical borrowing, see J. Peter Burkholder, "The Uses of Existing Music: Musical Borrowing as a Field," 851–70.

4. A description of the aesthetics of "collage" is not part of the scope of this study, as there is a vast body of literature concerning this topic. It is assumed that the reader is at least familiar with the topic.

5. See, for example: Bruna Della Torre, "Modelos Críticos: Antonio Candido e Roberto Schwarz Leem Oswald de Andrade," 183–84. To make matters even more difficult, there is a third and better-known Andrade: Carlos Drummond de Andrade, another writer affiliated with the Anthropophagy movement, whose poetry transcended the movement to the extent that some consider him the greatest Brazilian poet of all time.

6. Kimberle S. López, accessed September 10, 2021, at 28.

7. See, for example, Danilo Mercês Freitas and Mayara Ribeiro Guimarães, "A Antropofagia Musical na Poética de Mário de Andrade," *Revista Literatura em Debate* 9, no. 16 (2015): 42–56, http://revistas.fw.uri.br/index.php/literaturaemdebate/article/view/1726/1900.

8. It was on the banks of the Ipiranga River in São Paulo that the independence of Brazil was proclaimed in 1822. The piece is subtitled a "secular oratorio," because the text has a non-religious subject, and also due to the inclusion of choirs, soloists [or: a soloist], and orchestra (in a metaphoric way), as well as musical dynamic indications and cues for the entrance of instruments inside the text.

9. See Tiago de Oliveira Pinto, "Art Is Universal," 106.

10. Flávia Camargo Toni, "Mário de Andrade e Villa-Lobos," 43–58 at 54.

11. Ibid., 57.

12. For a comparison of the nationalist trajectories of Oswald and Mário de Andrade, see Renata Campello Cabral and Paola Berenstein Jacques, "O antropófago Oswald de Andrade," especially pages 25–26.

13. This statement is attributed to Hélio Oiticica, the plastic artist who gave the name *Tropicália* to an installation that was first exhibited in Rio de Janeiro in 1967, and became his most renowned artwork, considered a synthesis of the tropicalist movement. Within it, a penetrable (PN2, a geometrical structure mixing wood and fabric) included the sentence "purity is a myth," which updated the relationship of Brazil with the world. The installation challenged the myth of purity in art; incorporated some of the most popular experiences, such as the architecture and the way of community life in the *favelas* (Brazilian slums); and revealed the greatest tropicalist ambiguity: the simultaneous incorporation of mass culture—represented by the television and its profusion of images—and a posture that is both critical and apologetic. Oiticica aimed *Tropicália* to be "the most anthropophagic work of Brazilian art," which updated the anthropophagy of the late 1920s with its exaggerated tropical ambience, proposing what he coined a "super-anthropophagy," aiming to prevent the cultural colonialism still in existence among his generation of modernist artists. See Paola Berenstein Jacques, "Tropicália Brasília: A pureza é um mito," 150–51.

14. Viveiros de Castro, "Temos que Criar um Outro Conceito de Criação," 168–69. Caetano Veloso wrote something analogous: "while Mário de Andrade [. . .] had been the responsible, normative and organizing figure of modernism, Oswald [. . .] represented the radical fragmentation, the intuitive and violently iconoclastic force." See Caetano Veloso, *Verdade Tropical*, 255.

15. Arnaldo Daraya Contier, *Brasil Novo—Música, Nação e Modernidade: Os anos 20 e 30*, 14.

16. Thought by Marcos Napolitano quoted in Graziela Naclério Forte, "O Projeto Nacional dos Modernistas," 6.

17. Moacir Werneck de Castro, *Mário de Andrade: Exílio no Rio*, 60–61.

18. Of special importance is the seminal work of Paulo de Tarso Salles [*Villa-Lobos: Processos Composicionais*, Campinas: Unicamp: 2009] and Maria Alice Volpe [*Indianismo and Landscape in the Brazilian Age of Progress: Art Music from Carlos Gomes to Villa-Lobos, 1870s–1930s*, Austin: UMI Research Press, 2001]. Gil Jardim wrote a book titled *O Estilo Antropofágico de Heitor Villa-Lobos*, published by Philarmonia Brasileira in 2005.

19. As a parenthesis, it seems opportune to mention a picturesque incident connecting Mário and Oswald de Andrade with the Brazilian composer. The incident is narrated by Antônio Candido as follows: "In the 1920s, Oswald found Villa-Lobos in Europe and was surprised by a deficiency of the composer's culture, which led him to confuse Jules Romains with Romain Rolland and things like that. Back in Brazil, Oswald spoke of this in Dona Olívia Guedes Penteado's salon, stating that the great composer compromised us abroad. And entering into the exaggeration that took him when he was in a polemical vein, he ended up stating that he [Villa-Lobos] didn't even know music and was an instinctive ignorant. As it was alleged that he [Oswald] did not have the authority to say this, he replied more or less:

'It's not me who says. Mário [de Andrade], who understands, said that Villa doesn't know harmony or counterpoint.'

People were surprised, remembering that Mário had always said the opposite. Oswald then went further and explained:

'This is because Mário has no intimacy with you. To me he tells the truth.'

At this the discussion died, but one of those present could not get over the incident and telephoned Mário, reproaching him for his dubiousness: How could he think one thing and say another? He [Mário] protested, the caller gave the details, and Mário became angrily mad. He then set out to look for Oswald and, finding him by coincidence on 15th Street, called him to speak. But the friend disarmed him, replying simply, with the smiling clarity of his blue gaze:

'I lied.'" See Antônio Cândido, "Digressão Sentimental sobre Oswald de Andrade," 68.

20. Beatriz de Azevedo, "Antropofagia: Palimpsesto Selvagem," 17. Oswald's approach to punctuation, in particular, reflects Theodore Adorno's thought: "There is no element in which language resembles music more than in the punctuation marks. The comma and the period correspond to the half-cadence and the authentic cadence. Exclamation points are like silent cymbal clashes, question marks like musical upbeats, colons dominant seventh chords; and only a person who can perceive the different weights of strong and weak phrasings in musical form can really feel the distinction between the comma and the semicolon." Theodor W. Adorno, "Punctuation Marks," 300–301.

21. Kenneth David Jackson, *Cannibals Angels*, 121 and 229.

22. Oswald de Andrade, "O Artista," *Novíssima* II, no. 11 (Aug.–Sept. 1925): 32. The poem has been republished with updated orthography in Oswald de Andrade, *Poesias Reunidas*, eds. Jorge Schwartz and Gênese Andrade (São Paulo: Companhia das Letras, 2017), 290.

23. Oswald de Andrade, "Atelier," in *Oswald de Andrade: Poesias Reunidas*, eds. Jorge Schwartz and Gênese Andrade, 115.

24. Translation by Kenneth David Jackson. Two years later, on July 4, 1927, Villa-Lobos wrote from Paris a letter to Oswald de Andrade e Tarsila do Amaral with the following text:

Caros amigos Tarcila and Oswaldo	Dear friends Tarcila and Oswaldo
De Paris	From Paris
Um grito de admiração por esta carta! ...	A cry of admiration through this letter! ...
Pa! pa! pa!	Pa! pa! pa!
Pa! pa! pa!	Pa! pa! pa!
Pa!	Pa!
Pa!	Pa!
Pa!	Pa!
Para o Brasil	To Brazil
Cabareteio, mesmo sem o Jazz,	A cabaret number, even without Jazz
mas num forte zabumba de samba	but with a strong samba zabumba
cheio de catiras e mindinhos baianos	full of catiras and Bahian mindinhos

The original text (note the misspelling of the names) is found in Aracy Amaral, *Tarsila*, 409. Zabumba is a type of bass drum typical of Brazil, while catira (or cateretê) and mindinho (or miudinho) are both folk regional dances. When mentioning the Bahian mindinho, Villa-Lobos refers to a style of dancing samba in state Bahia, in which the feet of the dancers move in short steps, sliding on the floor. The composer used to call his second wife Mindinha (derived from her real name, Arminda), an affectionate nickname that reflected her diminutive stature, though they never officially married.

25. Richard Greenan, "Traditional Mutants," 26.

26. Ibid., 35. A previous section titled "The Tradition of Anthropophagy," 26–32, addresses the various stages of the development of Brazilian popular music.

27. The Brazilian pianist Anna Stella Schic called him the "indien blanc" [white (Amer)Indian] in her biography *Villa-Lobos: Souvenirs de l'indien blanc*. The Brazilian modernist poet Menotti del Picchia (1892–1988) was the first to call Villa-Lobos "o índio de casaca," roughly translated as "(Amer)Indian in a tuxedo." See C. Paula Barros, *O romance de Villa-Lobos*, 215.

28. Villa-Lobos's obituary in the *New York Times* referred to him as "primarily a folklorist." See "Villa-Lobos Dies, Composer Was 72," *New York Times*, November 18, 1959, 41.

29. Lisa M. Peppercorn, *Villa-Lobos: Collected Studies*, 86.

30. Béhague discusses "the fallacy that works of the great composers transcended national boundaries on the basis of their alleged universal character and appeal." Béhague, *Heitor Villa-Lobos* (1994), 146.

31. Ibid., 157. The last chapter of the book is entirely dedicated to an examination of Villa-Lobos's nationalism vis-à-vis theories of musical nationalism, particularly those advanced by Charles Seeger and Carl Dahlhaus.

32. Richard Taruskin, *Stravinsky and the Russian Traditions,*" ch. 12.
33. Béla Bartók, "The Influence of Peasant Music on Modern Music," 343.
34. Richard Taruskin, *"The Danger of Music" and Other Anti-Utopian Essays,* 134.
35. Robert Craft, preface to *A Book about Stravinsky,* xiv.
36. Margarita Mazo, "Stravinsky's *Les Noces* and Russian Village Wedding Ritual," 99.
37. He stated: "The music of Bach comes from infinite space in order to filter onto the earth as folkloric music; it is a cosmic phenomenon, which is repeated in individuals, scattering itself over the various parts of the globe in an endeavor to become universal." See *Villa-Lobos: Sua obra,* 2nd ed. (Rio de Janeiro: MEC/DAC/Museu Villa-Lobos, 1972), 187.
38. Manuel Negwer, *Villa-Lobos: Der Aufbruch der brasilianischen Musik* (Mainz: Schott Music, 2008), 8.
39. Tiago de Oliveira Pinto, "'Art Is Universal'—On Nationalism and Universality in the Music of Heitor Villa-Lobos," 113. Villa-Lobos's remarks are quoted from an interview held at the United Nations in New York (Registration no. 83.4, soundarchive of the Museu da Imagem e do Som, São Paulo). It is interesting to compare it with a statement by Stravinsky: "A man has one birthplace, one fatherland, one country—he can have only one country—and the place of his birth is the most important factor in his life." See Igor Stravinsky and Robert Craft, *Dialogues and a Diary* (London: Faber and Faber, 1968), 292–93.
40. A picturesque story about Villa-Lobos deserves to be mentioned. In an interview in New York, Villa-Lobos was asked about the use of Amerindian melodies in his music. He replied that he did use them, but that they were melodies so old that today's Amerindians did not know them. He was asked: "If the melodies were forgotten by the Amerindians of today, how did you manage to learn them?" Villa-Lobos quickly replied: "Through the parrots. Brazilian parrots have heard these melodies many years ago and have not forgotten them. They happen to live very long lives. I heard the parrots and wrote down the melodies." This anecdote appears in Irineu Franco Perpétuo, "Biografia Analisa Legado de Villa-Lobos," para. 1.
41. For a more detailed description of the reception of Villa-Lobos in Paris, see Anaïs Fléchet, *Villa-Lobos à Paris,* chapter III.
42. Béhague states that "in reality, the 'white, dressed-up Indian' discovered in his unique and modernistic way the soul of the music of Brazil of its own time. . . . He defined the sort of exuberant stylistic eclecticism that continues to characterize the present art music of Brazil." Béhague, *Heitor Villa-Lobos,* 155.
43. Leopoldo Waizbort, "Villa-Lobos: A invenção da identidade nacional," *Ensaios,* March 1, 2012, http://osesp.art.br/ensaios.aspx?Ensaio=25, para. 10 (accessed July 19, 2017).
44. Leopoldo Waizbort, "Como, quando e por que Villa desmentiu Benjamin," 27.
45. See Murilo Duarte Costa Corrêa, *O intempestivo e o desterritorializado: Oswald de Andrade e o lugar das ideias no Brasil,* Biblioteca on-line de Ciências da Comuni-

cação, 2012, http://www.bocc.ubi.pt/pag/correa-murilo-o-intempestivo-e-o-desterritorializado.pdf.

46. This is a statement by Villa-Lobos in interview granted to Magala da Gama Oliveira in August 1957. See *Presença de Villa-Lobos* (Rio de Janeiro: MEC, Museu Villa-Lobos, 1969, vol. 4), 98.

47. The *choro* and samba styles share many characteristics. Samba is "an Afro-Brazilian song and dance form strongly associated with Carnival. . . . The strength of popular culture that emanated from the urban middle classes was such that it propelled Brazil's most famous African-influenced popular music of all, samba, to the status of national icon in the 1920s and 1930s. In the eyes of intellectuals and the government, samba was a prime example of the racial harmony produced by years of miscegenation." See Tamara Elena Livingston-Isenhour and Thomas George Caracas Garcia, *Choro: A Social-History of a Brazilian Popular Music*, 15, 22.

48. During the 1920s, Villa-Lobos would bring the *choros* to the concert hall, turning the genre into a new kind of experimental, avant-garde music that developed in parallel with important compositions by Schoenberg and the Second Viennese School; Stravinsky's *Symphonies of Wind Instruments*; Ravel's *Bolero*, *La Valse*, and the opera *L'enfant et les Sortileges*; Bartok's String Quartet No. 3; and Varese's *Amériques*, *Hyperprism*, and *Octandre*, just to mention a few.

49. The phonograms were collected by Edgard Roquette Pinto (1894–1945) and archived in the National Museum in Rio de Janeiro.

50. Jane Pritchard, "Serge Diaghilev's Ballets Russes—An Itinerary. Part 1: 1909–1921," in *Dance Research: The Journal of the Society for Dance Research* 27, no. 1 (2009), 131, 156. The only possible confusion might arise from the performance of the pas de deux *L'Oiseau et le prince*, presented only once in Rio de Janeiro in 1913, and *The Enchanted Princess*, also presented only once in Rio de Janeiro in 1917. However, these are adaptations of pas de deux from other ballets. The two pas de deux in question seem to come, respectively, from the ballet *Bluebird* and Princess Florinde from *Sleeping Beauty* by Tchaikovsky, and not from Stravinsky's *Firebird*. According to Pritchard, it was common for Diaghilev's ballets to change numbers in response to cast and venue. All indications point to the conclusion that these performances were not an occasion for contact between Villa-Lobos and Stravinsky's music during these years. Pritchard, *Diaghilev and the Ballets Russes*, 137, 240–41.

51. Some confusion stems from the fact that, when Arthur Rubinstein was in Buenos Aires and about to leave for Brazil in 1918, Ansermet advised him to meet "an extraordinary musician in Rio capable of playing any modern work." See Vasco Mariz, *Heitor Villa-Lobos: Life and Work of the Brazilian Composer*, 12. It is uncertain, however, whether the musician in question was Villa-Lobos or Milhaud, whom Ansermet definitely met in Brazil. See Françoise Reiss, *Nijinsky: A Biography* (New York: Pitman, 1960), 167–68.

52. Claudel was a prominent intellectual, nominated for the Nobel Prize in Literature in six different years, and was the younger brother of the French sculptor Camille Claudel.

53. For example, upon his return to France in 1920, Milhaud wrote an article about Brazilian music in the *Revue Musicale*, where Villa-Lobos is depicted as a young man of robust temperament and full of boldness, but the article lacks details that would have identified him as already the most important force in Brazilian contemporary music, since by that time Villa had written more than a hundred compositions. See Darius Milhaud, "Brésil," *La Revue Musicale* 1, no. 1 (Nov. 1920), 61. According to the brother of Lucília Villa-Lobos, already in 1915 the newspaper O *Paiz* had indicated that the composer had about one hundred compositions under his belt. See Luiz Guimarães, *Villa-Lobos visto da plateia e na intimidade (1912/1935)*, 229.

54. Manoel A. Corrêa do Lago, "O Círculo Veloso-Guerra e Darius Milhaud no Brasil: Modernismo musical no Rio de Janeiro antes da Semana." Corrêa do Lago not only addresses the premieres of these and other modern orchestral compositions in Brazil, but also the possible acquaintance of Villa-Lobos with Stravinsky's compositions during the years preceding and immediately after 1920. His indirect acquaintance through piano transcriptions by Rubinstein and others is also highly speculative.

55. David P. Appleby, *Heitor Villa-Lobos: A Life*, 40.

56. Music Academy online, "Igor Stravinsky," para. 1, https://www.musicacademyonline.com/composer/biographies.php?bid=88 (accessed February 8, 2020). Stravinsky liberally insulted his peers: He called Rachmaninoff "a six and a half foot scowl"; he said that in order to write like Messiaen, "all you need is a large bottle of ink"; and that he couldn't help regretting Bartok's lifelong taste for his native folklore. According to Taruskin, "by now it is obvious that there were envy and repressed repentance in the barbs he [Stravinsky] hurled not only at Bartok but at all and sundry in his late memoirs." See Richard Taruskin, "Bartok and Stravinsky: Odd Couple Reunited?," *New York Times*, October 25, 1998, para. 21 (accessed July 19, 2017).

57. Washington Luiz Sieleman Almeida, "Villa-Lobos: Música e nacionalismo na República Velha," 74. This story, like many others, spread after appearing in Vasco Mariz's *Heitor Villa-Lobos, compositor brasileiro*, 42.

58. The year 1916 also saw the composition of the first recorded samba, "Pelo Telefone" (On the Telephone), a composition by Donga with lyrics by Mauro de Almeida. Donga was a *chorão*, a well-known guitarist and friend of Villa-Lobos. See Thomas G. Garcia, "The 'Choro,' the Guitar and Villa-Lobos," 63.

59. The dates are according to the third edition of the Catalogue of the Villa-Lobos Museum in Rio de Janeiro (a fourth edition is forthcoming). There is a lot of controversy concerning the veracity of those dates, as discussed in the subsequent chapters.

60. Paulo R. Guérios, *Heitor Villa-Lobos: O caminho sinuoso da predestinação*.

61. Lutero Rodrigues, "Villa-Lobos e a 'Descoberta do Brasil,'" 187–88.

62. Villa-Lobos's first trip to Paris occurred in 1923.

63. This may be the case if the publication dates of his early Amerindian compositions are indeed incorrect, a possibility that is addressed later in this study.

64. Béhague, *Heitor Villa-Lobos: The Search*, 43.

65. Oneyda Alvarenga, "Música Folclórica e Música Popular," *Revista Brasileira de Folclore* Ano IX, no. 25 (Sept/Dec. 1969): 228. http://docvirt.com/docreader.net/docreader.aspx?bib=RevBrFolcloLP&pasta=&pesq=Oneyda%20Alvarenga.

66. Bruno Kiefer, *Villa-Lobos e o modernismo na música brasileira* (São Paulo: Movimento, 1981), 72.

67. Glenn Watkins, *Pyramids at the Louvre*, 448–49.

68. Oswald de Andrade, "Anthropophagous Manifesto," aphorism 35 (see Appendix I).

69. Andrade, "Anthropophagous Manifesto," aphorism 9 (see Appendix 1).

70. Charles M. Joseph, *Stravinsky's Ballets* (New Haven, CT: Yale University Press, 2011), cover.

71. Ralph Waldo Emerson, "Quotation and Originality," 172.

72. Glen Watkins, *Pyramids at the Louvre*, 2–3.

73. The source of this quote is quite interesting. It was actually T. S. Eliot who asserted that "immature poets imitate; mature poets steal" in an essay about literary debts. "Due to a spoof feature in *Esquire* magazine in 1962, 'Immature artists imitate; mature artists steal' is sometimes misattributed to Lionel Trilling. Pablo Picasso has been credited with: 'Mediocre artists borrow; great artists steal,' and Igor Stravinsky with: 'A good composer does not imitate; he steals.'" See Ralph Keyes, *The Quote Verifier: Who Said What, Where and When*, 96.

74. Appleby, *Heitor Villa-Lobos: A Life*, 41.

75. The originality of Villa-Lobos's style will become evident in the detailed analysis of his works in the subsequent chapters.

76. *Villa-Lobos: Sua obra*, 3rd ed. (Rio de Janeiro: Museu Villa-Lobos, 1989).

77. L. Delarue Mardrus, "L'aventure d'un compositeur: Musique cannibal," *L'Intransigeant* (Paris), December 13, 1927, http://gallica.bnf.fr/ark:/12148/bpt6k792039k.item. This false testimony caused a stir in the Parisian audience and became one of the more picturesque and legendary stories about the composer.

CHAPTER THREE

The Sad Clowns of Carnival

Polichinelo and Petrushka

Tanto riso, oh quanta alegria
Mais de mil palhaços no salão! —Zé Keti and Pereira Matos

The modern street carnival in Rio de Janeiro is designated by the Guinness World Records as the biggest carnival in the world. According to tradition, both the street carnival with its "cordões carnavalescos" (carnival cords) and samba blocks, as well as the ballroom carnival, include the dazzling presence of masked revelers with the features of old people, clowns, devils, kings, queens, Amerindians, and Bahians, among others. The clowns are represented mainly by characters from the Italian Commedia dell'Arte, particularly Pierrot, Harlequin, and Columbina, who served as inspiration for a number of carnival marches. One of the most of famous of them has the title "Máscara Negra" (Black Mask)[1] by Zé Keti and Pereira Matos, winner of the First Competition of Carnival Music created in Rio de Janeiro in 1967.

The lyrics of the first stanza are translated as follows: "So much laughter, oh so much joy! More than a thousand clowns in the ballroom: Harlequin is crying for the love of Columbina in the middle of the crowd." Zé Keti (1921–1999) is the nickname of José Flores de Jesus, a talented Afro-Brazilian composer who also wrote protest songs against the military dictatorship, despite his timid personality. His partner, Hildebrando Pereira Matos, went into oblivion, and his coauthorship has been contested. This song presents a reversal in the love triangle of Pierrot, Columbina, and Harlequin, because, according to the story of the Commedia dell'Arte characters, it is Pierrot who ends up crying when Harlequin steals Columbina from him. A second ambiguity happens in the sad portrait of the crying clown, contrasting with the happiness that permeates Brazilian carnival. The tragic/comic figure of the Commedia dell'Arte clown was explored by both Villa-Lobos and Stravinsky.

In 1918, Villa-Lobos met and befriended the pianist Arthur Rubinstein, who later championed his music all over the world. The composer gave Rubinstein a copy of what would become one of his most important piano works, which he had just completed: *A Prole do Bebe Suite No. 1* (*The Baby's Family*) (1918), a cycle of eight miniature pieces dedicated to the composer's wife, who was herself a pianist. It is said that Villa-Lobos was inspired by listening to her playing Schumann's *Kinderszenen* and "Album for the Young." According to Wright, "the . . . suite has become Villa-Lobos's best-known piano composition, embodying a finely balanced mix of Debussy's ironic characterization, Ravelian clarity of texture, Milhaud's polytonal abandon, and an original application of 'Latin Americanisms.' It is the first enduring musical work of Brazilian Modernism."[2] The title of each of the movements of *A Prole do Bebe No. 1* gives the name of a doll and specifies the material of which it is made. The names of the dolls evoke the racial and ethnic diversity of Brazil in the early twentieth century, as well as the different social strata that make up the country's population.[3]

A Prole do Bebe Suite No. 1 (The Dolls, 1918)

I. Branquinha (A Boneca de Louça)—Little White Doll (The Porcelain Doll)
II. Moreninha (A Boneca de Massa)—Little Brunette Doll (The Dough Doll)
III. Caboclinha (A Boneca de Barro)—Little Mestiza Doll (The Clay Doll)
IV. Mulatinha (A Boneca de Borracha)—Little Mulatta Doll (The Rubber Doll)
V. Negrinha (A Boneca de Pau)—Little Black Doll (The Wooden Doll)
VI. A Pobrezinha (A Boneca de Trapo)—The Poor Little Doll (The Rag Doll)
VII. O Polichinelo—Punch
VIII. A Bruxa (A Boneca de Pano)—The Witch (The Cloth Doll)

There is one exception in the cycle: the seventh doll, Polichinelo, is the only one of male gender and the only one with a proper name; he is not given a descriptive title, nor is any material specified. The movement named after this doll became immortalized as an encore piece for many concert pianists, starting with Rubinstein, who changed the order of the cycle by moving it to the end, adding a repeat, and concluding with a glissando. Unlike the other dolls, Polichinelo does not represent a Brazilian ethnicity, but is based on a character from the Italian *commedia dell'arte*, Pulcinella, who first appears in printed texts in the early seventeenth century. His name derives from the Italian word *pulcino*, which refers to a day-old chick, and he is frequently depicted with a prominent beaklike nose. Italian actors exported the character to several European countries; in France he is known as Polichinelle, in Spain as Pulchinelo, and in England as Punch. It has been suggested that the Italian name comes from the corruption of a popular surname of the region, either Punchinello or Polsinelli.[4] When converted into Pulcinella, the name suffered modifications even within different parts of Italy, for example becoming Policenella in Padua.

Some of the *commedia dell'arte* characters, including Pulcinella, evolved into stock characters in puppet theaters in Europe and, later on, served as models for dolls. This explains the context of Pulcinella's musical representation as the puppet Petrushka,[5] his Russian counterpart, in Stravinsky's eponymous ballet of 1912, and as Polichinelo the doll in the piano composition by Villa-Lobos.[6] Stravinsky's original goal in composing *Petrushka* was to create "an orchestral piece in which the piano would play the most important part—a sort of *Konzertstück*."[7] Ultimately it became a ballet—a follow-up to *The Firebird*—at the request of Serge Diaghilev, and the piano remained as Petrushka's instrument.[8] *Polichinelo*, on the other hand, was conceived as a virtuosic miniature for solo piano.

In both compositions, the piano is the primary instrument, and there is an interesting visual connection between the piano and the figure of Pulcinella-Petrushka-Polichinelo. In his original form, he is dressed in a white blouse and trousers and wears a black mask over his face (Figure 3.1). The two colors not only suggest a reconciliation of the opposites of life and death, but they also create an association between the comic figure and the black and white keys of a piano.

Furthermore, Pulcinella's own character is reflected in the two compositions. Pulcinella has been often referred to as a subversive figure:

> He is the complete egotist. His good-humoured exterior conceals a ferocious interior and he cares no more for human life than for that of a flea. He delights in quarrels, makes a point of seeking them, and takes great pleasure in bloodshed. . . . A chameleon, despite the distinctiveness of this appearance, . . . yet

Figure 3.1. *Pulcinella*, drawn by Maurice Sand (1860).

behind all these there is an essential quality which we recognize as Pulcinella, just as we are aware of his nose and accent [whatever his disguise].⁹

The subversive nature of Pulcinella, as well as the duality that represents the reconciliation of life and death, is what Stravinsky explored through the subversiveness of the polytonality he associated with the character of Petrushka. When conceptualizing the work, Stravinsky

> was haunted by the image of a musician rolling two objects over the black and white keys of the piano, which led him to the idea of a bitonal effect made by combining the white-note C-major arpeggio with the black-note F-sharp major arpeggio. This double-sided sonority dominates Petrushka's scene (the first music Stravinsky wrote) and as the work progressed, it came to represent the conflicting sides of his character—the human versus the puppet.[10] (See Figures 3.3 and 3.4 below.)

Both *A Prole do Bebe* No. 1 (1918) and No. 2 (1921) reveal Villa-Lobos's experimentation with the use of multiple techniques, such as chords in seconds, fourths, and fifths, parallel motions, pentatonic and whole-tone scales, and so on. *Polichinelo* is a prime example of the use of *faixas sonoras*, or "sound bands," a term coined by Ernst Widmer.[11] "Sound bands" are characterized by the accumulation of multiple notes repeated very quickly through the alternation of both hands, in a toccata style. The final result is an emancipation of timbre, as the notes are not perceived individually, but as a timbre. In *Polichinelo*, sound bands also serve as a prime element for the articulation of the musical form, being produced through the superposition of the diatonic (white keys) and the pentatonic (black keys) of the piano, representing the black and white duality associated with the character of Pulcinella.

Figure 3.2. Villa-Lobos's sound bands in *Polichinelo*.
Created by the author, taken from Villa-Lobos score. Permission granted by the Brazilian Academy of Music.

Villa-Lobos demonstrates in his own terms a parallel trajectory not only with Stravinsky, but also with Schoenberg and the latter's emancipation of dissonance. Villa-Lobos experiments with the use of timbre for the creation of musical texture through the emancipation of pitch. As the composer stated, "I don't write dissonances to seem modern at all! What I write is a cosmic consequence of my studies, which resulted in my temperament analogous to Brazil's nature."[12] It is remarkable how the multiple procedures used by Villa-Lobos, such as sound bands, folk music quotations, the superimposition of diatonic and pentatonic, and the employment of ostinato techniques, converge to express the poetic content of the composition.

The black-versus-white juxtaposition is also the central element of the "Petrushka chord," characterized by the superimposition of the keys of C and F-sharp major, which are separated by the distance of a tritone:

Figure 3.3. A passage close to the beginning of the Second Tableau of Stravinsky's *Petrushka*, with the superposition of the triads of C major and F-sharp major, as performed by two clarinets at rehearsal 49.
Created by the author from the piano reduction of Petrushka by Igor Stravinsky.

A little later, during the second tableau, Stravinsky superimposes the white and black keys, expressed as F♯ major/G major, two keys that are a minor second apart. In the orchestral version, the ascending figures are played on a piano, the descending ones on clarinets.

Figure 3.4. A passage from the Second Tableau of Stravinsky's *Petroushka*.
Created by the author from the full score of Petrushka by Igor Stravinsky.

Rather than through a process of quotation or emulation, Villa-Lobos realizes the black and white dichotomy by juxtaposing, vertically, the diatonic and pentatonic scales into chordal/textural structures that produce sound bands. Stravinsky achieves the same effect through polytonality in horizontal layers—juxtaposing keys that are either a tritone or a semitone apart, the two most dissonant intervals in tonal music.[13]

Two Brazilian folk songs are quoted in *Polichinelo*. The first one is the most famous Brazilian nursery song, a circle dance called "Ciranda-cirandinha" ("Circle, Little Circle").[14]

Figure 3.5. The Brazilian nursery song "Ciranda-cirandinha" ("Circle, Little Circle"). Created by the author based on internet samples.

"Ciranda-cirandinha" is not simply a nursery song. Originally, the *ciranda* was a dance/song from the state of Pernambuco in the northeast region of Brazil, and as its name suggests, the participants hold hands while forming a circle. Early in its history, it was performed by fishermen's wives as they waited for their husbands to return from the sea.[15] Later on, it became a nursery song that is meant to be danced in a circle, where each child holds the hand of his or her neighbors. The verse structure of the *ciranda* usually asks for a child to go inside the circle and sing alone, while the others continue to sing joining hands and moving around with the circle.[16] Matisse's *The Dance* (1909–1910) (Figure 3.6) is a perfect illustration of the choreographic nature of a song like "Ciranda-cirandinha," where the characters have been likened to beanbag dolls because of their formless and unrestricted movements. Despite being a miniature composition and not a ballet, the choreographic nature of this nursery song, which is supposed to be danced while sung, creates another type of association between *Petrushka* and *Polichinelo*.

Figure 3.6. Matisse's *Dance I* (1909). For a Brazilian person, this painting will bring an immediate association with the nursery song "Ciranda-cirandinha," because it depicts exactly the way the song is supposed to be sung and danced.

Digital Image © The Museum of Modern Art / Licensed by SCALA / Art Resource, NY. © 2022 Succession H. Matisse / Artists Rights Society (ARS), New York

The other folk song quoted is "Viva o Zé Pereira" ("Long Live Zé Pereira"), whose refrain, according to tradition, is the motto that gave birth to street carnival in Brazil. The popular but inaccurate legend maintains that Zé Pereira was the nickname of the Portuguese shoemaker José Nogueira de Azevedo Paredes, who agitated the streets of Rio de Janeiro during carnival around 1850 by playing drums while announcing the beginning of the carnival celebrations. The practice continues to this day.[17] In 1869, Francisco Corrêa Vasques based a comic entr'acte titled "O Zé Pereira Carnavalesco" ("The Carnival of Zé Pereira") on this story. The play included a musical number, accompanied by drums, that was a parody of one of the most popular songs of the French burlesque, "Les Pompiers de Nanterre," which had been presented during that same season in Rio de Janeiro with great success.[18] "Les Pompiers de Nanterre" provided the tune of "Viva o Zé Pereira."[19]

The Sad Clowns of Carnival ～ 77

Zé Pereira

Figure 3.7. "Zé Pereira" is the popular carnival song that opens the carnival every year in Brazil.
Created by the author based on internet samples.

E viva o Zé Pereira!	Long live Zé Pereira
Pois que a ninguém faz mal	Who hurts no one
E viva a bebedeira	And long live drunkenness
Nos dias de carnaval!	During Carnival days!
Zim, balala! Zim, balala!	Zim, balala! Zim, balala!
E viva o carnaval!	And long live carnival!

The rhythmic introduction of the carnival song is prominently displayed in the low register of the piano in *Polichinelo*, enhanced by the forte dynamics and a percussive quality that highlights the association with carnival (Figure 3.8).

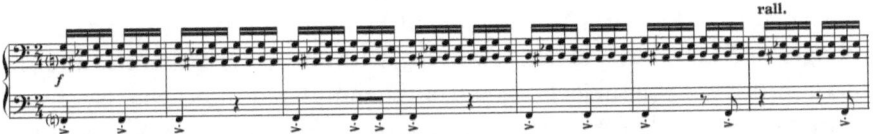

Figure 3.8. The accented notes in the low register represent a quote of the drumbeat introduction of the carnival song "Viva o Zé Pereira."
Created by the author, taken from Villa-Lobos score. Permission granted by the Brazilian Academy of Music.

The carnival quote in *Polichinelo* summons up another association with Stravinsky's ballet via *commedia dell'arte* characters. The three characters of *Petrushka* form a love triangle analogous to that of Pierrot, Harlequin, and Columbina, the most emblematic characters of the carnival in Rio de Janeiro. *Petrushka* tells the story of the loves and jealousies of three puppets: Petrushka loves the Ballerina, but she rejects him in favor of the Moor. Angry and hurt after losing the Ballerina, Petrushka challenges the Moor but is killed. Petrushka's ghost rises above the puppet theater as night falls to torment the magician puppetmaker who gave him life, only to collapse in a second death. As the unhappiest puppet story ever told, *Petrushka* represents the timeless tragedy of the human spirit and, as such, transcends its origins to attain a universal appeal.

Polichinelo is not a typical carnival character. However, Villa-Lobos cannibalizes him by placing him right at the center of Brazilian carnival, introduced by the famous motto that constitutes the so-called *grito de carnival*, the opening of the carnival celebrations. In doing so, he places Polichinelo at the same level as Pierrot, Harlequin, and Columbina (see Figure 3.9). Pierrot's Italian name was Pedrolino; he became Pierrot in nineteenth-century France. He wore white clothes made of out of flour sacks, and his face was painted white. Today he is known for his all-white face, like the moon, and a tear dangling from one of his eyes—the same character featured by Schoenberg in his *Pierrot Lunaire* from 1912, a contemporary of *Petrushka*. Pierrot suffers from unrequited love for Columbina, who loves Harlequin, and therefore becomes the butt of jokes. Pierrot became the precursor of all circus clowns. Harlequin, like Pierrot, is a servant of Pantaleon the merchant. Harlequin is a smart, lazy, and insolent rascal, a jumpy character who frequently performs acrobatic movements. He is a debaucher and likes to create confusion among the other characters. His costume consists of a colorful suit with diamond-shaped patches, and his face is smeared with mud. Columbina is also employed by the Court of Pantaleon. She is usually dressed in white and is courted by both Pierrot and Harlequin. In love with Harlequin, she sings and dances gracefully to enchant him, while Pierrot, sad and timid, is always left aside, suffering from his unrequited love.

The story of Pierrot, Columbina, and Harlequin is mirrored in the love triangle of Stravinsky's ballet, involving Petrushka, the Ballerina, and the Moor. It became the subject of some of the most famous carnival marches of all times, such as *Máscara Negra* (*Black Mask*, 1967), by Pereira Matos and Zé Keti, and *Serpentina* (*Serpentine*, 1949), by David Nasser and Haroldo Lobo. It was immortalized in *Pierrot Apaixonado* (*Pierrot in Love*),[20] a carnival march written in 1935 by Noel Rosa, one of the greatest names in Brazilian popular music, in collaboration with Heitor dos Prazeres.[21]

Um pierrô apaixonado	A passionate Pierrot
Que vivia só cantando	Who lived only by singing
Por causa de uma colombina	Due to Columbina
Acabou chorando, acabou chorando.	Ended up crying, ended up crying.
A Colombina entrou no botequim	Columbina entered the bar

Bebeu, bebeu, saiu assim, assim
Dizendo: "Pierrot, cacete!
Vai tomar sorvete com o Arlequim!"

Um grande amor tem sempre um triste fim
Com o Pierrot aconteceu assim
Levando esse grande chute
Foi tomar vermute com amendoim.

Drank right and left
Saying: "Pierrot, jackass!
Go get ice cream with Harlequin!"

A great love always has a sad end
With Pierrot it happened this way
After getting kicked
He went to drink vermouth with peanuts.

Figure 3.9. Pierrot, Harlequin, and Columbina, the three most emblematic characters of Brazilian carnival.
Harlequin and Columbina, Pierrot (1914) by F.X. Leyendecker for Vanity Fair

While the naïveté of "Ciranda-cirandinha" is obviously appropriate for a musical composition representing a doll, "Zé Pereira," with its permissiveness and praise of drunkenness during carnival, hardly makes sense in such a setting. By taking the two folk songs out of their original contexts and juxtaposing them within a noisy soundscape that includes the chordal/textural structures described above, Villa-Lobos produces a surrealist soundscape, a pure example of musical cannibalism of the highest order. Yet the composition predates the surrealist movement in Europe, which demonstrates how Villa-Lobos's intuition was in tune with contemporary aesthetic developments in Europe. The composition was completed a decade before the "Anthropophagus Manifesto" appeared, and its allusion to the attitude of mockery and debauchery that prevails during carnival demonstrates Oswald de Andrade's assertion that Brazilians already had a "surrealist language" prior to the European invasion.[22] The allusion is part of the process of dilution of opposites typical of cultural anthropophagy, and it brings *Polichinelo*'s carnival setting into direct relation with *Petrushka*, for the tale of the "immortal and unhappy hero of every fair in all countries"[23] is set in St. Petersburg's Admiralty Square in the 1830s during Shrovetide Fair, the winter carnival held before Lent.

In 1922, Arthur Rubinstein gave the premiere of *Prole do Bebe No. 1*. He changed the order of the compositions in the suite, ending the cycle with *Polichinelo*, as discussed above. The previous year, Stravinsky had decided to create a work for piano solo based on his ballet *Petrushka*. He called it "Three Movements from *Petrushka*" and dedicated it to Rubinstein, who championed it all over the world, including Brazil. Stravinsky's goal was to create a score that would be idiomatic to the piano and truly independent from the orchestral original. In other words, even though its material was drawn directly from the ballet, it should not be viewed as a piano transcription of the orchestral work. The composition is notorious for its technical and musical difficulties, ranking among the most challenging pieces for the piano. Villa-Lobos's *Polichinelo*, on the other hand, has always been a piano composition. It is noteworthy that "polichinelo" in Brazil is also the name given to the exercise known as "jumping jacks." The virtuosic technique used in *Polichinelo*'s performance, with its quick alternation of left and right hands, can be linked with the physical choreographic nature of jumping jacks. This extra layer of physicality and motion is another dimension that connects *Polichinelo* and *Petrushka*.

The miniaturist simplicity of *Polichinelo*, with its poetic representation of the *commedia dell'arte* character over multiple layers of connections, turned this piece into the most widely known composition for piano by Villa-Lobos. In the same year that Stravinsky wrote "Three Movements from *Petrushka*" for Arthur Rubinstein, Villa-Lobos started composing his most challenging work for solo piano, *Rudepoema* (Savage Poem), which he completed in

1926. *Rudepoema* is also dedicated to Arthur Rubinstein and was intended as a sound portrait of the Polish pianist. Ironically, it has been described as "*The Rite of Spring* meets the Brazilian Jungle."[24]

The importance of Petrushka within Stravinsky's output can be seen by observing that a sculpture of the character adorns the tombstone of Vaslav Nijinsky, the famous creator of the ballet role (see Figure 3.10). The statue was donated by Serge Lifar, another prominent dancer of the Ballets Russes, to whom Villa-Lobos dedicated his ballet *Uirapuru*.

Figure 3.10. Tombstone of Vaslav Nijinsky at the Montmartre Cemetery in Paris, featuring a sculpture depicting Petrushka.
Photo by Son of Groucho.

Notes

1. https://youtu.be/0iWTtISXmAU.
2. Simon Wright, *Villa-Lobos*, 32.
3. Angelis Jerke, *Musical and Sociological Implications of Villa-Lobos's Prole Do Bebê, No. 1*.
4. *Enciclopedia Italiana di Scienze, Lettere ed Arti iniziata dall'Istituto Giovanni Treccani*, s.v. "Pulcinella," accessed August 23, 2017, http://www.treccani.it/enciclopedia/pulcinella.
5. Another version of what is essentially the same character was later featured by Stravinsky in his neoclassical ballet *Pulcinella*, which premiered in 1920. Its libretto is based on an episode taken from an eighteenth-century Neapolitan manuscript entitled *Quatre Polichinelles Semblables* (*Four Identical Pulcinellas*).
6. There is another curious aspect about the evolution of the character's name. Both Pulcinella and Petrushka are names of male characters ending with the vowel "a," which is common in Italian and Russian. However, in Portuguese, traditionally male names end with the vowel "o" (hence, Polichinelo). Considering that all other dolls from *A Prole do Bebe* are female, whose names, therefore, end on the vowel "a," the name translation to Portuguese of the seventh doll made this movement stand out even more as an odd piece within the cycle.
7. Igor Stravinsky, *An Autobiography*, 31.
8. Angelo Cantoni, *The Language of Stravinsky*, 39.
9. John Rudlin, *Commedia dell'Arte: An Actor's Handbook*, 141. Another curious characteristic mentioned in the same page is that "Pucinella has a secret: he cannot help telling everyone everything." This justifies the expression "Pulcinella's secret" or "Polichinelo's secret," found in many countries, which means an open secret known by everybody.
10. Phillip Huscher, *Petrushka (1911)*, Chicago Symphony Orchestra program notes, https://cso.org/uploadedFiles/1_Tickets_and_Events/Program_Notes/Program Notes_Stravinsky_Petrushka.pdf.
11. Ernst Widmer, "Bordão e bordadura" (Assistant Professor diss., EMAC/UFBA, 1970), *ART Revista da Escola de Música e Artes Cênicas da UFBA*, no. 4 (Jan/Mar, 1982): 16.
12. Hellen Silva Cardoso, "Villa-Lobos: Uma 'melodia social,'" 184.
13. Technically speaking, Stravinsky uses polytonality (C major × F♯ major or G major × F♯ major), while Villa-Lobos uses polymodality (diatonic × pentatonic).
14. A coincidental similarity can be observed between the beginning of this nursery song and Mozart's *Üb immer Treu und Redlichkeit*, also known in its variant form as Papageno's aria in *The Magic Flute*.
15. Other sources state that the *ciranda* is a circle dance of Portuguese origin and originally danced by adults. Villa-Lobos wrote a cycle of sixteen *Cirandas* for solo piano, elaborate works in which folk materials (mostly nursery songs) are used as basis for complex structures, and where the original materials are transformed significantly

with great inventiveness. They became among his most important compositions for piano. Before that, he had already written a set of twelve *Cirandinhas*, in a similar vein however less adventurous that the set of *Cirandas*.

16. According to the third edition of the catalog of Villa-Lobos's works published by the Museum Villa-Lobos, the Brazilian composer wrote an orchestration for band of the nursery song in 1932.

17. The existence of a carnival recreational activity called Zé Pereira during the nineteenth century in Portugal suggests the strong Lusitanian influence in the emergence of such games in the carnival of Rio de Janeiro.

18. Jean-Paul Delfino, *Brasil: A música—Panorama des musiques populaires brésiliennes*, 74–75.

19. In 1932, Villa-Lobos released a set of 137 popular children's songs from various parts of Brazil arranged for chorus, under the title "Guia Prático: Estudo Folclórico Musical" (Practical Guide for the Study of Folk Music). This compilation was part of a larger plan to reform the musical educational system in Brazil. Later on, he produced five volumes of choral music from folk, religious, and civic sources also for instructional purposes under the form of "orpheonic singing" (*canto orfeônico*). Within the choral songs in the *Guia Prático*, Villa-Lobos created a choral version of "Viva o Zé Pereira" with the title "Viva o Carnaval," which is No. 135 in the collection. It is important to note that in this version of the song—where the compilation had an educational and civic purpose—the composer completely omitted from the lyrics the section that praises drunkenness. The same collection also includes a version of *Ó Ciranda, Ó Cirandinha* under No. 35, written homophonically for voice and piano (or to be performed in a purely instrumental version). Later on, the composer created piano versions of several of the 137 songs included in the Guia Prático, which were compiled into eleven albums of music for piano solo. Album 9, W359 includes *Ó Ciranda, Ó Cirandinha*, while Album 11, W473—the last one—concludes with *Viva o Carnaval*, an interesting and stylized version of *Viva o Zé Pereira* for piano solo. This last album was dedicated to the renowned Polish-American pianist Mieczyslaw Horszowski.

20. https://youtu.be/_wLpX1gp1YE.

21. Heitor dos Prazeres was one of the pioneer composers of samba. He participated as an instrumentalist, singer, and dancer in Josephine Baker's shows in Brazil and was hired by Orson Welles as choreographer for one of his films. After his wife's death, he became a prominent primitivist painter, producing a number of paintings on the theme of "Pierrot in Love."

22. The statement "We already had Communism. We already had Surrealist language. The Golden Age" appears in aphrorism 25 of the Manifesto (see Appendix I).

23. Richard Taruskin, *Stravinsky and the Russian Traditions*, 667.

24. Vivien Schweitzer, "Chaotic Yet Pensive, Pounding the Keys," *New York Times*, July 24, 2014, para. 1, https://www.nytimes.com/2014/07/23/arts/music/marc-andre-hamelin-plays-at-the-keyboard-institute.html (accessed July 29, 2017).

CHAPTER FOUR

~

Taking Flight with Two Ballet Birds

Uirapuru and Firebird

Uirapuru, uirapuru,
   Seresteiro, cantador do meu sertão. —Murilo Latini and Jacobina

The uirapuru is a restless and small bird, measuring less than five inches in length. Its scientific name is *Cyphorhinus aradus*, and it belongs to the Troglodytidae family. It basically feeds on fruits and insects, and its natural habitat is the Amazon forests. Its name in the Tupi language means "ornate bird," "borrowed bird," or "bird that is not a bird," and whose mission is to preside over the fate of other birds. Its singing is extremely beautiful,[1] and according to reports, its sounds make all the other birds silent, as if under a spell.

In Northern Brazil, there are several legends about the uirapuru. Researchers claim that this bird never repeats the same musical phrases and, for this reason, is considered by the natives as a supernatural being. After death, the bird's body and its nest are considered talismans, being highly sought after in the market. For the Tupi Amerindians, the uirapuru represents a god who acquired the form of a bird. Commercial establishments that carry the bird as an amulet are said to attract more customers. A male who carries one of its feathers becomes irresistible to women, and a woman who gets a piece of its nest will manage to live with the man she loves, who will remain faithful and in love forever.

The legends relating to the uirapuru inspired a number of artists, including the country song *Uirapuru* (1963)[2] by Jacobina and Murilo Latini, whose lyrics allude to the same idea found in the program of Villa-Lobos's composition: "Uirapuru, uirapuru, troubadour and singer from my countryside, sings the sorrows of my heart. The entire forest is silent when you sing. Everyone is silent to hear your song, that raises to heaven in a heartfelt melody, and reaches God as a sad form of prayer."

Several musicologists consider *Uirapuru* the composition where Villa-Lobos found his symphonic style, severing ties with the European influences of his previous works.[3] One of its contributions was to replace the romantic conventions surrounding the Amerindian with a new, nationalistic perspective where the native Brazilian becomes identified with an exuberant nature. In this new perspective, the Amerindian interacts with nature through legends that take place in a mythical, atemporal time.[4] *Uirapuru* is a tone poem/ballet based on the legend of a magic bird—the uirapuru, a species of wren that produces an elaborate song. Its Portuguese name is based on the language of the Tupi indigenous tribe, who considered the uirapuru a sacred bird.

Villa-Lobos placed the Amerindian of *Uirapuru* within an Edenic setting that incorporates the monumental aspect of the Brazilian rain forest with the mythical associations of Amerindian legends, a tropical setting not so distant from Russian fairy tales such as the Firebird. The story is based on legends that the composer supposedly learned during his travels.[5] One of the most

Figure 4.1. The uirapuru.
Photo by Dianes G. Marcelino.

famous of these legends states that, when the uirapuru starts singing, all other birds stop their songs to hear it. Other legends consider uirapuru the King of Love, through tales involving passion, jealousy, deception, and magical transformations, including the one created by the composer:

> Says one legend that the magical nocturnal singing of the Uirapuru was so attractive that the young female natives would disappear during the evening in search for this magical troubadour of the Brazilian forests, because the sorcerers told them that the Uirapuru was in fact the King of Love, the most beautiful Amerindian chief on earth.[6]

In Villa-Lobos's version of the legend, the uirapuru is a bird who is pierced by the arrow of an Amerindian huntress. The subject of a bird pierced by an arrow has a precursor in an art song written by Villa-Lobos in 1913, with the title *L'oiseau*,[7] which was based on the sixth fable from volume II of La Fontaine's *Fables*. The lyrics, which were taken directly from the original in French, are about the fate of a bird that is mortally wounded.

L'oiseau blesse d'une flèche by La Fontaine (in Villa-Lobos, *L'oiseau*, op. 10)	*Wounded Bird* by La Fontaine (in Villa-Lobos, *L'oiseau*, op. 10)[8]
Mortellement atteint d'une flèche empennée	Fatally struck with a feathered arrow,
Un Oiseau déplorait sa triste destinée,	A bird deplores its sad destiny,
Et disait, en souffrant un surcroît de douleur:	And says, suffering with increasing pain:
"Faut-il contribuer à son propre malheur?"	"Must we contribute to our own misfortune?"
Cruels humains, vous tirez de nos ailes	Cruel humans, you pull our wings
De quoi faire voler ces machines mortelles.	To produce deadly flying machines.
Mais ne vous moquez point, engeance sans pitié:	But do not mock, pitiless cattle:
Souvent il vous arrive un sort comme le nôtre.	Often a similar destiny awaits you.
Des enfants de Japet toujours une moitié	Half of the children of Japet[9] will always
Fournira des armes à l'autre.	Supply weapons to the other half.

If, as official sources suggest, *Uirapuru* was written in 1917,[10] it would be striking that Villa-Lobos's first breakthrough orchestral composition and Stravinsky's first composition for Diaghilev were both ballets based on fairy-tale legends about magic birds. The analogy goes even further, considering that sources indicate that *Uirapuru* was revised in 1934 and dedicated to Serge Lifar, the director of the Paris Opéra Ballet at the time. Lifar was considered Nijinsky's successor, making his debut with the Ballets Russes in 1923 and becoming its principal dancer and Diaghilev's lover until the latter's death in 1929.[11] *Uirapuru* was premiered as a ballet in Argentina in 1935 under the baton of its composer and with choreography by Nemanoff, without the participation of Lifar.[12]

Recent evidence demonstrates conclusively how *Uirapuru* was rewritten in Paris during the 1930s[13] as a reworking of *Tédio de Alvorada* (*Weariness at Dawn*),[14] an early composition that was written in 1916/17 and premiered in August of 1918. Studies show that the composer kept almost all of *Tédio de Alvorada* intact in *Uirapuru*, though sometimes changing the order, adding a few sections and expanding the orchestration.[15] Most likely, Villa-Lobos was motivated by the expectations of the Parisian public, interested in exotic images of Brazil, combined with his ambition to collaborate with the Ballets Russes.

The characterization of *Uirapuru* and *Amazonas* as ballet compositions is something that evolved over time, and constitutes a conceptual reorientation from symphonic poem to ballet. It is resultant from the shifting in the program from a Greek mythological subject to themes of Amerindian inspiration. The prototypes for the two works, respectively *Tédio de Alvorada* and *Myremis*, were initially conceived as symphonic poems, which, together with a contemporary composition titled *Naufrágio dos Kleônicos* (The Shipwreck of Kleonicos, 1916), constitute a trilogy based on Greek mythological themes. The trilogy was premiered in the first public concert of symphonic works by Villa-Lobos, which took place in Rio de Janeiro in 1918. Among them, only *Naufrágio dos Kleônicos* was characterized initially as a ballet, and was performed as such by the ballerina Norka Rouskaya one year after its creation.[16] The musical genres of *Uirapuru* and *Amazonas* oscillated between symphonic poems and ballets, most likely in attempts to have them performed as much as possible. According to research carried out by Charlotte Riom,[17] *Amazonas* was performed twice as ballet, both at the Municipal Theater in Rio de Janeiro: once in 1934, and the second time as part of a larger choreography in 2016. *Uirapuru* has a place apart in history of Brazilian ballet for having, until 2016, at least eight different versions, including its debut in Argentina, performances in São Paulo and Rio de Janeiro, and one performance in Spain.

Independently of the time when *Uirapuru* was completed, most of its avant-garde devices come from *Tédio de Alvorada*, written before Villa-Lobos had contact with the music of Stravinsky. Compared with *Tédio de Alvorada*, *Uirapuru* contains a more sophisticated orchestration, a result of the anthropophagic assimilation of Richard Wagner's orchestra, in a way that is found in several other compositions by the composer. Villa-Lobos's creativity and ability to manipulate orchestral sonorities led Olivier Messiaen to consider him one of the greatest orchestrators of the twentieth century.[18] Having studied with Rimsky-Korsakov, Stravinsky's orchestration of *The Firebird* also features Wagner's influence, though filtered through his teacher, who was also highly influenced by the German composer.

In addition to the instrumentation, the use of leitmotif technique in *Uirapuru* is also reminiscent of Wagner. However, while the Wagnerian leitmotif is supposedly associated with a person, place, or idea in all its recurrences, Villa-Lobos frequently uses the leitmotif in a completely different musical context and with a different meaning that is not necessarily associated with the same person, place, or idea. His originality rests in the use of the leitmotif transported into a different context, a resource that provides unity to the composition without necessarily keeping the typical associations attributed to the use of leitmotifs. Stravinsky also pursued the employment of a system of leitmotifs in *The Firebird*.[19]

Thematic Analysis

Contrary to the traditional dichotomy associated with the consecutive statement of two contrasting themes in the sonata form, the two main themes of *Uirapuru*—the "Theme of the Uirapuru" and the "Theme of the Jungle"—are presented simultaneously.

The Theme of the Uirapuru

The first person who notated the melody of the uirapuru bird was Richard Spruce in his expedition to the Obidos Indians on the Trombetas River on November 11, 1849, and January 6, 1859:

> There was no mistaking its clear bell-like tones, as accurately modulated as those of a musical instrument. Its "phrases" were short, but each included all the notes of the diapason; and after repeating one phrase perhaps twenty

times, it would suddenly pass to another—sometimes with a change of key to the major fifth—and continue it for an equal space. Usually, however, there was a brief pause before a change of theme. I had listened for some time before I bethought me of writing down its song. The following phrase is the one that oftenest recurred:

Figure 4.2. Uirapuru's song as notated by Richard Spruce.
Taken from Richard Spruce's 1908 book *Notes of a Botanist on the Amazon & Andes*.

Simple as this music was, its coming from an unseen musician in the depths of that wild wood gave it a weird-like character, and it held me spellbound for near an hour when it suddenly broke off, to be taken up again at so great a distance that it reached my ear as no more than a faint tinkling.[20]

More recently, American and German scientists found remarkable parallels between the singing of the uirapuru and works by Bach and Haydn.[21] According to them, the singing of the uirapuru favors perfect consonances over dissonant intervals or imperfect consonances, generating the perception of a tonal center.

In his composition, Villa-Lobos used the theme as notated by Richard Spruce. He keeps the presence of a perceived tonal center as described in Figure 4.3, below, as well as the zigzag motion of the melodic line in Richard Spruce's notation (see Figure 4.2, above). The stretching and shrinking of the generating motif, coupled with its rhythmic acceleration, mirrors the melodic behavior attributed to the typical singing of birds. Even the idea of the bird's sound fading in the distance "as no more than a faint tinkling" is also captured by the composer at the end of the theme. This seven-note

Figure 4.3. The song of the Uirapuru, captured as one of the main themes in Villa-Lobos's composition.
Paulo de Tarso Salles, Villa-Lobos: *Processos Composicionais*, 26.

motif is responsible for most of the main differences between the original composition *Tédio de Alvorada* and *Uirapuru*. In this sense, this generative motif plays the role of an *objet-trouvé* (ready-made), a term introduced by the plastic artist Marcel Duchamp in 1915 that represents a practice widely adopted by Dadaism and surrealism.[22]

The note C appears prominently through repetition and by its location between the highest and lowest notes of the motif. The polarization of the melody around this pitch allows us to consider that the melody is written on the Ionian mode of C. "The Theme of the Uirapuru" evokes the famous bassoon theme in the beginning of *The Rite of Spring*.[23] In *Uirapuru*, the placement of the tonal center C in relation of perfect fifth with the highest (F) and lowest (G) notes of the theme is equivalent to the tonal center A in the bassoon melody at the beginning of *The Rite of Spring*, demonstrated in the figure below.[24]

Figure 4.4. Beginning of the bassoon solo in *The Rite of Spring*.
Created by the author, taken from Igor Stravinsky's score.

In *Uirapuru*, the relationship of the highest (F) and lowest (G) notes of the theme reproduces the same relationship of perfect fifths present in the bassoon melody above (E-A-D). In *The Rite*, one can infer that the presence of the successive arrivals into the central note (A) polarize it as a "tonal center," whereas *Uirapuru*, polarized around C, can be seen as coming from the Ionian mode, as noted above. The kinship between the two themes is accentuated by their statement through woodwind instruments, the bassoon in *The Rite of Spring* and the flute in *Uirapuru*. In both cases, the narrow range melodies are based on nonfunctional, diatonic modality that creates, in principle, a static modal context. However, the staticity is compensated by a sense of motion produced through the rhythmic and metrical manipulation of the inner motifs, resulting in closed structures in both compositions, which are further explained in the next chapter.

In addition to rhythm manipulation, the completeness of the formal scheme is enhanced by other elements, such as the harmony, the contour of the melody, the placement of the fermatas, the counterpoint, and others, as addressed in a number of studies.[25] Of particular importance is the pitch material for the construction of the texture. In the case of *The Rite of Spring*, the pitch content of the tune is essentially an unordered, Aeolian, white-key, diatonic collection, with only one note missing (F): (A-B-C-D-E-[F]-G). At the last measure, a disturbance happens by the addition of a B-flat and a G-flat. However, the B-flat is a passing/neighboring tone, so the important disturbance is the G-flat, particularly because it is a cadential note that emphasizes the tritone interval with the C that ends the phrase. Through disturbances like this, combined with the intervention of other voices in countermelodies that use contrasting pitch collections, Stravinsky transforms original folk material such as the bassoon theme into abstract, cyclic pitch collections, which are symmetrically interlocked and complementary. While this aspect is not part of the scope of the present study, as it pertains to *The Rite of Spring*, it indicates that Stravinsky is able to achieve structural unity in the theme through the use of symmetries and complementarity.[26]

Within the use of leitmotif technique, Villa-Lobos also uses symmetry to create balance and unity. In the successive statements of the "Theme of the Uirapuru" throughout the composition, he manipulates the inner intervallic structure of the theme while maintaining a sense of symmetry. As demonstrated by Salles,[27] there are three occasions when the "Theme of the Uirapuru" appears in its complete form. The first statement happens in measures 5–16, where the theme presents a symmetric mirror intervallic structure as shown in Figure 4.5 below.

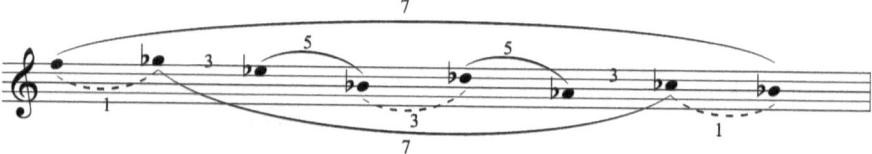

Figure 4.5. In its first appearance, the "Theme of Uirapuru" is written in the Mixolydian mode on D-flat, presenting a mirror symmetric structure around its axis in the middle. The numbers indicate the distance between the notes in terms of semitones.
Paulo de Tarso Salles, Villa-Lobos: *Processos Composicionais*, 55.

In its second appearance (mm. 136–142, with a variant on mm. 179–183, Figure 4.6), the symmetry is broken by eliminating the last note and changing some of the inner intervallic relations. Yet, a new balance is achieved because the last interval "complements" the first. In this case, the note C is polarized by the axis F–G formed by the extreme notes of theme in the Ionian mode, creating a new symmetry on a higher structural level.

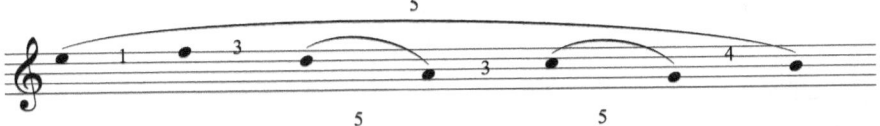

Figure 4.6. The "Theme of Uirapuru" in its second statement, written in the Ionian mode on C.
Paulo de Tarso Salles, Villa-Lobos: *Processos Composicionais*, 56.

The last full statement of the theme happens between mm. 146–158 (repeated in mm. 161–173) showing another apparent break of the symmetry. However, a new symmetry is once again achieved through the superimposition of proportioned structures, as demonstrated in Figure 4.7.

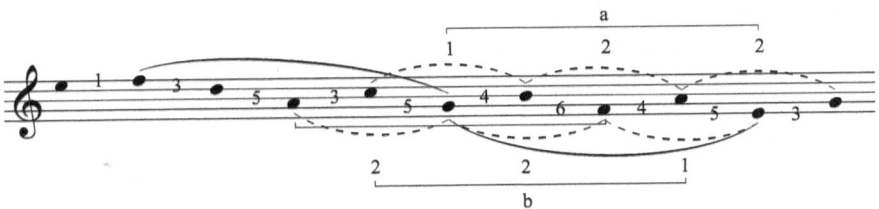

Figure 4.7. Interval asymmetries and symmetries in the last statement of the "Theme of the Uirapuru."
Paulo de Tarso Salles, Villa-Lobos: *Processos Composicionais*, 56.

Until the first G (upper full slur) we have a symmetrical arrangement of 3 and 5 semitones; afterward the intervallic relation is slightly asymmetrical (4-6-4-5). However, by observing the two intervallic relations of the two registers (dotted slurs) we notice the superposition of intervallic structures a and b (indicated through brackets), which show bilateral symmetry (mirror type symmetry).[28]

Here, one can make the argument that B is the polarized tonal center located between the lowest note E and the highest note F. This would imply a rare use of the Locrian mode.

The above shows intervallic manipulation as a unique feature of the composition style of Villa-Lobos: After starting with a symmetrical structure, he breaks the symmetry through intervallic manipulation. The asymmetrical result, paradoxically, reveals a new structure that, after further revision, results in a new kind of symmetry. In his own terms, Villa-Lobos redefines the concept of thematic development through the use of abstract coherence in the manipulation of symmetries. Though the "Theme of the Uirapuru" is reminiscent of the bassoon theme in *The Rite* and though both composers use symmetry and complementarity to achieve structural unity, their methods

The Theme of the Jungle

In contrast with the "Theme of the Uirapuru," the "Theme of the Jungle" has a more conventional structure of antecedent/consequent. This theme was already present in the original composition, *Tédio de Alvorada*, and is first introduced as a countermelody to the "Theme of the Uirapuru," starting in m. 3.[29] When brought to this new environment, the theme conjures a feeling of intoxicating beauty, moving slowly, mostly by conjunct motion, and building a sense of expansiveness and relentless abandon.

The antecedent begins with an incipit that features prominently the interval of tritone and ends with an appendix. While the interval of tritone in the beginning resolves in B-flat, the presence of C-flat in the theme implies the use of the Phrygian mode. Consequently, the antecedent constitutes a motion from I–V (B-flat–F) followed by an appendix, which prominently features the interval of major second imitated in inversion (*motif b*).

Figure 4.8. The recurrence of the tritone is prominently displayed. The interval of 2nd is also prominently featured as minor 2nd in the incipit within motif a (motion from C-flat to B-flat) and as major 2nd in the appendix (motif b). The appendix presents motif b in major second imitated in bilateral symmetry and augmentation (mirror inversion). The codetta is built on a sequence of minor 2nds over the span of a tritone (A-flat to D).
Created by the author, taken from Villa-Lobos's score with permission from the Brazilian Academy of Music.

The consequent starts with the same incipit and ends on the key center, B-flat, followed by a codetta featuring a chromatic, descending motion on the interval of tritone (A-flat—D). The codetta is related to the incipit, in the sense that the gesture of descending minor second is prominently featured. The climax of the theme happens around its golden section,[30] where the highest note (E-flat) is performed with *sforzato*. By featuring the interval of tritone in the "Theme of the Jungle" so prominently, a profound connection is made between the two main themes of the piece, allowing for a deep sense of thematic unity.

(a) Incipit of the "Theme of the Jungle"   b) Main cell of the "Theme of the Uirapuru"

Figure 4.9. Tritones appear prominently in the "Theme of the Jungle" and the "Theme of Uirapuru," producing an inner coherence between the two main themes of the composition.
Created by the author.

The interval of tritone displayed so prominently in the two themes continues to permeate the subsequent sections. For example, the "Theme of the Ugly Indian" that follows both of these two main themes displays several tritones (see Figure 5.5). Its successive repetitions of the pitch B-flat polarize it as a tonal center, reiterating what has been established as the key center for the "Theme of the Jungle." In the subsequent section (Tempo di Marcia), the B-flat remains in the double basses through most of the ostinato section.

Through the recurrence of intervals (tritone and major/minor second), as well as the polarization of certain notes (B-flat), Villa-Lobos expands the concept of tonality as a structural force. The interval of major/minor second is prominently featured throughout the piece, and its major/minor dichotomy is creatively explored. The tritone appears conspicuously in the "Theme of the Ugly Indian," while the dichotomy of major/minor second is characteristic of the "Theme of the Indian Huntress" (Figure 4.10):

Figure 4.10. Major/minor 2nd intervals prominently displayed in the "Theme of the Indian Huntress."
Created by the author.

The second statement of the "Theme of the Jungle" (mm. 31–67) presents a similar contour as the first, but in a contrasting register, tempo, dynamic range, character, and "tonality." The differences are significant, and the deformation of the theme is not accidental—it allows for new reiterations of the interval of tritone, which appears in the incipits, as well as between the high and low poles of the antecedent (A—D-sharp) and consequent (B—E-sharp), as demonstrated in Figure 4.11. Also noticeable is the permutation of intervals in *motifs a* and *b* (here notated as *a'* and *b'* to demonstrate the difference): The former becomes a major second, and the latter becomes a minor second.

Figure 4.11. Second statement of the "Theme of the Jungle." Dotted lines show the reiteration of the interval of tritone, while motifs a' and b' feature the interval of 2nd (major and minor, respectively). In this statement, the "Theme of the Jungle" is built over an octatonic scale, where C is missing and the E natural is a foreign, passing note inserted. When it appears at the end of m. 47, it is treated as a declination.
Created by the author.

The technique of purposely avoiding a pitch within a passage is used by Villa-Lobos to establish a process known as "polarization by exclusion,"[31] creating an urgency for the music to move toward the excluded pitch as its key center. In the present case, the ending of the "Theme of the Jungle" is prolonged until the arrival of the excluded pitch C, which appears in fortissimo over three octaves, sustained for four and a half measures until the end of the section (mm. 62–66). This is a remarkable feature: The process of development of the "Theme of the Jungle" at the coda is characterized by a motion from F-sharp to C, which once again reiterates the interval of tritone (Figure 4.12). The transformation of *motif b* into a minor second instead of a major second at the appendix receives a musical meaning: At the end of the consequent, the minor second creates instability, eliding into a chromatic, descending motion from F-sharp to the declination E-natural, which is the arrival point of the consequent. The instability created at the end of the consequent is followed by a long codetta, where the interval of major second reaffirms itself, as shown in Figure 4.12.[32]

Figure 4.12. Codetta of the second statement of the "Theme of the Jungle." A three note chromatic motif (F-sharp—E-sharp—D-double sharp) is reiterated through diminution (a1, a2, a3, a4), suffering a "modulation"—using the interval of tritone—that transforms the descending three-note half step motif (F-sharp—E-sharp—D-double sharp) into a descending three-note whole step motif (E-D-C).
Based on figure from Villa-Lobos: *Processos Composicionais* by Paulo de Tarso Salles, 151. Used with permission.

The point of arrival is the new polarized-by-exclusion center, "C," sustained by the violins in three octaves for four and a half measures.[33] In this way, the composer establishes a deep, inner connection between the intervals of tritone and major/minor second. In fact, the use of tritone, combined with the dichotomy of major/minor second as the main constructive intervals, constitutes a sort of "thesis" present with equal force in *Uirapuru* and *Amazonas*.[34]

The last full statement of the "Theme of the Jungle" happens over mm. 197–212 and is an enharmonic, almost literal, restatement of the first. More details are explained in chapter 5. While Villa-Lobos abandons the typical sonata relationship in *Uirapuru* by the simultaneous statement of the two main themes as melody/countermelody, he finds a new, original way to achieve symmetry of organization and unity in different structural levels of the composition. By using an analogous treatment in the subsequent appearances of both themes, he produces a new kind of symmetry that is described in Table 4.1 below. Only the first three statements of each theme are complete. The remaining appearances of the themes will be analyzed later.

Table 4.1. Structural symmetry and unity of the two main themes of Uirapuru (there is a reminiscent appearance of a fragment of the "Theme of the Uirapuru" at the very end [m. 369], which appears for programmatic reasons).

Theme of the Uirapuru	Theme of the Jungle
mm. 5–16 (repeated on mm. 72–83)	mm. 3–21 (repeated on mm. 70–85)
mm. 135–142 (repeated on mm. 179–183)	mm. 31–67 (repeated on mm. 98–134)
mm. 146–158 (repeated on mm. 161–173)	mm. 197–212
mm. 207–213 (partial, transfigured)	mm. 216–223 (only antecedent, deformed)
mm. 350–352 (shortened)	mm. 353–358 (only antecedent)

The program of the symphonic poem/ballet is transcribed below in its original form followed by its translation.[35]

UIRAPURU
Argumento de Villa-Lobos

(Conta uma lenda, que a magia do canto noturno do Uirapuru era tão atraente, que as índias se reuniam à noite, à procura do trovador mágico das florestas brasileiras, porque as feiticeiras lhes contaram que o Uirapuru era o rei do amor e o mais belo Cacique da terra).

Em uma floresta, calma e silenciosa, aparece um índio feio, tocando flauta. Em grupo alegre, surgem as mais belas selvícolas da região do Pará, que se decepcionam ao descobrirem o índio feio. Indignadas, enxotam-no brutalmente, com pancadas, empurrões e pontapés.

Por entre as folhagens das árvores, as índias, ansiosas, procuram o Uirapuru, certas de encontrarem um lindo jovem. Esta ansiedade é testemunhada pelos grilos, corujas, bacuráus, sapos-intanhas, morcegos e toda a fauna noturna.

Ouvem-se, ao longe, de quando em quando, alguns trilos suaves que anunciam o Uirapuru e irradiam contentamento em todo aquele ambiente.

Seduzida pelo mavioso canto do Uirapuru, aparece uma linda e robusta índia, de flecha e bodoque em punho, como uma adestrada caçadora de pássaros noturnos. Vendo o pássaro encantado, lança-lhe a flecha, prostrando-o por terra. Surpreende-se, porém, ao vê-lo transformar-se num belo índio que é disputado pelas índias. A caçadora que o ferira sai vitoriosa.

No auge da contenda, ouve-se o som fanhoso e agoureiro da flauta de osso. Temendo uma vingança, as índias procuram esconder o belo índio que é, porém, surpreendido pelo índio feio, feroz e vingativo que, atirando-lhe a flecha, fere-o mortalmente. Pressurosas, as índias carregam o belo índio em seus braços para a beira de um poço, onde, subitamente, ele se transforma num pássaro invisível, deixando-as tristes e apaixonadas a ouvir, apenas, o seu canto maravilhoso que desaparece no silêncio da floresta.

UIRAPURU
Script by Villa-Lobos

(A legend tells that the magic of the Uirapuru's night singing was so attractive, that the [Amer] Indian women gathered at night, looking for the magical troubadour of the Brazilian forests, because the witches told them that the Uirapuru was the king of love and the most beautiful Chief on the Earth.)

In a forest, calm and silent, an ugly (Amer)Indian appears, playing the flute. In a happy group, the most beautiful female Amerindians in the region of Pará appear as a happy group, but are disappointed to discover the ugly (Amer)Indian. Indignant, they brutally shoo him away with blows, shoves, and kicks.

Among the foliage of the trees, the (Amer)Indian women, anxious, look for the Uirapuru, certain that they will find a beautiful young man. This anxiety is witnessed by crickets, owls, nightjars, wild frogs, bats, and all the nocturnal fauna.

In the distance, from time to time, some soft trills can be heard announcing the Uirapuru and radiating contentment in the whole environment.

Seduced by the gentle singing of the Uirapuru, a beautiful and robust (Amer)Indian woman appears, with an arrow and a swagger in her hand, like a trained hunter of nocturnal birds. Seeing the enchanted bird, she shoots her arrow, prostrating him to the ground. She is surprised, however, to see him transform into a beautiful (Amer)Indian who is disputed by the (Amer)Indian women. The hunter who wounded him is victorious.

At the height of the strife, one can hear the prickly and foreboding sound of the bone flute. Fearing revenge, the (Amer)Indian women try to hide the beautiful (Amer)Indian, however he is surprised by the ugly, fierce, and vengeful (Amer)Indian who, shooting him an arrow, mortally wounds him. In a hurry, the (Amer)Indian females carry the beautiful (Amer)Indian in their arms to the edge of a well, where, suddenly, he turns into an invisible bird, leaving them sad and in love to hear only his wonderful song that disappears into the silence of the forest.

Notes

1. https://youtu.be/XsgXA_SQ7ws.
2. https://youtu.be/0J4kau5BYnM.
3. Simon Wright, *Villa-Lobos* (Oxford: Oxford University Press, 1992), 13. According to the Villa-Lobos Museum in Brasil, "Uirapuru is one of the first masterpieces by Villa-Lobos and begins a typical orchestral language of the composer." Museu Villa-Lobos, "Uirapuru," para. 1. Gil Jardim corroborates the above. See Gil Jardim, *O Estilo Antropofágico de Heitor Villa-Lobos: Bach e Stravinsky na Obra do Compositor*, 23.
4. Maria Alice Volpe, *Indianismo and Landscape in the Brazilian Age of Progress: Art Music from Carlos Gomes to Villa-Lobos, 1870s–1930s*, 324. This assertion suggests a connection with the surrealist movement that will be explored in chapter 9.
5. Villa-Lobos's travels are a matter of controversy. It is known that he related many fantastic stories about his explorations in the interior of the country. These stories became legendary texts that constitute fun reading but are certainly not true. However, leaving the fantastic stories aside, Villa-Lobos studied the folklore of the

country and used it, sometimes directly and sometimes indirectly, in his compositions. It is known that he went to Manaus, the capital of the state of Amazonas, in 1912 and organized two concerts whose programs survive. Lisa M. Peppercorn, *The World of Villa-Lobos in Pictures and Documents*, 47–48.

6. Kleide Ferreira do Amaral Pereira, "Influências Indígenas na Obra de Villa-Lobos," *Revista da Organização de Estudos Culturais em Contextos Internacionais*, Academia Brasil-Europa de Ciência da Cultura e da Ciência e Institutos Integrados de Pesquisa, no. 22 (1993): 2, n.p., http://www.revista.akademie-brasil-europa.org/CM22-04.htm.

7. The art song was published by Arthur Napoleão in Rio de Janeiro, 1987.

8. This opus 10 according to the published score corresponds to opus 23 according to the listing compiled by the composer.

9. Japet is Prometheus's father in Greek mythology, according to which, Prometheus created mankind.

10. *Villa-Lobos: Sua Obra*, third edition, 60.

11. In his autobiography, *Ma Vie*, Lifar recalls being with Diaghilev at his deathbed.

12. When arriving in Brazil in 1934, Serge Lifar asked for Villa-Lobos, saying that a visit to the composer was the first of his duties. He added that, a few days before his death, Diaghilev spoke about Villa-Lobos's talent and his desire to have him create a ballet with his music. On that occasion, Lifar choreographed and performed Villa-Lobos's *Jurupari*, based on his *Choros No. 10*. Two years before, Villa-Lobos dedicated his composition *O Papagaio do Moleque* (*The Kid's Kite*) to Lifar, followed by *Uirapuru* in 1934.

13. Luiz Fernando N. de Lima, "Notícia sobre o Primeiro Congresso Internacional Villa-Lobos," 6.

14. *Tédio de Alvorada* is based on a short piece of prose by Teixeira Leite describing the "infinitely slow process by which night turns to day" in a setting in ancient Greece. Wright, *Villa-Lobos*, 12. *Weariness at Dawn* responds to a nationalist convention at the time, where the sunrise represents Brazil as a young nation with a bright future.

15. The most recent study is the one by Manoel Corrêa do Lago and Guilherme Bernstein. See Manoel Corrêa do Lago and Guilherme Bernstein, *Uirapuru, Partitura de Estudo Comentada*. This article is particularly interesting in the way it demonstrates how a composition of essentially contemplative character that takes place in ancient Greece (*Tédio de Alvorada*) was transformed into a ballet full of action that happens in the Amazon forest. Another important study can be found in Paulo de Tarso Salles, "'Tédio de Alvorada' and 'Uirapuru': um estudo comparativo de duas partituras de Heitor Villa-Lobos," 2–9.

16. Charlotte Riom, "Contribuição de Villa-Lobos para a dança cênica," 76.

17. Ibid., 90–93.

18. Claude Samuel, *Olivier Messiaen: Music and Color. Conversations with Claude Samuel*, 194.

19. "Stravinsky confessed that he had not yet completely broken with all the devices covered by the term 'Music Drama' in his employment of a system of leitmotifs." Glenn Watkins, *Soundings: Music in the Twentieth Century*, 201.

20. Richard Spruce, *Notes of a Botanist on the Amazon & Andes*, Vol. 1, 101–02. In 1930, the book *A Amazônia que eu vi* by Gastão Cruls was published in Brazil. That book included the musical notation of the *Uirapuru's song* as notated by Richard Spruce, and is possibly the source for Villa-Lobos's theme.

21. Emily Doolittle and Henrik Brumm, "O Canto do Uirapuru: Consonant Intervals and Patterns in the Song of the Musical Wren," 55–85.

22. See Manoel Corrêa do Lago and Guilherme Bernstein, *Uirapuru: Partitura de estudo comentada*, 6.

23. Stravinsky's bassoon theme was taken from Juszkiewicz's anthology of Lithuanian folk songs. Elliot Antokoletz, *Twentieth-Century Music*, 95.

24. See Pierre Boulez, *Notes of an Apprenticeship*, 80.

25. See, for example, the analysis in Boulez, *Notes of an Apprenticeship*, 79–82.

26. For a detailed analysis of this aspect in *The Rite of Spring*, see Antokoletz, *Twentieth-Century Music*, 97–98.

27. Paulo de Tarso Salles, *Villa-Lobos: Processos Composicionais*, 55–56.

28. Ibid., 56. These are the only full appearances of the "Theme of the Uirapuru" in the piece.

29. According to Corrêa do Lago and Guilherme Bernstein, this theme was characterized by Luiz Fernando Valim Lopes as a "swan song" (the program of the piece states: "A swan sings softly, reclining on the waters of a lake; there is a deep lamentation in this elegy"). See Manoel Corrêa do Lago and Guilherme Bernstein, *Uirapuru, Partitura de Estudo Comentada*, 16. A similar swan song was created by Villa-Lobos for his symphonic poem/ballet *O Naufrágio dos Kleônicos* (The Shipwreck of Kleonicos, 1916), a composition contemporary with *Tédio de Alvorada*.

30. Assuming that the theme spans for a total of 58 beats, the golden section is located between beats 35 and 36, where the E-flat sforzato is located.

31. Term designated by Paulo de Tarso Salles in his study, *Villa-Lobos: Processos Composicionais*. See glossary of terms.

32. The transformative process occurring in cells a1 through a4 is described in Salles, *Villa-Lobos: Processos Composicionais*, 150.

33. On the downbeat of m. 130, the C is also doubled by the highest C of the piccolo, constituting the highest pitch in the score for the entire piece.

34. Current musicology attributes the connections between *Amazonas* and *Uirapuru* to other less structural factors, and these connections have been weakened when it was determined that the two compositions were probably written several years apart. In previous studies by Lisa Peppercorn, she posited that Villa-Lobos used to write compositions in pairs, and therefore *Amazonas* and *Uirapuru* were sister compositions that belong to the same group of ideas (Peppercorn, *Villa-Lobos: The Music*, 85). The present study will demonstrate in the subsequent chapters that the multiple correspondences between the two compositions suggest a meaningful inner connection that rescues Lisa Peppercorn's original statement.

35. "Villa-Lobos, Sua Obra," 2nd ed., 1972, MEC/DAC/Museu Villa-Lobos, 245.

CHAPTER FIVE

Dissecting Uirapuru

Caramuru, Caramuru
Filho do fogo, sobrinho do trovão! —Antônio Nássara and Sá Róris

The Brazilian fauna was one of the important nationalist elements that Villa-Lobos incorporated in his music. Besides *Uirapuru*, two other compositions inspired by birds come immediately to mind: The "azulão da mata" (blue-black grosbeak) was an important source of motivic material for the opening portion of *Chôros No.10*, while several birds of the Cariri Mountains appears prominently in Manuel Bandeira's poem set to music in Villa-Lobos's *Martelo* from *Bachianas Brasileiras No. 5*.

Three years after the premiere of *Uirapuru*, the carnival march *Caramuru*,[1] written by Antônio Nássara (1910–1996) and Sá Róris (1887–1975) was featured in the carnival of 1938, portraying Caramuru as the son of fire and nephew of thunder. The lyrics humorously include Brazilian birds, describing the character as someone who shot the *urubu* (a sort of black vulture), but missed the target, hitting instead the *gavião* (a middle-sized hawk). The title refers to the Portuguese sailor Diogo Álvares Correia, the first European to establish contact with the Tupinambá tribe. Confronted for the first time with a colonizer bearer of a firearm, the Amerindians named him Caramuru, which means "son of the thunder" in the Tupi language. Caramuru married an Amerindian woman called Paraguaçu, who became the first South American native to be received at the Palace of Versailles. He was immortalized in the epic poem *Caramuru* by Friar Santa Rita Durão, considered a precursor of the Indianist Romantic literature in Brazil that praised the noble savage. This is exactly the type of literature criticized by Oswald de Andrade and the anthropophagites, who sought a break with this literary tradition. Caramuru's narrative interweaves history and fiction, which, according to Janaína Amado, "can be considered to be Brazil's myth of origin."[2]

As noted in the previous chapter, the need to write music for the specific program of a ballet did not prevent Villa-Lobos from transplanting into *Uirapuru* most of the musical material from his earlier composition—*Tédio de Alvorada*—a symphonic poem about a landscape based on a text by Teixeira Leite Filho:

> In a sky inlaid with stars the sun, which has begun to rise, brings the first light and banishes nocturnal shadow. Slowly ghosts, along dark, deserted paths in the heart of the forest, by the banks of brooks and streams, are liberated, and crowd back to their sinister homes. Owls in flight return to their ancient lodgings, and the screams of other nocturnal birds fill the air. A swan begins to cry, softly floating on the waters of a lake, with immense profundity in the lament of his song. From the gloom the brightness of day is born, and as the light shines through, the stars vanish. The sun awakens the guard dogs in the palace of Argos, who howl in desperation. . . . In the solitude of night an old man wanders, lost—the slave of Agamemnon—the King of Kings. Dawn.[3]

The program of *Uirapuru* was written by Villa-Lobos and published in the score,[4] which contains written references to the various sections of the story in the body of the music. A more complete program appears in a typed page attached to the manuscript score:

> Tropical moonlight night. An ugly Indian appears in the calm and quiet forest, playing a nose-flute made of bones in a challenge to the magic bird that attracted the Indian maidens with its singing. The most beautiful Indian maidens come after the sound of the flute but are disappointed as they see the ugly Indian. The outraged Indian maidens banish him with brutality, battering, pushing, and kicking him. Anxiously, the Indian maidens search for the uirapuru through the foliage of the trees, hoping to find the handsome young Indian. Fireflies, crickets, owls, [illegible], frogs, [illegible], bats and all the nightly fauna witness the eagerness of the Indian maidens. Once in a while, one can hear soft trills announcing the uirapuru and filling the environment with joy. Seduced by the splendid song of the uirapuru, a beautiful and strong

Indian maiden emerges with a bow and arrow in her hands, like a skillful hunter of nightly birds. Seeing the enchanted bird, she shoots an arrow, and the uirapuru falls to the ground, pierced. The Indian maiden is surprised as she sees the bird transformed into a handsome Indian. He is disputed by the other Indian maidens, who have also chased him eagerly, but the Indian maiden who wounded him wins. At the height of the dispute, one hears the fiery and ominous sound of the ugly Indian's nose flute. The Indian maidens try to hide the handsome Indian, since they are afraid of the revenge of the ugly and evil Indian. However, the handsome Indian is caught by the terrifying Indian, who throws an arrow with fury and revenge, mortally wounding the handsome Indian. The Indian maidens carry the handsome Indian in their arms to the edge of a pond, where he suddenly transforms into an invisible bird. The sad and loving Indian maidens are left listening to the marvelous singing, which gradually fades into the depth of the quiet forest.[5]

Villa-Lobos framed the argument of the ballet as a rondo form (ABACA), with a one-measure introduction and an expressive coda. A brief analysis of the various sections follows.

Table 5.1. Formal structure of *Uirapuru*.

PART I			PART II		
The Uirapuru			The Handsome Indian		
A	B	A	C	A	Coda
Binary	Ternary	Ternary	Ternary w/ intro and codetta	Binary (abridged)	
1–134	134–184	185–226	227–340	341–364	365–375

Part I: The Uirapuru

Section A (mm. 1–67; 68–134. The section is repeated)

Written in binary form with two contrasting sections (*Poco Adagio* and *Tempo di Marcia*), the piece starts with an exquisite, one-measure introduction[6] that establishes the *Tristan chord* through a leap of tritone in the upper voice (Figure 5.1). The *Poco Adagio* occurs almost entirely over a pedal of this *Tristan chord*, in a sustained harmonic ostinato of seventeen measures in syncopated rhythm, alternating between horns and inner strings (second violins and violas). In this way, the composer asserts, from the very beginning, the Wagnerian influence that permeates the piece.[7]

Figure 5.1. Beginning of Uirapuru. The presence of the Tristan chord permeates the composition with a Wagnerian influence. The Tristan chord is slightly modified at m. 6 through semitone sliding, a typical compositional process of Villa-Lobos.

Based on figure from Villa-Lobos: *Processos Composicionais* by Paulo de Tarso Salles, 29. Used with permission.

According to the program, the syncopated ostinato of the *Tristan chord* is associated with the realm of the happy group of Amerindian girls, lured into the forest in search of the uirapuru. It is remarkable that the glissando on the top line in the first measure travels through a tritone from A to E-flat, since the tritone will be established as one of the most important constructive forces of the composition.

Over the seventeen-measure harmonic ostinato of the first section, the two main themes of the piece are introduced: The first violins state the "Theme of the Uirapuru," while the lower strings (cellos and basses) state the "Theme of the Jungle." The former is preceded by a three-note, chromatically descending motif (Figure 5.2), which is melodically connected with the

Figure 5.2. Beginning of the Prelude of the opera Tristan and Isolde and Uirapuru. Both examples feature an ascending leap from the upbeat followed by a descending line in semitones of three notes over a rhythm long-short-long.

Created by the author.

beginning of the Prelude of Wagner's opera *Tristan and Prelude*, and will reappear prominently in the connection of Sections A and C (mm. 224–226).

The reiterated motifs within the melody of the "Theme of the Uirapuru" start on different beats within the bars, with altered rhythms as the motif stretches and shrinks. The structure of the generating motif of the theme and its rhythmic treatment show a remarkable resemblance to the beginning of Stravinsky's *The Rite of Spring*. Considering that the rhythmic element has been considered one of the greatest breakthroughs of modernism through Stravinsky's music, this aspect deserves a more thorough analysis.

To a great extent, Pierre Boulez attributed the notorious reputation of the bassoon theme in the beginning of *Le Sacre* (*The Rite of Spring*) to the remarkable rhythmic development explored by the composer. In his analysis, he shows that the tune can be divided into four phrases, indicated by Roman numerals (see Figure 5.3). Each one of the phrases can be considered a variation of the same theme, because they employ the same thematic material. While the inner phrases, II and III, start on upbeats, the outer phrases, I and IV, start on the beat, with the latter creating a sense of rhythmic and thematic recapitulation. In contrast, phrase II conspicuously features the two triplets present in phrase I (notated there as a2), while phrase III features the remaining rhythmic components of phrase I (since a1, a3, and a4 find their correspondence in a6, a7, and a8). Therefore, rhythmically speaking, phrases II and III are complementary. In short, by breaking the symmetry, Stravinsky paradoxically produces a closed structure through reinterpretation of meter and rhythm, horizontal shifting of the phrases, and complementarity of materials (Figure 5.3).[8]

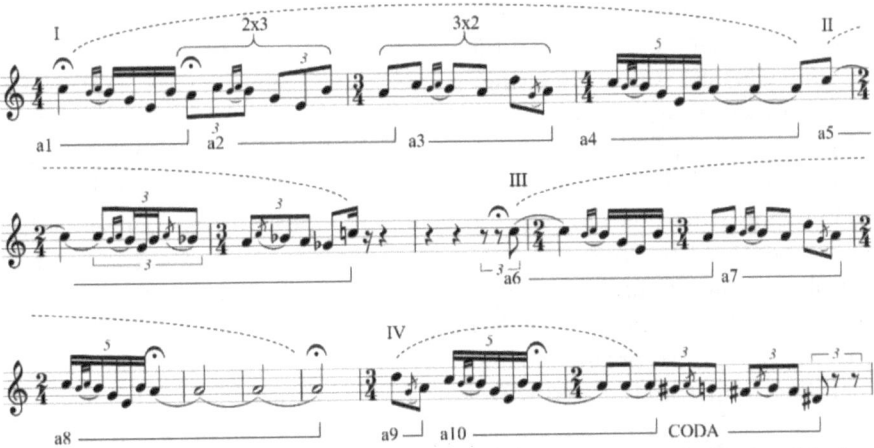

Figure 5.3. Analysis of the famous bassoon solo at the beginning of *The Rite of Spring*, according to Pierre Boulez.
Based on an illustration from *Notes of an Apprenticeship* by Pierre Boulez (1968), 79.

Within the microform, we can notice that the four-part structure of the phrases is reflected in the four inner motifs of phrase I, notated as a1, a2, a3, and a4. Therefore, the microform projects atomically what happens in the macro-structure, an almost fractal conception of music. Motif *a1*, with four short notes following a held note is a rhythmic retrograde of *motif a4*, with five short notes followed by a held note—an almost rhythmic palindrome. And *motifs a2* and *a3* are complementary in the sense that a2 has two triplets (2×3), while a3 has the combination of three groups of two eighth notes (3×2).

In the same fashion, the opening measures of *Uirapuru* also display structural balance due to its rhythmic structure. The theme is not a folk tune but has some familiar features, with its narrow range and a melody based on nonfunctional diatonic modality. Using Salles's analysis,[9] one can observe that, through the shrinking and expansion of melodic fragment B, the main motif achieves its complete form in fragments B3 and B6, through a zigzag statement of the sequence of pitches F—G-flat—E-flat—B-flat—D-flat—A-flat—C-flat (see Figure 5.4). When ordered from the key center D-flat (the axis between the upper and lower boundaries of the theme), they produce the Mixolydian mode on D-flat.

The rhythmic proportion of the six melodic cells of the theme (B1 through B6) present a process of shrinking followed by a stretching of the basic cell: 6.1>4.6<8.6 (B1-B2-B3); 5.6>3.6<8.5 (B4-B5-B6). In this way, Sections B1 through B3 are proportionally equivalent to Sections B4 through B6. The theme as a whole is framed by cells A and C, which complement the balance of the structure in its beginning and end phases. The rhythmic manipulation that happens in cells B2, B4, and B5 varies the same melodic figure of three notes, shifted metrically, and with a different duration for the last note (E-flat). Cells B3 and B6 are complete, while B6 is an accelerated version of B3. B1 is the generating cell that stands between the complete and shrunken versions of the melodic cells.

In conclusion, Villa-Lobos was able to produce a formal scheme that is proportionally balanced, developmental, and closed, like Stravinsky's bassoon theme in *The Rite of Spring*. While keeping the meter throughout, Villa-Lobos produced the horizontal shifting of the phrases, the expansion and shrinking of motifs, and their respective rhythmic complementarity. Despite the remarkable resemblance with *The Rite*'s bassoon melody, the "Theme of the Uirapuru" is so organically incorporated into the composition that the mention of anything related with plagiarism would be out of the question. One can hardly find a better example of musical cannibalism, a perfect metaphor of the quote (wrongly) attributed to Stravinsky: "a good composer does not imitate; he steals."

Figure 5.4. (a) Beginning of Uirapuru—violin theme. Ordered from the key center D-flat, the material of the "Theme of the Uirapuru" forms a Mixolydian mode (shown underneath). (b) Rhythmic structure of the theme, where the numbers indicate the durations of each melodic fragment in terms of number of beats.
Paulo de Tarso Salles, Villa-Lobos: *Processos Composicionais*, 167–168.

The first statement of the "Theme of the Uirapuru" polarizes D-flat Mixolydian as key center. The "Theme of the Jungle" is presented as countermelody in the low register of the texture by cellos, doubled by bass clarinet and double basses in the key center of B-flat Phrygian. The first section ends with a flute cadenza (at the repeat, played by the soprano saxophone) that represents the ugly, native invader of the forest, playing a nose-flute[10] (Figure 5.5).

It is interesting to observe that once again the composer explores a technique of polarization of the intervals major and minor seconds, as well as the tritone, at multiple levels. In m. 19, the flute's G-sharps form a harmonic tritone with the low D of the basses, while in mm. 20–23 the flute line emphasizes the note B-flat, aggregating this note to the interval of fifth (D-A) that sustains the harmony in the low register. This chord (D–A–B-flat) constitutes the basis of the next section, *Tempo di marcia*, performed by cellos and basses.

A more subtle effect happens in m. 23. Departing from C-sharp, the flute performs an arpeggiated figure based on a six-note collection that presents symmetrical properties that result in two tritones (C♯–G and F♯–C) separated by a half tone. A zigzag motion leads to the next measure, where the flute presents (starting on the upbeat) melodic tritones separated by a whole tone interval (C-sharp—G and A—D-sharp). These melodic tritones resonate harmonically in the upper register of the subsequent ostinato (G-sharp—D and F-sharp—C). Therefore, the flute line horizontally displays the intervallic properties that are featured in the ostinato that succeeds it. The technique

Figure 5.5. Theme of the Ugly Indian. This theme displays the polarization of the intervals of major and minor 2nd as well as the tritone.
Paulo de Tarso Salles, Villa-Lobos: *Processos Composicionais*, 149.

displayed is that of polarization of certain intervals—the tritone and the major second—displayed symmetrically in the analysis.[11]

Besides enhancing the inner coherence of the structure, the composer finds a way to provide an almost-seamless continuity to the work when going from a section to a contrasting one. This contradicts past criticism that accused him of producing works of rhapsodic character without the inner coherence found in composers who master the craft of thematic development. According to Salles, Villa-Lobos's critics attribute the absence of institutionalized formal procedures to a training deficiency, or to the instability of his temperament. Based on some testimonies, often extracted from their context, the judgments about the composer's musical production come to consider him as a naïvely intuitive composer, who, by a happy combination of forces of nature, occasionally obtains successful effects.[12] In fact, the procedure of organizing the transition to a new contrasting section through an anticipation of its features in the previous section is a traditional compositional process found frequently in a number of composers, such as Johannes Brahms (Figure 5.6):

Score

Figure 5.6. In the last movement of Brahms' Piano Concerto No. 2, the main theme has a ternary form, where the contrasting middle section constitutes a natural continuation and development of the last measure of the first section, as indicated above. A similar approach happens with the main theme of the 1st movement of Brahms' Piano Sonata op. 5 in F minor. This type of connection appears in many compositions by Brahms, including some of his art songs.
Created by the author.

The cadenza that constitutes the "Theme of the Ugly Indian" has an improvisatory quality and is highly chromatic,[13] contrasting with the diatonicism of the "Theme of the Uirapuru," a feature explored in an analogous way by Stravinsky in The Firebird.[14] In the latter, the dichotomy between the chromatic and the diatonic is a way of differentiating the human and the fantastic worlds of the story (the chromatic is associated with the world of Kaschei and the Firebird, while the diatonic is associated with the human world of Ivan and the princesses).[15]

In Uirapuru, the diatonic realm associates the magic bird with the Handsome Amerindian, the "noble savage" being identified with nature, a metaphor resultant from the fact that the diatonic system is a product of the harmonic series, which is also identified with nature. In contrast, the Ugly Amerindian represents the "primitive savage" and is identified first by a twelve-tone chromatic collection conspicuously presenting the tritone and, at the end, by an eight-tone, non-diatonic collection, as demonstrated in Figure 5.26. Villa-Lobos's "noble savage" is not defined as such by virtuous features. His nobility rests in his identification with nature, by the fusion of his identity with the local fauna.[16] While musically the materials are highly contrasting and contradictory (diatonic versus chromatic), they guard an inner coherence—all the themes polarize the intervals of tritone and major/minor second. A more detailed discussion about the multiple realms explored in the composition appears at the end of the chapter.

The Tempo di Marcia section that follows occurs over an ostinato march rhythm formed by the hemiolas of the accompaniment (Figure 5.5 above, starting on m. 25). It is a march in triple meter, where the "Theme of the Jungle" is transformed to represent the beating of the ugly native by the young native maidens, who drive him out of the forest. This section displays many primitivist characteristics of Brazilian modernism, such as the presence of an ostinato rhythm with irregular accents, the predominance of conjunct motion, and parallelisms, which became associated with Villa-Lobos's style of representing the Amerindian in his music.[17]

Rather than pure leitmotif technique, the reappearance of the "Theme of the Jungle" with distinct meaning and character in different sections of the work constitutes a unifying element of a different nature. The aggressiveness of the native maidens toward the male figure of the ugly Amerindian recalls a depiction of the female as a warrior, a distant but noteworthy connection with the mythological amazons.[18] The section ends with a powerful and harsh chord, whose notes are derived from a shortened octatonic collection that complements the octatonic associated with the "Theme of the Jungle" during the persecution scene (Figure 5.7).

Dissecting Uirapuru — 113

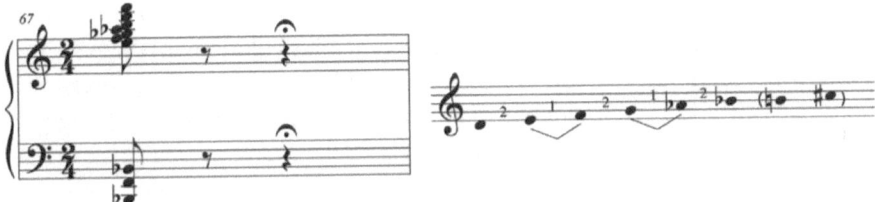

Figure 5.7. Final chord of section A of Uirapuru. This chord is derived from an incomplete octatonic collection (the notes missing appear in parenthesis).
Created by the author.

The entire Section A, including the introduction, is repeated in the score. The difference is that the flute solo representing the nose-flute is performed at the repeat by a soprano saxophone, and part of the "Theme of the Uirapuru" is performed by a solo violin in the upper register (mm. 77–83). Such repetition makes sense only when performing *Uirapuru* as a symphonic poem. Several performances and recordings tend to eliminate the repetition, as it would make obscure the connection with the program of the ballet.[19]

Section B (mm. 134–184)

The ternary form of Section B is framed by a passage where the various members of the nocturnal animal and insect kingdoms are represented over a new background ostinato. The ostinato formed by the piano and basses playing softly in hemiolas at the low register suggests a nocturnal atmosphere. Time stands still, while multiple noises randomly break the silence of the dark forest. The noises are produced by a texture in eight layers, formed by figures performed by the bass clarinet, double basses with piano, English horn, oboe, xylophone, first violins, and flute.

The atmosphere created is one that can be associated with impressionism/tenebrism[20] in its attempt to suggest the depiction of a nocturnal atmosphere, where the animals and insects of the Amazonian fauna practically stop to hear Uirapuru's song, as described in the legend. The "Theme of the Uirapuru" appears prominently in one of the layers, played by the flute, and heard among an onomatopoeia of sounds representing glowing worms, crickets, owls, enchanted toads, bats, and other insects performed by the other layers of the texture. This chiaroscuro soundscape is the result of the timbristic combinations, which carry a descriptive meaning that mirrors the universe of the tropical noises.

Scholars detected Stravinsky's influence in the construction of this passage, through the anthropophagic assimilation of a similar passage from the symphonic poem *Chant du Rossignol* by Stravinsky. In the "mechanical nightingale song" scene by the Russian composer, the melody of the singing bird played by the oboe is framed by different musical elements exposed by other instruments in the contrasting high and low registers of the orchestral texture.[21] Villa-Lobos conducted the premiere of this piece in Brazil one year before completing his score of *Uirapuru*.

It is possible to identify here a surrealist aesthetic collision achieved through the multilayered texture: The diatonic nature of the "Theme of the Uirapuru" expressed in the first collection contrasts with the chromatic, exotic pitch collection of the remaining sounds, which presents a mirror symmetry (second collection in Figure 5.8). When the passage reappears on mm. 177–184, it is abridged, and some of the sounds are eliminated (the xylophone, oboe, English horn, and bass clarinet). When this happens, the new pitch collection of the remaining sounds still maintains a mirror symmetry.

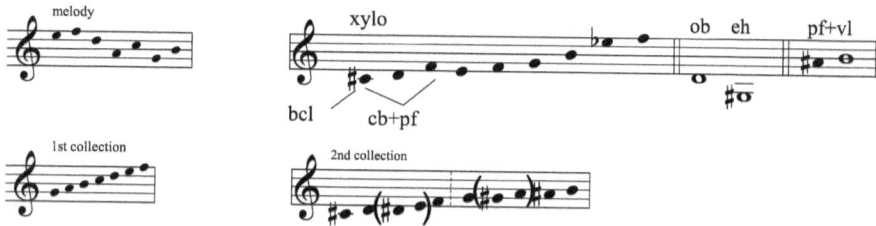

Figure 5.8. The passage in mm. 134.143 depicts the nocturnal insects and animals in contrast with the uirapuru. The line on top describes the pitches used for the various motifs, and the line below shows their corresponding ordered pitch collections, demonstrating that the uirapuru is represented by a diatonic collection, while the combined remaining sounds are represented by an exotic pitch collection of 10 notes that present a mirror symmetry. When this passage is restated in an abridged form at mm. 177–184, some of the sounds are eliminated (the xylophone, oboe, English horn and bass clarinet), but the collection representing the remaining pitches maintains a mirror symmetry. The notes eliminated at the repeat appear in parenthesis in the 2nd collection.
Paulo de Tarso Salles, Villa-Lobos: *Processos Composicionais*, 114.

Within this multilayered passage, the entrances of the various instruments, while precisely and not randomly written, give the perception of an embryonic use of aleatory music mirroring nature's behavior. The figures enter unexpectedly in seemingly random places within the measures, though their entrances are clearly notated. The atmospheric effect is reminiscent of impressionism, while the representation of "noise" is associated with futurism and the shock of musical materials is a surrealist. In the subsequent chapters of this study, it will be demonstrated how this sort of collision is fully realized in *Amazonas*, where Villa-Lobos's language becomes much more radical, transporting his innovations to the next level.

The framing of Section B by this aleatory passage produces a ternary form that contrasts with the binary nature of Section A. The rhythmic middle section features the "Theme of the Uirapuru" within another layered structure, representing one more example of use of the leitmotif technique as a unifying element not necessarily associated with the same *leit*-idea. In the present case, the material previously used to represent the singing of the uirapuru is now brought to a different context. Starting with a motif of two notes, new notes are gradually added in zigzag through a process of summation, ending with a full statement of the motif of the Uirapuru with eleven notes.[22]

Figure 5.9. Restatement of the Theme of the Uirapuru through a process of summation. Though questionable, an argument can be made that the process of summation employed is derived from the Fibonacci series.
Created by the author.

This new variant of the theme is quite dramatic and intense, identifying with the primeval power of the unleashed forces of nature. The theme is presented in counterpoint with an energetic, quasi-ostinato of double basses and parallel triads on violas and cellos with trombones.[23] The percussive ostinato nature of the passage brings a primitivist character to the whole section B. While Sections A and B of the composition are clearly contrasting, the presence of the uirapuru theme in both as a leit-theme serves as a unifying factor. The process of summation found in Section B (Figure 5.9) contrasts with the shrinking and stretching of motifs present in the "Theme of the Uirapuru" as introduced in Section A. Summing up, Villa-Lobos achieves unity through the use of numerous devices, such as leitmotifs, with renewed meaning; complementarity of binary and ternary forms; complementarity of procedures when handling short motifs (stretching and shrinking as opposed to summation); expressive complementarity (lyric/expressive versus rhythmic ostinato); and the association of multiple realms with different characters, as indicated in Table 5.4 below.

While Villa-Lobos has been criticized for his inability to handle thematic materials and achieve unity in larger compositions, the above demonstrates exactly the opposite—a highly original approach in handling musical materials, which allows him to achieve unity through structural plurality of complementary materials and procedures. This reflects the composer's desire to express in his music the exuberance of his country in all its monumentality.

Restatement of Section A (mm. 185–226)
The first restatement of Section A starts at rehearsal number nine, where the pictorial nature of the music is achieved through structural metaphors. One of them is a unifying element that permeates the section but does not appear in the beginning of the piece: a pulsating, bell-like, B-natural pedal, which will become a leitmotif associated with the magical realm of Amerindian legends, where the ritual of transformation takes place. This leitmotif is orchestrated with the distinctive colors of the piano, celesta, and harp harmonics performing in octaves. In later passages, other notable timbres are added, such as cello harmonics (m. 187); glockenspiel and chimes (m. 208); viola plus cello harmonics (m. 350); and bass harmonics (m. 371).

This section can be subdivided into three phases: the appearance of the Beautiful Huntress; the transformation scene (where the two main themes are again presented simultaneously); and the conclusion, a modulatory bridge that leads into the most contrasting section of the rondo form (Section C).

Table 5.2. Segmentation of the first restatement of Section A.

Phase I	Phase II	Phase III
Appearance of the Indian Huntress	Transformation Scene	Bridge
185–196	197–215	216–226

a. Phase I: Harmonic Recapitulation

A long B-natural pedal by cello and harp harmonics, reinforced by the celesta, gives a supernatural ambience to the background. The syncopated rhythm representing the Amerindian maidens supports rotating harmonies around the *Tristan chord*,[24] constituting a sort of harmonic recapitulation, which prepares the entrance of the Beautiful Huntress, represented by a repeated, bell-like motif of a descending second (Figure 5.10). The Huntress's motif is reminiscent of *motif b* from the appendix of the "Theme of the Jungle" (Figure 4.8). By placing it over the syncopated harmony that represents the Amerindian maidens, it positions the huntress within their realm, while at the same time connecting her, metaphorically, with the jungle through *motif b*.[25] The Huntress's motif has a distinctive timbre that alternates the combination of soprano sax and celesta with glockenspiel and flute, heard over the supernatural atmosphere of the passage. Curiously, the passage sounds like an inversion of the memorable introduction of Gershwin's "Summertime" from *Porgy and Bess*, which premiered a few months after *Uirapuru*. The inverted motif in "Summertime" is shifted horizontally in the measure, so that it starts in the second beat instead of the downbeat. The attentive listener would certainly recognize how much the sonority of Gershwin's harmony recalls the alternating half-diminished chords in *Uirapuru*, which are the product of the nontraditional, octatonic collection used by Villa-Lobos, another manifestation of the presence of the *Tristan chord*. The use of bells in Gershwin's motif promotes an even closer association.

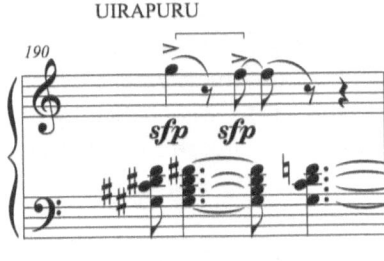

Figure 5.10. The motif representing the beautiful Amerindian huntress in Uirapuru. The non-traditional octatonic collection used by Villa-Lobos presents a symmetry in the alternation of tones and semitones.
Created by the author.

Throughout this introductory passage, the noises of the forest remain, with their peculiar aleatoric sounds provided by periodic interventions of woodwinds and percussion. Among those sounds, a flute motif (later performed by oboe and English horn an octave lower) resembles, in inverted form, a passage of *The Rite of Spring*, performed by piccolo, E-flat clarinet, and piccolo trumpet (Figure 5.11).[26] The idea of an abrupt, chromatic motion of repeated notes that dives into emptiness was already present in *Tédio de Alvorada*, written in 1916, demonstrating that it was conceived originally by Villa-Lobos before he had any contact with *The Rite of Spring*.

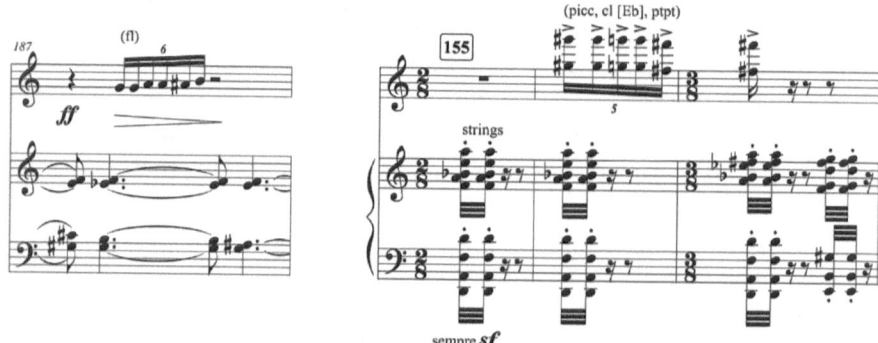

Figure 5.11. Fast, chromatic motion of repeated semitones diving into the vacuum in The Rite of Spring (right) and in the form of an inverted variant in Uirapuru (left).
Paulo de Tarso Salles, Villa-Lobos: *Processos Composicionais*, 30 and 31.

b. Phase II: Thematic Recapitulation

The thematic recapitulation corresponds to the passage of transformation of the uirapuru into a Handsome Indian.[27] At rehearsal ten, the "Theme of the Jungle" is restated enharmonically on the Phrygian mode over A-sharp, enharmonic to the original statement in B-flat (see Figure 4.8). The only major difference is that the codetta becomes a diatonic descent of fifth from G-sharp to C-sharp (mm. 211–215), instead of the original chromatic descent over a tritone. As in the Exposition, the two main themes are presented simultaneously, the transformation represented by the deformation of the "Theme of the Uirapuru," which is performed in this passage by the oboe. The theme is written in the Dorian mode on D-sharp, the axis between the lowest and high points of the theme, as well as the ultimate point of arrival (Figure 5.12). The absence (polarized by exclusion) of C-sharp in these statements of the "Theme of the Uirapuru" is compensated by its presence at the arrival point of the "Theme of the Jungle," which is prolonged by cellos and basses until the beginning of the next segment (mm. 213–215). As the C-sharp is reached, a triple iteration of the Beautiful Huntress's motif, performed by the harps, celesta, and clarinet, ends Phase II of the section.

Figure 5.12. The transformation of the uirapuru into a handsome Indian is achieved through the deformation of the "Theme of the Uirapuru" over the Dorian mode.
Created by the author.

Described above are a number of elements that, combined, produce an impressionist soundscape. They reveal several innovative elements, such as the use of dissonances, deformation of themes, search for rare timbristic effects, and syncopated rhythms that carry an expressive meaning and latent potential for structuring the musical form. These innovations will explode into a liberation of a much larger arsenal of resources and techniques that will stretch the boundaries of the musical language in *Amazonas*, where primitivism reveals itself with its utmost primeval intensity.

c. Phase III

The conclusion of Section A is a bridge presenting the final and incomplete statement of the "Theme of the Jungle," performed *piu mosso*, and including only the antecedent (Figure 5.13). While the theme still shows a movement I–V, this statement is deformed and built over a non-traditional octatonic pitch collection that produces an exotic, non-diatonic realm.[28] One can assume that this is product of a metaphorical intervention: The magic realm that coincides with the arrival of the beautiful Indian Huntress affects the natural realm of the forest, which is now defined by the new, exotic pitch collection. The exotic octatonic pitch collection representing this new sphere displays a certain symmetry in the arrangement of whole tones and semitones and is essentially a variant of the octatonic realm of the Beautiful Huntress, which was presented previously (see Figure 5.10). The ostinato ringing of chimes, glockenspiel, and piano over the pitch B-natural accompanying the theme (not shown on Figure 5.13) once again displays a resemblance with the introduction of the accompaniment of "Summertime" by Gershwin, which also uses a quite similar bell sound, with the employment of glockenspiel. This orchestration device became a symbol of "tenebrism" in our collective subconscious, which associates this sound with a nocturne atmosphere and the world of dreams. After all, "Summertime" is essentially a lullaby that can be subliminally connected with the nighttime setting of this scene in *Uirapuru*.

120 ～ Chapter Five

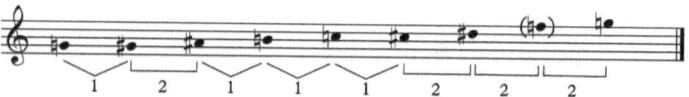

Figure 5.13. Final statement of the Theme of the Jungle. Only the antecedent is stated, deformed in relation to its first statement in the beginning of the piece (Fig. V-9). This statement of the theme is built over an exotic octatonic collection, which is a variant of the octatonic material associated with Indian Huntress (see Fig. V-10). Note that the absence of the pitch F in the octatonic collection is compensated by its emphatic repetition in the figures performed by the piccolo and saxophone in octaves in other parts of the texture between mm. 216–227, as well as its presence in the Huntress' motif that appears in mm. 221–223.
Created by the author.

The exotic octatonic collection brings a magic realm to the forest, related with the preceding transformation scene. The "Theme of the Jungle" is followed by another restatement of the motif of the Beautiful Huntress (mm. 221–223, shown on the upper line of Figure 5.13a), and concludes dramatically with a powerful return of the three-note chromatic motif that was first introduced at the beginning of the piece in the high register of the first violins (top line of Figure 5.14), this time stated in unison by cornets, horns, English horn, and clarinets. As explained previously in Figure 5.2, this three-note motif is derived from the beginning oboe motif of the Prelude to Wagner's *Tristan and Isolde*. With its return at the end of the first part of *Uirapuru*, it serves as a frame to this portion of the piece. Section C starts at rehearsal number thirteen, located near the golden section of the composition.[29]

Figure 5.14. The three-note chromatic motif above frames Part I of Uirapuru.
Created by the author.

Part II: The Handsome Indian

Section C (mm. 227–340)

The Allegretto creates an atmosphere of excitement for the celebration following the transformation of the uirapuru into a Handsome Indian. Almost the entirety of Section C is unified by the use of an ostinato that ends at a codetta, indicated below as Phase 5. The ostinato, which is not strictly rigorous and is performed mainly by the timpani with the periodic intrusion of other instruments, starts as a four-measure figure, changing to a two-measure figure near rehearsal sixteen. Section C can be subdivided into five segments or phases:

Table 5.3. Section C is formed by five segments connected by pedals (except the cantus firmus, which is introduced by a descending chromatic scale).</tt>

Phase 1	Phase 2	Phase 3	Phase 4	Phase 5
Opening	Celebration	Cantus firmus	Indian theme	Conclusion
227–238	239–268	269–292	293–325	326–340
	pedal E	Connected by descending chromatic scale	pedal B-natural	pedal G

Analogous to Part I, Section C also introduces two main themes, which will be denominated "Celebration Theme" and "Handsome Indian Theme."

"Celebration Theme"

This theme has a palindromic form (a b a b' a) with a recurring choriamb motif (long—short—short—long) that gives it a distinct character. Besides being palindromic, this theme starts and ends on E, the pitch at the axis between the highest and lowest note of the theme. Its exotic pitch collection combines the main intervals of the piece (a tritone obtained through a chromatic motion of semitones, and a major second).

Figure 5.15. The "Celebration Theme." Its pitch material comes from the combination of an ascending chromatic motion over the span of a tritone, followed by three whole-tone steps.
Created by the author.

"Handsome Indian Theme"

While probably written by Villa-Lobos, this theme presents the typical characteristics of the music of the Brazilian Amerindians, with its small range, repeated notes, small intervals with the predominance of conjunct motion, and use of non-functional, diatonic modality. The theme is written on a pentatonic pitch collection using only the white keys. The two pitches remaining to complete a full diatonic scale from this pentatonic are part of the accompaniment.[30] The contour of the theme indicates that G is polarized as key center. The "Handsome Indian Theme" features a *quartus paeon* motif.[31] In its original form, the theme is symmetrical: The *quartus paeon* motif frames a central portion where another motif (F—G—B natural) ascends to a climax and descends to the original point of departure (A—G—F).

Figure 5.16. The "Handsome Indian Theme."
Created by the author.

Melodically, this central portion of the theme brings to mind a melody of the Pareci Amerindians called Nozani-ná, which Villa-Lobos used in other compositions, such as his *Choros No. 3*, as well as his own version of Nozani-ná with the title "Canção Indígena." The example below demonstrates the assimilation of the national culture into the anthropophagic compositional process of the composer.

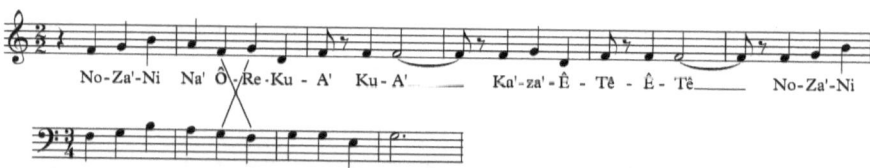

Figure 5.17. Transcription by Edgard Roquette-Pinto of the Pareci song Nozani-ná, according to phonogram 14.597 (transposed one tone up for comparison). The permutation of the F and G in the second measure would produce the same melody of the central portion of the "Handsome Indian Theme," which appears in the bottom line.
Created by the author.

The above is further corroborated by observing that, rhythmically, the *quartus paeon* is also found in *Canide Ioune Sabath* (yellow bird), an Amerindian theme collected by Jean de Lery, which Villa-Lobos used in other occasions, such as the *Three Amerindian Poems* of 1926 (see Figure 5.18).[32] If the "Theme of the Uirapuru" stylistically emulates the behavior of a singing bird (see Figure 4.3), the "Handsome Indian Theme" emulates the behavior of Brazilian Amerindian songs. The recurring repetitions, with slight variants, immerse the listeners in the Brazilian rain forest, witnessing an Amerindian pagan ritual enhanced by the addition of Brazilian percussion instruments within the ostinato (*coco*, *tamborim*, and *surdo*).

Figure 5.18. Beginning of the Amerindian song Canide Ioune Sabath.
Created by the author.

Ironically, while the primitive characteristics of the "Handsome Indian Theme" are compared with the music of the Brazilian Amerindian natives, it is interesting to note that this theme, as well as the "Celebration Theme," were already present in *Tédio de Alvorada*. Both themes are strongly related, one being almost a variant of the other—their recurring motifs are basically the same, the *quartus paeon* of the "Handsome Indian Theme" being an augmented variation of the choriamb motif of the "Celebration Theme," which is another display of thematic unity.

Figure 5.19. The inner relationship of the "Celebration Theme" (above) and the "Handsome Indian Theme" (below) is expressed through their analogous contour.
Created by the author.

The opening of section C displays prominently the beginning of an ostinato figure on timpani, cellos, and cornets, where the interval of perfect fifth is reinforced by horns and violins. It is a typical feature of the composer to articulate the musical form through a recognizable harmonic entity, such as the perfect fifths in this case.[33]

The "Celebration Theme" is presented (Phase 2) in an imitative fashion, respectively by the bassoons plus xylophone (mm. 239–243); viola plus English horn (mm. 247–251 and mm. 255–259); and violins plus cornets *piu mosso* at rehearsal number fifteen. Around the golden mean of Section C (m. 269),[34] the "Handsome Indian Theme" is introduced as a *cantus firmus* in augmentation (Phase 3), played by double basses, bassoons, contrabassoon, and tuba.[35] A pedal of B-natural connects with the next phase, which introduces the "Handsome Indian Theme" proper at m. 293 (Phase 4).

After the last statement of the theme by the trombones, the music gradually subsides. The concluding section starts with an ascending chordal progression of almost-parallel triads harmonizing an ascending line over the pitches F-G-A-B-D-E, where the predominance of whole tones (with one exception) should be remarked. This section contrasts substantially with all the preceding phases of section C, particularly because it somehow returns to a whole-tone realm that was absent in the previous phases, which were essentially modal. Half of the almost parallel chords that harmonize the ascending melodic line are augmented triads, which are a product of the whole tone scale (Figure 5.20). This surrealist intervention of a new harmonic realm anticipates the progression of exotic, polytonal chords representing the grief of the Amerindian maidens at the end of the piece (Figure 5.30), where the same melodic line transposed a whole tone above (with one exception) is harmonized by similar chords.[36] While this feature enhances and gives unity to the composition, the timbre of violins with harp and celesta in both passages reinforces the magical nature of their realms.

The piano intones an ascending Lydian scale on the white notes, associated with the Handsome Indian. This line, started on the piano, ends on a sustained B-natural on the flute—almost its highest pitch—while a solo double bass descends in contrary motion (over the Locrian mode on C) to-

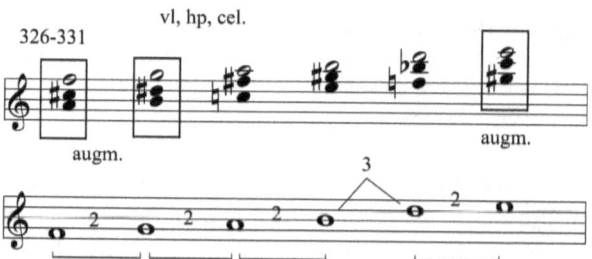

Figure 5.20. The concluding phase of Section C reintroduces a whole-tone realm through an ascending line harmonized by almost parallel chords.
Created by the author.

ward the open low C string (Figure 5.21). Within this poetic and impressionist soundscape, time seems to stop through a gradual *rallentando* ending on a fermata, which sustains the extreme pitches of the composition.[37] As this point is reached, the harp performs a *glissando cadenza ad libitum* that ends on a fermata over low B. The last sound of Section C is the open V string of the double bass against the B-natural sustained by the other instruments. With this, the interval of minor second reaffirms itself, gaining a new dimension as it is resultant from the contrary motion of the two extremes of the orchestra, each one performing the interval of tritone. This "constructive thesis" becomes an important element in the articulation of the musical form.

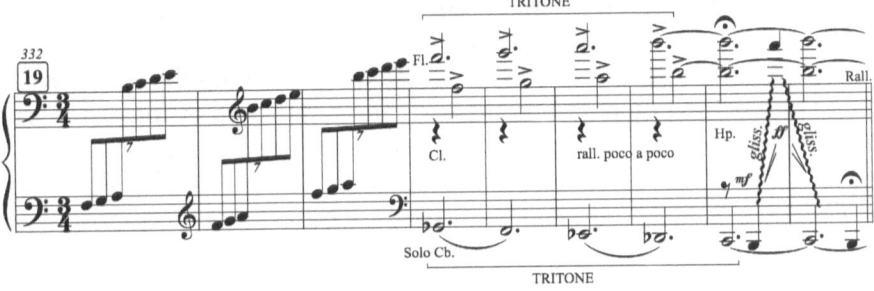

Figure 5.21. The bass solo and a flute solo perform a contrary motion over the interval of tritone, ending Section C on a minor 2nd (separated by several octaves).
Created by the author.

Final Statement of Section A (mm. 341–364)

The final statement of Section A is written in an abridged, binary form, the first part Moderato and the second part Grandioso. The Moderato section corresponds to the flirtation of the Indian Maidens and the Beautiful Huntress with the Handsome Indian. The former is represented by their typical, syncopated motion of vagrant chords circling the *Tristan chord* and, here, reinforced by accented notes by the third horn. The subsequent flirtation of the Beautiful Huntress is represented, consecutively, by her typical bell-ringing effect of intervals of major second (clarinet and harp) and minor second (soprano saxophone and celesta). The flirtation of the Indian Maidens happens over their syncopated motion, bringing back their sphere from the beginning of the piece (the syncopated harmonies of vagrant chords are not shown in the figure below). The undulating motion around the *Tristan chord* is reinforced by accented notes on the third horn until the arrival of the motif of the flirtation of the Beautiful Huntress, displayed by the dichotomy of major/minor second. The whole passage happens over the leit-timbre of a bell-like B-natural ostinato, pulsating on chimes, piano, and harmonics on cellos and violas (not included in the example below). This keeps the supernatural atmosphere of the narrative throughout the passage.

Figure 5.22. **The flirtation of the Indian Maidens interrupted by the flirtation of the Beautiful Huntress.**
Created by the author.

The thematic recapitulation is abridged, restating the two main themes consecutively, instead of simultaneously: the "Theme of the Uirapuru" stated this time by the clarinet (mm. 350–352) and the "Theme of the Jungle" by cellos and basses doubled by bassoons and contrabassoon (mm. 353–357). Both themes are shortened and introduced in the same original key centers as in the Exposition.[38] The background maintains the B-natural pedal, reverberating on chimes, piano, and lower string harmonics.

The Grandioso segment occurs over an F pedal, obtained through a tritone leap from the B-natural pedal of the Moderato. It features a new thematic material that consists of a series of parallel triads in rhythmic acceleration on every measure (four eighth notes–triplet eighth notes–four sixteenth notes, including a sixteenth rest), creating a sense of urgency with the increase of dynamics.

A *molto allargando* in the last two measures (mm. 362–363) over an orchestral *tutti* builds an almost unbearable tension that resolves in the dynamic climax of the composition. During this passage, an interesting process takes place. The upper voice (celesta, flutes, and piccolo) performs a series of parallel, descending chromatic sixteenth sextuplets, where the top and bottom chords at the extremes of each line come from complementary pitch collections of whole tone scales (Figure 5.23). The sum of the two complementary whole tone scales produces all twelve notes of the chromatic spectrum. Through this synthesis between the chromatic and whole tone collections, Villa-Lobos produces a bridge between Wagner and Debussy, two of his most important influences assimilated through musical cannibalism.

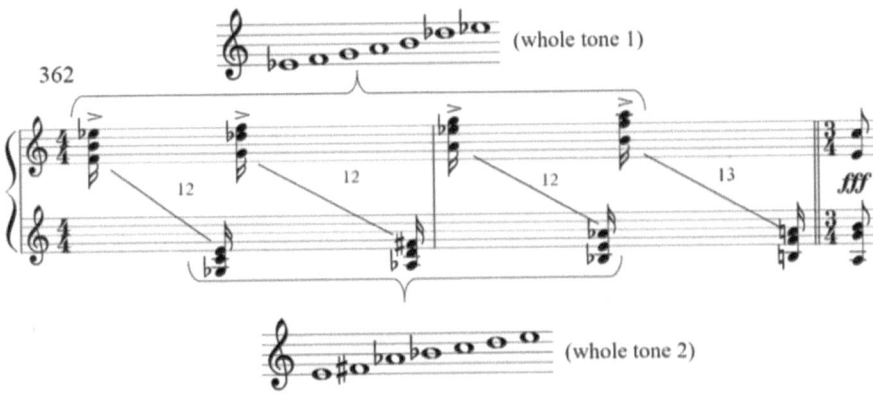

Figure 5.23. A synthesis between the chromatic and whole tone collections produces a bridge between Wagner and Debussy.
Created by the author.

The chord progression in the final cadence is also remarkable. The last chord of Section A (m. 363) is built over a pentatonic whole-tone collection, which resolves into a pentatonic "white collection" at the downbeat of the coda (essentially, an A-minor chord with seventh and ninth, as seen in Figure 5.24).

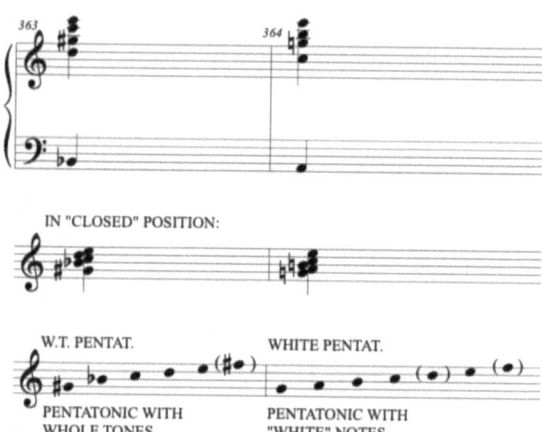

Figure 5.24. The top system shows the simplified chord progression in the connection of the last Section A with the Coda by eliminating the doublings of voices. The analysis demonstrates that the first chord is derived from a pentatonic collection of whole tones that resolves in a pentatonic collection of white notes.
Created by the author.

If, horizontally, Villa-Lobos achieved a synthesis between the whole-tone and chromatic collections (Figure 5.23), vertically he achieves a synthesis between the whole-tone and white-note pentatonic collections (Figure 5.24). In mm. 362–363, he produces, horizontally, the synthesis of the whole tone and the chromatic, which metaphorically embodies the synthesis between Romanticism, as represented by Wagner, and modernism, as represented by Debussy. The synthesis of emblematic musical languages is one of the highest achievements of musical cannibalism, and it is further corroborated at the coda (see Figure 5.31). Vertically, the cadential chord progression connecting the conclusive A Section with the Coda happens through two pentatonic collections, one formed by whole tones and the other formed by a "white" tone collection.[39]

Coda (mm. 364–374)

The last measures of the composition constitute a statement of ultimate thoughts at the conclusion of the piece. The Coda is announced by the powerful chord built over the pentatonic "white" collection, as shown in Figure 5.24 above, leaving only a high E hanging with the unexpected entrance of the violinophone, an exotic, violin-type string instrument that amplifies its sound through a metal horn attached, instead of the usual wooden sound box of the standard violin.

Dissecting Uirapuru ~ 129

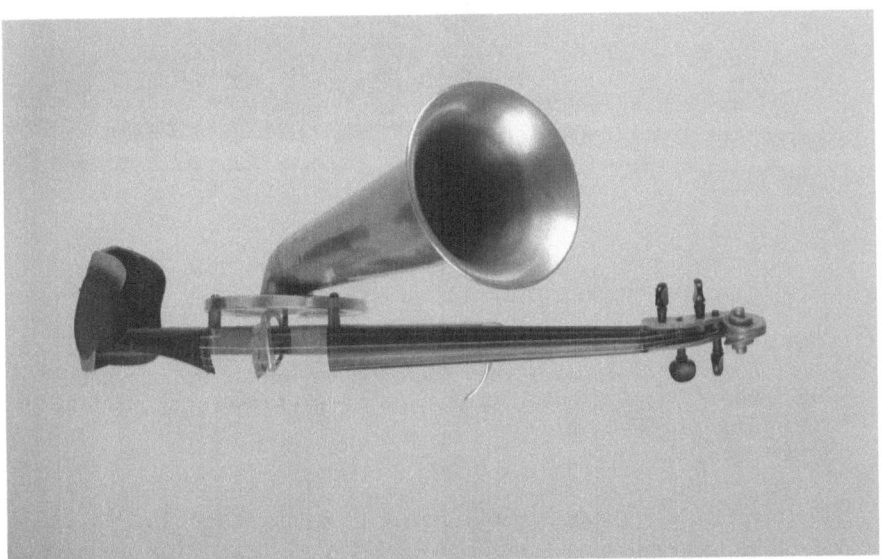

Figure 5.25. The violinophone.
Photograph by Jordi Puig. Used with permission from the Museu de la Música de Barcelona.

The violinophone can project well, and its whining sound provides the timbre for the "Theme of the Ugly Indian," which is reintroduced at the opening of the Coda. With this abrupt change from a *tutti* to a monophonic texture, the violinophone brings the high E down two octaves using the opening motif of the "Theme of the Ugly Indian" from Figure 5.5.

Within its eleven measures, the Coda concludes the composition with the successive appearance of the main characters of the story, each one represented by a different harmonic realm.

a. Appearance of the Ugly Indian, who pierces the Handsome Indian (non-diatonic realm) This new statement of the "Theme of the Ugly Indian" is written over an eight-note scale system (E—F-sharp—G/G-sharp—A—B— C—D-sharp), which might be described as an interesting combination of the scales of harmonic major and minor. Therefore, the representation of the Ugly Indian within a non-diatonic realm is maintained (Figure 5.26). It is interesting to observe that the long notes with fermatas delineate an E-major chord with the ninth (indicated with brackets under the notes), while the remaining short notes suggest a harmonic minor scale.[40] The three arpeggios derived from the incipit of the original theme that appears on m. 19 are separated by a permutation of the notes F-sharp—A—B, shown in the figure with brackets.

Figure 5.26. The "Theme of the Ugly Indian" can be recognized by its opening motif of a descending major 7th chord performed in arpeggio on the violinophone, stated a perfect 5th above its original statement on m. 19 in the beginning of the piece.
Created by the author.

The piercing of the Handsome Indian with an arrow happens through a flute arpeggio over the diatonic white collection.

b. Death and Transfiguration (of the Handsome Indian, and his transformation into the Uirapuru) (diatonic modulating to a black × white realm) The death of the Handsome Indian is presented in the white diatonic realm through a flute cadenza, while his transfiguration in *rallentando* has the intervention of a flattened VI step (presented enharmonically as a G♯) that will lead the previous E pedal to a B-flat pedal, a tritone apart. Metaphorically, the music is taken from the white-notes realm of the Handsome Indian to the modal realm of the uirapuru (Figure 5.27).

Figure 5.27. The final stage of the transformation of the Handsome Indian into the uirapuru, around rehearsal 24.
Created by the author.

The violinophone intones for the last time a reminiscence of the "Theme of the Uirapuru," his farewell song in Mixolydian C, performed through violinophone harmonics. The ethereal sound of this reminiscence highlights the intangibility of the final incarnation of the bird, this time transfigured as a forest spirit, "its sweet song diminishing into the silence of the forest," according to the program.

Figure 5.28. Uirapuru's farewell song in C Mixolydian.
Created by the author.

The violin solo resumes afterward by playing a G-minor, bi-harmonic, ascending scale that represents the uirapuru disappearing in the distance, supported by the "Polichinelo chord" of black and white notes in the piano and woodwinds. The melodic line departs from the B-flat pedal and concludes on a suspended G that hangs, solitary, above the texture, fading in the distance, prolonged until the end of the piece. This G is the only note of the ascending bi-harmonic scale that does not appear in the black and white harmony of the Polichinelo chord sustaining the violin.[41]

The idea of a programmatic transfiguration of the main character of a composition being represented by an ascending line of the violin ending on a high G was also used by Alban Berg in his Violin Concerto (Figure 5.29). The bi-harmonic, ascending scale of *Uirapuru* was substituted by the twelve-tone row used by Berg, and the B-flat major chord with added sixth of the Violin Concerto stands in for the "Polichinelo chord" of *Uirapuru*. The violin line in Berg's composition represents the ascent of Manon Gropius's soul toward heaven,[42] while the one in *Uirapuru* represents the flight of the bird, disappearing in the distance. The latter is supported by a variant of the Polichinelo chord, combining the black and white keys of the piano, while the harmony in Berg's Violin Concerto is reminiscent of the ending of Mahler's "Song of the Earth," which is associated with the idea of eternity.[43] *Uirapuru* premiered on May 25, 1935, in Argentina, while the score of Berg's Violin Concerto is dated August 11, 1935.

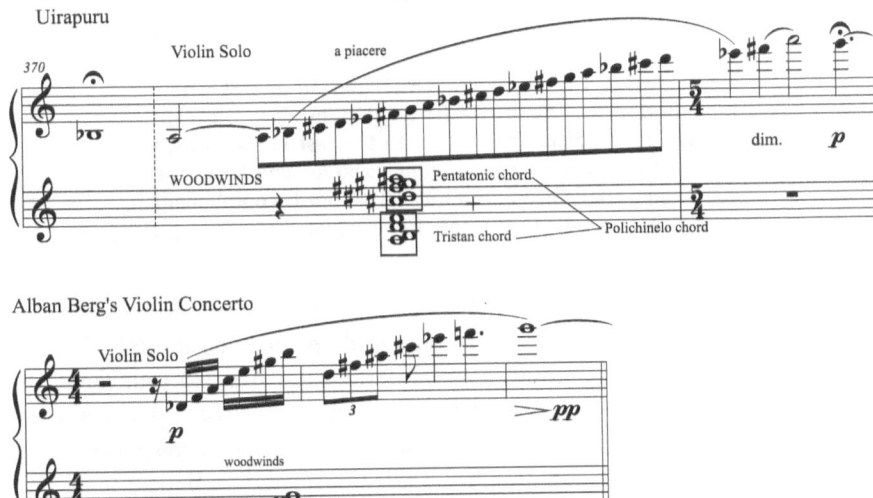

Figure 5.29. The last violin solo in Uirapuru (upper system) compared to the last ascending gesture of the violin soloist in Berg's Violin Concerto (lower system), and the supporting cords in simplified form.
Created by the author and used with permission. © 1936, 1996 by Universal Edition A.G., Wien.

c. Grief of the Amerindian maidens (chromatic realm) In the last five measures of the piece, there is a return of the leitmotif of the magical realm (the bell-like ringing of B-natural through accented notes on harp, piano, celesta, and bass harmonics). The grief of the Amerindian Maidens is represented by a transfiguration of their realm. While originally it was characterized by syncopated *Tristan chords* (Figure 5.1), here the rhythm suffers an augmentation coupled with a *rallentando*, while the *Tristan chord* is replaced by a progression of exotic, polytonal chords (Figure 5.30). The upper voice moves in whole tones and is reminiscent of the ascending line at the end of section C (Figure 5.20) with the exception of an E-natural, which functions as a leading tone toward the last harmony of piece. The exotic polytonal chords that harmonize the upper line include all four variants of the augmented triad, bringing the Indian Maidens to a fully chromatic realm that represents their grief.

Figure 5.30. The upper voice executes an almost whole tone motion (G—A—B—C-sharp—[E natural]—F), except for the E-natural in the second to the last chord, which breaks the symmetry and functions as a leading tone. The augmented triads present in the last 4 chords complement each other to encompass the 12 notes of the chromatic spectrum.
Created by the author.

d. Conclusion (synthesis of whole-tone and chromatic realms) At the beginning of this formal analysis, it was asserted that the first four measures of *Uirapuru* quote the beginning of the Prelude from *Tristan and Isolde* by Wagner. Analogously, the last two measures of *Uirapuru* correspond to the last five measures of the same prelude. As demonstrated by Salles:

> Villa-Lobos transformed this quotation in a sort of whole-tone variation [See Figure 5.31] that evokes Debussy's music. This may be considered as a sort of musical trope, since two different sources (Wagner and Debussy) are merged with a completely different meaning.[44]

Figure 5.31. Comparison of the endings of Villa-Lobos's Uirapuru and Wagner's Prelude from Tristan and Isolde.
Paulo de Tarso Salles, Villa-Lobos and National Representation by means of Pictorialism, 341.

In the figure above, the top line shows the last six measures of *Tristan*'s Prelude, the middle system shows the last two measures of *Uirapuru*,[45] and the third system contains the analysis, which shows how the melodic line at the end of *Tristan*'s Prelude is transformed into the whole-tone line in *Uirapuru*'s ending. Villa-Lobos keeps the first and last notes of *Tristan* (G and A-flat) and permutates the remaining three notes, while allowing the addition or subtraction of semitones: B-natural becomes B-flat (plus C with the addition of a semitone); E-flat becomes E-natural (plus D with the subtraction of a semitone); and F-natural becomes F-sharp. The process above exemplifies the way Villa-Lobos has been able to cannibalize the music of other composers, regurgitating it into a new realm of his own, a powerful and poetic soundscape that stands as a testament of the originality of the accomplishments of a distinguished composer.[46]

Pictorialism in Uirapuru

Villa-Lobos uses a sophisticated system of metaphors to represent the various characters in *Uirapuru*. Each element in the story is represented within a different realm, and each realm is represented by a specific pitch collection; individual pitch centers; and distinctive timbres, textures, or identifiable rhythmic patterns or intervals. The table below summarizes the musical representation of each one of the characters in the story.[47]

Table 5.4. While each character in *Uirapuru* is represented within a specific realm, the realm might change depending on the needs of the program.

	Measure Nos.	Music Material	Realm
Uirapuru	5–16 & 72–83 136–142 & 179–183 146–158 & 161–173 207–212 350–352	D♭ Mixolydian C♯ Ionian B Locrian G♯ Dorian D♭ Mixolydian	Diatonic
Rain Forest	3–18 & 70–85 31–48 & 98–115 197–212 216–226 353–358	B♭ Phrygian Octatonic A♯ Phrygian Exotic collection A♯ Phrygian	Modal/octatonic
Indian Huntress	190–192 213–215 & 221–223 246–247	Major/minor 2nd Major 2nd Major/minor 2nd	Diatonic/chromatic
Indian Maidens	2–17 & 69–84 185–225 341–357 371–374	Tristan chord Vagrant chords Vagrant chords Chromatic 12-tone	Chromatic
Handsome Indian	293–298 (repeated)	Pentatonic	**Pentatonic ("white")**
Ugly Indian	19–24 & 86–91 364–366	Chromatic 12-tone 7-note collection	**Chromatic/ non diatonic**

On several occasions, *Uirapuru* presents pictorialism in a similar way as the one found in *The Firebird*, but then, it goes beyond that. Villa-Lobos uses polymodality to express the interaction of two different characters, for example, by the combining the Phrygian and Mixolydian modes in the beginning, where he places the "Theme of the Uirapuru" and the "Theme of the Jungle" simultaneously, incorporating both within a "nature realm." At the beginning and end of Section B, the uirapuru is placed within the nocturnal environment of the jungle, surrounded by insects and other nocturnal animals. The "Theme of the Uirapuru" is diatonic, while the combination of the remaining animals and insects belongs to an exotic realm (Figure 5.8). The contrast is charged with significance. Furthermore, the composer allows the realm associated with a certain character to change, depending on the needs of the program. For example, to express the grief of the Indian Maidens after the death of the Handsome Indian, they are moved into a chromatic realm that uses all twelve notes of the chromatic spectrum; the "Theme of the Uirapuru" changes timbre and mode in the different sections, according to the program; the "Theme of the Jungle" is also modified to satisfy the needs of the musical narrative; and the realm of the Ugly Indian changes when he returns at the end of the piece.

Villa-Lobos also makes a distinction between the nature realm of the forest and the magical realm, where the legend takes place. The tolling of a B-natural pedal—associated with the magical realm—is presented with an unusual combination of timbres: first with the combination of piano, celesta, and harp with flute and soprano saxophone, and on other occasions incorporating glockenspiel, chimes, and string harmonics. This realm can be associated with a pictorial style that combines impressionism and tenebrism.

The orchestration has a crucial role for pictorialism. The subject theme of *Uirapuru* is particularly suited for the poetic language of Villa-Lobos, a magical bird that is like Orpheus—when the uirapuru sings, all other birds stop their song to hear it. The unusual sound of the uirapuru is represented not only by the obvious choice of the flute, but also through other timbres, such as the violinophone harmonics or the oboe, during the section of the piece where the uirapuru transforms into the Handsome Indian.

The composer had to find a different solution for the representation of another musical element in the story: the nose-flute, played by the Ugly Indian. The nose-flute is an instrument also known as *tsin-hali*, which is used by the *Nambiquara* tribe from the northern region of Mato Grosso state in Brazil.[48] The flutes belonging to the indigenous tribes found during the Roosevelt-Rondon expedition to the Amazon basin constituted a group of complex ceremonial instruments, associated with their mythology. One cannot underestimate their importance as sacred instruments. There were many different types of flutes, and for the indigenous man they were considered dangerous beings; they were kept in a secluded place, because they were not supposed to be seen or touched by women. The dangerousness of the flutes for the indigenous man had various meanings and origins. The music produced by the flutes should be understood as if the flute itself were a living being producing the sound, like a narrator.[49]

In addition to representing the nose-flute with a regular flute, the author uses the timbre of the soprano saxophone and the violinophone to capture the timbristic quality of the unusual wind instrument in different sections of the music. Other remarkable examples of the timbristic palette of the composer are the representation of the Indian maidens, by a homogenous choir (horns in the beginning, then violins or low register clarinets, plus bassoons in other sections); the Indian Huntress, by the combination of soprano saxophone and celesta; and the original illustration of a nocturnal atmosphere, through figurations in the low register of the piano with basses. The onomatopoeia of the forest is particularly suited for the depiction of the various members of the nocturnal animal and insect kingdoms through creative associations of instruments, and the transformation of the Uirapuru into the Handsome Indian is prepared by a glissando gesture of a muted cornet in unison with the English horn.

Pictorialism partially replaces the traditional idea of motivic development. In his expressive language, Villa-Lobos works with timbres, textures, metaphors, and their interactions to imbue the sounds with poetical meaning. As a result, his music becomes more visual and concrete when compared, for example, with Stravinsky, whose ballets are more motion-oriented. The pictorialism described above implies the predominance of an impressionist and tenebrist soundscape, under the latent influence of Wagner. This is felt through the use leitmotif technique and quotations of the *Tristian chord* that permeate the entire composition. The apparent nod to Wagner's romanticism is balanced by the setting of *Uirapuru* within a mythical time more in line with contemporary influences of the avant-garde, and the revolutionary findings in science in the beginning of the twentieth century.

The avant-garde aesthetic is expressed in the use of modern composition techniques, including noises, onomatopoeia, aleatory music in embryonic state, and primitivist elements such as simple tunes of folk character, block-like chords, and ostinatos. Despite these modern techniques, the predominant soundscape is mostly impressionist and still under the influence of a post-Romantic harmony. The imagery is that of a dreamlike soundscape where the natives interact with a benevolent nature. Images are depicted through sounds: The onomatopoeia is present, and suggestive images are communicated through metaphors. While this is a predominantly impressionist feature, it is also imbued of surrealist overtones through the dreamlike atmosphere, coupled with the juxtaposition of contradictory musical materials within a mythical ambience.

With *Uirapuru*, Villa-Lobos conciliated the post-Romantic aesthetics with impressionism, adding primitivist tinges that provided a bridge toward the future.⁵⁰ The latter is achieved through broken ostinato that provide rhythmic randomness, pedal tones, polyrhythms, and insightful uses of harmonic textures close to atonalism, such as sound agglomerates and polytonality. *Uirapuru* is a modernist composition in its successful cannibalization of Wagner and Debussy. However, the aesthetics of the future were fully realized not in *Uirapuru*, but in *Amazonas*.

Notes

1. https://youtu.be/EtxnrAgUxcw.
2. Janaína Amado, "Caramuru," 784.
3. Wright, *Villa-Lobos*, 13.
4. Heitor Villa-Lobos, *Uirapuru* (New York: Associated Music Publishers, 1948).
5. Translation of a typed page attached to the autograph P. 39.1.2 (full score) held by Museu Villa-Lobos, Rio de Janeiro.
6. The musical gesture is remarkably expressive and constitutes a typical case of "sound stain," a compositional device used by the composer in numerous occasions and explained in the glossary of terms.
7. An enlightening explanation of the Wagnerian influence on *Uirapuru* appears in Salles, *Villa-Lobos: Processos Composicionais*, 28–36. On a few occasions (measures 6, 14, and 16), the chord is slightly changed through a process called by Salles "semitone sliding," explained in the glossary of terms. No matter the slight modifications, the *Tristan chord* asserts itself as the harmonic environment for the entire section.
8. Boulez, *Notes of an Apprenticeship*, 79–81.
9. Salles, *Villa-Lobos: Processos Composicionais*, 167–68
10. The nose-flute is an instrument used by several Amerindian tribes in Brazil, and phonograms of its playing had been collected by Villa-Lobos's friend Roquette Pinto in one of the Roosevelt-Rondon expeditions. This flute cadenza has remarkable similarities with the flute solos of Debussy's *Syrinx* and the *Prelude to the Afternoon of a Faun*. See José de Carvalho Oliveira, "Simetria, Invariâncias e Organicidade Escalar, Um Estudo Sobre Padrões e Similaridades em Villa-Lobos e Debussy," 305–08. The long solo cadenza was borrowed from the beginning of the composition *Tédio de Alvorada*, which was reused in *Uirapuru*.
11. Salles, *Villa-Lobos: Processos Composicionais*, 148.
12. Salles, *Villa-Lobos: Processos Composicionais*, 245.
13. Scholars have observed the "Straussian inflections" present in the theme, constituted by unresolved chromatic appogiaturas, which promote an oriental character in works such as the opera *Salomé*. See Manoel Corrêa do Lago and Guilherme Bernstein, *Uirapuru, Partitura de Estudo Comentada*, 11.
14. It is known that Stravinsky's distinction between the forces of good and evil through the use of diatonicism and chromaticism is reminiscent of Rimsky-Korsakov's *Golden Cockerel* (1907).

15. Cross, *The Cambridge Companion to Stravinsky*, 148. In *The Firebird*, the chromaticism of Kaschei is resultant from the use of the octatonic scale borrowed from Rimsky-Korsakov to represent the character.

16. "Another convention of romantic Indianism present in the program written by Villa-Lobos is the opposition between the 'primitive' Indian and the noble savage, represented respectively by the Ugly Indian and the Handsome Indian. The identity of the latter, however, is not established by the noble character of the good savage, as convened by Romantic Indianism, but by its fusion with the local fauna within a mythical universe." Volpe, "Villa-Lobos e o Imaginário Edênico," 36.

17. Gabriel F. Moreira, "O Elemento Indígena na Obra de Heitor Villa-Lobos: observações musico-analíticas e considerações históricas" (Masters diss., UDESC, 2010), especially chapter 3.

18. In the sketches for the *Rite of Spring*, Stravinsky gave the title "Amazons" for the section of the Glorification, which serves as an analogous justification for the wild behavior of the female characters as they honor the "Chosen One" in the ballet. This provides another subliminal connection between *Uirapuru* and *The Rite*. See Richard Taruskin, "The Rite Revisited," 200.

19. Zanella dos Santos attempts to give a coherent explanation to justify the repetition in terms of the program, but his solution can hardly be justifiable in a ballet performance. See Daniel Zanella dos Santos, "Narratividade e Tópicas em Uirapuru (1917)," 115–16.

20. Tenebrism is used here as an Impressionist device reminiscent of the chiaroscuro painting technique. In painting, it is characterized by the use of violent contrasts of light and dark, where darkness becomes the dominating feature of the image.

21. See Manoel Corrêa do Lago and Guilherme Bernstein, *Uirapuru, Partitura de Estudo Comentada*, 13.

22. While not indicated in the published score, this section starting on m. 144 apparently represents the Amerindian maidens dancing as they recall the singing of the Uirapuru. Zanella dos Santos, "Narratividade e Tópicas, 119–20.

23. The triadic parallelism in *Uirapuru* will evolve into the quartal parallelism of *Amazonas*, which corroborates the idea in this study that despite premiering before *Uirapuru*, *Amazonas* uses a more modern language than the latter.

24. The process of rotating harmonies around the *Tristan chord* is explained in the glossary as a compositional process called semitone sliding.

25. The motif in question is that of a descending major second, annotated in Figure 5.9 as motif b1.

26. Salles, *Villa-Lobos: Processos Composicionais*, 30–31. The author also shows how Villa-Lobos's ascending motif played by the flute is similar to the oboe motif at the opening of the Prelude to Wagner's opera *Tristan and Isolde*.

27. In order to depict the atmosphere of transformation, Villa-Lobos uses an original combination of instruments: English horn and muted cornet performing a glissando followed by a descending chromaticism (mm. 197–198). The same gesture appears at mm. 205–06 through violins performing *sul ponticello*. This is

one of the numerous examples of the composer's mastery and originality in the manipulation of timbres.

28. The "Theme of the Jungle" is accompanied by a pedal harmony on an eleventh chord not shown in the musical example.

29. Considering that *Uirapuru* has 375 measures, the golden mean would be around m. 231, which is relatively close to m. 227, where the second part actually starts. An analogous type of symmetry appears on *Amazonas*. In the latter case, a corresponding type of ostinato starts in the most contrasting section of the rondo (section D), but the golden mean is not located there, but at the place where an important fugato starts (m. 127, rehearsal 15).

30. The C-sharp in the accompaniment plays the role of a passing tone.

31. According to Greek prosody, the *quartus paeon* in quantitative verse corresponds to a foot of three syllables followed by a long one.

32. The anthropophagic assimilation of so many influences eluded past musicologists. For example, Tarasti stated that the leitmotif Miremis from *Amazonas* (see Figure 6.7) is a "direct quotation from melodies notated in Jean de Lery's well-known travel description, printed in 1554." He presumed that the beginning of *Canide Ioune Sabath* was the source of the Miremis leitmotif, when in fact, any possible similarity is simply a consequence of the simplistic and primitive nature of Amerindian melodies. Tarasti, *Heitor Villa-Lobos*, 359.

33. Salles, *Processos Compositionais*, 147.

34. Considering that section C has 114 measures, the golden mean would be close to m. 270, while the cantus firmus starts on m. 269.

35. Villa-Lobos consciously explored the connections of the Amerindian music with Gregorian chant, namely the use of conjunct motion and compensated leaps of thirds; rhythm based on the inflection of the text; modal material; and ritual function. Villa-Lobos referred to the eternal beauty of plainchant as a strong influence on his aesthetics. Paulo Renato Guérios, *Heitor Villa-Lobos: o caminho sinuoso da predestinação*, 123.

36. When this melodic line appears at the end of the piece to represent the grief of the Amerindian maidens, the last note is altered, so that the last two notes stand at a semitone relationship.

37. Strictly speaking, there is another occasion (m. 63) where the piccolo briefly reached the highest note of the score. However, it is in this section that extreme notes are sustained within the texture with the obvious intention of being juxtaposed for structural reasons.

38. The "Theme of the Jungle" is written enharmonically in A-sharp Phrygian, including only the antecedent, before being interrupted at the Grandioso.

39. Potentially, one could infer an attempted synthesis between the whole-tone and the diatonic through incomplete collections, because the F-sharp is missing in the whole-tone pentatonic collection, and D and F are missing from the pentatonic white collection.

40. Zanella dos Santos, "Narratividade e Tópicas," 150.

41. This particular version of the "Polichinelo chord" of white and black notes is incomplete: Besides missing the G, it also lacks the E-natural and C-natural. The four white notes that belong to the chord form a version of the *Tristan chord*, which juxtaposed against the pentatonic collection of black notes form the Polichinelo chord.

42. Manon Gropius was the daughter of Walter Gropius and Alma Mahler, most often cited as the "angel" and dedicatee of Berg's Violin Concerto. The pitch G (from Gropius) reached at the end of the final ascending line of the violin has a symbolic meaning associated with the program of the concerto.

43. See Watkins, *Soundings: Music in the Twentieth Century*, 19–20 and 379. It is a remarkable coincidence that the last violin solo line in Uirapuru goes from B-flat to a high G, because in Berg's Violin Concerto, a secret program connects the lives of Alban Berg and Manon Gropius in a similar way. The last sound of the concerto connects the B-flat (as the lowest note of the harmony, representing "eternity"), which stands for Berg, with the high G of the solo violin, which stands for Gropius. Poetically, this procedure symbolizes the encounter of Alban Berg and Manon Gropius in eternity.

44. Salles, "Villa-Lobos and National Representation," 341.

45. In the manuscript score, there is a note indicating "exit of the Ugly Indian" that does not appear in the published score.

46. See Maria Alice Volpe Volpe, "O Manuscrito P38.1.1 e a 'tabela prática' de Villa-Lobos," 299–309. The article describes a possible methodology used by the composer to justify the convergence of the chromatic and whole-tone collections in the composition process of *Tédio de Alvorada* and *Uirapuru*.

47. While there is an overall agreement that Villa-Lobos represented each character of *Uirapuru* within a specific realm, different authors provide distinct analytical interpretations. A different interpretation is given by Maria Alice Volpe in her study found in Volpe, *Indianismo and Landscape*, 308–18.

48. See Edgard Roquete-Pinto, *Rondônia 1912*, n.p. A compact disc accompanies the publication, allowing us to listen to the sound of a nose-flute.

49. A description of the multiple types of flutes discovered during the Roosevelt-Rondon expedition appears in Pedro Paulo Salles, "'Nozani-Ná' e As Flautas Secretas dos Homens-Da-Água," 41–125.

50. According to Salles, "initially, Debussy was his [Villa-Lobos's] musical hero, opening doors to a new world of sound, but Stravinsky revealed to him the possibilities behind musical 'barbarisms' that could be more faithful representations of a national identity." Paulo de Tarso Salles, "Ritual Dance, by Villa-Lobos: A Music Topic in the Tropics," in *Anais do III Simpósio Villa-Lobos: Novos Desafios Interpretativos* (São Paulo: ECA – USP, 1917), 80.

CHAPTER SIX

~

Breaking Treaties

Amazonas *and* Le Sacre du Printemps

> *Eu vou, eu vou*
> *pras matas do Xingu.* —Klécius Caldas and Rutinaldo

The Brazilian Amerindian has been frequently portrayed in carnival marches. Most of the time, the lyrics depict the Amerindian as a picturesque reveler, sagacious, always outsmarting others, and a rapturous and irresistible conqueror of females. The lyrics of the first stanza of the carnival march *Índio do Xingu* (The Xingu's Amerindian, 1965)[1] by Klécius Caldas (1919–2002) and Rutinaldo (1927–2004) praises the happiness of the Amerindian life and can be translated as follows: "I will go, I will go to the forests of Xingu. The Amerindian lives for free, eats his prey, and walks naked." The Xingu River is the fourth largest tributary of the Amazon River, and the only area from Amazonia where the continuity of the indigenous occupation since prehistory until the present can be clearly demonstrated, hence its importance. In 1961, the Brazilian government created the Xingu National Park, an indigenous protected reserve that became home to indigenous peoples representing the four major aboriginal language families in Brazil: Tupi, Arawak, Carib, and Gê.[2] This happened two years after Villa-Lobos's death.

In the same year, a renewed interest in the Amerindian has spread through Brazilian carnival, when the composers Haroldo Lobo and Milton de Oliveira circumvented censorship, launching the malicious march *Indio Quer Apito* (The Amerindian Wants a Whistle),[3] taking advantage of a fashionable joke involving Mrs. Sarah Kubitschek, wife of the president of Brazil at the time, Mr. Jucelino Kubitschek.[4] In subsequent years, the renewed Amerindian fever generated a number of songs that kept the same playful spirit, including "Indio do Xingu," until the composer Jorge Ben Jor came up with an ecologically conscious song titled "Todo Dia Era Dia de Indio" (Everyday was Amerindian's Day, 1981).[5] The lyrics state that the "Amerindian was very cheerful before the arrival of the white man colonizer, able to keep the ecological balance, and the purest example of fraternal harmony and happiness. However, today their sad song is the lament of a race who was once very happy, because in the old days every day was Amerindian day." When Oswald de Andrade stated in the Anthropophagous Manifesto that "happiness is the ultimate proof," he was referring to the Amerindian, since "before the Portuguese discovered Brazil, Brazil had discovered happiness."[6]

While *Uirapuru* seems to have been written later than the official date, as an offspring of *Tédio de Alvorada*, a similar process must have happened with Villa-Lobos's work *Amazonas*, which was derived from *Myremis*, a symphonic poem/ballet written in 1916 and premiered in 1918. One difference that comes to mind is that the program of *Amazonas* preserves the narrative of *Myremis*, transposing it to the new Brazilian tropical environment, while *Uirapuru* changes completely the program narrative of *Tédio de Alvorada*.[7] Unfortunately, all materials of *Myremis* are considered lost, making it impossible to compare it with the score of *Amazonas*.[8]

The ballets *Amazonas* and *Uirapuru* have been considered sister compositions—they are both framed as symphonic poems/ballets, with a similar instrumentation, displaying features of a primitivist aesthetic, and composed in the same year, according to official sources.[9] Lisa Peppercorn states that Villa-Lobos "often wrote his compositions in pairs or groups, and though there are musical differences between *Uirapuru* and *Amazonas*, they both belong to the same group of ideas."[10] Contributing to the confusion surrounding composition dates are statements by different musicologists. Vasco Mariz mentions that "in 1918, when preparing the National Institute of Music orchestra for a concert of his music, Villa-Lobos had a hard time convincing the *spalla* (concertmaster) to play his symphonic poem *Amazon*."[11] He was probably referring to *Myremis* and not *Amazonas*. Wright states that: "the projected first performance of *Amazonas* in Brazil at the time of its composition was abandoned as, at the rehearsal, the string section had tied handkerchiefs to their bows as a protest at the new and incomprehensible sounds expected of them."[12]

Amazonas is a more avant-garde and experimental composition than *Uirapuru*. Its orchestration amplifies that of *Uirapuru* by adding one piccolo, one E-flat clarinet, one sarrusophone, two alto trumpets (in F), and a viola d'amore playing with scordatura.[13] An analysis indicates that *Amazonas* is a step forward from *Uirapuru* in the same way that *The Rite of Spring* evolved after *The Firebird*. This is a musicological challenge. If we assume that *Uirapuru* was written in the early 1930s to be premiered in 1935, it would be unlikely for Villa-Lobos to use a more avant-garde aesthetic to write *Amazonas* years before *Uirapuru*, to be premiered in 1929, yet this seems to be the case according to the most recent studies.[14] Current musicology discredits Villa-Lobos's reliability in dating his works, considering it an attempt on the part of the composer to magnify the importance of his pioneering musical achievements. According to Mário de Andrade, Villa-Lobos altered the dates of his compositions in his autobiography, presenting some of them as being created earlier than they actually were: "I feel obliged to doubt the dates of which the composer backdates several of his works, with the presumption of becoming a brilliant pioneer in everything."[15] Loque Arcanjo corroborates the above, stating that, "by changing the dates of the compositions and positioning them as previous to the real dates of their creation, the composer presented himself as a more modern musician."[16] This is not unheard of. The painter Giorgio de Chirico's reputation suffered a similar type of disapproval of his late works due to his habit of backdating his paintings, as if later pictures had been created back in the 1910s, during the high point of his career.

The act of backdating has been explained by David Appleby as the composer indicating the date when the spiritual conception of the work took place and not when the composition was committed to paper.[17] As in the case with de Chirico, there are probably deeper reasons for this to happen, reasons of an aesthetic nature. The two contemporary artists lived during the time when Niels Bohr won his first Nobel Prize in Physics and Henri Bergson wrote his seminal text, *Duration and Simultaneity*. Bergson's notion of art rejects the conventional notion of cause and effect, invoking a more intuitive approach to reality. His approach is in line with Villa-Lobos's cannibalism, through the rejection of the conventional workings of the intellect in order to reveal a truer, more fluid nature of reality.

> Art has no other object than to set aside the symbols of practical utility, the generalities that are conventionally and socially accepted, everything in fact which masks reality from us, in order to set us face to face with reality itself. . . . Art is certainly only a more direct vision of reality itself.[18]

Current musicologists are excessively hasty in assuming that *Amazonas* was actually written in the late 1920s and *Uirapuru* in the middle 1930s, in periods close to their premieres. In doing so, they tend to dismiss Villa-Lobos's originality as derivative, placing greater importance in the nationalistic aspects of his music. Despite their differences, the two compositions present enough aspects in common to suggest that they belong to the "same group of ideas," as suggested by Peppercorn.[19] Their kinship is substantial, and numerous examples of common features are presented throughout this study.

When writing *Uirapuru*, Villa-Lobos clearly went back to *Tédio de Alvorada*, keeping the original material almost in its entirety. The comparison of the scores of *Tédio de Alvorada* and *Uirapuru* led to important conclusions, particularly the fact that certain innovative features of Villa-Lobos's compositional process were already present in *Tédio de Alvorada* and, therefore, before the composer had contact with Stravinsky's works.[20] It is possible that he also kept substantial materials from *Myremis* when writing *Amazonas*. The comparison of the synopsis of both works corroborates it, and the use of violinophone[21] in both *Amazonas* and *Uirapuru* (an absent instrument in *Tédio de Alvorada* and *Myremis*) is also telling of the connection between the two works, since these are the only two compositions in the entire body of Villa-Lobos's work that include this instrument. Both *Amazonas* and *Uirapuru* combine influences from Wagner and Stravinsky. In *Uirapuru*, the Wagnerian influence is stronger, while in *Amazonas*, the influence of Stravinsky is predominant, which is another indication that *Uirapuru* looks toward the past and *Amazonas* toward the future. Despite being shorter, *Amazonas* approaches the rondo form in a more complex and sophisticated way than does *Uirapuru*.[22]

Above everything, both *Amazonas* and *Uirapuru* belong to a great number of compositions where Villa-Lobos has recycled previously written works, a practice that he kept for most of his professional career. Recent musicology displays a fascination in unveiling the creative process of the Brazilian composer, by demonstrating in minute detail the operations—usually called *beurbeitung*—which Villa-Lobos made explicit when reforming previously written works. Within the context of the Villalobian anthropophagic style, this process should be viewed as a specific case of self-cannibalism, in order to allow us to better understand its characteristics while at the same time differentiate it from similar practices that happened throughout the various periods of music history.[23] There resides one of the great examples of craftmanship of the Brazilian composer: the miraculous ability to assign new meanings to the same musical passage through a process of self-cannibalism, so that it aligns effectively and naturally to a context completely foreign to the one for which the musical passage was initially created.[24]

The synopsis of *Amazonas* has a number of elements in common with Stravinsky's *The Rite of Spring*. In his analysis of *The Rite*, Pieter van den Toorn writes that the work lacks a specific plot or narrative and should be considered as a succession of choreographed episodes.[25] Yet, there is a libretto written in Stravinsky's hand, which translates as follows (Table 6.1):[26]

Table 6.1. Synopsis of *The Rite of Spring* according to a libretto written in Stravinsky's hand.

Vesna sviashchennaia is a musical-choreographic work. It represents pagan Russia and is unified by a single idea: the mystery and great surge of the creative power of Spring. The piece has no plot, but the choreographic succession is as follows:
Rite of Spring: synopsis
First Part: THE KISS OF THE EARTH The spring celebration. It takes place in the hills. The piper's pipe and the young men tell fortunes ["Augurs of Spring"]. The old woman enters. She knows the mystery of nature and how to predict the future. Young girls with painted faces come in from the river in single file. They dance the spring dance. Games start ["Dance of the Abduction"]. The Spring Khorovod ["Spring Rounds"]. The people divide into two groups, opposing each other ["Ritual of the Rival Tribes"]. The holy procession of the wise old man ["Procession of the Sage"]. The oldest and wisest interrupts the spring games, which come to a stop. The people pause trembling before the great action. The old men bless the earth ["The Sage"]. *The Kiss of the Earth*. The people dance passionately on the earth, sanctifying it and becoming one with it ["Dance of the Earth"].
Second Part: THE GREAT SACRIFICE At right the virgins hold mysterious games, walking in circles ["Mystic Circles of the Young Girls"]. One of the virgins is consecrated and is twice pointed to by fate, being caught twice in the perpetual circle. The virgins honor her, the chosen one, with a marital dance ["Glorification of the Chosen One"]. They invoke the ancestors ["Evocation of the Ancestors"] and entrust the chosen one to the old wise men ["Ritual Action of the Ancestors"]. She sacrifices herself in the presence of the old men in the great holy dance, the great sacrifice ["Sacrificial Dance"].

The ritualistic aspect of Stravinsky's composition, leading to the sacrifice of the chosen one who dances herself to death, is analogous to the ritualistic bathing of the Amerindian virgin in *Amazonas*, who concludes her dance by plunging into the "abyss of her own desire." The key idea of *The Rite*, "the mystery and great surge of the creative power of Spring" in prehistoric Russia, is analogous to the barbaric power of *Amazonas*, conveying "how multiple forces have broken loose.... This gigantic fresco evokes the mystery of Amazonas, the strong poetry of the earth, water, forest and primitive people."[27]

Myremis's literary program narrates a Greek-inspired legend written by Villa-Lobos's father, a story about a beautiful Greek virgin, blessed by the gods of mythology, who bathes in the river Archeló, entering into conflict with monsters and divine powers. It is said that the program of *Amazonas* is the composer's adaptation of the original *Myremis* program, setting it into a Brazilian landscape, similar to what happened between *Tédio de Alvorada* and *Uirapuru*:[28]

> A beautiful virgin maiden, consecrated by the gods of the Amazonian forests, welcomes dawn by bathing in the waters of the Amazon, the Marajoara river. This river sometimes would show its loathing of the daughters of Atlantis, but in honor of their beauty, he would also sometimes calm down the tides of its eternal river currents. The maiden enjoys herself, invoking the sun with ritual gestures, displaying her divine body in graceful movements so it could be contemplated by the sunrays of the king star or mirrored in the undulating surface of the river. The more the Indian maiden sees her shade drawing the contours of her beauty in the cold and indolent screen, as no one has ever idealized, the more she feels proud of herself in such brutal sensuality. While the virgin goes astray, the god of the tropical winds blows a perfume with tenderness and love, but the maiden ignores his supplications, dancing and giving herself to her wild pleasures as a naïve child. Wrathful with her disdain, the jealous god of the winds takes the chaste scent of the Marajós' daughter to the profane region of the monsters. One of the monsters detects the maiden and, incited by desire to possess her, advances, destroying everything in his way. As he approaches unperceived, he contemplates the maiden with ecstasy and desire. He tries to hide, but his image is reflected by the sunlight on the gray shadow of the girl. Seeing her shadow transformed and pursued by the monster, the horrified and disoriented virgin plunges into the abyss of her own desire.[29]

The scenery of *Amazonas*, with an Amerindian virgin, representative of Brazilian nature, who is bathing at dawn, is connected with the rise of Brazil as a monumental nation in ascension, providing the nationalist setting for the music. This allowed Villa-Lobos to conceive through music the fulfillment of the dreams of an exotic nation, full of natural resources and potentialities.

Amazonas and *The Rite of Spring* had their premieres in Paris exactly sixteen years apart. *Amazonas* was premiered on May 30, 1929, as part of the Concerts Poulet, while the Rite of Spring was premiered on May 29, 1913, at the Théâtre des Champs Elysées. Adolphe Piriou, an orchestra member in the second violin section, recalled how, after the warm reception of *Amazonas* by the public, a riot ensued in the audience between opponents and supporters for the reception of Varése's work, *Amériques*, which was premiered in the same concert.[30] The apparent scandals or riots in the premiere performances of the *Le Sacre* (*The Rite*) and *Amazonas* in Paris have served to further build speculation about the connections between the two compositions.

Villa-Lobos's Orchestral Palette

The Rite of Spring uses an unusually large ensemble, with over twenty-one different woodwind and eighteen brass instruments, including eight French horns, which are also present in *Amazonas*. Besides their sheer number, Stravinsky calls for instruments that had rarely been scored for in orchestra music before, such as alto flute, piccolo trumpet, bass trumpet, and Wagner tuba, and achieves a distinctive sound through the manipulation of instrumental registers. Villa-Lobos also uses a large orchestra with unusual instruments such as the violinophone,[31] viola-d'amore, and the simultaneous use of contrabassoon and sarrusophone, which has been compared with the use of two contrabassoons in Schoenberg's *Gurre-Lieder*, premiered in the same year as *The Rite of Spring*. All of these compositions were influenced by the expansion of Wagner's instrumental ideas. *Amazonas*'s distinctive sound comes from the masterful use of the instruments, their unique combinations and performance techniques, as well as their potentiality to reflect, metaphorically, the literary and visual contents of the piece, which led Olivier Messiaen to proclaim Villa-Lobos as one of the greatest orchestrators of the twentieth century.[32]

A good comparative example of the orchestrations is the soundscape in the beginning of the two compositions. Stravinsky represented, through sounds, "the great surge of the creative power of spring" and the "awakening of nature, the scratching, gnawing, wiggling of birds and beasts." He imagined the woodwinds as a "swarm of string pipes (*dudki*)."[33] Villa-Lobos represented the rain forest also through figures in the woodwinds, with insects, birds, and other animals, as well as the forces of nature combining water (the current of the Marajoara River) and air (the God of Winds). Both composers depicted the wilderness through periodic interventions of aggressive and mysterious figures by the woodwind instruments, as demonstrated in the comparison of the two examples in Fig. 6.1.

Figure 6.1. The Primitivist soundscapes at the beginning of *Amazonas* (a) and the *Rite of Spring* (b, score in C), showing a similar use of woodwind instruments. Some of the voices have been omitted.
Created by the author.

The compositions also feature other types of comparable musical gestures with similar orchestration (Figs. 6.2 and 6.3). In Fig. 6.2, examples *a* and *b* are taken from *Amazonas*, while example *c* is from *The Rite of Spring*. In example *a*, Villa-Lobos produced a parallel, chromatic, descending gesture of staccato notes that dives into emptiness, which is similar to the gesture in example *c*, though the latter ends on the beat, producing a sense of arrival. Example *b* is similar, but more sophisticated. The descending parallel motion

Figure 6.2. Descending staccato gestures in *Amazonas* (a & b) and the *Rite of Spring* (c).
Created by the author.

of the various voices is not chromatic, but it features diatonic parallelism of "white notes" on the upper line, while the lower line presents parallelism of two pentatonic scales, one with white notes and the other with black notes.[34]

In Fig. 6.3, example *a*, taken from *Amazonas*, Villa-Lobos produced an ascending motion of three octaves using an exotic scale that juxtaposes a whole tone with a chromatic tetrachord, while Stravinsky's ascending motion, seen in example *b*, spans over two octaves and is diatonic (E-flat—B-flat—F—C).

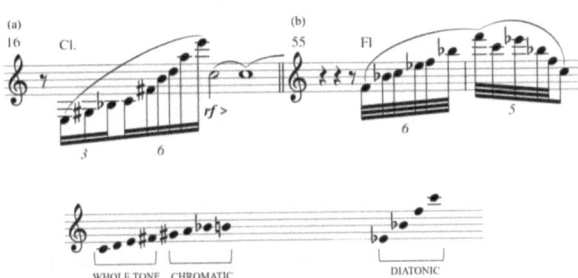

Figure 6.3. Ascending, multi-octave gestures in *Amazonas* (a) and the *Rite of Spring* (b).
Created by the author.

All of these are essentially the result of the experimentalism of the time, reminiscent of the influence of Wagner in post-Romantic works.[35]

Another interesting comparison is the use of string harmonics by both composers. Stravinsky shows a preference for harmonic glissandos over one string, while Villa-Lobos prefers harmonic arpeggios on multiple strings. He explores this technique in unusual instruments, such as the violinophone, harp, and even the viola d'amore, performing with scordatura. Fig. 6.4c adds a comparison with the traditional use of harmonic glissandi in Varèse's *Amériques*, considering that the revised version of this piece premiered together with *Amazonas* in the same concert.

Figure 6.4. Use of string harmonics by Stravinsky (*Rite of Spring*, a), Villa-Lobos (*Amazonas*, b), and Varèse (*Amériques*, c).

Amériques. Music by Edgard Varèse. Published by Casa Ricordi Srl, a company of Universal Music Publishing Group. International Copyright Secured. All Rights Reserved. Used with kind permission of Hal Leonard Europe BV (Italy)

A unique case in orchestra literature is the *Dance for the Enchantment of the Forests* in *Amazonas*. Villa-Lobos obtains a supernatural effect by combining string harmonic arpeggios on the violinophone and viola d'amore with scordatura, while most of the strings perform arpeggios over undetermined pitches, by playing between the bridge and the string holder. The bell-like notes of the celesta (doubled by a muted F trumpet an octave below not shown in Fig. 6.5) bring to mind the magical realm of the Amerindian legends also present in *Uirapuru*.[36] The unique combination of instruments and the use of divisi for the strings is meant to represent an untamed landscape where the universe of noises emanating from the forest builds a non-tempered soundscape distant from the European traditions.

Villa-Lobos's mastery of orchestration led to an erroneous view about its importance in comparison with other qualities. When addressing the piano version of *Amazonas*, Tarasti condemned what he viewed as lack of thematic-symphonic unity. "According to an old anecdote, if one takes the orchestra away from Berlioz, the bad harmony remains, while if one takes the orchestra away from Mahler, nothing remains. This may hold true also for Amazonas."[37] Such a unidimensional view of Villa-Lobos's orchestral palette

Figure 6.5. Arpeggios in the Dance for The Enchantment of the Forests
Paulo de Tarso Salles, Villa-Lobos: *Processos Composicionais*, 194

cannot be sustained, because his mastery of orchestration lies exactly in making it an integral part of the conception of the music. Mário de Andrade poetically described the orchestra in *Amazonas* as a "monster crawling painfully forward, breaking branches and falling trees, tonalities and composition treatises,"[38] a statement that could certainly be applied with equal force to *The Rite of Spring*. It corroborates Villa-Lobos's statement: "After *Amazonas*, I lost the modesty and shyness of writing bold things."[39]

Texture Articulating Form

Musicologists tend to agree that one of Villa-Lobos's most important contributions to modernism concerns the role of musical texture in his compositional process, which becomes so fundamental that it has the power to replace other elements in the articulation of the musical form. An overview of the score of *Amazonas* in terms of texture reveals a structure of four sections, framed by a two-measure introduction and a two-measure coda:

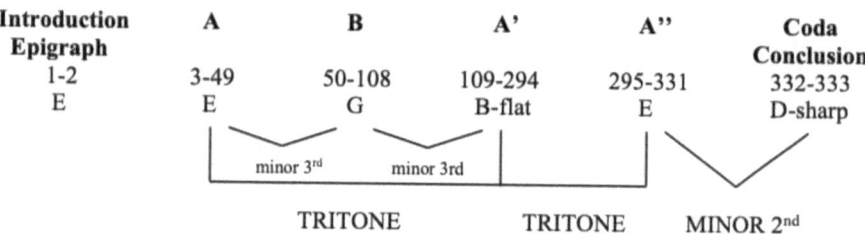

Figure 6.6. Formal structure of Amazonas in terms of texture (the second line represents measure numbers and the third line represents the key centers, within an expanded conception of tonality)
Created by the author.

Rather than in terms of tonality, the harmonic language should be understood in terms of "polarized key centers," where certain notes function as poles of attraction that are used as formal and unifying factors for the composition. From this perspective, each section is separated from the previous by a pedal note at a distance of a minor third from the previous polarized key center. Combined, they constitute a tritone motion from E (key center of the whole composition) to B-flat, going back to E, and concluding unexpectedly in D-sharp at the very end. Consequently, while E is the key center, the tritone and minor second are the "polarized intervals" of the composition, which recalls a similar procedure in *Uirapuru*. By bringing to the fore the two most dissonant intervals of tonal music (tritone and minor second), Villa-Lobos gives his contribution to the emancipation of dissonance, which was approached in so many different ways by composers under the influence of Schoenberg, Stravinsky, and Bartok.

The initial, monophonic texture of the first measure introducing the Miremis leitmotif sets the pattern for future transitions.

The ending of section A is punctuated by an abrupt reduction of density, with the six or seven voices being reduced later to a single voice (English and

French horns unison) approximately four measures later. . . . The English and French horns perform the motif G—A-flat—G, which is a modified reiteration of the initial motif.[40]

A modulation leading to a B-flat pedal by the violinophone (mm. 107–108) serves as transition to the next section A', which starts with the theme of the "Sensual Dance of the Amerindian Girl." Section A' is the textural climax of the piece, intensified by clashes of minor seconds and the use of ostinatos and expanded percussion. This section is notated as A' to reflect the idea of a *textural recapitulation*, due to the use of a prolonged pedal note (or notes) inserted within the accompaniment. Section A' ultimately leads to a sustained E on the double basses (m. 294, *arco uniti*),[41] which serves as an initial pedal point and transition into the final section [A"]. Such procedure can be considered a *tonal recapitulation*[42] of the first section. As it will be noted later, this section continues to explore the use of ostinatos of minor seconds, suddenly interrupted by a brutal tam-tam hit indicating the abyss and ultimately leading into the conclusive section, *Prestissimo*, and ending in the two measures of the coda.

The brief analysis above reveals an original approach on the part of the composer when dealing with the aspect of musical form and unity. From this perspective, the structure of *Amazonas* combines the interaction of rondo (the alternation of contrasting sections with the periodic recurrence of the first section) and variation forms, through use of *textural* and *tonal recapitulations*.

Thematic Analysis

A central aspect of *Amazonas* is the use of leitmotif as unifying factor. From a thematic perspective, one can detect a rondo form expressed as **ABACAD(AB)A** through the use of a leitmotif for the reiterations of the refrain A.

The various reiterations of A have in common the recurrence of the Miremis leitmotif as thematic generator, stated for the first time in the initial two measures of the work in the form of an epigraph. This leitmotif (Fig. 6.7) is formed by the repetition of the note E (Mi) leading only once into its lower neighbor D (Re), resulting in MI-RE-MI(s) or, for the purposes of this analysis, the "Miremis leitmotif."

This leitmotif serves as a unifying factor for the whole composition, because all themes of the recurring A sections are derived from it. The leitmotif was taken from Villa-Lobos's previous composition *Myremis*,[43] which used the same leitmotif within a totally different context. The use of this leitmotif

Table 6.2. Thematic Musical Form of *Amazonas*.

INTROD.	PART I					PART II	PART III	
	EXPOSITION					MIDDLE SECTION	RECAPITUL.	CODA
Introduction	A	B	A	C	A	D (A B)	A	Coda
Epigraph								Conclusion
1–2	3–36	37–49	50–67	68–99	100–113	114–285	286–294	295–333
E	E	Black & White	White diatonic	non-tempered A	B♭	12-tone chromatic	F-E A	E-D♯

Figure 6.7. The Miremis leitmotif
Created by the author (copied from the score).

demonstrates Villa-Lobos's flexibility in adapting the same music material into different contexts depending on his programmatic needs. This can be characterized as a sort of self-cannibalism, a procedure that Villa-Lobos adopted until the end of his days, when he included in his last compositions appropriations of materials from earlier works. In this particular case, this procedure of self-cannibalism works particularly well because the melodic and rhythmic simplicity of the Miremis leitmotif, with its small range and predominance of conjunct motion and repeated notes, is characteristic of Amerindian melodies. It made seamless the transplantation of a Greek legend into an Amerindian myth.[44]

Section A

The themes of the recurring A sections are all derived from the Miremis leitmotif (Fig. 6.8).

Figure 6.8. Themes of the Recurrent A Sections.
Created by the author.

The Miremis leitmotif generates two other motifs that are used prominently in subsequent passages. For the purposes of this analysis, those motifs are denominated the "Sigh Motif" (a descending minor second, Fig. 6.9a) and the "Enchantment Motif" (Fig. 6.9b): the "Sigh Motif" is derived from the Miremis leitmotif by transforming the major second incipit into a minor second (see mm. 46–49), while the "Enchantment Motif" is generated by an inversion of the major second incipit (see mm. 70–78).

Figure 6.9. The "Sigh Motif" & "Enchantment Motif."
Created by the author.

Section B

The two appearances of Section B display a contrasting theme that is reserved for climactic moments and in this way stands out as a secondary theme (Fig. 6.10). This secondary theme is a homorhythmic brass chorale, characterized by great rhythmic richness and parallel seventh chords, which combine black and white pitch collections (only the tuba notes come from the "pentatonic black" pitch collection).[45]

Figure 6.10. Secondary theme in Section B as performed by the trombones and tuba (horns and trumpets double those voices an octave higher).
Created by the author.

In its second appearance (m. 269), the theme is abridged and distorted but still clearly recognizable through its rhythm (Fig. 6.11).

Breaking Treaties ～ 157

Figure 6.11. Second Statement of the Secondary Theme.
Created by the author.

Despite its rhythmic complexity, the ample use of parallel motion constitutes a "return to simplicity." It is one of the resources used by the composer to metaphorically represent primitivism and closeness with nature, particularly when writing music of Amerindian inspiration.[46]

Section C

The main theme in Section C is a melody of improvisatory character played by the E-flat clarinet starting on m. 73. The theme is written as a melody built over the twelve notes of the chromatic scale. The melody presents not only great rhythmic richness and variety, but also a wide range that explores the acoustic tension of the interval major seventh through the insistent repetition of notes (F-sharp/F-natural) in the upper register of the instrument. Such acoustic tension has also been explored by Varèse on multiple occasions through the insistent repetition of dissonant intervals in loud dynamics on the upper woodwind register.[47] In the example below (Fig. 6.12b), the excerpt from Varèse's *Amériques* displays the acoustic tension of the interval minor second separated by an octave in the high register. Interestingly, *Amériques* (revised version) and *Amazonas* were premiered in the same program in 1929.

Figure 6.12. Excerpt from E-flat clarinet solo in *Amazonas* (a) and similar use of dissonant repetition in Varèse's *Amériques* (b). In both cases, pitches are written as they sound.
Example a comes from Paulo de Tarso Salles, Villa-Lobos: *Processos Composicionais*, 107. Example b includes a few measures taken from *Amériques* by Varèse. Used with permission.

Section D

A typical feature of the rondo form is to present the greatest contrast in the most distant section from its refrain. Section D starts one-third of the way into the piece, close to the golden section of the composition.[48] The melody initially characterized as the "Sensual Dance of the Amerindian Girl" constitutes an eleven-tone theme (Fig. 6.13), where the distinctive absence of E—the key center of the composition—is polarized by exclusion.[49]

Figure 6.13. The Theme of the "Sensual Dance of the Amerindian Girl."
Created by the author, based on a score by Villa-Lobos.

In essence, Villa-Lobos's *Amazonas* is bounded by two complementary thematic aggregates. On one side, we have a collection of recurrent themes derived from the Miremis leitmotif, where the themes polarize E as the key center. On the other side, we have the theme of the "Sensual Dance of the Amerindian Girl," which is an eleven-tone theme that also polarizes (by exclusion) E as the key center, the latter providing contextual unity to the two main themes. The quasi ostinato flow of Section D comprises a continuous block of 171 measures, which, by itself, balances the cumulative combination of the remaining sections.

Table 6.3. Structural Balance in *Amazonas*

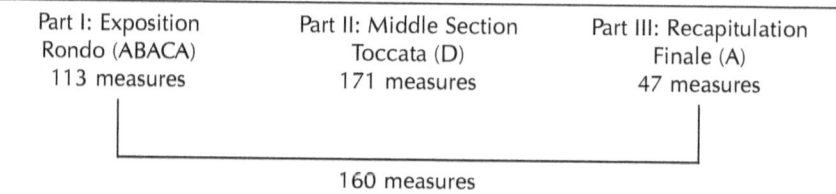

Notes

1. https://youtu.be/OjOkRD0PIl8.
2. See Seth Garfield, "A Nationalist Environment: Indians, Nature, and the Construction of the Xingu National Park in Brazil," 139–67, https://www.jstor.org/stable/3513749.
3. https://youtu.be/T85tj-5ed6s.
4. See Renato Vivacqua, *Música Popular Brasileira*, 117.

5. https://youtu.be/v2bbqD-7i6M.
6. See Appendix I, aphorisms 40, 42, and 47.
7. Both *Tédio de Alvorada* and *Myremis* belong to a group of early compositions by Villa-Lobos of Greek inspiration, typical of the time. Together with a third, the ballet *Naufrágio dos Kleônicos* (Shipwreck of the Kleonicos), they were performed in the first public concert dedicated to Villa-Lobos's compositions in August 1918 in Rio de Janeiro. See Lutero Rodrigues, "Villa-Lobos: a temática grega," in *Anais do III Simpósio Villa-Lobos*, 140.
8. According to Wright, the narrative of the story was printed in the program booklet of the first performance, which took place on August 15, 1918, at Teatro Municipal do Rio. This printed program is not available at the Villa-Lobos Museum in Rio de Janeiro. Wright, *Villa Lobos*, 12. However, Lutero Rodrigues had access to the program and stated that "it is easy to see that [*Myremis* and *Amazonas*] have the same text, transposed from Greece to Brazil. See Lutero Rodrigues, "Villa-Lobos: a temática grega," 141.
9. Museu Villa-Lobos, *Sua Obra*, 3rd edition (1989), 52, 60.
10. Peppercorn, *Villa-Lobos: The Music*, 85.
11. Mariz, *Heitor Villa-Lobos: Life and Work*, 11.
12. Wright, *Villa-Lobos*, 19.
13. During the Baroque era, the viola d'amore was usually tuned specifically to each piece performed through scordatura. A standard tuning appeared in the end of the eighteenth century as A2-D3-A3-D4-F#4-A4-D5. The tuning Villa-Lobos elected for *Amazonas* is D3-F#3-Bb3-D4-E4-Bb4-D5.
14. See, in particular, Manoel Corrêa do Lago and Guilherme Bernstein, "Do Tédio de Alvorada ao Uirapuru," 544–45. It should be noted that *Amazonas* premiered during the 1920s, toward the end of the period when Villa-Lobos wrote some of his most experimental music, particularly the Choros. By the time *Uirapuru* premiered, the composer was writing in the neoclassical style of his Bachianas Brasileiras.
15. Mário de Andrade, "Villa-Lobos," *Mundo Musical*, quoted in Coli, *Musica Final*, 171.
16. Loque Arcanjo, *O Ritmo da Mistura*, 44.
17. "The dating of Villa-Lobos's compositions is often a problem. When asked when a certain work was written, Villa-Lobos frequently would provide the date when the work was conceived, rather than the date when it was written down or published." Appleby, *Heitor Villa-Lobos*, 20.
18. Bergson, *An Essay*, 157. The quotation above is an updated translation. The original translation reads: "So art, whether it be painting or sculpture, poetry or music, has no other object that to brush aside the utilitarian symbols, the conventional and socially accepted generalities, in short, everything that veils reality from us, in order to bring us face to face with reality itself." See https://archive.org/details/laughteranessay00berggoog.
19. Peppercorn, *Villa-Lobos: The Music*, 85.

20. See Salles, "Tédio de Alvorada e Uirapuru." As for the composer's acquaintance with Stravinsky's music, there is no common agreement, but the evidence points in the direction that this happened in the 1920s, during Villa-Lobos's stays in Paris.

21. In *Amazonas*, also written as "cítara de arco" (bowed sitar). Villa-Lobos employed a number of unusual instruments in his orchestrations, such as solovox, sarrusophone, novachord, and multiple percussion instruments typical of Brazil. It would be unlikely for him to use the violinophone only in those two compositions if they were written so many years apart. A curiosity is that in July 1930, Villa-Lobos used the violinophone in substitution to the *violino piccolo* when conducting Bach's *1st Brandenburg Concerto* in São Paulo (see Mário de Andrade, *Musica Doce Musica*, 181). This practice today would certainly cause a heart attack on the proponents of historically informed performance, but at the time was received positively by Mário de Andrade, who praised the way the violinophone blended well with some of the wind instruments.

22. More details about the discussion concerning Villa-Lobos's practice of backdating his works appears in chapter 9.

23. In commenting over the remodeling of *Myremis* into *Amazonas*, Mário de Andrade stated: "The remodeling and inspiration into an Amerindian context gave it new life, and I especially like this unceremonious way in which Villa-Lobos attributes to the same music the possibility of expressing either Greece or the savage of Marajó, in the same way as Handel who converted love arias into arias dedicated to Christ in his oratorio *Messiah*." See Mário de Andrade, *Música, Doce Música*, 196.

24. Two particularly telling examples of this process can be found in the transformation of *Tédio de Alvorada* into *Uirapuru*: The first is the transformation of the opening flute solo of the original composition into the flute cadenza that represents the ugly Amerindian at rehearsal two (see Fig. 5.5); and the other is the transformation of an exotic *belle-époque* dance from the second page of *Tédio de Alvorada* into the Tempo di Marcia at rehearsal three of *Uirapuru*, which according to the program features the entrance of the Amerindian maidens. See Manoel Corrêa do Lago and Guilherme Bernstein, *Uirapuru: Partitura de estudo comentada*, 34.

25. Pieter Van der Toorn, *Stravinsky and The Rite of Spring*, 26–27. An ironic curiosity is that Van der Toorn mentions that "the rhythmic turbulence of the 'Glorification of the Chosen One' . . . at one time suggested an Amazonian scene. The Amazon idea was later abandoned as inappropriate and unworkable." Van der Toorn, 25. The same was expressed by Taruskin (see Richard Taruskin, "The Rite Revisited," 200).

26. Stravinsky and Craft, *Stravinsky: In Pictures and Documents*, 75.

27. Renato Almeida, *História da Música Brasileira*, 456.

28. When comparing side by side the literary programs of *Myremis* and *Amazonas*, it is observed that the text is essentially the same, except by the action being transposed from Greece to Brazil. There is complete correspondence in all aspects of

the two programs, something that does not happen between *Uirapuru* and *Tédio de Alvorada*, where the plot is substantially changed.

29. *Villa-Lobos: Sua Obra*. 2nd edition, 186–87.

30. Pellecer, "Adolphe Piriou," n.p. Concerning the premiere of *Amazonas*, Tarasti writes that "the concert was a great success, even a scandal" and that the critic of *La Revue Musicale* was confused by the novelty and perplexity of its musical form. Tarasti, *Villa-Lobos*, 358.

31. No musicological study to date has referred in more details to the composer's indication for the use of the bowed sitar (*cítara de arco*) as a solo instrument in *Amazonas*. All live performances and recordings use the violinophone. This is an interesting curiosity, because all the possible instruments known as "bowed sitars" have substantial technical and sound limitations, which make us wonder which instrument Villa-Lobos had in mind when conceptualizing the work.

32. Anna Stella Schic, *Villa-Lobos, o índio branco*, 79.

33. Taruskin, *Stravinsky and the Russian Traditions*, 874.

34. The C-flat on the lower line is a passing note to allow the pentatonic scale to be distributed around six sixteenth notes.

35. Salles states that the greatest influence of Wagner found in Villa-Lobos's work is in the field of orchestration, as well as the use of leitmotifs in his symphonic poems. Salles, *Villa-Lobos: Processos Composicionais*, 24. The influence of Wagner's orchestra on Stravinsky comes through his teacher Rimsky-Korsakov, whose operas were deeply inspired by Wagner's compositions in this genre.

36. This is the realm where the transformation of the *Uirapuru* into the Handsome Indian takes place. It is characterized by a pulsating, bell-like, B-natural pedal, performed by the piano, celesta, and harp harmonics in octaves, therefore, with a similar timbre as the one found in *Amazonas* (see chapter 5).

37. Tarasti, *Heitor Villa-Lobos*, 359.

38. Mário de Andrade, *Música, Doce Música*, 157.

39. Kiefer, *Villa-Lobos e o modernismo*, 44.

40. Salles, *Villa-Lobos: Processos Composicionais*, 196. Salles is referring to the Miremis leitmotif and its transformation into the "Sigh Motif," described in the thematic analysis. The successive reiteration of the "Sigh Motif" is a variant of the Miremis leitmotif, with its characteristic major second changing into a minor second and projecting in the distance the ending of the piece, where the tonal center E is led abruptly into a D-sharp as the last note.

41. Being a cellist, Villa-Lobos frequently explored the open IV string of cellos or basses in crucial moments of his compositions (for example, the ending of his *Bachianas Brasileiras No. 1* for cello ensemble). This makes it even more remarkable that *Amazonas* ends on a D-sharp played by the basses, for *not* ending on their open string, as one could reasonably expect.

42. The word *tonal* is being used here under an amplified concept of tonality in terms of polarized key centers.

43. The letter *y* does not exist in the Portuguese alphabet anymore. However, it existed when Villa-Lobos wrote his composition *Myremis*. For the purposes of this study, the title *Myremis* will be used when referring to the early symphonic poem by the composer, and the spelling *Miremis* will be used when referring to the leitmotif in the symphonic poem *Amazonas*.

44. The transplant of a Greek legend into a tropical Brazilian environment happened likely in order to satisfy the appetite of the French public of the time for primitive and exotic settings. The transplantation is so subtle that it led Eero Tarasti to wrongly attribute the Miremis leitmotif as a "direct quotation from melodies notated in Jean de Lery's well-known travel description, printed in 1554," more specifically the tune *Canide Ioune* Sabath (see Fig. 5.18). Tarasti, *Heitor Villa-Lobos*, 359. The latter was, indeed, used by Villa-Lobos when writing his different settings of *Three Amerindian Poems* in 1926, but a possible similarity with the Miremis leitmotif is simply a consequence of the simplistic and primitive nature of Amerindian melodies.

45. A final brass glissando in m. 40 prepares the last chord of the theme. It seems that the part of the second and fourth horns have wrong notes on the published score. Those horn parts are written in E, and the sounding pitches contradict the D minor chord that appears in the equivalent place of the piano version.

46. Moreira, "O Estilo Indígena," 29.

47. More details concerning the exploration of such acoustic tensions appear in Paulo de Tarso Sales, *Villa-Lobos: Processos Composicionais*, 106–07.

48. Considering that Amazonas has 333 measures, section D starts near one-third into the composition (m. 114). However, the fugato section starts on m. 127 (rehearsal 15), which is located really close to the golden section.

49. Concepts such as "polarization by exclusion" appear in the glossary of terms at the end of the book. It is a resource that provides an expansion of the concept of tonality through the idea of a "key center" that functions as a pole of attraction. However, in this case, the key center is not produced by its gravitational power, but by its absence as a key center in a certain passage. This creates an expectation fulfilled by the prominent appearance of the absent key center in the subsequent passage immediately after.

CHAPTER SEVEN

Diving into the *Amazonas*

Quem é que viu uma índia por aí
Não é Bororó, Tupiniquim, nem Guarani. —Milton de Oliveira
and Haroldo Lobo

The carnival march *Pele Vermelha* (Redskin, 1939)[1] was written by Milton de Oliveira (1916–1986) and Haroldo Lobo (1910–1965), two of the most renowned composers in the history of carnival in Rio de Janeiro. Its refrain is translated as follows: "Whoever saw an Amerindian girl out there? She's not Bororó, Tupiniquim, or Guarani. She is . . . a redskin, the color of parsimon." Bororó, Tupiniquim, and Guarani are Amerindian tribes in Brazil. The apparent feeling of discrimination in the lyrics should be viewed under the perspective that the beauty of the Brazilian woman was one of the hottest topics of the carnival songs, and most of the songs differentiated Brazilian women based on the color of their hair or their skin.

This march was written in 1939, only four years after the premiere of *Uirapuru* by Villa-Lobos in Argentina. It earned second place in the popular music contest organized by the Departamento de Imprensa e Propaganda do Estado Novo, during Getúlio Vargas's government, in the event "Popular Music Day," created to define which were the favorites for the carnival of 1940. Held on the soccer field of América Futebol Clube, the "Popular Music Night" elected first in the march category *Dama das Camélias* (Lady of the Camellias) by João de Barro and Alcyr Pires Vermelho, awarding the second prize to *Pele Vermelha*. Villa-Lobos was president of the jury and insisted on the victory of *Dama das Camélias*, being criticized for his choice because although it was a beautiful song, it was not necessarily a carnival march.

The same competition included the renowned composition *Aquarela do Brasil* (Brazilian Watercolor)[2] by Ary Barroso in the samba category. The song was not classified among the top three, because as an "exaltation samba," it was not considered a carnival song. The incident caused Barroso to severe relations with Villa-Lobos.[3] *Aquarela do Brasil*, known in the United States simply as "Brazil," became one of the most emblematic Brazilian compositions of all times, earning the designation of "song of the century" by the Academia Brasileira de Letras in 1997.

Villa-Lobos's larger compositions have been criticized for an apparent lack of a coherent and unified musical structure, something that has been attributed to deficiencies in his development as composer.[4] Many of his works are viewed as displaying an apparent freedom of form, where multiple sections are randomly juxtaposed, lacking the type of thematic unity and motivic development inherited from Beethovenian models. According to Paulo de Tarso Salles, even the current Brazilian musicology does not "know for sure what the style of our most important composer consists of, his technique, his strategies in the handling of form and harmonic material, we barely know most of his works."[5]

The composer denies any lack of technique: "I am a sentimentalist by nature and at times my music is downright sugary, but I never work by intuition. My processes of composition are determined by cool reasoning. Everything is calculated, constructed."[6] The analysis below will demonstrate that a revision is necessary in order to pinpoint the true value of the originality of Villa-Lobos's contributions. Underneath the apparent indiscipline, one can detect an uncommon sense of architecture that has been missed in the evaluations by most musicologists until the present day.

Formal Analysis

Introduction: Epigraph

The brief, two-measure introduction of *Amazonas* serves as epigraph by presenting concise music material, in concentrated form, from which the main themes of the composition are derived. In those two measures, the Miremis leitmotif is first enunciated by the French horn in m. 1 in a sort of "call from the jungle." While the last E of the horn is sustained through the next measure, the same motif is repeated in the same octave by the viola d'amore in m. 2.

Throughout the composition, the manipulation of the Miremis leitmotif is always associated with the way in which the Amerindian girl interacts with other elements of the environment and the narrative. The last note

Figure 7.1. The Introduction of the Miremis Leitmotif.
Created by the author.

of the leitmotif (E) constitutes the polarizing key center for the composition and is harmonized by a dissonant chord that produces a clash through the simultaneous presence of B-natural and B-flat, forming a major seventh, which creates an acoustic tension explored in the piece under the form of its inversion (minor second).

The chord has two layers. The first layer features the harmonic version of the melodic interval of Miremis, with E and D playing simultaneously in their original registers. The second layer is formed by a sequence of diminishing intervals (perfect fifth—augm. fourth—perfect fourth) over the polarized key center E and distributed among the different woodwind instruments (flute, English horn, and clarinet). In other words, the chord is a combination of the harmonic interval of Miremis with the so-called first Webernian archetype, a chord formed by the superposition of an augmented fourth (enharmonically written as a diminished fifth) and a perfect fourth (Figure 7.2a). According to Menezes, the first Webernian archetype is originated from the Wagnerian archetype—the *Tristan chord*—with the suppression of its central interval of third (Figure 7.2b).[7]

This sort of chord reveals Villa-Lobos's original approach to harmonies derived from Wagner's *Tristan chord*, which Schoenberg denominated "vagrant

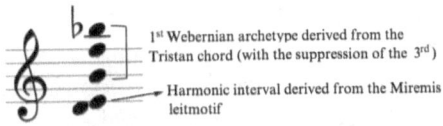

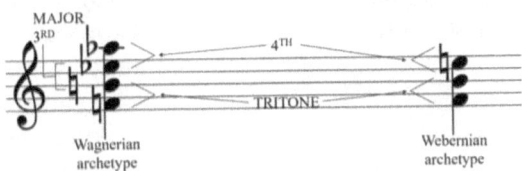

Figure 7.2. The first chord present in *Amazonas* (a) and the 1st Webernian Archetype (b), which is derived from the Wagnerian Archetype by eliminating the interval of major 3rd (written enharmonically as diminished 4th). The resulting chord is formed by the superposition of a diminished and a perfect 4th.
Created by the author.

chords,"[8] due to their tonal ambiguity. Those chords appear prominently in the works of Schoenberg, Berg, and Webern, as well as other composers such as Bartok and Debussy.[9]

As demonstrated previously, *Uirapuru* prominently features the *Tristan chord* throughout the piece, and Wagner's influence permeates the work. Therefore, the use of the first Webernian archetype—a chord derived from the *Tristan chord*—at the very beginning of *Amazonas* is another corroboration of the connections between *Amazonas* and *Uirapuru* and another expression of musical cannibalism.

The introduction and conclusion of *Amazonas*, as two-measure framing structures, reveal a motion from E (the polarizing center of the Miremis leitmotif) to a low D-sharp, reached through an abrupt descent at the end of the piece. The minor second clash that results from the prevalence of E as the tonal center throughout the composition, in contrast with the final D-sharp, is anticipated by the polarization of the interval minor second in multiple key moments throughout the piece, as this analysis will demonstrate. The emphasis on the two intervals—minor second and tritone—as well as the major second that is characteristic of the Miremis leitmotif, represents Villa-Lobos's response to the emancipation of dissonance endorsed by many composers in the beginning of the twentieth century. The same sort of "compositional thesis" is found in *Uirapuru*, which brings again the idea that a more profound relationship exists between the two compositions, something the current musicology tends to weaken when assuming that their dating is incorrect, and, in fact, they were written later than the official published dates, as well as several years apart from each other.

The ending of *Amazonas* is musically very similar to the ending of *The Rite of Spring*, as the comparison of their piano reductions demonstrate in Figure 7.3 below. The final measures of both start with the harsh dissonance of a minor second clash in the upper voices (inverted minor second in the case of *Amazonas*), followed by a chromatic ascending motion (a glissando, in *Amazonas*), and ending with a plunge into the depths of the low orchestra register toward a short dissonant chord, where the interval of second is again stressed.

The endings in the orchestra versions (Figure 7.3b) are even more telling. In *Amazonas*, the last chord is built with two major seconds superimposed (one of them enharmonically spelled as a diminished third) and separated by a distance of a major third. In *The Rite of Spring*, a minor second is placed above a major second, also separated by the distance of a major third. In the original version, the low part of the final chord of *The Rite* spells the word "DEAD" from the bottom up (Figure 7.3a).

Figure 7.3. Comparison of the piano reductions of the endings of *Amazonas* (top) and the *Rite of Spring* (bottom), followed by the final chords of *Amazonas* and the *Rite of Spring* in closed position (b).
Created by the author from the piano reductions of *Amazonas* and the *Rite of Spring*.

Part I: Exposition

Section A: Contemplation of the Amazon; Jealousy of the God of Winds; The Amerindian Girl's Mirror; The Treason of the God of Winds (m. 3–36)

In *Amazonas*, the music evolves from the literary program through the interaction of multiple layers of musical metaphors. The sustaining pitch, E, in the viola d'amore throughout the entire segment of the *Contemplation of the Amazon* represents a metaphor of love for the solid body of the Amerindian girl, whose physical presence is placed against the undulating motion of "dark" woodwinds (chalumeau register of clarinets plus bassoon), representing the waters of the Marajoara River. The timbre of the viola d'amore, as it sustains the E, metaphorically represents an expression of love, and the appogiaturas an octave above by the flutes over the same pitch represent the swimming motions of the girl through tone painting.[10] The combination of dark woodwinds representing the murky waters of the river, with their movement in parallel fifths and fourths, is associated with nature through another metaphor, since these are prominent intervals in the harmonic series.

Figure 7.4. Beginning of *Amazonas*, featuring multiple musical metaphors (other incidental sounds representing elements of the surrounding nature have been omitted).
Paulo de Tarso Salles, Villa-Lobos: *Processos Composicionais*, 190.

The above representation of water produces a primitivist soundscape through the combination of a number of rudimentary elements that give a naïf quality to the music. Rhythmically, the motion adheres to the metrical pulse; melodically, it evolves mostly by conjunct motion; and harmonically, it presents parallel fourths and fifths. The dynamic circularity with hairpins following the undulating motion of the woodwinds strengthens the cyclic conception of life present in the Amerindian culture.

A detailed analysis of the initial seven measures of *Amazonas* can enlighten the originality of Villa-Lobos's pictorial method of using structural metaphors. After the initial statement of the Miremis leitmotif in the first two measures, the woodwinds start the figuration that represents the murky waters of the Marajoara River.

The lines of the 1st clarinet and 1st bassoon form a whole tone scale, while the 2nd bassoon and bass clarinet form the complementary whole tone scale, so that the combination of the two include the 12 notes of the chromatic spectrum. The intervals among those four voices are also constant; however, the 2nd bassoon breaks the regularity (though keeping a symmetry of 5ths with the 1st bassoon).[11]

Figure 7.5. Woodwind chords representing the waters of the Marajoara river.
Paulo de Tarso Salles, Villa-Lobos: *Processos Composicionais*, 191.

The break in regularity produced by the second bassoon creates a gap resultant of the augmented second between the first and second notes of its tetrachord. However, ultimately the second bassoon line is in balance with the first bassoon line, with its display of diminished and augmented fifths symmetrically weaving around a perfect fifth axis.

Another astonishing example of the pictorial nature of the music is the transitory character of delicate structures that the composer doesn't hesitate to destroy. In m. 6, a disturbance is produced in the texture due to an aggressive chromatic intervention in ***fff*** of tuba, bass trombone, contrabassoon, sarrusophone, and double basses, representing a big, creeping animal on the riverside. This intervention of the low instruments, and the metaphorical creature they represent, is reflected on the surface of the water that has been created by the clarinets: The fourths between the top clarinet lines become thirds, while the bass clarinet produces a brief chromatic figuration in eighth notes on the third beat. The original whole tone motion of the first clarinet is transformed into a non-traditional octatonic scale, which alternates symmetrically groups of one or two tones and semitones (Figure 7.6).

Figure 7.6. Structural metaphors in the early measures of *Amazonas*.
Paulo de Tarso Salles, Villa-Lobos: *Processos Composicionais*, 191.

As seen above, each layer of the texture features a musical metaphor, and their interaction produces structural effects, where each note finds its reason for being. This could hardly be associated with the image of a rebellious and intuitive composer whose talent masks a certain lack of technique. The connections between these structural metaphors,[12] resonating among themselves, are what determine the development of the musical material.

An analogous process continues in the subsequent sections of the work. In the *Jealousy of the God of Winds* passage, the undulating chromatic motion of the flute—a timbristic metaphor representing the God of Winds comparable to the representation of love for the body of the Amerindian girl by the viola d'amore—contrasts with the diatonic pedal of the strings, sustaining harmonic notes in fifths (omitted in the figure below). In this instance, the chromatic disturbance by the low brass and woodwind instruments in m. 8 reflects on the surface in the clarinet solo, which produces a shrieking effect, written with an octatonic material (bottom line of Figure 7.7), while the remaining clarinets and bassoons (followed by piano and harp) continue the representation of the river.

Figure 7.7. Similar chromatic disturbance in low brass and woodwinds reflects again in the surface of the water represented by clarinets (other voices in the passage have been omitted).
Paulo de Tarso Salles, Villa-Lobos: *Processos Composicionais*, 38.

It shouldn't go unnoticed that, at the end of the first clarinet figuration, a transposed variant of the incipit of the Miremis leitmotif (E-D-E) appears in the high register under the form F—E-flat—F-sharp. Salles explains the remarkable semantic meaning of the passage (mm. 8–10):

> While the note, E, floats in the surface of the water, being momentarily covered by them, the action of the wind whips the water with its chromatic motion, resulting in rinforzatti in the woodwinds. Meanwhile, the low register of the flute

playing in *ff* dynamics produces a wide range of transient sounds. The chromatic disturbance produced by bass trombone, tuba, contrabassoon, and sarusophone (m. 8) produces the octatonic figuration in the clarinet, which, after a quick ascending motion of over two octaves, features a distorted statement of the Miremis leitmotif incipit, written as F—E—F-sharp. As soon as this event ceases, the viola d'amore returns with the E pedal, one octave above the initial one.[13]

The first, proper theme starts at m. 10, performed by the oboe, beginning sequentially and based on a whole-tone collection. This theme represents the Amerindian girl giving herself to her wild pleasures, its sensuality being associated with the alterations in the last beat of every measure, alternating between a major third and a tritone. These alterations seem almost palpable, a portrayal of the sensual gestures of the girl. When they happen, the God of the Winds responds accordingly, by transforming the chromatic undulating triplets into sixteenth notes. After m. 14, the girl's theme further develops through a nine-tone pitch collection that alternates sequences of two semitones with a whole tone, ending on the key center of E an octave lower, reached through a tritone (Figure 7.8). It depicts how the Amerindian

Figure 7.8. Main theme of Section A as performed by the oboe and flutes. Created by the author.

girl goes astray in her brutal sensuality, ignoring the loving advances of the God of the Winds, while the interval of tritone establishes itself as a major constructive force. The jealousy of the God of the Winds is represented by a thematic aggregate of two voices: the oboe theme plus its countermelody in the form of a chromatic flute ostinato.

Analogous procedures permeate the entirety of Section A in the subsequent passages, corroborating the pictorial quality of the music through interactive textural layers formed by the various instrumental families. The result is a soundscape where "foreground and background textures" replace the traditional concept of melody with accompaniment.[14] Over the background texture, sound objects appear and disappear in multiple registers, new textures come and go, and the rhythmic energy intensifies and subsides.

At rehearsal number two, the representation of *The Amerindian Girl's Mirror* is created through an imitation between flute (and later oboe at m. 22) and English horn on the interval of the sixth (plus octave), while at rehearsal number three—*Treason of the God of Winds*—the process is intensified with the addition of more and more textural layers. The reappearance of the chromatic theme of the God of Winds in the oboe at rehearsal number four contrasts with the "white diatonic" nature of the background, still representing the undulating motion of the Amazon River in a colorful combination of harp, piano, and string harmonics in tremolo sul ponticello. The intensification of the processes within this remarkable impressionist backdrop leads into the first climax of the piece, which takes place in Section B.

Section B (m. 37–49): Wrath of the God of Winds

As shown in Figure 6.10 of the previous chapter, the theme of this section is based on a black and white pitch collection and produced by parallel seventh chords performed homorythmically by the brass, within a rich rhythmic contour. A countermelody in parallel seventh chords in the strings (except basses) at m. 39 contrasts with the secondary theme by being based on a nine-tone, exotic pitch collection. This collection displays the successive reduction of the number of semitones alternating with whole tones (three semitones—one whole tone—two semitones—one whole tone—one semitone—one whole tone), as shown in Figure 7.9 below.

Figure 7.9. The string countermelody.
Created by the author.

The literary program indicates that this secondary theme represents the *Wrath of the God of the Winds*. After its statement, the texture is reduced, essentially, to two elements at rehearsal six: water (clarinets and bassoons, as in the beginning of the piece) and air (French horn). The chromatic motion initiated by the horn (representing the God of the Winds) takes the initial E a tritone upward to B-flat, and is followed by an ascending line started by flutes and harp that is based on a seven-note pitch collection of two whole-tone trichords mediated by a semitone motion. It represents the God of the Winds catching the scent of the Amerindian girl in the distance, in a process characterized by an upward motion that raises the key center E—that represents the girl—over the span of four octaves (Figure 7.10). The process constitutes a remarkable example of tone painting.

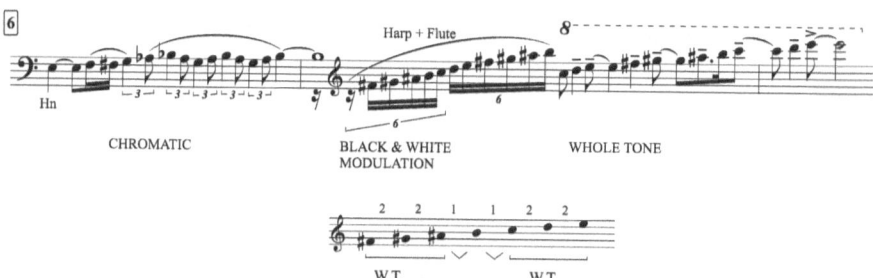

Figure 7.10. The melodic motion represents the God of the Winds catching the scent of the Amerindian girl in the distance. The line initiated by the harp and flutes is based on a 7-note pitch collection represented by two whole tone trichords—one on black keys and the other on white keys—mediated by two semitones.
Created by the author.

The section ends with successive reiterations, on English and French horns (joined in the last two iterations by the third trumpet), of the "Sigh Motif" (A-flat—G), a modified version of the incipit of the Miremis leitmotif (E—D—E converted into A-flat—G—A-flat). As explained previously, this profound transformation of the major second into a minor second projects the distinctive ending of the piece in D-sharp, a minor second below E, the key center of the composition.

Figure 7.11. Successive reiterations of the "Sigh Motif" constitute a variant of the Miremis incipit.
Created by the author.

Section A: The Prayer of the Amerindian girl (m. 50–67)

The return of Section A is based on a new variant of the main theme, under the form of the *Theme of the Prayer of the Amerindian Girl* (Figure 6.8b, second example, starting on m. 53). This section takes the composition into a new, more mystical realm, where unique orchestration devices create an impressionist background texture. It sounds like an onomatopoeia of nature, combining arpeggios of harmonics in the cellos and viola d'amore, harp harmonics, muted horns, and accented notes on flutes and clarinets. The main element is the *Theme of the Prayer*, whose first section is accompanied by arpeggiated cello harmonics, and the second section is accompanied by arpeggiated harmonics of the viola d'amore. In this way, the first part of the theme is harmonized through a diatonic realm, while the second half is harmonized through a whole tone realm, explained in Figure 7.12.[15] One should notice that the notes of the pitch collection produced by the two whole-tone tetrachords on the bottom left can be arranged in a sequence of fifths: C-G-D-A-E-B-F♯-C♯, making the collection diatonic.

Against the elegant simplicity of the "Theme of Prayer," performed with the unusual timbre of the violinophone, the English horn intones a countermelody derived from the "Enchantment Motif," while the other voices punctuate the texture with different figures, musical gestures that create dissonant accents on the first and third beats. Among these gestures, the first

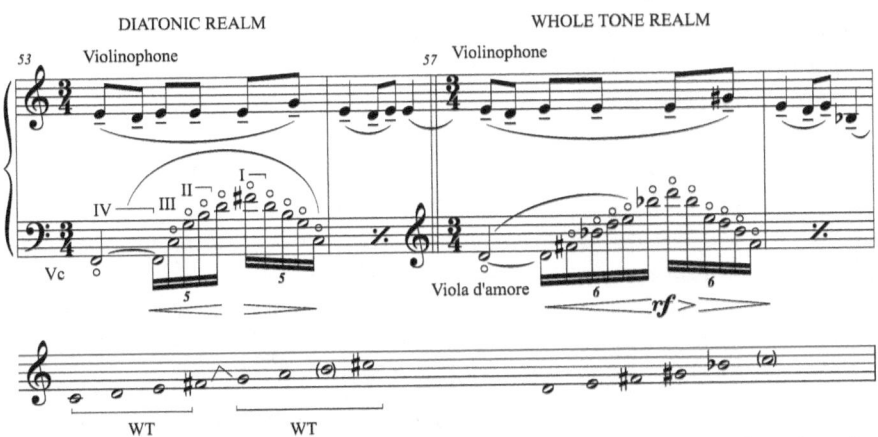

Figure 7.12. The first half of the Theme of the Prayer is written within a diatonic realm formed by the combination of two whole-tone tetrachords that are a semitone apart. The pitch B-natural does not appear in the two voices above, but is found in figurations performed by other voices not shown. In the second half, the distorted theme is written within a whole tone realm, where the pitch C does not appear in the two voices above, but is found in figurations performed by other voices.
Created by the author.

Figure 7.13. The "Sigh Motif" in the 1st clarinet & the incipit of the Miremis leitmotif in the muted 1st horn are presented simultaneously, both inverted.
Created by the author.

horn reiterates an inversion of the incipit of the Miremis leitmotif, while the first clarinet states an inversion of the "Sigh Motif" (Figure 7.13).

The combination of so many thematic elements (the "Theme of the Prayer," the incipit of the Miremis leitmotif, the inversion of the "Sigh Motif," and the "Enchantment Motif"—all derived from the Miremis leitmotif) makes the texture metaphorically charged with an inner coherence. It is important for the "Theme of the Prayer" to be brought to the foreground, while all the remaining elements remain subsidiary as onomatopoeic components. At its conclusion (rehearsal 8, m. 61), the "Theme of the Prayer" resolves on middle C, and Section A concludes within a diatonic environment stressing the white-key notes collection, which sensitively adheres to the spiritual ambience of the section. The purity of the white diatonic collection at this arrival point is a poetic depiction of the religious connotation of the "Prayer of the Amerindian Girl." An important detail that should not go unnoticed is the accentuated attack of the two flutes into the harmonic interval D-E, the major second that stands for *Miremis* and appears at the very end of the section (m.66) in rallentando. This harmonic interval on crescendo is what prepares the entrance of the next section.

Section C: Dance to the Enchantment of the Forests (mm. 68–99)

The mystical atmosphere of the previous section prepares the entrance of the *Dance to the Enchantment of the Forests*, where an extraordinary impressionist soundscape creates the framework for the violins to intone the "Enchantment Motif" (see Figure 6.9 in chapter 6), followed by a virtuosic, contrasting melody of rhapsodic character by the E-flat clarinet starting at m. 73 (Figure 6.12a shows an excerpt from this theme). The soundscape takes the listener into the universe of noises built on a non-tempered realm, by asking the string players to perform arpeggios over sounds of undetermined pitches performed in the space between the bridge and the string holder of the instruments (see Figure 6.5 in chapter 5). This soundscape starts and ends with a pedal point A, the subdominant of the key center E.[16]

This is not a typical primitivist rhythmic dance based on an ostinato rhythm. According to comments by the composer, the freedom of the melody by the E-flat clarinet evokes the presence of a forest being, a bird or spirit, that sings freely, flowing over the steady stream of arpeggios of the impressionist soundscape. It is an edgy melody full of nuances that develops sinuously across the entire range of the instrument and is interrupted on two occasions (at m. 81 and m. 89) by brutal, cluster-like chords that seem to be randomly placed, recalling the beginning of the Sacrificial Dance of *The Rite of Spring* (Figure 7.14). When this happens, the E-flat clarinet intones a motif that is a variant of the incipit of the Miremis leitmotif, transformed into a minor second (F—E—F instead of F—E-flat—F). During this intervention, the only pitch not present is B-flat, which is polarized by exclusion. This B-flat becomes the ultimate resolution of the subdominant pedal present in the beginning and end of Section C, arriving monophonically in the form of a pedal sustained by the violinophone, connecting Parts I and II of the composition (mm. 107–110).

Figure 7.14. Brutal cluster-like chords (lower system) below theme on E-flat clarinet, flute, and piccolo.
Created by the author.

Analogously to the end of Section B, Section C ends with successive reiterations of the "Sigh Motif," this time in the low register of the first flute.

Figure 7.15. Analogous endings of sections B and C.
Created by the author.

Section A: Conclusion of Part I (mm. 99–108)

At the end of Section C, the texture gradually rarefies in diminuendo with the successive departure of the string divisi, and the conclusive section starts over the A pedal, which remains almost until the end. This conclusive section functions as codetta to Part I, starting with new arpeggios of the low strings plus viola d'amore and violinophone. A bell-like, abridged version of the main theme is stated, sounding like a reminiscence and performed by the first bassoon echoed, through a bell-like imitation, by the first clarinet (Figure 7.16), ultimately leading into a solitary B-flat in the violinophone, which connects with the next part of the composition.

Figure 7.16. Abridged version of the main theme at the end of Part I of *Amazonas*.
Created by the author.

In this way, Part I starts and ends monophonically, beginning with E—key center of the composition—and ending on B-flat, the lowered V degree, constituting a tritone motion I-V♭. Its preparation by a subdominant pedal point (A) bears a resemblance with the traditional tonal procedure of a full cadence (tonic-subdominant-dominant), and it demonstrates a remarkably original treatment of the idea of tonality in the author's compositional process.

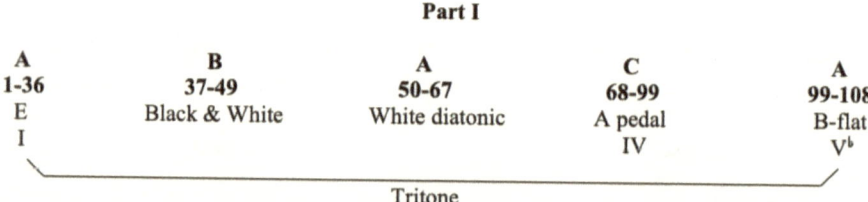

Figure 7.17. Harmonic plan of Part I of *Amazonas*, presenting a motion I—IV—V♭. It demonstrates the importance of the interval of tritone.
Created by the author.

Part II: Middle Section

Section D: The Sensual Dance of the Amerindian Girl; The Monster's Region; The Monster's March; The Girl's Happiness; A Monster Stands Out (mm. 109–285)

The middle section of *Amazonas* is unified by the inexorable motion of the monsters under the form of a toccata, the placement of which in the piece, as well as its programmatic implications, is equivalent to the Sacrificial Dance of *The Rite of Spring*. Both pieces provide an apocalyptic vision where an unrelenting rhythmic vortex concludes with the death of a virgin woman.

Within the ostinato primeval motion of the toccata, Section D can be subdivided into five segments, which shows another level of symmetry in relation to Part I, which is also segmented in five parts (A B A C A). Table 7.1 demonstrates the partitioning of the Middle Section.

Table 7.1. Structure of the middle section of *Amazonas*
(line 3 displays the measure numbers on which each section begins and ends; line 4 shows the number of measures in each phase).

PHASE 1	PHASE 2	PHASE 3	PHASE 4	PHASE 5
Sensual Dance of the Amerindian Girl	Fugato	Miremis and Enchantment	Happiness of the Amerindian Girl	Treason of the God of the Winds
109–113	114–166	167–215	216–268	269–285
5	53	49	53	17

The *Theme of the Sensual Dance of the Amerindian Girl* is the second main theme of *Amazonas* (see Figure 6.13 in chapter 6). Its sensuality lies in the abundant chromaticism and the melodic contour, which forms a rounded and sinuous curve, starting on G-flat and ending on F. The minor second formed by the horizontal extremes (first and last notes) of the theme is complemented by the major seventh, which is its inversion and is formed by the highest and lowest pitches of the theme (Figure 7.18). Therefore, the minor second becomes a polarized interval in the sphere of this theme.

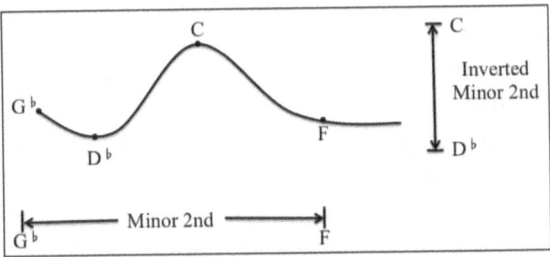

Figure 7.18. Melodic contour of the Theme of the Sensual Dance of the Amerindian Girl.
Created by the author.

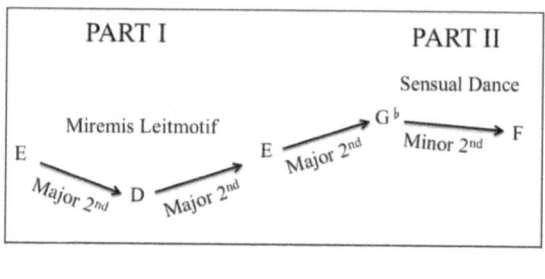

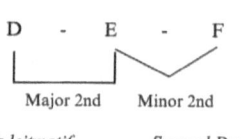

Figure 7.19. The Miremis leitmotif at the beginning of Part I polarizes the major 2nd, while the Theme of the Sensual Dance at the beginning of Part II polarizes the minor 2nd.
Created by the author.

Like the Miremis leitmotif that permeates Part I, it is first stated monophonically (here, by a solo cello), and the melody includes all chromatic pitches except the E-natural, which is saved through polarization by exclusion to be presented prominently at the Recapitulation (Part III). A comparison of the two main thematic materials of the composition reveals a remarkable structural coherence. The Miremis leitmotif is the unifying force behind Part I of *Amazonas*. It polarizes the interval of major second through the lower neighbor of E, and when the E is reached in m. 3, it is prolonged, through insistent repetition, for eighteen measures until the downbeat of m. 19. The "Theme of the Sensual Dance of the Amerindian Girl" unifies Part II of *Amazonas*. It polarizes the interval of minor second, ending on F, which is prolonged as a pedal, also for eighteen measures (basses, mm. 114–131). The "Theme of the Sensual Dance" also polarizes E, in this case, by exclusion.

The second phase starts with the setting of the toccata at m. 114, through a relentless ostinato that characterizes the region of the monsters. Through a process of densification, more and more instruments join the inexorable rhythm, in a process of complementarity of the dactyl metrical unit (long-short-short).

At m. 119, a new set of cluster-like chords indicates the arrival at the *Region of the Monsters*, preparing the entrance of a fugato, which is located right at the golden section of the composition (m. 127).[17] The chords in this passage are analogous to the ones in the "Dance to the Enchantment

Figure 7.20. The toccata moves inexorably with an underlying complementary dactyl rhythm.
Created by the author.

of the Forests" (Figure 7.14 above), except for the F-natural in the right hand, which becomes sharp in the current passage. They are reminiscent of the chords in the *Sacrificial Dance* of *The Rite of Spring* (Figure 7.21b).[18] The chord in *Amazonas* is the result of a cluster effect, combining black and white notes, similar to Villa-Lobos's conception in *Polichinelo* (see chapter 3). It demonstrates the composer's taste for combining the white against the black keys of the piano.

Figure 7.21. Cluster-like chords in the Region of the Monsters performed by the piano and brass in *Amazonas* (upper system) and beginning of the Sacrificial Dance in the *Rite of Spring* (lower system).
Created by the author.

The subject of the fugato is the "Theme of the Sensual Dance" and is stated successively in the clarinet, violins, and flutes plus oboes, within key centers established using the concept of polarization by exclusion (bottom line of Table 7.2 below). The successive iterations form a sequence of

Table 7.2. Successive statements of the fugato subject happen over keys that form a sequence of major 3rds followed by a tritone.

1st statement	2nd statement	3rd statement	Episode	4th statement
Clarinet	Violins	Fl., picc., & ob.	mm. 139–150	Brass
mm. 127–130	mm. 131–134	mm. 135–138		mm. 150.5–154
B	D#	G		C#

major 3rd — major 3rd — tritone

major thirds, followed by a tritone for the last statement of the subject by the brass. This last statement by the brass has the title "The Monster's March" written in the score.

A bridge over a G-sharp pedal leads to phase three, located at the center of Section D. Phase three is programmatically charged and brings back elements from Section A ("Jealousy of the God of the Winds") at the beginning of the composition, with one major difference—while in its original form, the "Theme of the Amerindian Girl" interacted with the God of the Winds through their polyphonic statement in two voices (flutes in unison versus oboe solo, Figure 7.8); here, the two voices appear separately, one after the other. The "Theme of the Amerindian Girl" starts on m. 167, performed by the F trumpets and, through a four-measure bridge (mm. 175–178), turns into the representation of the God of the Winds, with its chromatic, wavelike motions combined with dynamic hairpins. On m. 189, the B-flat trumpets pick up the "Theme of the God of the Winds" and convert it into the "Enchantment Motif," reiterated a number of times and altered in subsequent iterations, converting the original major seventh into a tritone, which also appears prominently at the end of the "Theme of Amerindian Girl." The pictorialism is evident: The God of the Winds brought the scent of the Amerindian girl to the region of the monsters, ending in a series of consecutive iterations of the "Enchantment Motif" in cantabile. Villa-Lobos produces a sonorous description through musical gestures that mirrors the programmatic nature of the narrative (Figure 7.22).

The procedure above has a subtlety that might pass unperceived. While in its original form the "Theme of the Jealousy of the God of the Winds" appears as a thematic aggregate of two contrasting elements on the flutes and oboe (Figure 7.8), in phase three of Section D, the contrast is minimized—the two elements are presented consecutively and with the same timbre of trumpets. This demonstrates Villa-Lobos's original method of incorporating traditional procedures within a modernist outfit. In this case, texture replaces harmony. While in the sonata form, the contrast of themes of the exposition is reduced in the recapitulation by their restatement in the same tonality; in this example, the contrast of the two voices is minimized by presenting them monophonically and with the same timbre.

Figure 7.22. At the center of Section D, a restatement of the "Jealousy Theme" from Section A is presented as a programmatically charged episode.
Created by the author.

A bridge between rehearsals twenty and twenty-one (m. 209–215) introduces an important modification to the ostinato: the complementary rhythm described in Figure 7.20 is broken, while a superimposition of triple meter over the pulse of the march produces a metrical modulation, shown in the figure below. As the metric modulation takes place, several voices start an ascending chromatic motion in crescendo, leading to the climatic passage of the middle section (phase 4).

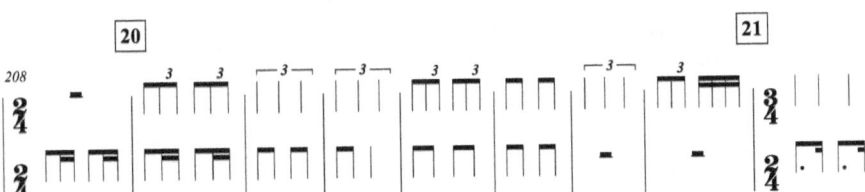

Figure 7.23. A metric modulation happens in the bridge between rehearsals 20 and 21, leading to the next phase of the middle section, characterized by a polymeter. During the bridge, a number of voices start an ascending chromatic motion in crescendo, which prepares the new climatic passage.
Created by the author.

Phase four is a complex orgiastic passage in piu mosso, where the combination of duple and triple meters into a frenzied polymeter supports the statement of the "Theme of the Happiness of the Amerindian Girl." This is, in fact, a climactic statement of the theme of the sensual dance in augmentation, over four octaves in the cellos, violins, oboes, French and English horn, and piccolo.[19] When this theme in augmentation is introduced, the Brazilian percussion instruments (*matraca*, *bumbo*, and *pandeiro*) join in triple meter. The texture also includes a number of other harmonic

Figure 7.24. Skeleton of the beginning of phase 4, displaying only the lowest voices of the texture. Multiple other elements have been omitted in order not to overload the analysis. The basses continue the ostinato rhythm of the march, while the cellos present a wave like motion in counterpoint in triple meter. The upper voice of the cellos introduces the main theme of section D in augmentation, and this theme is doubled over four octaves by other instruments.
Created by the author.

and polyphonic elements that form a highly chromatic and dissonant accompaniment to the theme.

This climatic moment starts at the golden mean of section D and is one of the most daring moments in the composition.[20] By introducing the main theme in augmentation, performed in fortissimo over four octaves, in polymeter, accompanied with Brazilian percussion instruments, the entire texture sounds like an erotic version of carnival brought into the Brazilian jungle.

This phase essentially continues until the end of the section; however, it is interrupted by the statement of an abridged version of the "Theme of the Treason of the God of the Winds" from Section B (see Figure 6.10 in chapter 6), performed again by the brass (mm. 269–281). The reprise of this theme articulates Section D into its last phase, and at the end of its statement the march gradually disintegrates through diminuendo and rallentando. A monster stands out, represented by perfect fifths in the low part of the texture (Figure 7.25), and the section ends on a fermata over a ten-note harmony in *pp*, where the pitches A and F are missing.

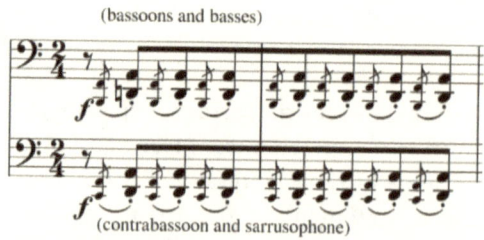

Figure 7.25. "A Monster Stands Out" through the remarkable combination of sarrusophone and contrabassoon in recurring 5ths, doubled an octave above by bassoons and basses.
Created by the author.

The restatement of themes from Sections A and B within the end of Section D constitutes a noteworthy, nontraditional treatment of the rondo form. In principle, one would expect that the restatement of thematic materials from Sections A and B would happen after Section D. Instead of confining himself within the archetypes established in absolute music, the author anticipates their return, making them part of Section D. Villa-Lobos conveys the idea of wrath as product of the jealousy of the God of the Winds, who takes the chaste scent of the Amerindian girl to the secular region of the monsters. This produces an original treatment of the rondo form, achieved through an inversion of the arrow of time. The last two phases of Section D are not simple restatements of themes, but connect, through time, two distant sections of the piece. Villa-Lobos combines spontaneity of expression with deliberate mastery of development technique, approaching musical form as a flexible process of manipulation of time.

As happens with great artists, life and art are entangled. Technical procedures cannot be separated from the poetic meaning of the musical contents. While a different composer might have preferred to adhere to academic norms, Villa-Lobos lets his intuition dictate the structure of his music, and in this case, he produced an inversion of the arrow of time. This idea brought to a different context might justify the speculation that his habit of predating his compositions represented something more profound than a simple attempt to be regarded as a more original composer than he actually was.

Part III: Recapitulation and Coda

The last part of *Amazonas* depicts the conclusion of the program, when the Amerindian girl is confronted by the monster. The part is centered around two themes, one derived from the Miremis leitmotif depicting the girl, and a new theme that depicts the monster's anxiety. The manipulation of the two themes as they interact among themselves and with the surrounding soundscape is once again charged with structural metaphors.

Section A: The Monster's Anxiety; The Deceptive Mirror; The Discovery (mm. 286–294)

Instead of a main theme and a secondary theme, or a melody with its countermelody, Villa-Lobos presents in concentrated form numerous elements interacting among themselves through foreground and background textures. After the Vivo middle section, the Adagio tempo in 4/2 constitutes a circular return to the beginning of the piece, which, despite being written in tempo Andante, is in practice only slightly faster than the Adagio.

The two key centers polarized by exclusion at the end of the previous section (A and F) appear prominently. The A returns as a pedal at the very beginning, connecting in the distance with the subdominant pedal in Section C of Part I (see *Dance to the Enchantment of the Forests*, starting on m. 68). This pedal constitutes the base of the background texture. The F is featured prominently in the "Theme of the Monster's Anxiety," which is performed in the most unusual setting, by the violinophone and the contrabassoon separated four and a half octaves (Figure 7.26, upper two lines). The F functions as an axis (C for the violinophone), because besides being the starting and ending points of the theme, it is located between the extreme notes. Through bilateral symmetry, the F stands a minor third apart from the highest and the lowest pitches of the theme. At the end of the theme, the F is prolonged as a pedal in parallel with the A in the double basses.

An abridged theme representing the Amerindian girl appears *en dehors*, performed in *fff* by the oboes in unison in the low register (Figure 7.26, lower line). This theme constitutes both a thematic and a timbristic recapitulation, by recalling the first theme proper of *Amazonas*, which was introduced in m. 10. The juxtaposition of the two themes forms the foreground texture, symbolizing two contrasting elements—the girl and the monster—and polarizing two centers, E and F, which are one semitone apart: E associated with the girl and F associated with the monster.

Figure 7.26. The theme of The Monster's Anxiety is presented by the contrabassoon and violinophone separated by four and a half octaves. The polarized F appears as the lowest note in the texture, complementing the A pedal of the double basses and bass trombone. Another theme representing the Amerindian girl is performed by the oboe in fff en dehors. The simultaneous statement of two contrasting themes in counterpoint, one polarizing F and the other polarizing E, reaffirms once again the polarization of the interval of minor 2nd as the main "thesis" of the composition.
Created by the author.

Besides the already mentioned A pedal, the background texture includes a number of other elements, such as: a divisi of double basses plus a solo flute reiterate the inversion of the Miremis leitmotif incipit separated by two octaves (Figure 7.27a); the strings inner voices recall the initial representation of the river during the *Contemplation of the Amazon* section, by performing a similar undulating motion in tremolo vibrato sul ponticello (Figure 7.27b); short chords depict the monster by using an eleven-tone collection where the note F is missing (Figure 7.27c). As explained above, the polarized center F embodies the monster by appearing prominently as a pedal in the "Theme of the Monster's Anxiety" and by being polarized by exclusion in the cluster-like chords.[21]

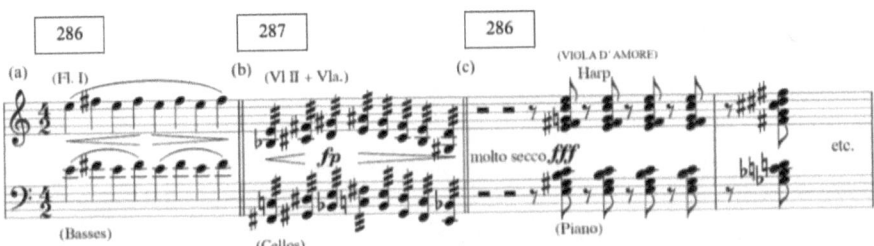

Figure 7.27. In addition to the A pedal on the lower divisi of the basses, the background texture includes a) reiterated inversions of the incipit of the Miremis leitmotif; b) the undulating motion of the water represented by strings in tremolo sul ponticello; c) short chords, representing the monster, built over an 11-tone pitch collection, where F is missing (polarized by exclusion, the F represents the key center of the monster). Created by the author.

As the dramatic climax of the story's narrative, this recapitulation includes various elements where the score graphically illustrates the storyline through the interaction of the layers of the texture. For example, "The Deceptive Mirror" is where the image of the monster is reflected by the sunlight over the gray shadow of the girl (Figure 7.28). It is depicted by the alternation of short and aggressive eighth notes over D on the low woodwind instruments, and the short cluster-like chords in the piano, harp and viola d'amore pizzicato. In this quick dialogue, the upper voice of the texture reiterates the fast alternation of D and E, a mirror image of the incipit of the Miremis leitmotif, which is associated with the Amerindian girl.

Immediately after, two trumpets in *ffff* double the oboes on the "Theme of the Amerindian girl" (mm. 289–290). As the monster tries to grab the girl through a brass descending glissando in *ffff*, an unexpected leap of minor

Figure 7.28. The Deceptive Mirror is illustrated metaphorically by the alternation of quick 8th notes, where the upper voices reiterate an inversion of the incipit of the Miremis leitmotif (D-E instead of E-D).
Created by the author.

ninth distorts the theme of the girl, when she suddenly becomes aware of the presence of the monster (Figure 7.29). This abrupt distortion sounds like a cry of terror, denoted in the score as **rfff>**. The expressionist leap of minor ninth constitutes an inversion of the incipit of the Miremis leitmotif (the major second E—D)—already anticipated in "The Deceptive Mirror"—into a minor second across an octave (D—E-flat).

Figure 7.29. The abrupt leap of minor 9th at the end of the last statement of the girl's theme stands out as an expressionist cry of horror, notated with a rfff>. The effect can be compared with the "Deceptive Mirror," where the reflection of the image of the girl is confused with the reflection of monster, producing a major 2nd separated by octaves (D—E, Fig. VII-28). In other words, in this case the recognition of the monster is expressed through a cry of despair featuring a minor 2nd separated by an octave (D—E-flat), which sounds like as shriek.
Created by the author.

A progressive crescendo and accelerando builds up the tension, and a descending whole tone scale *affretando* at the end of the section dives into the open E string of the double basses, hanging solitary in a long fermata (Figure 7.30).[22] A similar idea of a descending line plunging into the vacuum was also used by Stravinsky in *Le Sacre du Printemps*.[23]

Figure 7.30. A descending figure based on a whole-tone pitch collection plunges into the vacuum with a sense of urgency, leaving a solitary E-natural hanging on the double basses through a long fermata. The idea of a descending line of a few notes plunging into the vacuum was also used by Stravinsky in Le Sacre, however the descending line in the latter is chromatic.
Created by the author.

Coda: The Fight of Desire; The Abyss; The Precipice (295–333)

Starting with one single voice, the Coda is based on a process that mirrors the narrative through the combination of densification and diminution of the multiple voices. In the background texture, the voices join successively, producing a rhythmic ostinato through complex complementarity, as shown in Figure 7.31. All the elements that will be described below combine to represent what the composer wrote in the score as *The Fight of Desire*. Another symmetry appears in the macro-from: If the Recapitulation section brought us back to the sphere of Part I, the use of ostinato in the Coda constitutes a return to the sphere of Part II, "The Monster's March," which happens over an ostinato with complex rhythmic complementarity.

Figure 7.31. The ostinato in the Coda features complex rhythmic complementarity in different levels. The combination of multiple rhythms represents "The Fight of Desire" notated in the score. This example shows the most important voices, but there are others that have been omitted. The underlying complementary rhythm is modified during this section as some of the voices suffer a process of diminution described below.
Created by the author.

Besides the rhythmic complementarity, some of the voices go through a process of diminution, where the durations of the notes within the rhythmic pattern are reduced. Each one of the ostinatos is based on a different material: the ostinatos of violas and cellos are derived from the Miremis leitmotif, with the reiteration of major seconds in a way that recalls the juxtaposition of the black and white pitch collections; the ostinato of the basses contrasts by featuring the interval of minor second, a variant of the "Sigh Motif;" the brass produces bell-like reiterations of an ascending fourth between C and F, which recalls a diatonic pitch collection; and woodwinds and first violins reiterate fast ascending scales over a sequence of white and black notes, going to higher and higher registers.[24] The dialogue of the latter is combined with a stretto, where figures imitated between violins and woodwinds become gradually closer. The combination of densification, diminution, and stretto of contrasting materials produces a powerful drive that represents the struggle of the Amerindian girl trying to escape from the monster (Figure 7.32), which justifies the title "The Fight of Desire" for this section. All these voices combined constitute the background texture and are accompanied by a crescendo of twenty-five measures.

Figure 7.32. The coda of *Amazonas* starts at pppp dynamics, where various voices enter successively. The top three lines show a process of rhythmic intensification through diminution in some of the voices. The two lower lines (mm. 303–318) show a process of stretto that happens through imitation between violins and woodwinds. Combined within a gradual crescendo of 25 measures, this section represents the girl trying to escape from the monster and ends abruptly with a loud hit of the tam-tam on m. 320. Created by the author.

The processes of densification, diminution, and stretto, combined with the continuous crescendo, generate a cumulative build up that drives the music forward to a climax. This procedure is reminiscent of a long tradition started with Beethoven (see Figure 7.33). For example, the endings of the first movement of his last three symphonies include a basso ostinato that produces a motion from a low climax (*tiefpunkt*) to a high climax (*höhepunkt*).

Figure 7.33. Ostinato figures present at the end of the 1st movements of Beethoven's Symphonies 7, 8, and 9. The ones in Symphonies No. 7 and 9 in particular create hypnotic effects similar to the ostinato in Amazonas, due to the undulating chromatic nature of their construction.
Created by the author.

Within the powerful background setting described above, the foreground texture features "The Fight of Desire" through the interaction of the "Theme of the Amerindian Girl" with the "Theme of the Monster's Anxiety," ending climatically in a violent hit of the tam-tam sustained by a minor second (F—G-flat). The "Theme of the Amerindian Girl" enters at rehearsal thirty (m. 315) performed by trumpets and oboes in *ff* and the "Theme of the Monster's Anxiety" enters two measures later performed by tuba, contrabassoon and sarrusophone (Figure 7.34).

Figure 7.34. Foreground texture of "The Fight of Desire" section at the coda. The "Theme of the Amerindian Girl" (trumpets and oboes) is once again confronted with the "Theme of the Monster's Anxiety" (tuba, contrabassoon, and sarrusophone). The doubling in octaves of both themes has been omitted. The section ends at the lower edge of "The Abyss," where low instruments sustain a minor 2nd (F—G-Flat) in octaves under a violent hit of the tam-tam.
Created by the author.

The "Theme of the Monster's Anxiety" is polarized by F: It starts and ends on F—the axis located a minor third between the highest and lowest notes of the theme. The "Theme of the Amerindian Girl" is a variation of the main theme, conveying her struggle through deformation. It features

Figure 7.35. At the coda, the Miremis leitmotif suffers an important transfiguration metaphorically representing the Amerindian girl's struggle with the monster.
Created by the author.

the conflict between E and E-flat (enharmonic of D♯) fighting for predominance, as well as the conflict between the intervals of major (E/D) and minor (E-flat/D) second. This constitutes a major transfiguration of the Miremis leitmotif (Figure 7.35).

Instead of ending in a tritone like in the previous statements, the "Theme of the Amerindian Girl" ends on a minor second (indicated as y1 in Figure 7.34), reminiscent of the "Sigh Motif," and echoes a major third above (y2). This final motion is interrupted at the golden section of the Coda by a fermata on a tam-tam hit in *fff*, while the low wind instruments sustain a minor second F/G-flat on the low register of the texture. This minor second (plus octave) in the low register, located close to the golden section of the Coda,[25] represents the lower edge of "The Abyss."

As the sounds subside during the fermata, the previous complementary rhythm motion is retaken by the background texture for six and a half more measures, while the transfigured "Theme of the Amerindian Girl" is stated one last time. Here, the intensification of the processes leads to a voluptuous cluster of white versus black notes in tremolo legato Prestissimo, which represents the vastness of "The Abyss." In m. 330 the tremolo in crescendo bursts in a loud and short note at the high register of the texture, representing the top edge of "The Abyss" (Figure 7.36).

Figure 7.36. The black and white dichotomy is first expressed melodically through ascending scales, then harmonically as sound stains through tremolos legato between the black and white keys, and finally as a minor second (plus octave) performed harmonically between piccolo and E-flat clarinet at the edge of "The Precipice."
Created by the author.

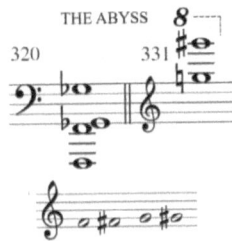

Figure 7.37. The upper and lower extremes of "The Abyss," and its musical material.
Created by the author.

In conclusion, the top and bottom edges of "The Abyss" are connected in the distance by two intervals of minor second (plus octave, shown in Figure 7.37).

The monster follows the girl to the edge of "The Precipice" through chromatically descending parallel chords by the brass and low woodwinds in m. 330. The initial cluster combines all the notes of the A-flat major scale, with A-flat as the top voice (trumpets in F) and D-flat on the lowest voice (contrabassoon and bass trombone). The descending motion of all the voices representing the monster is chromatic, with the exception of the lowest voice, which descends over an octatonic scale reaching the E at the bottom of the texture. This E represents the Amerindian girl (Figure 7.38). It is remarkable that the missing note in this octatonic scale (E-flat) is polarized by exclusion and will appear enharmonically as a D-sharp at the end of the piece.

Figure 7.38. The fff descending chromatic motion of the brass diving into the vacuum represents the monster following the girl into "The Abyss." The lowest voice is the only non-chromatic one: it is based on a descending octatonic pitch collection that ends on the E-natural, which represents the Amerindian girl. The remarkable absence of E-flat in the octatonic collection implies that this note is polarized by exclusion, appearing prominently as the last note of the piece, enharmonically spelled as D-sharp.
Created by the author.

The final gesture of *Amazonas* has been described in Figure 7.3. The descending motion into "The Precipice" occurs over a whole tone pentatonic pitch collection, where the G is missing (Figure 7.39). It is an original and bold descending motion in whole tones over a span that covers seven octaves—the full span of the orchestra range–from A7 down to D#1. The polarized by exclusion key center G is both an axis in the last chord of the piece (b) and the missing note in the pentatonic material of the descending line that antecedes it (a). In the piano version of *Amazonas*, it appears prominently as the top edge of "The Abyss," preceding the plunge into "The Precipice."

Figure 7.39. Ending of *Amazonas*, representing the plunge of the girl into the "abyss of her own desire," followed by the monster. The final tetrachord is analogous to the one found at the end of Le Sacre du Printemps (see Fig. 7.3a).
Created by the author.

It is interesting to note that, in the piano version of *Amazonas*, the notes on the downbeat of m. 331 (which represent the upper edge of *The Abyss*) are inverted. One can argue that it might have been "better" if Villa-Lobos had inverted the interval also in the orchestra score so as to make the G-natural appear as the top note. On the other hand, the A that initiates the descent into the precipice in the orchestra score is preceded by a G-sharp, which functions as a leading tone.

Figure 7.40. Comparison of orchestra and piano versions of the ending of *Amazonas*.
Created by the author.

Another remarkable feature can be observed in the macro-form. Both the recapitulation and the coda conclude with descending whole tone scales with a powerful drive forward. The whole-tone materials in both sections are complementary, producing an elegant sense of completion to the Part III of the composition (Figure 7.41).

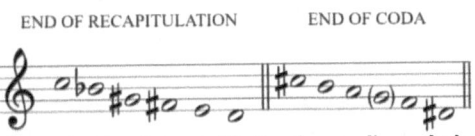

Figure 7.41. In part III, the descending whole tone materials at the end of the recapitulation (see Fig. VII-30) and the Coda (see Fig. VII-39) are complementary.
Created by the author.

Summarizing, in Part III of *Amazonas*, we observe a number of devices connecting its two sections, which provide a sense of unity and completion in the concluding portion of the piece. The recapitulation restates themes previously featured in Part I and introduces a new element through the monster that stands out, while the coda introduces an ostinato rhythm that is reminiscent of Part II. Therefore, Part III is a synthesis of Parts I and II.

Both sections in Part III are built over the confrontation of two themes: one representing the Amerindian girl and the other representing the monster's anxiety. Both display a powerful drive forward toward their endings, concluding with descending whole tone motions that plunge downward toward a note on the low register of the double basses. The recapitulation presents a semitone motion from F—representing the monster—toward E-natural, a note associated with the Amerindian girl. The Coda also presents a semitone motion, in this case from E—representing the Amerindian girl through its theme based on the Miremis leitmotif—toward D-sharp. The latter, which is the last note of the coda, is connected in the distance with the E, last note of the recapitulation. Therefore, the motion of a semitone is also present on a higher hierarchical level of the macroform, featuring the interval of minor second as a major constructive force, a "thesis" for the composition process that stands in contrast with the major second that characterizes the Miremis leitmotif in the microform.

The Metaphorical Power of *Amazonas*

The scenery of *Amazonas*, with the image of an Amerindian virgin bathing at dawn, symbolizes Brazilian nature and became identified with the rise of Brazil as a monumental nation. *Amazonas* became the embodiment of the natural essence of a country in search of its national identity, allowing Villa-Lobos to fulfill the dreams of an exotic nation, full of natural resources and potentialities.

Through anthropophagy Villa-Lobos built in *Amazonas* his personal cosmic world. The structure of the piece grows out of melodic cells in the same way that a rain forest germinates out of the seeds of individual plants. Differently from *Uirapuru*, where the use of leitmotif technique follows a more conventional approach, the leitmotif Miremis in *Amazonas* serves as a generating cell from which the main themes derive. The combination of this treatment of motivic development and the use of structural metaphors allows for the poetic content of the music to represent sonorous allegories of synesthetic nature.

> [The elements of Amazonas] appear like voices, sounds, noises, thuds, whirring sounds, symbols coming out of meteorological phenomena, of geological accidents and irrational beings. It is the rowdy impudence of the virgin land.[26]

Through metaphors, the music reaches other dimensions of perception, where sounds depict the most tangible ingredients of the environment. Villa-Lobos absorbed the visual and sonorous potential of nature and folk materials, discovering a new musical potentiality in the synesthetic relation of the senses. After the first performance of *Uirapuru* in the United States on February 12, 1945, the critic of the *New York Times* detected this unique feature by stating that "it may be said of Villa-Lobos's scoring that in places one scents as well as hears the forest, sees the play of light, is aware of the tropical night and its strange enchantment."[27]

In *Amazonas*, the metaphors reached an even more sophisticated level. For example, the depiction of the Amazonian waters encompasses not only the representation of their sound, but also their fluidity, their density, translucency, thickness, and color, translated musically through structural metaphors. They give a synesthetic dimension to the music, leading to a pure sensation of time and space within a new auditory universe of perception, very much in line with the revolutionary findings in science during the beginning of the twentieth century.

A New Conception of Musical Space

The conventional depiction of extra musical elements of the traditional tone poem (known as tone painting) is still present in *Amazonas*, through the wavelike motions of the woodwinds to represent the water in the section *Contemplation of the Amazon,* or the undulating chromatic motion of the flutes to depict the God of the Winds. Another type of pictorialism, one of symbolic nature, also permeates *Amazonas.* The themes derived from the Miremis leitmotif are associated with the Amerindian girl, and the way this theme is altered in different sections of the piece reflects how the girl interacts with the surrounding environment and the other elements of the story. For example, the final distortion of the theme shown in Figure 7.29 depicts a cry of terror. The religious realm of the *Prayer of the Amerindian Girl* (mm. 50–67), set over a "white" diatonic pitch collection, is distinguished from the profane or secular realm of the monsters, starting at rehearsal fourteen, which is set on a chromatic pitch collection encompassing the twelve notes of the octave. The realm associated with nature is expressed through harmonies or chords built in fourths or fifths (for example, strings in mm. 14–17), which is the basis of the diatonic system. The unusual use of string instruments performing arpeggios over the region between the bridge and string holder (see Figure 6.5 in chapter 6) evokes the magical realm of the *Dance for the Enchantment of the Forests* (mm. 70–97).

On top of these various manifestations of pictorialism, Villa-Lobos transcended the illustrative nature of the traditional tone poem through structural metaphors. While each layer of the texture is built independently, and its pitch contents or musical material might conflict with the materials of other layers, the multiple strata frequently interact with each other. A disturbance in one layer is reflected in the behavior of another layer. This was exemplified in detail in Figure 7.6. Such pictorialism or tone painting replaces the traditional idea of motivic development, a practice that goes beyond the romantic tradition of illustrating through sounds something outside of the sphere of absolute music. Through structural metaphors, the music becomes more visual than ever. The interaction of sounds doesn't happen only at the polyphonic level, but also thorough the interaction of the musical figures on the page. The intervention of certain figurations in one layer of the score can impact the behavior of the main melodic line in another layer, making the music more palpable, visual, and concrete.

The final result is a "spatialization" of sound, in an art that is traditionally regarded as unidimensional, an art that unfolds in time. Musical notation becomes not only the representation of sound, but an illustration of something happening outside of the sonorous realm, or in other words, the musical notes represent images as much as they represent sounds. The score becomes more conscious of its semiotic nature, in its ability to defy the conventions of the graphic representation of sound, almost as if the notes on the page were yelling at us: "I am not a sound!" In his poetic expression,

Figure 7.42. *The Treachery of Images (This is not a pipe)* by Rene Magritte, 1928–1929, same year of the premiere of Villa-Lobos' *Amazonas* (1929).
Digital Image © 2021 Museum Associates / LACMA / Art Resource, NY. © 2022 C. Herscovici / Artists Rights Society (ARS), New York

Villa-Lobos works with timbres, textures, metaphors, and their interaction in the architecture of the musical form, a process in line with the questionings about the ability of graphic representation in painting exemplified in Magritte's *The Treachery of Images* (Figure 7.42).

It is known that in painting these questionings led to the elimination of perspective, first through an emphasis in the two-dimensionality of the canvas, and ultimately into abstractionism, which was a reaction against the artificiality of representation. This new spatial conceptualization of sound in *Amazonas* brings a synesthetic condition where sound and image are amalgamated. It allows for Villa-Lobos's style to develop in parallel with the breakthrough achievements in the visual arts, which will be addressed in more depth in chapter 8. It also hints at one of the theses of this text, namely, that the aesthetic innovations of Villa-Lobos display a prevalence of surrealist elements.

A New Conception of Time

Most of the listeners at the time were struck by the rhythm in *The Rite of Spring*, considered the great novelty Stravinsky brought to modernism in music. Critics even commented that Stravinsky had sacrificed melody and harmony on behalf of rhythm. Today, we know that to a great extent the rhythmic novelties of *The Rite* are heavily indebted to folk music. Bartok observed: "Even the origin of the rough-grained, brittle and jerky musical structure backed by ostinatos, which is so completely different from any structural proceeding of the past, may be sought in the short-breathed Russian peasant motives."[28]

Villa-Lobos did not use jolting asymmetrical rhythms like Stravinsky. They are not typical of Brazilian folk music, but other devices such as syncopations, hemiolas, and asymmetrical subdivisions of the beat are abundant and bring a modernist tinge to the music. These devices are usually present in multiple layers of texture, sometimes in counterpoint with Amerindian-derived themes, providing richness and contrast. For Villa-Lobos, it is not the rhythm but the texture that has a primordial role in the construction of the music, to an extent that it became common place among musicologists to focus their analysis in the behavior of the textures within the music.

Villa-Lobos also brought another major contribution to Modernism that is not as apparent as his manipulation of textures. It is the way he reconceptualized the meaning of time in music, something he achieved with particular force in *Amazonas*. He accomplished this through two main approaches. The first one is the use of ostinatos, which like in *Le Sacre* brings a primitive touch to the music. Villa-Lobos's ostinatos feature the repetition of simple melodies or motifs of small range, creating a ritualistic ambience through music that is simultaneously repetitive, static, and visceral.

Within the context of the program, ostinatos represent music that is atemporal, like the myths and legends associated with the conception of the work. They recall the idea of the "eternal return," conceived by Mircea Eliade,[29] for whom the primitive man associates all nature, words, and activities with some kind of sacred meaning. For the primitive man, almost everything is embedded with religious significance: a virgin consecrated by the gods, the eternal river currents, the invocation of the sun-god, and the natural elements (wind, water, and light, the latter represented by the sun). Critics saw in Amazonas a gestating world, "music that reflects the cosmic instability of the first days of creation,"[30] hence, the presence of the God of the Winds, of the waters, the monsters, the bathing ritual and its invocation of the sun, and others. These are all manifestations of the sacred, called hierophanies. Through them, the elements of nature become sacred manifestations, symbols of something else.

When this happens, the sequential chronology of historical time is substituted by the recurrence of a sacred, atemporal time, perpetuated in the circular return to "the conditions of the world in which the sacred originally appeared."[31] Villa-Lobos's ostinatos metaphorically represent the ritual, the reenactment of the myths, where the transformation of profane time—that inexorable motion through the arrow of time—into a sacred atemporal time takes place.

> [The ostinato] evokes abstract concepts about primitive populations, such as technical simplicity, ritual repetition, and the construction of music not due to melodic or harmonic interest, but because of the experience of time dilation in its counterpart: its reduction to short cycles with little or no short-term changes.[32]

In *The Rite of Spring*, the two main hierophanies are related with the consecration of space (the earth, which ends the first part with the ritual of the "Kiss of the Earth") and time (represented by the asymmetrical ostinato of the *Dance Sacrale*, leading into the sacrifice of the "chosen one"). They translate the reenactment of the ritual of eternal return preconized by Eliade into sacred time. In *Amazonas*, the atemporal universe surrounding the river is confronted with the profane world of the region of the monsters. When the God of the Winds—a manifestation of hierophanized nature—takes the scent of the virgin to the region of the monsters, a hierophany is produced through the ostinato march that ritualizes this sphere, bringing it to a sacred realm. It is within this realm that the virgin is confronted with the monster, who comes from a chaotic and profane world, and ends with the Amerindian virgin plunging into "the abyss of her own desire."

The second method Villa-Lobos uses to re-conceptualize time is through an original approach toward the musical form as a process. In the evolution of the symphonic poem, Liszt first introduced the concept of the cyclic form when translating a poem into music. Debussy is credited with revolutionizing musical form by rejecting the formal practices of romanticism in works such as his *Prelude to the Afternoon of a Faun*, which translated symbolist poetry into an elusive ternary form.[33] It was Debussy who said that the duty of modern composers was to "find the symphonic formulae best suited to the audacious discoveries of our modern times."[34]

Villa-Lobos's formula was through his rejection of the sonata principle and a new attitude toward the idea of restatement and recapitulation in the rondo form, by giving new meaning to the leitmotif. Instead of a recurring leitmotif throughout the piece, each new appearance of the theme is at the same time derived from the Miremis leitmotif and imbued with a new meaning. While the provenance from the Miremis leitmotif in the gestation of each theme is easily recognizable, each new appearance of Section A does not have any more the function of a ritornello or recapitulation of Section A but constitutes a break in the linearity of narrative. This circular and evolutionary return to the beginning can arguably be conceived as an inversion of the arrow of time.

It is important to remember that "for the native indigenous culture, 'music' is not something discreet and distinct from the ritual, from the performance, or from cosmology. We are the ones who have the category 'music,' with which we categorize what the other [the native] does."[35] In other words, if music itself is a hierophany, a manifestation of the sacred, Villa-Lobos treated musical form as a dynamic, constructive process. In doing so, the idea of a circular return is expressed in *Amazonas* both through the use of ostinatos and through the recurrent return of the Miremis leitmotif within the rondo form, a new conceptualization of time in music.

While in *Uirapuru* Villa-Lobos built a bridge between Wagner and Debussy, in *Amazonas* he engendered the compatibility of Wagner's Romanticism and Stravinsky's Primitivism, two apparently contradictory aesthetics. All the elements addressed above contribute to a new assessment of Villa-Lobos and his place within the development of music in the modern era, which will be addressed in the last chapters.

Notes

1. https://youtu.be/pZdSqD1vfB0.
2. https://youtu.be/yOqu-zlY7AY. This is the first recording of the piece, interpreted by Francisco de Morais Alves and arranged by Radamés Gnattali.
3. Sérgio Cabral, *No Tempo de Ari Barroso*, 185.
4. Mário de Andrade, for example, stated that Villa-Lobos's head was "full of poorly digested learnings, with huge flaws in his training." FláviaToni, "Mário de Andrade e Villa-Lobos," 57. José Maria Neves wrote that Villa-Lobos's major works have mixed quality and are not elaborated using methods of traditional composition technique. Neves, *Villa-Lobos, o choro*, 25.
5. Paulo de Tarso Salles, "Villa-Lobos: Desafiando a Teoria e Análise," 81
6. Ewen, *American Composers Today*, 252–53.
7. Menezes, *Apoteose*, 84. The abundant presence of this chord in many of Webern's compositions made the author characterize it as the first Webernian archetype. For more details, see Appendix 2.
8. Schoenberg, *Structural Functions of Harmony*, 44–50. See glossary of terms.
9. Menezes, *Apoteose*, 74.
10. Isis de Oliveira, "The Structural Metaphors in *Amazonas*," 235.

11. See Salles, *Villa-Lobos*, 190. The tetrachords are notated according to Forte's classification (Forte, *The Structure of Atonal Music*). The analysis of this section that follows comes from Paulo de Tarso Salles's text mentioned above. The manipulation of intervals that break and reconfigure symmetries has already been observed in the thematic analysis of the "Theme of the Uirapuru" in chapter 4.

12. Terminology borrowed from Isis de Oliveira, "The Structural Metaphors in *Amazonas*," 233–34.

13. Salles, *Villa-Lobos: Processos Composicionais*, 37–38.

14. Ibid., 192.

15. It is important to understand the notation for the harmonics: the ones for the viola d'amore correspond to the sounding pitches. The harmonics of the cellos correspond to the fingering positions to perform the harmonics, so the actual sounding pitches are: C–G–D–F-sharp–A–C-sharp.

16. As a reminder, the terminology is used within the context of an expanded conception of tonality.

17. Considering that *Amazonas* has 333 measures, the golden section appears close to m. 127.

18. The chords in the Sacrificial Dance are transposed recurrences of the famous "Augurs chord," which according to Stravinsky was the foundation of the whole ballet *The Rite of Spring*. Due to its ambiguity, this chord became a radical moment in music history. See Daniel Chua, "Rioting with Stravinsky," 59–109.

19. This is another important similarity between *Amazonas* and *Uirapuru*. In the latter, a *cantus firmus* in augmentation appears close to the golden section of the most contrasting section of the rondo form of the piece (see analysis of Part II of *Uirapuru* in chapter 4). In *Amazonas*, the theme in augmentation also appears relatively close to the golden section of the most contrasting section of its rondo form.

20. Considering that section D has 174 measures, the golden mean is close to m. 216, exactly where the section called *Happiness of the Young Amerindian Girl* starts.

21. Based on the current analysis, one can detect that there were note mistakes in the manuscript score (string parts) that were transferred to the published editions (both the Max Eschig edition and the critical edition published by the Brazilian Academy of Music).

22. The performance of *Amazonas* works better with the availability of basses with five strings, to allow the low E to be performed on an open string and the final D-sharp at the end of the piece to be performed on the fifth string.

23. This same idea also appears in a different context on *Uirapuru* (Fig. 5.11).

24. The imitation of rapid scales over the white vs. black keys between violins and woodwinds is derivative of the *Polichinelo* chord. When brought to this section of *Amazonas*, it emphasizes the latent interval of minor second fighting for predominance at the end of the piece.

25. Considering that the coda has thirty-nine measures, the golden section is located slightly before m. 320, where the tam-tam hit indicating the low part of the abyss is located.

26. Mário de Andrade from "Música, doce Música," as quoted in Neves, *Villa-Lobos, o choro*, 86, and translated by Béhague, *Villa-Lobos: The Search*, 57–58.
27. Downes, "Villa-Lobos Guest at the City Center," 21.
28. Quoted in Richard Taruskin, "Bartok and Stravinsky," para. 6.
29. Eliade, *The Myth of the Eternal Return*.
30. França, *A música no Brasil*, 34.
31. Eliade, *The Encyclopedia of Religion*, 315.
32. Moreira, "O Elemento Indígena na Obra de Villa-Lobos," 204. Another important study about the use of rhythmic ostinatos as a defining characteristic of primitivism found in Villa-Lobos's music appears in Guilherme Bernstein, *Sobre Poética e Forma em Villa-Lobos: Primitivismo e Estrutura nos Choros Orquestrais* (Curitiba: Editora Prismas, 2015).
33. Brown, "Tonality and Form," 143.
34. Debussy, *Monsieur Croche*, 241, and *Debussy on Music*, 297.
35. Waizbort, "Villa-Lobos e seus Índios," 143.

CHAPTER EIGHT

Toward a New Assessment of Villa-Lobos

Papai Adão, papai Adão
Papai Adão já foi o tal. —Armando Cavalcanti and Klécius Caldas

Eva, me leva
Pro paraíso agora. —Haroldo de Campos and Milton de Oliveira

The carnivalization of biblical themes was a frequent theme of the carnival marches. The carnival song *Papai Adão* (Father Adam)[1] by Armando Cavalcanti (1914–1964) and Klécius Caldas (1919–2002) was one of the big hits of the carnival in Rio in 1951. The lyrics state: "Father Adam, father Adam, father Adam once was the top. Today it is Eve who maneuvers thanks to the serpent. A vine leaf, an Eve with poor judgment, a treacherous snake, and paradise was gone!" The humorous lyrics comment on female supremacy, giving a subliminal nod to Oswald de Andrade's exaltation of matriarchy.

One year after *Papai Adão*, themes from the book of Genesis returned again to carnival, this time by the renowned duo of composers Haroldo Lobo and Milton de Oliveira. The first stanza of the carnival march "Eva" (Eve, 1952)[2] translates as follows: "Eve, take me now to paradise. If I have too many clothes, I throw the clothes away." It conveys the typical carnival debauchery, with another nod to Oswald de Andrade in its praise of the nakedness of the primitive. Songs about Adam and Eve have appeared in great number in the carnival of Rio de Janeiro since the 1930s.

The birth of Heitor Villa-Lobos in Brazil coincided with the modernist explosion that started in Europe during the *Belle Époque*.[3] The main characteristic of modernism was the concerted attempt to make art progressive—"modern"—and achieve this through a break with tradition. While a number of artists insisted that their works were an extension of previous trends in art,[4] there is no question that modernism caused a rupture with the most established traditions rooted in Western culture. Art is a powerful tool that allows us to connect with our inner and external realities, and the beginning of the twentieth century is perhaps the most eventful period in the history of art, a time when the avant-garde of the arts and sciences changed forever the way we comprehend the world. The multiplicity of trends in the arts has been labeled with a variety of "isms"—impressionism, expressionism, fauvism, Dadaism, surrealism, futurism, cubism, and many others. Every movement had its visionary artists who inspired generation after generation, leaving an important legacy. The innovations promoted by these artists found their correspondence in the revolutionary discoveries in sciences, redefining the paradigms according to which we perceive the world.

The beginning of the twentieth century coincided with a complete revision of the Western notions of reality through new conceptualizations of time, space, matter, energy, and light, the elemental coordinates that defined reality for the modern man. In the sciences, it led to a rupture with the notion of reality as perceived by an observer in a privileged position, the Galilean idea of the existence of inertial frames of reference in time and space. In human thought, the rules of conventional logic of the empirical method, where phenomena were understood as products of the laws of cause and effect, were questioned. The multiple manifestations of modernism in art were products of an evolution present in all fields of knowledge, which produced a profound impact on the way Western civilization perceived "truth." It also allowed a dialogue among the various forms of artistic expression, opening the possibilities for dramatic works to become musical, music to become visual, and literature to become sculptural, promoting a full entanglement of the arts. Ultimately, modernism in the arts and the revolutionary discoveries in the sciences produced a new conceptualization of the universe, reaching a point where science revealed the counterintuitive way the universe functions and became practically incomprehensible to us. Art became more and more divorced from audiences, producing literary works that were set free from syntax, visual artworks without images, and music without sounds, centered on noises, all of this paving the way for abstractionism.

The most influential achievement in the visual arts of the time, the one that became a common ground to all the different styles that emanated from modernism, was the violation of perspective, that monumental discovery in painting that dominated Western visual arts from the fifteenth to the twentieth century. Ultimately, the reactions against linear perspective by the multiple styles in the beginning of the twentieth century tacitly eroded Euclid's notion of space, which was reflected in the system of single-point perspective. Most of the visual arts movements introduced the idea that a painting can have multiple points of view, a major departure from established tradition. This idea of multiple points of reference found its correspondence in music, through musical styles that rejected the notion of tonality as defined in the musical practice of previous centuries. In the same way that the visual arts broke with the notion of single point perspective, music broke with the notion of a home key around which all the other keys gravitate, and composers found different ways to approach tonality. In doing so, they found inspiration in the arts of cultures that were divorced from Western European traditions, such as the early cultures that preceded ancient Greece, the previously unexplored cultures from the East, the world of dreams and inner psyche explored by Freud, the spontaneity of the naïf art of children, the ritualistic art of Africa and Oceania, and others.

Within this apparent chaos, it was the visionary artist and the revolutionary scientist who led the path to the future, producing wide-scale and far-reaching transformations in Western society. Artists from the Anthropophagy movement in Brazil cannibalized not one, but several aesthetical European styles. They assimilated those styles while at the same time incorporating elements from the syncretic Brazilian culture, producing artworks impregnated of profound expressive meaning and whose originality rested in the cohesion of those multiple influences, internal and external. As the most emblematic representative of the anthropophagic aesthetics in music, Villa-Lobos produced works that synthesized fundamental artistic findings, making him a pivotal figure within the modernist movement.

Villa-Lobos, the Visionary Romantic

Considering that the major aesthetic movements associated with modernism and the breakthrough discoveries in sciences during the beginning of the twentieth century happened in Western Europe, the eruption of a modernist language in Villa-Lobos is almost a mystery. He practically learned on his own the techniques of multiple European composers—Wagner, Debussy, Stravinsky, and others—combining apparently incompatible styles with his personal findings.[5] He assimilated those techniques by devouring and regurgitating them into his own soundscape in such a way that the sonorous result guards an elusive connection with the original sources.

This anthropophagic assimilation is highly original and intuitive. The resultant exoticism is sophisticated and seductive, causing misunderstanding among scholars and critics, many of whom viewed the composer's pioneering achievements as derivative, as demonstrated by the reception of *Uirapuru* when it was presented for the first time in 1945 to the North American audience:

> Critics found *Uirapurú* pleasing enough, with Downes detecting "outbursts of sensuous song." Paul Bowles, one of Thomson's composer-hires at the *Tribune*, noted a "nineteenth-century predilection for musical picture making" and, invoking one of his boss's least favorite composers, labeled Villa-Lobos "a southern Sibelius." In sum, *Uirapurú* was no more and no less than a piece of "color music," as Bowles called it: ingratiating but conventional, its sanitized jungle raising none of the vexing questions associated with Caliban's domain.[6]

Villa-Lobos has since been characterized as a tropical impressionist, a view that has persisted into twenty-first-century critique:

> In the earlier works the influences are clear to see. *Uirapurú*, a depiction of a rare Amazonian bird of blazing colours in its version for full orchestra, sounds as if Villa-Lobos had just rushed home after hearing Stravinsky's *The Rite of Spring* for the first time and copied down as much of it as he could remember.[7]

Such statements either corroborate the controversy surrounding the genesis of the modernist language of Villa-Lobos or can be traced back to discrimination against a composer from outside of the European circle. The influence of *The Rite of Spring* over generations of composers until our days became almost common place, to an extent that anything modern is traced back to it. Not even Stravinsky became immune to this preconceived attitude.[8]

Since pioneering achievements add value to artistic work and leverage recognition to the composer in terms of originality, the genesis of modernism in Villa-Lobos becomes a controversial subject, difficult to elucidate in the midst of his personal statements vis-à-vis the writings of his promoters and historians.[9] The nationalist features of his music, for example, have been used both to promote it and to encapsulate his achievements within the frame of an "exotic folklorist." Villa-Lobos's nationalism is a form of conscientious self-expression traced back to his roots, but not necessarily localized due to the vastness of the country's territory.

> Yes, I am Brazilian and very Brazilian. The rivers and the seas of this great Brazil sing through my music. I do not put brakes or restraints, nor suppress the tropical exuberance of our forests and our skies, to be instinctively incorporated into everything I write.[10]

The nationalism evident in compositions such as *Amazonas* and *Uirapuru* is not a result of the incorporation of folk motifs. It is related with the descriptive qualities of the landscape, because at the time, it was the landscape that constituted the embodiment of the national identity of Brazil. Villa-Lobos incorporates in his representation of the landscape some of the most important ingredients of nature: the sounds of the forest, its animals, insects, and monsters; the Amerindian inhabitants; and the sunrise as representation of the potentialities of a young nation. This feature can be used as one of the arguments concerning the incidence of surrealism in Villa-Lobos's music: the *deterritorialized* aspect, which associates the music with the mythological nature of the collective unconscious of the nation.[11]

As Wisnik has noted, the musical representation that is found responded to the needs of the society to represent the image of a nature abundant with resources, making evident the huge potentialities of the nation, and projecting a positive vision of the possibilities for the future. This "grandiose and eloquent view of Brazil" was embodied by the sound masses created by Villa-Lobos, in which "the indulgence of sound effects motivates and engages the internal language of his music, its dissonant harmonies, multiform rhythms, varied timbres, and expansive melodies. The fortissimos do not convey tension but overflowing energy, and surplus of youthfulness."[12] In short, what is found is an idealization of the expectations still present in the collective mindset of a country that continues to struggle to realize its potential in order to achieve grandeur—an image that has yet to be realized. We can say that instead of reflecting the country in his music, Villa-Lobos pioneered the creation of a national musical image of Brazil that corresponded to the demands of society. His grandiloquent language, with masses of sound and juxtaposition of textures, was the embodiment of the aspirations of the nation. Through the exaltation of its nature, Brazil could boast its potentialities against the traditional culture of the European colonizers and the technological prowess of North America.

Yet Villa-Lobos never abandoned the expressive quality of his music, which is ever present even in his most dissonant and complex compositions. This seemed unforgivable to a twentieth-century avant-garde more interested in cerebral experiments, which took classical music through paths that gradually drifted further away from the audience. The visceral quality of Villa-Lobos's compositions and their ability to elicit emotions remained ever present in all the phases of his career:

> Brazil has the geometrical shape of a heart. Every Brazilian has this heart. Music goes from one soul to another. Birds talk through music. They have hearts. Everything we feel, is felt through our hearts. The heart is the metronome of life, and a lot of people forget that. . . . If someone could put a metronome on the top of the Earth, maybe we would be closer to peace.[13]

According to Alex Ross, among twentieth-century composers most influenced by *The Rite of Spring* is Stravinsky's near-contemporary, Edgard Varèse, who had attended the 1913 premiere: "[Varèse] was particularly drawn to the 'cruel harmonies and stimulating rhythms' of *The Rite*, which he employed to full effect in his concert work *Amériques* (1921), scored for a massive orchestra with added sound effects including a lion's roar and a wailing siren."[14] The revised version of *Amériques* was premiered together with *Amazonas* in 1929 in Paris. When Varèse asked Villa-Lobos's opinion about *Amériques*, Villa-Lobos reluctantly said that to him the piece sounded like a "block of sonorities." Later on, he told his wife that he thought this sort of modern music "meant absolutely nothing to him."[15] Boulez vehemently criticized composers who imitated Stravinsky in the use of innovative devices in order to sound modern. Villa-Lobos's aesthetic position, however, reveals lucidity both in terms of technical originality and poetic content:

> I have not and will not assume any position or attitude toward recent trends and techniques of music; I think that, if my works were studied profoundly and seriously, one would realize that I have a very personal and different style from the others. I admire any art innovation, but I criticize and condemn that which does not take into consideration the logical laws of humanity.[16]

Villa-Lobos attempted to build Brazil under the form of a sonorous image that could be identified with the society of the country. This was achieved by turning the social imaginary into a stereotype, a musical language with a symbolism of images that attempt to contemplate the pluralistic universe of the country and translate it into music. In doing so, Villa-Lobos brought an external reality into his works under the form of semiotic symbols that represented myths, nature, and social characters, allowing audiences to identify some of the elements present in his discourse as folk elements.[17]

Ultimately, the romanticism of Villa-Lobos can be traced back as one of the dimensions of the anthropophagic impulse, the magic of human existence,[18] and the conviction that intuition and mysticism helps creativity to navigate among the stars.[19]

Villa-Lobos, the Visionary Primitive

The discovery of non-Euclidean geometry threw into question the traditional conventions of perspective in the visual arts and suggested the existence of multiple dimensions, as well as other perspectives in which reality would look very different.[20] This brought into question the thoughts that have served as the foundation for the development of logic and sciences for our civilization for over two thousand years, where Euclid's *Elements* had been considered the most successful and influential textbook ever written. Primitivism became one of the most compelling and influential artistic responses to this new conception of reality. Artists intuitively understood that primitive art had the ability to grasp a new formulation of time, space, matter, and energy. Gradually their artworks started to incorporate the absence of linear perspective, the use of simple outlines, emotional distortions of figures, symbolic signs such as hieroglyphs, and energetic rhythms resulting from the use of repetitive ornamental patterns.

Wisnik posited that the constructive forces of Brazilian modernism lie in the tension between futurism and primitivism, understood as the adoption of cosmopolitan techniques concomitant with the representation of a magical and savage world. This happened within a cultural context divided between the eagerness to accompany the modernity of the Second Industrial Revolution—a role assumed by the vibrant futurism—and the realization that the Brazilian roots, in particular the ones of indigenous and African descent, demanded a primitivist aesthetic treatment.[21] The Anthropophagy movement became the prevailing model in Brazil, being conceptualized from the standpoint of the primitive Amerindian who coexisted with the modern artist in the same historical moment, which did not prevent the African element from also being incorporated under the form of endocannibalism.[22]

Composers such as Stravinsky and Villa-Lobos used folklore as generative stimulus, rather than as an aesthetic goal. Villa-Lobos did not use quotation in *Amazonas* or *Uirapuru*, and even our now widespread knowledge of Stravinsky's use of folk music during his Russian period should be understood under the prism of the abandonment of quotation as a constructive principle. Both composers "distilled the folk melodies into mosaic-like components and redeployed them in an imaginary ritual drawn from 'first times.'"[23] They represent instances where the use of folklore reflects a search for truth without authenticity. The most influential composers in the beginning of the twentieth century used folk themes and the popular music of their countries to extract from them the possibility of a total emancipation from the tonal system hegemony. Like Stravinsky's, Villa-Lobos's primitivism carries the powerful raw expression of music emanating from nature prior to the arrival of culture.[24]

Villa-Lobos's abandon of the sonata principles did not lead to a rhapsodic treatment of the themes, but to a treatment more in line with the modernist aesthetic: In the macroform he displayed a predilection for structures of contrasting sections, such as rondo; in the microform, the individual sections were formed by juxtapositions of contrasting textures, where divergent or complementary elements coexisted. Villa-Lobos's contributions should not remain at the periphery of the modernist movement. His profound connection with modernism propelled him to use polytonal and atonal combinations, polyrhythms and instrumental novelties, together with a primitivist aesthetic treatment of the subject themes, particularly when representing the Amerindian.

As part of the process that led to a new conception of reality, the paradigm shift that caused the collapse of Euclidean geometry in science and the Renaissance perspective in art brought a common element in practically all the areas, ranging from the arts to sciences and philosophy—an attempt to unify and integrate the various fields of knowledge. From Wittgenstein's attempt to codify all knowledge into a single standard language of science,[25] to Einstein's search for a unified theory that integrates relativity and quantum mechanics, the world celebrated the pioneering achievements of artists, scientists, and philosophers. This integrative process allowed a dialogue among the arts, where literature could be imbued with a sculptural quality,[26] music became more visual, and the visual arts became more dramatic through the incorporation of motion.[27] One of the revolutionary aspects of Villa-Lobos that became evident in this study is the synesthetic nature of his music, which brings a spatial element to the time-related nature of an art that unfolds in time.[28] This can be considered another expression of the attempt of unification mentioned above, a parallel to Einstein's definition of the spacetime continuum.

In the beginning of the twentieth century, a preoccupation with the nature of time became one of the most researched subjects in science, art, and philosophy. This had particular ramifications for music, which is an art that unfolds in time. It found contrasting interpretations in the works of two prominent thinkers who received the Nobel prize half a dozen years apart: Albert Einstein in physics (1921) and Henri Bergson in literature (1927). The role of duration and simultaneity was central to the findings of both of them. For Bergson,

If everything is in time, everything changes inwardly, and the same concrete reality never recurs. Repetition is therefore possible only in the abstract: what is repeated is some aspect that our senses, and specially our intellect, have singled out from reality, just because our action, upon which all the effort of our intellect is directed, can move only among repetitions. Thus, concentrated on that which repeats, solely preoccupied in welding the same to the same, intellect turns away from the vision of time. It dislikes what is fluid, and solidifies everything that it touches. We do not *think* real time. But we *live* it, because life transcends intellect.[29]

For Bergson, reality becomes what we experience as the global sum of a continuous flow of sensations. Duration is a "dynamic process that permits us to reflect all at once—simultaneously—on the inner unconscious experience that constitutes our memory."[30] Our intellect is subordinated ("a contraction") of a greater power, the vague intuition that is exercised in the deep unconsciousness. Therefore, the experience of time as "duration" can best be understood through intuition and not through a mathematical rendition of chronological time. "Bergson denied to science any possibility of understanding of the physical reality, because scientific symbols and units, as intellectual constructs, are not reflective of the continuous manner in which the individual experiences time."[31]

While it is in the domain of artists to illuminate, imitate, and interpret their surrounding world, revolutionary artists are those who are able to intuitively anticipate the major changes in paradigms of society. Artists intuited the major discoveries in the beginning of the twentieth century through multiple interpretations. More than any time before, revolutionary artists were praised for their pioneering achievements, since "the essence of the *avant-garde* myth is that the artist is a precursor; the truly significant work of art is the one that prepares the future."[32] In this context, Villa-Lobos contributions are reexamined below.

Villa-Lobos, the Naif

One of the most important characteristics of the child's world is the non-linearity of time, where causality's laws of sequence from the Age of Reason are violated:

> In the child's magical worldview, the subjective act of wishing can effect changes in the objective world of "out there." Einstein's conception of relativity and the later notion of quantum mechanics confirmed that the observation and thoughts of the observer enter into the calculations and measurements

of the "real world." Children at play, artists at work, and scientists measuring quantum effects share this in common: they are all creating reality.[33]

One of the early departures from traditional Renaissance perspective was naïve art, characterized by its simplicity and spontaneity of expression. In the visual arts, it was characterized by a recurrent use of pattern combined with an unrefined use color and composition plan in a flat surface, where the effects of perspective are erroneous when present at all. The importance of naïve art has been recognized by major artists. Van Gogh stated that "a child in the cradle has the infinite in its eye,"[34] and Picasso expressed a similar thought: "It took me four years to paint like Raphael, but a lifetime to paint like a child."[35] Composers such a Debussy with his *Children's Corner Suite* or Bartok with *Mikrokosmos* approached, in their own way, the world of the child.

The quotation of nursery songs in the suites, *A Prole do Bebê*, and other works of the same nature constitutes a different expression of primitivism, one that depicts interior emotional realities. Villa-Lobos drew a parallel between the mentality of the child and the mentality of the primitive man. "In the case of educating primitive man, the missionaries utilized elements of native folk music already linked to his social and religious life. Similarly, it is best to base the child's first musical instruction on folk songs he already knows."[36] However, *A Prole do Bebê* is not music for children or young musicians, such as Bartok's *Mikrokosmos*. It is music that brings the simplicity of children's tunes into a modern, sophisticated, and virtuosic sphere, like *Children's Corner* by Debussy. It is music that brings the artist closer to an instinctive perception of the world without intellectual restraints, a sort of naïf-imbued self-consciousness. The quotation of a children's round dance within a perpetuum mobile setting in *Polichinelo*, for example, can be regarded as an expression of the nonlinear time associated with the world of the child.

Villa-Lobos, the Cannibal Primitive

As a reaction against idealized classical forms, one of the types of primitivism referred to a return to more distant origins of expression, prior to the beginning of recorded Western culture inherited from the ancient Greek civilization through the findings of Euclid. When confronted with the Amerindian, the Western European found "the ultimate other," someone who performed the worst possible conceived form of barbarism: the eating of human flesh. In attempting to grasp such heresy, one of the strategies was to place the Amerindian within a more familiar context, creating a role reversal. For example, in 1542 the Spanish explorer Francisco de Orellana conducted the first expedition to the northern region of Brazil. As his expedition navigated the waters of the river on its way to the Atlantic Ocean, they battled warrior women who commanded a large group of Amerindians. The natives succeeded in chasing away the Spaniards. Orellana ironically immortalized the river by naming it after the warrior women of Greek mythology: the amazons. This explains not only the origins of the name of the river, but also unusual connections that appeared throughout the years.

A curious association concerns Stravinsky's *The Rite of Spring*, the most emblematic work in the orchestra literature to display a primitivist aesthetic. It played the same seminal role in music that Picasso's *Les Demoiselles D'Avignon* had in the visual arts. As a catalyst of the avant-garde, *The Rite* became the most influential composition of the century, and Boulez summed up its importance: "This ritual of 'Pagan Russia' attains a dimension quite beyond its point of departure; it has become the ritual—and the myth—of modern music."[37] It seems paradoxical that for the Parisian public the choreography and costumes of *The Rite of Spring*, with "the use of headbanded, bent, and stamping figures performing line and circle dances," as well as the bearskins, the embroidery decoration analogous to beadwork, and the percussive nature of the music appeared as "clearly redolent of early cowboy and Indian movies."[38] These features reflect a Russian and Western European fascination with Amerindian culture, which brings to *The Rite of Spring* a subliminal relation with the primitivism of *Amazonas*.[39]

Figure 8.1. Costuming and choreography from the ballet the *Rite of Spring* (1913).

The Brazilian primitivism advocated by the Anthropophagic Manifesto had many characteristics in common with the primitivism developed by European artists, above all in its praise of a social system in harmony with nature and the rest of the planet. The concept of the primitive is that of a person who has achieved wisdom by engaging with concrete and natural phenomena, instead of resorting to means of communication and experiences that are artificially created and, therefore, are superfluous and artificial. Yet, the main feature that differentiated Brazilian primitivism from the European is that Brazilian artists positioned themselves as *mestizos* living among the primitive people, rather than expressing a nostalgic feeling for a paradise lost in the distant past (European primitivism of the prehistoric civilizations) or in a distant place (European primitivism concerning the civilizations of Africa or Oceania). In order to see themselves as primitive, all Brazilian artists needed to do was look into their own backyard.

The Anthropophagous Manifesto does not look into cannibalism as an exclusive Amerindian practice. For them, the European also practiced cannibalism, under the form of the eucharist ritual, where Christ's body and blood are transubstantiated into bread and wine so as to be consumed by the believers. However, this type of cannibalism is considered low and negative, because "when speculative, it creates science. It takes detours and moves around. We arrived at degradation. The low anthropophagy clustered in the sins of catechism—envy, usury, slander, murder. We are acting against this plague of the supposedly cultured and Christianized peoples."[40] The text of the Anthropophagous Manifesto invokes the French Renaissance philosopher Michel de Montaigne, who stated that civilized cultures often participated in more barbaric acts than primitive cultures. Cannibalism is, therefore, a universal law, "The only law in the world. Masked expression of all individualisms, all collectivisms. Of all religions. Of all peace treaties."[41]

The nationalism of the Brazilian primitivism is implied in the idea that the primitive person is more authentic than one who has been culturally assimilated through colonialism. They praise the naturalism of the primitive who lives in harmony with nature, believes in the stars, and is against the dogmatic European ideas that subjugated and destroyed nature. The Marxist influence on Oswald de Andrade made him embrace the need for a revolution to achieve the goal of independence from colonialism. "Our independence has not yet been proclaimed . . . reality without complexes, without madness, without prostitutions and without penitentiaries in the matriarchy of Pindorama."[42] Despite becoming politically independent from Portugal, according to the Anthropophagous Manifesto, Brazil remained a culturally assimilated colony. However, the indigenous population remained coherent in their politics of distribution of goods in contraposition to the "civilized" political systems, with their migration movements in opposition to urban sclerosis, and with their disdain for speculative sciences and objectified ideas, symbolically represented in the Anthropophagous Manifesto by the study and categorization of plants in Botany or the study in conservatories.

Brazilian primitivism favored tribal mysticism instead of European monotheism by positioning against the dogmatism of the Catholic religion predominant in the country, since Brazil is the largest Catholic country in the world. The Manifesto used cannibalism to appropriate history, by indicating that "We made Christ to be born in Bahia. Or in *Belém do Pará*."[43] The negation of religion is enhanced through references to Freud's *Totem and Taboo*, one of the most speculative texts of the father of psychoanalysis. The book purports that all manifestations of modern society are shaped by the primitive culture of origin, in a movement from totemistic to taboo societies, from matriarchal to patriarchal systems. The shift from primitive to civilized is viewed negatively in the Anthropophagous Manifesto, because it consolidated paternal authority as the foundation of culture, and patriarchy is considered a corrupt system because it represents the system imposed by the European colonialist fathers. Oswald de Andrade proposes a reversal, by praising a totemistic cannibalism, one that places matriarchy at the center. He does that by exalting maternal family relations, identifying the country as the mother of its people, and attributing to female goddesses the central place in religion: Guaraci, goddess of the sun is the mother of the living, and Jaci, goddess of the moon is the mother of the plants. Villa-Lobos anticipated this view by placing women at the center of the two ballets investigated in this study: the bathing (Amer)Indian virgin of *Amazonas* and the beautiful native huntress in *Uirapuru*. Despite its unique features, in essence Brazilian primitivism remained faithful to the overall trend of the movement, the nostalgia for the primitive: "before the Portuguese discovered Brazil, Brazil had discovered happiness. . . . Happiness is the ultimate proof. In the matriarchy of Pindorama."[44]

One of the main characteristics of primitivism is the creation of works that express internal visions and that do not necessarily conform with external appearances. The primitive "does not separate the chronological time and the real space of the objective world from the artist's inner mythopoetic vision."[45] This feature is particularly powerful in the connection of Brazilian primitivism with surrealism. In this sense, primitive artists attempt to depict realities from a world beyond the limitations of the existence of the conventional three dimensions. Primitivism became one of the most compelling and influential artistic responses to the new conception of reality that appeared in the beginning of the twentieth century. Artists intuitively understood that primitive art had the ability to grasp a new formulation of time, space, matter, and energy that was more in line with the new scientific discoveries. Gradually, they started to incorporate in artwork the absence of linear perspective, the use of simple outlines that displayed a preference for curves rather than straight lines, emotional distortions of figures with a preference for elongated forms, the absence of shadows, and the presence of energetic rhythms featuring repetitive patterns.

The cyclicity of the perception of time by the primitive man, described in the religious concept of "eternal return" by Mircea Eliade, expresses the primitivist belief that "one is able to become contemporary with or return to the 'mythical age'—the time when the events described in one's myths occurred."[46] The cyclicity of time, as opposed to the linearity of its flow from the past into the future, was perceived to be in line with the new conception of time posited by the Theory of Relativity, with its counterintuitive idea of simultaneity. *The Rite of Spring* as a ballet can be considered a series of episodes, where the use of the same material in the beginning and the end of a section serves to announce that the section is about to end and a new episode will start. In *Amazonas* the principle of restatement of the same material serves a programmatic purpose more in line with the idea of an "eternal return." This study already demonstrated how the use of ostinatos and the recurrence of motifs in *Amazonas* are an artistic expression of this concept.

The primitive man creates hierophanies by investing objects with magical powers. In the ritual act, he produces a space that is sacred and a time that is mythical and atemporal. Tribal art reflects the hierophanies by portraying the reality of the world of spirits and ultimately reflects an interest centered on the search for the primeval beginning, the exploration of the chaos that preceded creation. European artists associated this quest with a fascination for the stylistic attributes present in the artworks from Africa and Oceania, as well as the archaic and peasant art of Europe and Asia. Villa-Lobos however, simply turned to his own country to find inspiration in the music, myths, and legends of the Amerindians. By substituting a mythopoetic inner vision for "real" space, the primitive man creates a new space that might be understood beyond the rudimentary simplicity of two-dimensional painting. Artwork of primitive people frequently display a dynamic surface, where each piece fills its own space and creates its own world. Not only references to background can disappear, but also the artwork can be seen equally well from any direction. This multidirectional spatial orientation can be regarded as an expression of space more in line with suggestions about the possibility

Figure 8.2. Ancient petroglyphs (Utah, USA).
Photograph by the author.

of the existence of multiple dimensions and perspectives from which things might look very different—a reality beyond the limitations of the three-dimensional world in its conventional representation.

One can argue that, with the abundant use of structural metaphors in *Amazonas*, Villa-Lobos metaphorically transcended the limitations of the linearity of musical perception by producing a spatialization of the sound. This feature alone, which has been overlooked until recently, could place Villa-Lobos in a unique position within the avant-garde of modernism. The evolution in the conceptualization of time and space displayed from *Polichinelo*, through *Uirapuru* to *Amazonas* are a singular achievement that sets Villa-Lobos's primitivism quite apart from Stravinsky's. Curiously, the chronological order in the composition of these three works becomes meaningless in this scenario, where physical time loses its reason of being. Even the anthropophagic feature resultant from the seductiveness of cultural outreach and the potential of appropriation as a creative impulse demonstrate that Villa-Lobos's compositional method turned out to be primitivism in its purest expression.

Villa-Lobos, the Cubist

Cubism presented the world with a new way to visualize space, which was the first creative alternative to Euclid's views in more than twenty-two hundred years. Essentially, cubism is a breakthrough in conceptualizing space, which justifies the claim that it is associated mostly with the visual arts, and not with music, which belongs to the sphere of the performing arts associated with time. However, the beginning of the twentieth century brought us the solution to puzzling features of time and space through Einstein's brilliant demonstrations that space and time are relative to each other and only the speed of light is constant and mediates time and space. In other words, the discovery established that space and time are relative to each other, that they combine to form the next higher dimension called the spacetime continuum, and that there is no such thing as an inertial frame of reference. The latter was the basis of Euclidean geometry for the conceptualization of the vanishing point used in Renaissance perspective.

The above led to the speculation that cubism is a way to conceptualize space (and time) according to the same principles of the Special Theory of Relativity. In a cubist painting, all sides of an object are presented simultaneously, so, in fact, the entire reality is "all there" and in the "everlasting now." What one sees in a cubist painting is analogous to the reality perceived by an observer travelling at the speed of light, which is the only possible absolute—and unattainable—frame of reference. The seminal importance of cubism can be summarized in the fact that it posed the first new way of perceiving space in art since the classic geometrical system formulated by Euclid so many centuries before.

> Cubism breaks with Renaissance perspective. It views objects relatively: that is, from several points of view, no one of which has exclusive authority. And in so dissecting objects it sees them simultaneously from all sides—from above and below, from inside and outside. . . . Thus, to the three dimensions of the Renaissance which have held good as constituent facts throughout so many centuries there is added a fourth one—time.[47]

Parallels between the artistic and scientific findings of Picasso and Einstein are remarkable: Despite claims to the contrary—both by Picasso and Einstein—the correlation of the artistic and scientific findings is evident.[48]

> Picasso and Einstein believed that art and science are means for exploring worlds beyond perceptions, beyond appearances. Just as relativity theory overthrew the absolute status of space and time, the Cubism of Georges Braque and Picasso dethroned perspective in art.[49]

Figure 8.3. *Girl with a Mandolin* (Picasso, 1910). This is an example of analytic cubism that combines multiple perspectives in one picture by breaking down the natural form of objects into geometric shapes.

Digital Image © The Museum of Modern Art / Licensed by SCALA / Art Resource, NY. © 2022 Estate of Pablo Picasso / Artists Rights Society (ARS), New York

In cubism, spatial simultaneity corresponds to different points of view presented all at once, instead of a succession of perspectives. This notion of spatial simultaneity was drastically new, because the sum of those different viewpoints reconstructs the object in its entirety, allowing us to capture the essence of the object and, more profoundly, the very essence of reality itself. Einstein's approach to simultaneity shares with cubism the notion that there is no single preferred frame of reference. And the reduction of the subject to geometrical forms also constitutes an attempt to approach the essence of reality, while at the same time bringing art closer to science.

According to Angelo Cantoni, Picasso's cubist period coincides almost entirely, chronologically and stylistically, with Stravinsky's Russian period.[50] What in Picasso is viewed as *art nègre* is equivalent to the Russian art in Stravinsky—and the Amerindian art in Villa-Lobos. In music, cubism can be viewed as presenting two different aspects. The first one is *collage*, which in *The Rite of Spring* appears in multiple levels. As a whole, *The Rite* can be considered a sequential collage of almost independent episodes, a sequence of Cartesian planes, particularly useful if we consider the possibility of higher dimensions. The musical continuity resembles the type of cinematic editing that impacts the large-scale form. In this sense, it reflects a geometrical approach in the architecture of the musical form. On a lower hierarchical level, Stravinsky displays virtuosity in his manipulation of musical objects, disassembling and reassembling them in a different fashion so as to renew their significance. This is almost a trademark of his personal style. During his Russian period, themes derived from folk melodies are built up progressively bit by bit, piled up in layers only to be reassembled shortly afterward in cubistic collages and montages. Within this process, "musical materials slice into one another, interact and superimpose with the most brutal edges, thus challenging the musical perspective and logic that had dominated European ears for centuries."[51]

Stravinsky's process of fracture and purposeful reassemblage contrasts with Villa-Lobos's process of summation, or contraction/expansion, which appear prominently in the treatment of Uirapuru's theme (see Figures 4.3 and 5.9 in previous chapters). In the macro-form, Villa-Lobos introduces his own cubistic approach, where musical materials were sliced into one another and elements were combined through clipping, collage, and juxtaposition. This geometric approach to musical form brings a tendency toward abstractionism, which challenged two of the most fundamental characteristics of the classical music that preceded it: the use of perspective through polyphony and the use of logic, obtained through motivic development, which culminated in the sonata form. Polyphony was replaced by a textural treatment where background and foreground textures coexist. Motivic development evolved into a sophisticated system of structural metaphors, a new conception of space in music. In it, musical ideas interact through resonance among themselves, producing sonorities whose meaning transcends the literary structure of the program. At the same time, one finds a high degree of rhythmic and harmonic autonomy among the various layers. In this regard, his cubistic approach is quite different from the one by Stravinsky.

While both composers explore the superimposition of ostinatos to create stratification of the texture, for Stravinsky, a number of times, the layers are in heterophony, a typical characteristic of the Russian folksong. Heterophony implies the combination of more voices than are apparent, because while similar, heterophonic voices should be considered separately. In *The Rite of Spring* the multiple layers can create structures of great density, with up to fourteen layers. Villa-Lobos also creates textures of great density, but his approach is that of background and foreground textures interacting through structural metaphors, without the use of heterophony.

The other cubist aspect in *The Rite of Spring* is subtler. What we see in Picasso's abandonment of perspective is equivalent to Stravinsky's abandonment of traditional, fixed meter. In the same way that Picasso's paintings can display double profiles or the simultaneous views of the same object under multiple points of view (see Figure 8.4), Stravinsky's music navigates over multiple metrical shifts.

> Just as Picasso and his colleagues show the same object at the same time from various simultaneous profiles, Stravinsky presents the same themes from different metrical perspectives. The composer essentially resorts to two methods: use of constant meter with shifting of motifs with respect to the bars and the use of changing meter. The two categories are not always rigidly separated from each other but often mutually interact.[52]

Villa-Lobos does not explore meter changes in the compositions addressed in this study. However, as stated by the Brazilian composer Francisco Mignone,

> While the Russian composer fights against the metronomic monotony of the ancient symmetrical rhythm, through the displacement of the barline, alternating meters but conserving throughout the value of the 8th and quarter notes, Villa-Lobos flees, frees himself from the arithmetical game, using violent displacement of the rhythmic accent, creating a world of contradictions and rhythmic conflicts, highly effective.[53]

Figure 8.4. *Woman in Hat and Fur Collar* (Picasso, 1937). The subject appears both in frontal and profile views.

Used with permission from Art Resource, NY. © 2022 Estate of Pablo Picasso / Artists Rights Society (ARS), New York.

Villa-Lobos, the Futurist

If cubism displayed a focus on a new conceptualization of space, futurism was a movement that predominantly addressed the component of time by negating history. Futurists attempted to glorify the technological achievements of modernity by focusing on the present with a vision toward the future: "The futurists found they could pull the future into the present by representing sequential frames of individual frozen moments within a single canvas. [In doing so] they proposed a new way to see time, just as the cubists inserted a multitude of different perspectives into one work and thereby invented a new way to envision space."[54]

The relationship between cubism and futurism is noteworthy in one of the most prominent artworks of the time, Marcel Duchamp's *Nude Descending a Staircase No. 2*.

Figure 8.5. Duchamp's *Nude Descending a Staircase No. 2* (1912)
The Philadelphia Museum of Art / Art Resource, NY. © Association Marcel Duchamp / ADAGP, Paris / Artists Rights Society (ARS), New York 2022

Both cubism and futurism imply the idea of simultaneity, of the frozen moment, of the everlasting now. And, both relate to the only absolute frame of reference, which is the speed of light. In essence, futurist artworks aim to represent the reality of motion as viewed from the only absolute frame of reference—as the speed of light is approached, time dilation is produced tending to achieve the stage when all reality is frozen into an everlasting now. This echoes the relativity phenomenon both in science and art, where a new sense of time fostered insights available only through the simultaneous projection of multiple elements.

The attempts to display a new depiction of time on the canvas led artists from different fields to try to capture these dislocations of the coordinates of time and space. One year after Duchamp's *Nude*, the poet Blaise Cendrars—who would later have an important relationship with Oswald de Andrade in the formulation of the Brazilwood Manifesto during the 1920s—claimed in 1913 to have written the first simultaneous poem in his *Prose du transsibérien*. This was considered by Apollinaire "the first attempt at simultaneous writing where the contrast of colors trains the eye to read at once the multiple aspects of the poem; just as a conductor reads at a single glance the superimposed notes of an orchestral score."[55] Similarly, the Anthropophagous Manifesto has been compared with a musical score: the repetition and echo effect applied to certain words and sentences suggest a possible reading that is horizontal and vertical, keeping similarities with the reading of a musical score, which is a process that brings out the concept of simultaneity.

In the same year, Stravinsky unleashed the *Rite of Spring*, where one can argue that the audible contraction, expansion, and stasis of the three compact cells that articulate the opening of the *Danse Sacrale* as analyzed by Boulez are a sort of study on the concept of time dilation.[56] In addition, the pervasive use of polyrhythm in *Le Sacre* is entirely analogous to the breakthrough that Duchamp achieved in his *Nude Descending a Staircase*:

> Some of the score's most electrifying moments come when opposed rhythmical strands are piled on top of one another. Such superimpositions amount to a musical collage, creating a form of highly organized chaos. This was the expansion of polyrhythm, one of modern music's most essential innovations, way beyond anything conceived before.[57]

Polyrhythms also permeate the scores of Villa-Lobos, with the added effect of multilayered textures, where not only opposed rhythmical strands are mingled, but also multiple themes and contrasting materials in different modes coalesce. Instead of chaos, structural metaphors bring unity to the multiplicity of simultaneous events, producing a complex system where each layer complements the other in a beautiful synthesis that builds a new cosmic universe where musical time acquires a new significance.

Futurism as an artistic and social movement, celebrated technological advances and urban modernity. As such, it emphasized the beauty of machines, speed, violence, motion, and change, praising the life in industrial cities. In music, futurism can be associated with the incorporation of noise as valid musical material. In the same way that Duchamp's *Nude* generated a scandalous controversy leading even to cartoonist satires of the painting, the dynamic rhythms and dissonances of *Le Sacre du Printemps* became the ultimate apotheosis of noise, whose detractors nicknamed the work *Le Massacre du Printemps*. If primitivism belonged to the sphere of what the classical musical tradition would call "pre-music," the incorporation of noise became "post-music," compositions that were not music anymore.

The forces unleashed in Villa-Lobos's works assimilated the new sounds of the techno-society in conjunction with the demolition of the established systems. Those are the same forces that represent the urge of creation in *Le Sacre*—the barbaric forces of nature and the turbulence of sprouts and plants germinating from soil—the same forces that allowed for the emergence of a dense and diverse world of new possibilities for the representation of nature and reality. Like Stravinsky, Villa-Lobos incorporated sound blocks, sound bands, and sound stains[58] in an atonal setting that included noises within the multilayered texture. Beyond Stravinsky, in *Uirapuru* and *Amazonas*, he also incorporated aleatoric sounds that belong to the non-tempered universe of tropical noises, as well as sounds produced by string instruments in the region between the bridge and the string holder of the instruments. Ironically, these sounds were meant to represent an untamed landscape, where the universe of noises emanating from the forest builds a non-tempered soundscape distant from the European traditions—therefore, a universe quite distant from the technological prowess celebrated by the futurists.

Villa-Lobos, the Abstractionist

When Einstein discovered relativity, he became a celebrity, yet his theories were far beyond the comprehension of most people, including his physicist colleagues. Later discoveries in the field of quantum mechanics stretched the level of incomprehension even further. Besides being counterintuitive, it was almost impossible to convey with words or images the incredible insights that changed the paradigms that had been ingrained in the collective psyche of our civilization for so many centuries. An analogous process took place in art. The various art movements in the beginning of the twentieth century gradually started to present the public with an ever-increasing number of unrecognizable forms. Never before had the general public felt that the art of its own civilization had become so incomprehensible.

> For the first time since natural philosophers began to inquire into the nature of the universe, scientists had created models of reality that humans, the most visual of the animals, could not visualize. The concepts of general relativity, it seemed, could be precisely expressed only by the use of abstract mathematical symbols. . . . Non-Euclidean geometry, the unimaginable arcane space supposedly confined to mathematics, became the new basis of physical reality and art without an image became a major new style in art.[59]

"What I admire most in your art," says Einstein, "is the universality. You don't say a word but the whole world understands." "True," answers Chaplin, "but your glory is even bigger; the whole world admires you when nobody understands you."

Figure 8.6. Charlie Chaplin and Albert Einstein were relatively close friends and the quote above is attributed to their encounter during the premiere of Chaplin's film City Lights.
Einstein photograph by Orren Jack Turner, Princeton, N.J (1947). Chaplin photograph by P.D. Jankens (1915).

If art without an image is what defined abstractionism in the visual arts, music without sound, or conversely, music made of noises is what characterizes abstractionism in music. It is in this sense that compositions such as *The Rite of Spring* or *Pierrot Lunaire* became the epitomes of modern music, through the glorification of dissonance. At the premiere of *The Rite*, one critic wrote:

this is the most dissonant music ever written. I would say, after a first and very imperfect hearing, that never has the system and cult of the wrong note been practised with such zeal and persistence as in this score; that from the first bar to the last whatever note one expects is never the one that comes, but the note to one side, the note which ought not to come.[60]

No matter the level of intricacy of the phenomena being investigated, the scientist's approach includes aesthetical considerations in the search for elegant solutions to the most complex problems. Even the most exoteric findings in physics in the quest for the mysteries of the universe included representations that embody simplicity, symmetry, balance of proportions, and unity of foundations. For example, "in Einstein's 1905 papers, aesthetic arguments reappeared with a force unseen in centuries."[61] A permanent link exists between aesthetics and the fundamental laws of nature. As the new reality reduced the laws of physics to a non-Euclidean conceptualization of space, abstract painting in the second decade of the twentieth century assumed that space had an inherent geometry and many abstract artworks started to be organized geometrically.

An analogous process happened in music. Abstractionism became related to atonality and serialism. The relationship with atonality exists because the absence of a single frame of reference in the new conceptualization of space was equivalent to the absence of a key center unifying a composition. In atonalism, each note has the same relative importance as all the others. In serialism, starting with Schoenberg's twelve-tone system, the notes of a composition became organized geometrically in the composition through manipulation of rows.[62] The mathematical operations of inversion, retrogression, and others reflected a geometric approach to composition. "Serial thinking is something that's come into our consciousness and will be there forever: it's relativity and nothing else," posited Stockhausen.[63] In contrast with Stravinsky, Villa-Lobos did not explore serialism during his career. Yet, he flirted with atonalism through stylistic incursions into a new harmonic universe. The numerous devices that he employed—from the various incidences of polarization by exclusion to the eleven-tone theme of the sensual dance of the Amerindian girl in *Amazonas*; from sound stains and clusters to the creation of twelve-tone conglomerates—imbued his music with an abstract quality.

Abstractionism in art is a product of ambiguity, the questioning of the capacity of art to accurately depict reality. In music, abstractionism associated with atonality can be traced back to the *Tristan chord*, whose ambiguity constitutes a radical moment in music history, as it "pushes the boundaries of the tonal system to create a yearning for death that is satisfied when Isolde's dissonances dissolve into the consonant totality of the final cadence."[64] This study demonstrates that the process of cannibalization of Wagner and Debussy in *Uirapuru* led in the direction of an abstractionism that is not fully realized. Isolde's death finds its poetic correspondence in the death of the handsome Amerindian at the end of the ballet, together with his transfiguration into the magic bird.

When compared with the *Tristan chord*, the Polichinelo chord has a more abstract potential, because it is a sonority that stands out by itself. The description of the "Augurs chord" from *The Rite of Spring* according to Frederick J. Smith applies with equal force to the Polichinelo chord, as he states that this chord "was never conceived intellectually . . . there is no harmonic analysis called for. . . . It was this bodily placing of hands which gave birth to the sound and not some theoretical idea that made it possible."[65] Despite their similarities, there is also an important difference between the Polichinelo chord and the Petrushka chord, because the latter is devoid of tonal functionalism, while the former is devoid of an intellectual conceptualization.

The Augurs chord stands as the twentieth-century counterpart to the *Tristan chord*, as both express the same kind of ambiguity that places them as radical moments in the history of music. The Augurs chord has central importance in the conception of the *Rite of Spring*:

> this chord was the inception of the *Rite of Spring*, according to Stravinsky. The sketches suggest that it might not be the very first idea on the opening page, but Stravinsky intuitively believed it to be the initial inspiration—the first in significance if not in time. 'It was rather a new chord,' he claimed, not only in its notes but in its rhythmic accents which, according to the composer, were 'the foundation of the whole [work],' as if it were the biological pulse of the ballet. Thus the opening sonority of the 'Augurs of Spring' is the emblem of the *Rite*; in the words of Robert Craft, it is the 'motto chord.'[66]

The explanation of the Augurs chord became the quest of modern musicology: Due to its significance as the foundation of the ballet, the understanding of this chord promised to unlock the language the entire composition. Such an important landmark demanded a theoretical justification. However, due to its ambiguity, it suffered the same kind of destiny as the *Tristan chord*, triggering multiple contrasting analytical explanations under different approaches.[67] Ultimately, the Augurs chord stands by itself as a landmark exactly due to this ambiguity, which epitomizes the emancipation of dissonance advocated by Schoenberg.

The abstractionism in Villa-Lobos music is of a different nature. What Villa-Lobos's approach in *Amazonas* has in common with Stravinsky's in *Le Sacre* is a similar aesthetic that prizes conceptual rudimentariness over perceptual beauty. Starting with *Uirapuru*, the composer used dissonant harmonies combined with syncopated rhythms and unusual timbre effects, which reflect an impressionist aesthetic with overtones from tenebrism. This aesthetic exploded in *Amazonas* into sound stains, noises, sound aggregates, and blocks, where the rhythmic contours widely expanded the possibilities of choice of the musical materials. This apparently indiscriminate release of sound energy has been called by Mário de Andrade an "almost music" (*quasi musica*), because the sound ceases to function as a constructive element of a logical structure,[68] almost in the same way as Stravinsky conceived the Augurs chord. In this sense, it guards a parallel with Schoenberg's twelve-tone aesthetic. Schoenberg's approach reflects an attempt of approximation towards a primordial condition. Emotionally, both attitudes carry a connotation of urgency that seems to stem from a consideration of the raw materials of the musical art, the atomization of the musical note.

When sound stops being a constructive element, Villa-Lobos reaches, in *Amazonas*, one of his utmost expressions of abstractionism through atonality. This is when, more than ever, he adds a more palpable element to the music, in the form of structural metaphors. The sound represented in the score is not the sound of the music emanating from the musical instruments, as much as the word tree is not a tree, and the pipe in Magritte's *Treachery of Images* (Figure 7.42) is not a pipe. The employment of sound aggregates as independent sonorous objects, as well as the use of structural metaphors, transform music into a more spatial and concrete state of being, a form of music pictorialism that is a spiritual precursor of the *musique concrète* of Pierre Shaffer.[69] In this lies the ultimate ambiguity of Villa-Lobos's music: He subverts its sonorous nature by converting it into a visual representation on the page. Ironically, this is when the abstract quality of his music acquires concrete significance.[70]

Final Thoughts

For several decades, the evaluation of Villa-Lobos was based on problematic formulations regarding his biography and compositional style. His biographies emphasized fantastical and legendary aspects of his life, recognizing that these views were promoted by the composer himself. Incongruencies that appeared in the first biographies were reproduced in later ones, creating a body of literature of questionable veracity. Most of his travels around the country, which supposedly allowed him to collect folk material used in his nationalist works did not occur; and his habit of predating compositions to look like an avant-garde composer at a time that valued above all originality, takes away the credibility of his achievements.[71] His relationship with the dictatorial government of Getúlio Vargas in Brazil characterized him as an opportunist.

Early musicologists considered Villa-Lobos an *enfant terrible*, a composer who wrote rhapsodic works due to lack of technical proficiency in basic compositional skills such as harmony, form, and polyphony. Absent a formal education, Villa-Lobos has been considered a talented and intuitive musician, who used these qualities to compensate for his lack of ability in the manipulation of thematic materials. While recognizing the composer's originality, Mário de Andrade criticized his spontaneity and impetuosity, which, according to him, resulted in multiple repetitions, unevenness, and abuse of musical effects.[72] Later musicologists assessed a lack of inner coherence and irrefutable logic in Villa-Lobos's works. Other composers initially received the same reception, yet today we can hardly negate the skillfulness in artists such as Schoenberg, Bartok, and Stravinsky. Similarly, Villa-Lobos's notes are chosen with impeccable refinement, providing structural solidity on an almost-Beethovenian level. Yet, it still prevails the view that Villa-Lobos's style lacks traditional motivic development and his music displays the nonadherence to the typical archetypes of tonal music for which he has always been criticized. Today, the justification is different:

> Traditional analytical approaches based on the concepts of classical formal logic are of little use not only when applied to Villa-Lobos music, but also to most of the early 20th century music. . . . The coherence does not rest in the development of thematic material typical of European symphonic music, but in the evolution of the sonorous potentialities of the musical conception.[73]

While the music of a modern composer needs to be analyzed with the correspondent analytical tools proper for the times and style in question, this study demonstrated that a number of traditional analytic approaches adhere perfectly to the study of Villa-Lobos's music, and the expansion of these methodologies to include Set Theory, Interval Cycles and Octatonism provides greater lucidity to the understanding of his compositional process. His works reveal the inner coherence that corroborates the composer's statement that he operates with "strict and severe control of consciousness."[74] The simultaneous presence of elements from multiple trends of the avant-garde in the music—primitivism, surrealism, naïvism, and others—reveal how much Villa-Lobos was in synch with the aesthetic developments of his time. Even the naivete present in his music is sophisticated and should not be confused with the criticism of naivete in his composition technique.

The challenge of comprehension resides in the fact that the multiplicity and complexity of the compositional processes of Villa-Lobos is such that it results in "open works"—compositions whose interpretation and multiple meanings are inexhaustible. This study revealed the exploration of a large number of techniques, such as manipulation of symmetries; creation of hidden polyphony through zigzag figurations; use of vagrant harmonies, polytonality, sliding of semitones, and chords built in non-traditional intervals (fourths, seconds, etc.); interval recurrence and polarization of key centers; abundance of polyrhythms and uneven beat subdivisions; treatment of ostinatos; and others. Independently from connections of certain musical elements with those of other composers, through anthropophagy Villa-Lobos was able to create a highly original universe of auditory appreciation. The final result is a system of interconnected musical events charged with visceral emotion and poetic meaning, achieved through structural plurality, where everything is "all there" and "at once."

Structural plurality is translated into a high degree of rhythmic and harmonic autonomy among the various layers of the texture. Villa-Lobos's abandon of the sonata principles did not lead to a rhapsodic treatment of the themes, but to a treatment more in line with a modernist aesthetic. In the macroform, the composer displays a predilection for structures of contrasting sections, such as rondo. In the microform, the individual sections present contrasting textures, where divergent or complementary elements coexist. This corresponds to a cubistic compositional approach, where musical materials are sliced into one another and multiple elements are juxtaposed over one another through cutting and sliding.

All the above considerations point to the plurality of aesthetics that were incorporated into the Villalobian style through anthropophagy. Yet, it remains to address the incidence of surrealism, which due to its importance is purposely left for the last chapter. The elucidation of the nature of the music by the Brazilian composer through this methodology brings a new perspective for the appreciation of his sound palette. Villa-Lobos is buried in his hometown, and his tombstone reads: "I consider my works to be letters to posterity, written without expectation of an answer."[75] The response likely rests within the music itself, lingering among the sounds of works such as *Amazonas*, *Uirapuru* and *Polichinelo*, sounds of an original voice waiting to be rediscovered.

Notes

1. https://youtu.be/wt9yCN-b_Lo.
2. https://youtu.be/kODIh-rDJug.
3. Though the timing of the beginning of modernism is a topic of controversy, many authors agree that it began during the *Belle Époque*.
4. For example, in a letter to Nicholas Slonimsky, Arnold Schoenberg stated: "I personally hate to be called a revolutionist, which I am not. What I did was neither revolution nor anarchy." Slonimsky, *Russian and Soviet Music*, 158.
5. Travassos, *Modernismo e música brasileira*, 29.
6. Hess, *Representing the Good Neighbor*, 133. The misspelling of *Uirapuru* has been maintained.
7. Fairman, *Total Immersion*, n.p.
8. "There is no composer whose name is more narrowly attached to a single work or, let us say, a single series of works. Stravinsky is, in the first place, *Le Sacre*; *Petrushka, Renard, Les Noces,* and *Le Chant du Rossignol* form a constellation of which the importance cannot be denied, but the magnetic pole always remains that *Sacre*, yesterday scandalous, today a pretext for animated cartoons!" Boulez, *Notes of an Apprenticeship*, 72.
9. Travassos, *Modernismo e música brasileira*, 29.
10. Ribeiro, *O Pensamento Vivo*, 13.
11. This aspect is further explained in chapter 9.
12. Wisnik, *O Coro dos Contrários*, 167–71.
13. Ribeiro, *O Pensamento Vivo*, 13.
14. Ross, *The Rest Is Noise*, 137.
15. Appleby, *Heitor Villa-Lobos*, 76.
16. Fernando Lopes Graça as quoted in Jamary Oliveira, *Black Key versus White Key*, 33–34.
17. Melo, Cleisson. *Villa-Lobos: Do Simbólico Ao Semiótico*, 215.
18. "Magic and life. . . . And we knew how to transpose mystery and death with the help of a few grammatical forms." Anthropophagous Manifesto, aphorism 26 (see Appendix I).
19. "Let's get rid of ideas and other paralyses. By means of itineraries. Let's believe in signs, in sextants and in the stars." Anthropophagous Manifesto, aphorism 45 (see Appendix I).
20. Henderson, *The Fourth Dimension* (1984), 205.
21. Wisnik, *O Coro dos Contrários*, 166–67.
22. More details about this matter appear in chapter 9 and in Appendix 1.
23. Watkins, *Pyramids at the Louvre*, 99.
24. Maia, *Villa-Lobos: Alma Brasileira*, 20.
25. Kandel, *The Age of Insight*, 9.
26. For example, through the concretist aesthetic of the Noigandre poets, which is not part of the scope of this manuscript. For more information about the Noigandre movement, see Thompson, "Pound and Brazilian Concretism."

27. As, for example, in the artworks produced under a futurist aesthetic.

28. This topic is discussed further below in the section "Villa-Lobos, the Abstractionist."

29. Bergson, *Creative Evolution*, 46.

30. Bob Fowles, "Is This Where I Am," bobfowleslifedrawing1 (blog), http://bobfowleslifedrawing1.blogspot.com/2019/01/is-this-where-i-am-going.html.

31. Miller, *Einstein, Picasso*, 24. The polemics generated from his encounter with Einstein might have had an impact on Einstein's being awarded the Nobel Prize for his discovery of the photoelectric effect (the corpuscular nature of light and electromagnetic radiation, which later allowed for the development of the theory of wave-particle duality in quantum mechanics), and not for his formulation of the Theory of Relativity.

32. Hughes, *The Shock of the New*, 366.

33. Shlain, *Art and Physics*, 148.

34. Argüelles, *The Transformative Vision*, 167.

35. Scigliano, *Michelangelo's Mountain*, 296.

36. Vassberg, "Villa-Lobos: Music as a Tool of Nationalism," 60. The text refers to the choral singing used by Catholic missionaries that formed the pedagogical basis for their catechesis of the native Brazilians in the sixteenth century.

37. Watkins, *Pyramids at the Louvre*, 100.

38. Ibid., 90.

39. In his sketches for the *Rite of Spring*, Stravinsky put the title "Amazons" for the section of the Glorification, which at the time was referred to as *Dikaia pliaska* (wild dance). It is said that this section was based on a story of the mating of amazons and Scyths that served as justification for the wild or martial behavior of the women in the honoring of the "Chosen One" in the Rite. See Richard Taruskin, "The Rite Revisited," 200.

40. Anthropophagous Manifesto, aphorism 48 (see Appendix I).

41. Ibid., aphorism 2 (see Appendix I).

42. Ibid., aphorisms 50 and 51. Pindorama is how the Amerindians referred to Brazil. The word can be translated as "land of palms."

43. Ibid., aphorism 13. Bahia is one of the largest states of Brazil, while Belém (Bethlehem) is the capital of the state Pará, located in the northeast region of the country.

44. Ibid., aphorisms 40, 42, and 43.

45. Shlain, *Art and Physics*, 150.

46. Doniger, "Foreword to the 2004 Edition of *Shamanism: Archaic Techniques of Ecstasy*," xiii.

47. Gideon, *Space, Time and Architecture*, 436.

48. The author Linda Dalrymple Henderson dismissed the possibility that cubism is an expression of the spacetime continuum under the argument that its multidimensionality refers to a fourth *spatial* dimension, while the fourth dimension in the spacetime continuum is time. See Henderson, *The Fourth Dimension* (2013).

49. Miller, *Einstein, Picasso*, 4. Perhaps the answer rests in a reevaluation of the theories of Henri Bergson.

50. Cantoni, *The Language of Stravinsky*, 165.

51. Benjamin, "How Stravinsky's *Rite of Spring*," para. 5.

52. Cantoni, *The Language of Stravinsky*, 166.

53. Francisco Mignone, "Villa-Lobos na Música Sinfônica" (Lecture given on October 27, 1966), in *Presença de Villa-Lobos* (Rio de Janeiro: MEC, Museu Villa-Lobos, 1969, vol. 3), 92. What Mignone characterized as "a world of contradictions and rhythm conflicts" can be viewed as another example of the incidence of surrealist aesthetic in Villa-Lobos's compositional method.

54. Shlain, *Art and Physics*, 205–6.

55. Guillaume Apollinaire, "Simultanisme-Librettisme," *Les Soirées de Paris*, 323–24. The text of the poem was printed alongside an abstract painting by the artist Sonja Delaunay, so painting and poetry complemented each other in the production of *simultanéism*.

56. Watkins, *Pyramids at the Louvre*, 99.

57. Benjamin, "How Stravinsky's *Rite of Spring*," para. 13.

58. An explanation of these terms appears in the Glossary of Terms (See Appendix II).

59. Shlain, *Art and Physics*, 343–45.

60. Pierre Lalo, 'Considerations sur "Le Sacre du Printemps,"' Le Temps, 5 August 1913, reprinted in Lesure (ed.), Le sacre du printemps: Dossier de Presse, pp. 33–4; the translation is taken from Hill, *Stravinsky: The Rite of Spring*, 93.

61. Miller, *Einstein, Picasso*, 238.

62. In the same way that parallels between Picasso and Einstein have been addressed by multiple authors such as Miller, parallels between Einstein and Schoenberg (relativity and twelve-tone composition) have been the subject of a number of texts. See, for example, "Composing Einstein: Exploring the Kinship of Art and Science," by Edvin Østergaard.

63. Jonathan Cott, *Stockhausen; Conversations with the Composer*, 101.

64. Daniel K. L. Chua, "Rioting with Stravinsky," 64.

65. Frederick J. Smith, *The Experiencing of Musical Sound*, 70 and 178.

66. Chua, "Rioting with Stravinsky," 63

67. Ibid. The article by Chua summarizes most of the different interpretations.

68. As demonstrated in this study, this is actually not true. The *perception* of a lack of logical structure that persists among musicologists, and the reception of Villa-Lobos's music as disturbingly dissonant by audiences of the time, hide the fact that Villa-Lobos's edifices of sound are chosen with impeccable refinement for the construction of the musical form.

69. Waizbort mentions another example of Villa-Lobos's work as a harbinger of *musique concrète*. The composer's transcription of the Amerindian Paresi song *Mokocê-cê-makà* includes a sort of out-of-tune acceleration, which is the result of some mechanical failure of the phonograph at the time of recording. This is one of

the phonograms collected by Roquette-Pinto during the Roosevelt-Rondon expedition to the interior of Brazil. By incorporating the technical hiccup in the composition, instead of rendering the original "correct" version, the composer is anticipating procedures associated with *musique concrète*. See Waizbort, *Como, Quando e Por Que*.

70. This aspect can be traced back to aphorism 45 in the Antropophagous Manifesto ("We are concretists"), and provides a parallel to the concretist movement in poetry of the Noigandres in Brazil during the 1950s.

71. During the VI Villa-Lobos Symposium sponsored by the Universidade de São Paulo between September 29 and October 1, 2021, the scholar Luiz Fernando Lopes presented the lecture "Narradores não confiáveis: Os catálogos de Villa-Lobos como obra de ficção" (Unreliable Narrators: Villa-Lobos's catalogs as fiction works), where he addressed the fact that in the area of Villalobian studies, there is an increasingly established consensus that the composer lacked the truth about certain facts of his biography, especially in relation to the beginning of his career. The lecturer stated that "the various catalogs dedicated to the work of Villa-Lobos contain many inaccuracies and seem to suffer from a defect of origin: the composer's lack of commitment to documenting the facts of his production . . . this defect of origin contaminates with fictional elements his biographies and his catalogues."

72. Travassos, *Modernismo e música brasileira*, 49; Nasser, "Villa-Lobos e a elaboração de linguagem. 49–50.

73. Salles, *Villa-Lobos*, 197. According to him, "Villa-Lobos music requires specific analytical strategies, similar to those developed for the study of the music of Schoenberg, Bartók and Stravinsky throughout the 20th century." See Paulo de Tarso Salles, "Villa-Lobos: Desafiando a Teoria e Análise," 81.

74. This statement appears under comments and considerations about Musical Education in a text by Villa-Lobos published in the Latin American Musical Bulletin in 1946. See *Presença de Villa-Lobos* (Rio de Janeiro: MEC, Museu Villa-Lobos, 1971, vol. 6), 96.

75. Appleby, *Heitor Villa-Lobos*, 183.

CHAPTER NINE

Villa-Lobos, The Surrealist

Quem foi que inventou o Brasil?
Foi seu Cabral, foi seu Cabral
No dia 21 de abril
Dois meses depois do carnaval. —Lamartine Babo

Before addressing how surrealism is manifested in the music by Villa-Lobos, it is interesting to observe that surrealism has been embedded in Brazilian culture for a long time, as postulated by Oswald de Andrade in the Anthropophagous Manifesto, when he proclaimed that "we already had the surrealist language" in the aphorism 25 of his Manifesto (see Appendix 1). As a starting point, let us examine the carnival march *História do Brasil* (History of Brazil),[1] which, despite having been written in 1933—after the establishment of surrealism as a major aesthetic movement in France—can illustrate the particular nature in which surrealism is manifested in Brazilian culture. The lyrics of the song are as follows:

História do Brasil	History of Brazil
Quem foi que inventou o Brasil?	Who invented Brazil?
Foi seu Cabral, foi seu Cabral,	It was Mr. Cabral, it was Mr. Cabral,
no dia 21 de abril	on April 21st,
dois meses depois do carnaval!	two months after carnival!

Depois, Ceci amou Peri	Afterwards, Ceci loved Peri,
Peri beijou Ceci	Peri kissed Ceci,
ao som . . . ao som do Guarani!	to the sound . . . to the sound of Guarani!
Do Guarani ao guaraná	From Guarani to guarana;
Surgiu a feijoada	the feijoada appeared
E mais tarde o Paraty.	and later on, the Paraty.
Depois, Ceci virou Iaiá,	Afterward Ceci turned into Iaiá,
Peri virou Ioiô.	Peri turned into Ioiô.
De lá pra cá tudo mudou!	Since then, everything changed!
Passou-se o tempo da vovó.	Granny's time has passed.
Quem manda é a Severa	Today Severa is in charge,
E o cavalo Mossoró!	as well as Mossoró, the horse.

The song was written by Lamartine Babo (1904–1963) and became a major hit in the carnival of Rio de Janeiro in 1934, one year before the premiere of *Uirapuru* in Argentina. Already in its first stanza, the author curiously does not ask who "discovered" Brazil, but who *invented* it, showing that the country was actually a creation of the Portuguese colonizer, represented by Admiral Pedro Álvares Cabral. This major historical figure, who shares the same status as Christopher Columbus to North Americans, is treated in an informal way: "seu Cabral," translated here as "Mr. Cabral." The lyrics also suggest that the date of the discovery of Brazil is not particularly relevant: In fact, the discovery of Brazil is a subproduct of carnival, which existed previously, providing a surrealist reversal of history.

In the continuation of the song, other important references to Brazilian identity are presented: the main characters of the opera *Il Guarany* by Carlos Gomes, the Amerindian Peri, symbol of the noble savage, and Cecilia, the daughter of the Portuguese colonizer. *Il Guarany* (*O Guarani*, in Portuguese) is the most famous Brazilian opera in history, the highest symbol of "high art" that stands in diametrical contrast with the unpretentious style of the carnival march.[2] Brazil's history continues from the opera *Il Guarany* to the Amazonian plant guaraná, considered an aphrodisiac. The word *guaraná* means "eyes of the gods" in the Amerindian language. In Tupi-Guarani mythological tradition, guaraná originated with a deity killing a beloved native child. However, in this particular context, guaraná refers to a famous non-alcoholic carbonated drink made of guaraná, which competed against Coca-Cola, a product imported from another imperialist nation. By way of guaraná, Brazilian history takes us from the opera to the culinary taste of feijoada, the most famous dish of Brazilian kitchen, accompanied by Paraty, the Brazilian liquor derived from sugarcane.[3]

A new twist in history happens afterward, with the introduction of the words *Ioiô* and *Iaiá*, which in Brazil were the honorifics used by African slaves to address young people who were children of the owners of the house. In this case, since the Amerindian Peri was engaged to Ceci (*Iaiá*, the daughter of the Portuguese colonizer and slave owner), he became *Ioiô*, the soon-to-be son-in-law. With few words, the composer introduces in the song the social/ethnic configuration of the country, formed by Amerindians, Portuguese colonizers, and African slaves.

Since then, everything has changed! Granny's time has passed, meaning that Brazil left its early stages in history, and through modernization entered in the Industrial Age of the 1930s. The new times are represented by Severa and the horse Mossoró, who became in charge of the country. In this quick coda to end the song, the composer concludes by refering to Severa, the mascot of the Portuguese soccer team;[4] and Mossoró, a nationally bred horse, winner of the first Grand Prix in Brazil in 1933. Both animals represented popular sports of the 1930s, soccer remaining until today the most important sport practiced in Brazil. This elementary and unpretentious song stands out as a masterpiece of economy of resources to synthesize the cultural spirit of the country. Brazilian identity is summarized in these few lines as a combination of three simple elements: the miscegenation of races, sports and food, where the latter provides a subliminal connection with the nutritional nature of anthropophagy.

The previous chapter indicated that since the end of the nineteenth century, visual artists played a fundamental role in evoking visionary images that corresponded to revolutionary discoveries in the field of science. This is how the great artistic styles of the modern era emerged—impressionism, expressionism, fauvism, Dadaism, primitivism, surrealism, cubism, neoclassicism, and several others. The most revolutionary artists of the twentieth century were constantly changing their styles in order to express the fervent intensity of a succession of new discoveries. Picasso's prolific work is usually categorized in several periods: the Blue, the Rose, the African-influenced, the analytic cubism, synthetic cubism, neoclassicism, and surrealism. Stravinsky's output is usually categorized into three periods: the Russian, the neoclassic and the serial. Also prolific, Villa-Lobos underwent several periods. After departing from the European influence of his early works, he underwent the period of the founding of Brazilian nationalism, the experimental period of the *choros*, the neoclassical period of the *Bachianas Brasileiras*, and the final synthetic period of his late works. This categorization does not take into account his prolific musical production as an educator during the Vargas government.

Given that music is a more abstract artistic field, styles are often defined using analogies with the fields of plastic arts or literature. Contemporary musicology tends to emphasize the styles that are considered more comprehensive within the field of music, such as impressionism inherited from France, expressionism inherited from Germany and Austria, primitivism from Bartok and the Stravinsky of the *Rite of Spring*, neoclassicism coming a little later, and others. While all these musical styles find a match in the visual arts, not all plastic styles find a match in musical styles. For example, it would be difficult, although not impossible, to find fauvist manifestations in the field of music.

The phenomenon described above explains why the Brazilian anthropophagic style is usually defined from the framework of the painting *Abaporu* by Tarsila do Amaral. Considering the comprehensive character of the anthropophagic style, its resulting aesthetics is often seen as the product of a culture recreated independently and that produced works of art impregnated with dense, profound and hybrid multicultural characteristics. Brazilian music of the period, of which Villa-Lobos is the main representative, should be studied within the same framework of cultural anthropophagy.

Like fauvism, surrealism is usually best known for its manifestations in visual arts and literature, having subsequently migrated to other artistic fields such as theater and cinema. The main ingredients of surrealism are usually described in terms of its emergence from Dada, with its radical approach of mockery towards the establishment; its admiration for Marxist ideas inciting social rebellion against the tenets of capitalist society, and the influence of Freud, which led to the notion that more authenticity of art expression can be found in the exploration of the subconscious.

From Primitivism to Surrealism and Anthropophagy

As a movement that evolved from Dada, surrealism incorporated the same ideas of valorization of primitive thought and simplification of the poetic language for the expression of an authentic art.[5] Both primitivism and surrealism found in the instinctive element, in the magical thought and in the forces of the unconscious the path for art renewal, and these ingredients found their way into Brazilian modernism. Dadaists and surrealists approached primitivism through a concern with the inner expression of the artist, either through intense emotion and spontaneous sentiment, or through the incitement of the subconscious, which leads to psychic automatism and catharsis in search for the elemental origin of art.[6] In a lecture given at the Sorbonne in 1923, Oswald de Andrade demonstrated lucidity when stating that the twentieth-century artist was looking for emotional sources, for the concrete and metaphysical origins of art. Primitivism preaches "savage thinking," the myth-poetic thinking that participates in the logic of the imaginary, and which is savage in opposition to the cultivated, utilitarian and domesticated thinking.[7]

The psychic automatism proposed by Breton, "the actual functioning of thought. Dictated by thought, in the absence of any control exercised by reason, exempt from any aesthetic or moral concern,"[8] had already found its parallel in the inclusion of the elements of invention and surprise in the Brazilwood Manifesto, written in the same year as Breton's. Surrealist automatic writing is one in which the author begins to write whatever comes to mind in hopes of unlocking the unconscious mind to reveal truth in the art form. Literary automatism was further consolidated in the Anthropophagic Manifesto, where K. David Jackson notices that

> the particular qualities of this avant-garde prose include short, dense sentences dominated by each word's expressiveness. The writing is elliptical, full of images which treat reality with poetic techniques—suggestion, allusion, metaphor, simile, pun, onomatopoeia. The use of syntactic alterations and neologisms in a collage of images achieves style of poetry in prose, based on free association of ideas and images.[9]

A sort of writing automatism is suggested by Mário de Andrade in his "Extremely Interesting Preface" to *Paulicéia Desvairada* from 1922, where he states: "when I feel the lyrical impulse, I write without thinking everything that my unconscious screams. I think later: not only to correct, but also to justify what I've written."[10] It is interesting to note that this precedes the publication of Breton's *First Manifesto of Surrealism*. Psychic automatism is only one of the manifestations of surrealism.

The notion of the cannibal had been already present in the sixteenth-century humanism of Montaigne, as well as in works by Voltaire and Rousseau. However, it was mainly the Dada movement that transformed it into an aesthetic venture. European cannibalism manifested itself through a disturbing language, a form of verbal aggression that generated outrage through the use of allegories and violent images. Literary examples can be found in *Il Negro* (The Black Man) by Marinetti, a "grotesque tale of Western cannibalism and futurist eroticism;"[11] in the two-issue 1920 French Dadaist magazine *Cannibale*; and in the *Manifeste cannibal dans l'obscurité* (Cannibal Manifesto in Darkness), both by Picabia and published in the *Dadaphone* magazine in 1920. As such, the image of the cannibal belonged to the same set of ideas that accompanied the introduction of the Primitivist aesthetic, the magical element introduced by Lévy Bruhl and the Freudian importance of the subconscious. Oswald de Andrade's anthropophagy drank from the same source,[12] and like the European movements also valued the magical, instinctive, and irrational components of human existence. The originality of Andrade's approach rests in turning the cannibal into "an aggressive symbol capable of subverting the primitivism then in vogue in Europe, in order to rewrite colonial history and invert the relationship between center and periphery."[13] Oswald de Andrade thus transformed cannibalism into a metaphor of a creative process that would generate a Brazilian art that was modern and autonomous.

The cannibalism introduced by the Dada movement also migrated to surrealism, acquiring a sexual connotation by way of Freud. For example, Salvador Dalí's postmodern works from his last surrealist period promoted a radical aesthetic turn through cannibalism, where "Dalí's ultimate purpose was not the fulfillment of dreams, nor a new revolutionary poetics, but, to use his own words, the conversion of aesthetic surrealism into edible surrealism."[14] Besides a direct reference in his painting *Cannibalism d'automne*, Dalí "also underlined what he called 'the colossal nutritive and cultural responsibility of Surrealism' in his tract 'The Conquest of the Irrational.' There, he described culture as an indispensable meal for a society more and more seduced by irrationality."[15] The surrealist flirting with cannibalism derives from the same Freudian source as the Anthropophagy movement, the idea that sexual desire may be nothing more than a disguised appetite for human flesh. Not by chance, it was Salvador Dalí who rewrote Breton's motto ("Beauty will be convulsive or it will no longer be") with an anthropophagic bias: "Beauty will be edible or it will no longer be."[16]

In its essence, surrealism combined two opposing influences. It started with the subconscious exploration of dreams, through André Breton's First Manifesto, an approach clearly subjective and connected with Freud and his investigations about the world of dreams. In the Second Manifesto of 1930, it took a more pragmatic and objective approach through the influence of Marxist materialism, which to an extent was not compatible with the subjectivity of Freud. This combination produced an ambiguous quality to surrealist philosophy, after all, the surrealist exaltation of subjectivism goes against the materialist nature of Marxism. The materialist dimension of surrealism

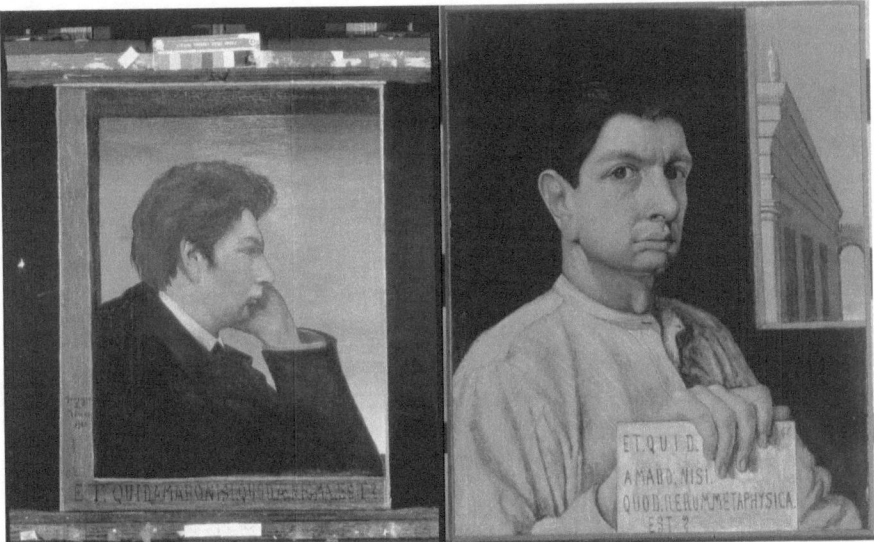

Figure 9.1. Two self-portraits, 1911 and 1920 by Georgio de Chirico.
Two images used with permission.
1. Art Resource, NY (1911 portrait). © 2022 Artists Rights Society (ARS), New York / SIAE, Rome
2. bpk Bildagentur / Sammlung Moderne Kunst / Pinakothek der Moderne/Bayerische Sta / Art Resource, NY (1920 portrait). © 2022 Artists Rights Society (ARS), New York / SIAE, Rome

of the second manifesto, however, allowed Breton to claim a more proactive side to surrealism, arguing that the surrealist attitude was not incompatible with a more operational elevation of thought. It gave more validity to his statement in the previous manifesto: "Can't the dream also be used in solving the fundamental questions of life?" he claimed.[17] His argument, in essence, was against an excessive rationalization, a reaction against the use of logical thought. In doing so, surrealism aimed, in fact, to approach the mysteries of existence, which are found in the enigmatic settings where the abrogation of our sense of time and space is achieved. This is exemplified in the text inserted in Giorgio de Chirico's self-portraits, which reads "Et quid amabo nisi quod aenigma est?" ("What shall I love if not the enigma?").

Despite the fact that both movements derive their forms of cannibalism from Dada, there are differences. The influence in surrealism is essentially expressed in the discovery of the unconscious through the exploration of the dream and psychoanalysis, while in Anthropophagy it is related with the anthropologic view expressed in Freud's *Totem and Taboo*. In a reinterpretation of Freud, the anthropophagic transformation of taboo into a totem means a return to a matriarchal system in opposition to capitalism, which is the owner of power and inheritance represented by colonialism in the patriarchal system.[18]

Both anthropophagy and surrealism preached violence through the promotion of a revolution. Cannibalism is the supreme act of savagery, the ultimate taboo, the thread that separates civilization from barbarism, which the Anthropophagy movement converted into an aesthetic maneuver. In contraposition, André Breton was explicit in his proclamation that surrealism was first and foremost a revolutionary movement, which aimed to revolutionize life through art by producing powerful and at the same time highly disturbing creations.[19] Anthropophagy proclaimed the "Caraib Revolution,"[20] which followed what Oswald de Andrade considered the sequence of revolutions that led to the state of society at the time: the French, the Romantic, the Bolshevist, and the Surrealist Revolutions. In doing so, he places surrealism as the immediate predecessor of Anthropophagy:

> Surrealism is one of the best pre-anthropophagic movements: the liberation of man as such, dictated through the unconscious and turbulent personal manifestations, was undoubtedly one of the most exciting spectacles for any anthropophagous heart that in recent years has accompanied the despair of the civilized man.[21]

This statement demonstrates the value that Oswald de Andrade placed in the primitivist valorization of the magical, instinctive and irrational elements of the human condition. Andrade's aversion to the logical-linear discourse inherited from the European colonizer led him to produce the manifesto in a surrealist language, where the unsystematic character and telegraphic style of aphorisms produce a multiplicity of interpretations through the juxtaposition of images and concepts, resembling a surrealist creation. Like most aesthetic movements of modernism, it had a strong connection with the visual arts, and was in fact inspired by the painting *Abaporu*[22] (Figure 1.1) by Andrade's future wife, Tarsila do Amaral. While until recently the surrealist connections of this painting have been relegated to a superficial and distant plane, more recent scholars identified Tarsila's deliberate and systematic engagement with the principles of surrealism:

> Her engagement was not one of pure emulation; instead, she turned the surrealists' penchant for satire and desire to disrupt hierarchical schema back on itself, parodying the images and ideas put forth by the movement to create a counter modernism. Amaral's sardonic appropriation of surrealism's formal languages and subversive strategies was the very factor that made Abaporu the catalyst of the anthropophagite movement.[23]

In music, the surrealist element can be interpreted in different ways. Edgard Varèse, whose revised version of *Amériques* was premiered together with Villa-Lobos's *Amazonas*, stated that his work *Arcana* was drawn from a dream sequence. While similar claims can hardly apply to Villa-Lobos's compositional method, it is curious that the composer Willy Corrêa de Oliveira published recently an essay about Villa-Lobos where he detected the incidence of dreams in the composer's method:

> The music he came to listen to during his world travels; things, sounds, images that only he was able to hear: like one who hears stars, in DREAMS, under the eyelids, multiple (unheard) noises and crystalline drops of fairy tale songs. . . . The *logic of dreams* hides from the awake man. Villa-Lobos—alchemist—transmuted *dreams* into musical realities; from fragments of *dreams* he sewed musical works—with the logic that escapes the vigilant man. Villa-Lobos, even "pre-destined," was a man awake. But with the gift of landing at night while working, and receiving from it ways of chaining, welding, which rule in *dreams*, however frighten us by day.[24]

There are also other composers whose music display surrealist inclinations, but this is due to their associations with painters or writers who clearly belonged to the surrealist movement. While such examples imply the indirect use of surrealism as a compositional process, surrealism appears in Villa-Lobos's music as an aesthetic component, through the incorporation of timeless myths associated with an Edenic imaginary. This process evolved in parallel with a similar treatment of Brazilian subjects by Tarsila do Amaral. In her paintings, the myth is created through ambiguity resultant from an "escape without hesitation from reality,"[25] where stylization reduces subjects to basic shapes. Their composition is achieved through regrouping of these shapes in a new order evocative of a theatrical set that constitutes a peculiar world with new connections and unexpected perspectives. These unexpected worlds found in Tarsila's paintings are also found in some of Villa-Lobos's musical compositions, such as the nocturnal dreamlike environment of *Uirapuru* and the mysterious landscape of *Amazonas*, which converges into a nightmare populated by monsters.[26]

It was in Villa-Lobos's apartment in Paris that Tarsila do Amaral and Oswald de Andrade were introduced to Benjamin Péret, a surrealist poet who in 1925 became the chief editor of the journal *La Révolution Surréaliste*. Péret was later associated with the Anthropophagy movement through his Brazilian connections. His wife, Elsie Houston, was a prominent Brazilian lyric singer and interpreter of Villa-Lobos's music, who performed the soprano part in the premiere of the *Suite Sugestiva*, his conspicuously surrealist composition. The incorporation of the myth in anthropophagic/surrealist works allowed for the creation of an exhilarating strangeness aimed to shake the audience out of its complacency and undisputed acceptance of established norms. It impregnated the works with the convulsive beauty defined by Breton, "the uncontrolled fusion of apparent opposites into one another in such a way as to embody both extremes without subsuming either, [which] was at the core of surrealist production and served as a mechanism for transgressing traditional boundaries and expected classifications."[27]

This fusion of opposites also appears in the structuralist theory of Claude Lévi-Strauss, the renowned French anthropologist who spent a number of years studying the Amerindians through expeditions in Brazil's interior. Lévi-Strauss posited that people think in terms of opposites—such as high and low, life and death, male and female, the raw and the cooked[28]—and that every culture can be understood in terms of these opposites. Structuralism implies the analysis of cultural systems in terms of the structural relations among their elements, and one of Lévi-Strauss's greatest and at the same time most controversial contributions, was the notion that due to their structural character, there is a homology between music and myth: "Music is able to overcome the aforementioned binary oppositions, which form the basic principle of mythical thought and language—the essence of human thought as it exists in their unconscious structures. Myth and music are instruments that overcome these oppositions by making up for the lack of logic."[29]

By viewing myths as exhibiting structures similar to musical constructions, Lévi-Strauss believed that analytical processes used for musical analysis could be applied to mythological structures, allowing us to better understand the pattern forming nature of the human mind. In addition, both music and myth are able to induce affective communication, "the pleasant illusion that contradictions could be surmounted and difficulties resolved." In the same way that the conflicts found in the narrative of a myth are resolved in the end, a musical composition has a cathartic function where "every melodic phrase or harmonic development offers an adventure" that ultimately leads to a cathartic experience for the listener.[30] Based on these contentions, the liberating and cathartic experience of music can be interpreted as the convulsive beauty advocated by surrealism, allowing the prospection that surrealistic elements are particularly evident in Villa-Lobos's anthropophagic works of mythological character, of which *Amazonas* and *Uirapuru* constitute emblematic examples.

The incorporation of myth is one of the most fundamental expressions of surrealism in the tropical anthropophagic art. While European surrealism is expressed in the irrationality of the dream, in Brazil, primitive irrationality is articulated in the alogical expression of the myth, which served Anthropophagy to criticize Brazilian history through its colonial past. At the same time, it served to establish a utopian horizon, in which the matriarchy of the primitive community would replace the patriarchal bourgeois system of the European colonizer and the capitalist system.

Anthropophagy advocated for the assimilation not only of surrealism, but the whole myriad of modernist styles developed in Europe. Through the practice of anthropophagic appropriation, Brazilian artists such as Tarsila do Amaral, Oswald de Andrade and Villa-Lobos turned their artworks back on themselves to produce a sardonic palimpsest of modernist tendencies. Yet, within the dialectic integration of multiple modernist influences, it was surrealism that uttered the last word, after all

> the real flesh of the Manifesto, the part that is truly cannibalized, is surrealist, since Surrealism is directly mentioned twice: "Heritage. Contact with the Carib side of Brazil. Où Villegaignon print terre. Montaigne. Natural man. Rousseau. From the French Revolution to Romanticism, to the Bolshevik Revolution, to the *Surrealist* Revolution and Keyserling's technicized barbarian. We push onward [. . .] We already had Communism. We already had *Surrealist* language. The Golden Age."[31]

The expression without restraint of imagination and the magical element through the incorporation of the myth connects surrealism with anthropophagy. As to the subconscious, which is considered an essential element of the Freudian surrealism, it is diluted in music through the carnivalization of surrealism.

The Carnivalization of Surrealism

In order to understand the Brazilian version of surrealism, it is necessary to reread the meaning of the idea of carnivalization proposed by Bakhtin,[32] by giving it an anthropophagic bias. Carnival is a striking and omnipresent feature in Brazilian culture, a celebration that occupies an absolutely central place in the identity of the country, and it produces a carnivalized conception of the world and life. The great strength of Bakhtin's theory comes from the consideration that carnival as a comic rite has the power to counteract an official culture of serious tone, creating a parallel universe, a second life that generates a duality in our perception of the world. According to Bakhtin, this double perception of the world has always been present since the dawn of humanity.

Carnival and its precursors seem to possess a seminal principle of human existence, a sort of primordial form of civilization. Bakhtin elevated carnival to a position where it is directly linked to everyday life and, in fact, is confused with life itself. Poetically, carnival is an effective way of living life, even if in a transitory way, becoming a form of aestheticization of human existence. By taking this stance, our life can be seen as an ideal form resurrected by carnival, in which our existence becomes reduced to a situation that is both dreamlike and real.

This second life created by carnival has a utopian character of universality, which the Anthropophagy movement rescued: the search for freedom, equality between people without hierarchies, where the absence of rules and taboos predominates. Therefore, carnival can be interpreted as the anthropophagic transformation of taboo—the official culture, which has a serious tone and represses the unconscious impulses of man—into a totem, the liberation of the collective desires anchored in the image of the Amerindian. The collective desires are associated with sexual freedom, valorization of nudity, full idleness, paradisiacal life, unconscious creativity, and happiness. This perspective brings out an artistic language anchored in satire, parody, creative decontextualization, and the aesthetics of collage, which frequently display the approximation between distant and/or disparate elements and humor. "As a result, this provisional elimination, at the same time ideal and effective, of hierarchical relations between individuals, created in the public square a particular type of communication, inconceivable in normal situations."[33] Anthropophagy—like carnival—produces an inversion of the world. Carnival language uses a reverse logic, which creates a new world in reverse, where antinomian pairs are swapped: the superior versus bottom; the scholar versus popular; the high versus low. World and life are turned upside down.

The transgression of sacred values by carnival revelers appears in the outlandish behavior of the surrealist artists, and it is redolent from the out of proportion Dada irreverence. Poetic surrealism does not make concessions to courtesy or adequate social behavior. It is the eccentric side of surrealist that toys with reality, defies logic, and provokes a confusing mental state. Nobody personified more this attitude than Salvador Dalí, with his extravagant statements and eccentric lifestyle. His behavior finds a correspondence in Villa-Lobos eccentricities: In the late 1920s, Villa-Lobos spent four years in Paris (1927–1930) and covered his apartment at the Place St. Michel with an exotic and colorful wallpaper. He had a suit (or pajamas) made to exactly match the wallpaper, which he used to receive prominent artists and dignitaries at home. The effect was of Villa-Lobos's head walking within the apartment over an invisible body as he received his guests.[34] Other characteristics of the Brazilian composer's eccentricities that made him a picturesque and controversial figure, such as his habit of distorting facts about his biography, his fictional travels across the country, his pseudo-collection of folk materials, and even his habit of predating several of his compositions could be related to the typical irreverence of surrealism.

This feature of surrealism reveals a penchant for humor, parody, and satirical irony through the representation of shocking images that defy logic, while introducing a bizarre super-reality. Both the surrealist and the anthropophagic avant-gardes were connected with primitivism, as a method of liberation from the trauma resultant from the process of culturalization (in the case of surrealism) or colonization (in the case of anthropophagy). They were also catalysts of revolutions, as explained previously.[35] In a way, both movements sought to bring back the romantic allure of the dream, the enchanted moments erased by the bourgeoise civilization: the poetry, the passion, imagination, the magic, the myth, the revolution, and the utopia. Surrealism and anthropophagy aimed to break with causality logic through a detour toward the past or the subconscious, combined with the creation of a modern mythology.

Brazilian surrealism had one special dimension that distinguished it from its European counterpart: the carnivalization of art. In Brazil, particularly in Rio de Janeiro, the carnival has a side of social satire and mockery of the authorities, as well as a general reversal of day-to-day rules and norms. This feature mirrors surrealism's "rebellion against convention, moral codes, and the inhibitions of the conscious mind." It includes circus elements, with people wearing costumes and masks, allowing them to lose their everyday individuality and experience a heightened sense of social unity. This idea is expressed in Oswald de Andrade's assertion that "we were never catechized. Instead, we produced Carnival. The Amerindian in costume of senator of the Empire."[36]

In the beginning of the twentieth century, Brazilian carnival was characterized by the *cordões* and *ranchos carnavalescos* (carnival rows), so appreciated by the young Villa-Lobos, and which proliferated mainly in Rio de Janeiro, then capital of the country. The *cordões* were groups of organized revelers who paraded through the streets in a row, with their participants dressed in costumes, walking and dancing one after the other. At the front of the parade was the group called *Abre-Alas* (Open the Way), made up of people dressed as Amerindians who, in large numbers, danced like savages blowing ox horns as if they were trumpets, producing hisses and inventing words that imitated the language of the natives.[37] They were followed by other groups wearing costumes of clowns, old people, nobility, devils, *baianas*,[38] and several other types of characters.[39]

It was one decade after Villa-Lobos's birth, right at the turn of the nineteenth century, when the genre of the carnival march began to become a prominent musical genre in Rio de Janeiro.[40] Very few artistic manifestations reflected so creatively the spirit of the time. Their lyrics were chronicles of the life in the city, the features, virtues, and vices of the people. Frequently with a mocking tone, many of those songs are virtually untranslatable. For example, a famous carnival march of Portuguese origin from 1917 called *A Baratinha* (The Cockroach)[41]—the year when Villa-Lobos arguably "conceived" *Amazonas* and *Uirapuru*—was about a cockroach, an insect that subliminally anticipates the surrealistic ants of Dalí's paintings such as *The Persistence of Memory*.[42] Here is an attempt to translate an excerpt from the surrealist lyrics:

Perna de porco, é presunto,	Leg of pig is ham
Mão de vaca, é mocotó,	Cow's hand is "mocotó"[43]
Quem quiser viver feliz,	Anyone who wants to live happily
Deve sempre dormir só . . .	Should always sleep alone . . .

Like other modernist artists, Villa-Lobos spent substantial time in Paris, first from 1923–1924, when he met Oswald de Andrade, Blaise Cendrars, Erik Satie and Jean Cocteau, among others, at the studio of Tarsila do Amaral; and from 1927–1930, when he met Edgard Varèse, Pablo Picasso, Leopold Stokowski, and Aaron Copland. By the time of his second trip, Josephine Baker was already the great sensation of Paris. In 1929 she toured Brazil, staying as guest in Oswald de Andrade's farm while in Rio de Janeiro. Baker was famous for her *dance sauvage* and her costume, which consisting of only a short skirt of artificial bananas and a beaded necklace, became an iconic image and a symbol of the Jazz Age and the 1920s. Legend says that this surrealist banana costume was conceived in a dream of Jean Cocteau. Among the hits of Josephine Baker is the Brazilian carnival march *Chiquita Bacana* (1948),[44] which was lost in translation as *Chiquita Madame de la Martinique*:

Chiquita Bacana lá da Martinica	Nice little lady from Martinique
Se veste com uma	dresses with
Casca de banana nanica.	a nanica[45] banana peel.
Não usa vestido, não usa calção	Does not wear a dress, does not wear shorts

Inverno pra ela é pleno verão	Winter for her is midsummer
Existencialista (com toda razão!)	Existentialist (with all reason!) [46]
Só faz o que manda o seu coração.	Only follows what her heart dictates.

This carnival song explores the idea of sexual liberation inherited from France through the exotic setting of Martinique, a colony of France. *Chiquita* is a female name, and *bacana* is a Portuguese slang word that means "cool" in the sense of stylish and trendy. So, Chiquita is a cool girl from Martinique who loves to walk around naked, while audiences loved the poetic and surrealist connection of the rhyme *bacana* with banana. In the same way, Martinica was just an excuse for the appropriation of the name for the rhyme with nanica, the most popular variety of edible bananas in Brazil. In fact, it was Brazil and not Martinique, the stereotypical "banana republic," an underdeveloped tropical and fertile Eden, where banana could be viewed both as a symbol of the country and a phallic object.[47] In later shows in Paris, Josephine Baker was accompanied on stage by her cheetah pet, called "Chiquita." Often the animal would escape into the orchestra pit, terrorizing the musicians.

Though the song *Chiquita Bacana* came later, in 1939 the fixation with bananas had been already introduced in the musical comedy *Banana da Terra* (Banana of the Land), a Brazilian film that belonged to the tradition of self-deprecating carnival movies. João de Barro, one of the scriptwriters was the cowriter of both *Chiquita Bacana* and the carnival march *Yes, nós temos bananas* (Yes, We Have Bananas),[48] which became the big hit of Brazilian carnival in the previous year (1938),[49] which included the following excerpt:

Yes, nós temos bananas	Yes, we've got bananas
Bananas pra dar e vender	Bananas to give away and to sell
Banana, menina, tem vitamina	Bananas, young lady, are full of vitamins
Banana engorda e faz crescer.	Bananas fatten you up and make you grow.
Vai para a França o café, pois é!	Coffee goes off to France, sure enough
Para o Japão o algodão, pois não!	And cotton to Japan of course
Pro mundo inteiro homem ou mulher	To the whole world, for men or women
Bananas para quem quiser.	There are bananas for anyone who wants them.

The movie *Banana da Terra* marks the first time that Carmen Miranda, the "Brazilian bombshell," performed the song *O que que a baiana tem* (What Is It That the *Baiana* Has?)[50] wearing the famous costume of *baiana*, which included an elaborate hat in the form of a turban decorated with fruits. The *baiana* represented the Afro-Brazilian woman from state Bahia[51] who sold food on the streets of Rio de Janeiro. Thus, the banana migrated from Josephine Baker's skirt to Carmen Miranda's iconic hat. Months after the release of *Banana da terra*, Baker returned for a second tour in Brazil and performed the same song, *O que que a baiana tem*, in Rio de Janeiro, wearing a *baiana* costume in homage to Carmen Miranda, and on the same stage where the latter performed it a few months prior.[52] That was the occasion when Miranda was discovered by an American agent who took her to the United States in May of 1939 to make her a sensation on Broadway and Hollywood, where by 1945, she was the highest-paid entertainer.[53]

Ultimately, Carmen Miranda became the muse of Tropicália, the Brazilian artistic movement of the 1960s that revived the idea of cannibalism, and therefore is known today as the Second Anthropophagic Movement (see chapter 1). Tropicália was an anarchist and anti-authoritarian movement during the country's military dictatorship that used Cultural Cannibalism to

Figure 9.2. The bananas migrated from Josephine Baker's skirt during her dance sauvage to Carmen Miranda's hat-turban, decorated with tropical fruits.
Josephine Baker (1927) by Walery; Carmen Miranda (1943) Billboard 1943 Music Yearbook

incorporate American pop culture aiming to promote a countercultural revolution. Its hybrid model mingled traditional Brazilian rhythms with electric guitars and psychedelic elements. Many Brazilians saw such hybridization as a negative adulteration of authentic national music, a similar criticism suffered by Carmen Miranda, who years earlier created a stereotyped image of Brazil as it was viewed by North Americans.

Villa-Lobos's trajectory followed that of Josephine Baker and Carmen Miranda. His international career as composer took him to Paris during the years when Baker became a great sensation there, and he visited extensively the United States between 1944 and 1949, which were peak years in the career of Carmen Miranda. Villa-Lobos was deeply influenced by the urban folklore and popular music of his country, where carnival in Rio de Janeiro was the most emblematic manifestation, a kaleidoscope of surrealistic impressions that marked his development as composer. Since his youth, Villa-Lobos appreciated the customs of the old carnivals in Rio de Janeiro, which led him to revive the *cordões carnavalescos* on his own initiative in 1940.[54] In the same year, he became president of the jury of a carnival songs competition that happened in the field of a soccer team.

His hometown, Rio de Janeiro, is known as the "marvelous city," immortalized in the carnival march *Cidade Maravilhosa* of 1935, which became the anthem of the city. Both Carmen Miranda and her sister Aurora sang this song numerous times, making it immensely popular. The eulogy of the "marvelous" is at the core of the surrealist movement, alluded to by André Breton in the First Surrealist Manifesto of 1924: "Let us not mince words: the marvelous is always beautiful, anything marvelous is beautiful, in fact only the marvelous is beautiful."[55] The *marvelous* is defined as exacerbated beauty, mirrored in the perpetual anxiety underlying the human experience. The experience of the marvelous has been qualified as "convulsive beauty," manifested in the artist's strivings to be part of the unconscious divine.

Breton was convinced that the colonized possessed a sort of natural or immediate contact with the marvelous, due to the fact that the interaction of the primitive with nature is not mediated by reason. Since surrealism gains access to the marvelous through an immersion in the senses, the natural landscape provides the ideal setting for the engagement with the marvelous. Alejo Carpentier corroborated the idea of "the marvelous" as being an innate Latin American characteristic that preceded the advent of surrealism, echoing Oswald de Andrade's statement that "we already had surrealist language."[56] As Carpentier asserts, "the marvelous begins to be unmistakably marvelous when it arises from an unexpected alteration of reality . . . perceived with particular intensity . . . that leads it to a kind of extreme state [estado limite]."⁵⁷ It is this aspect that will be explored when examining the incidence of surrealism in Villa-Lobos's aesthetic.

The Anthropophagic Surrealism

One of the great criticisms of today's approach of multiculturalism refers to the attempt to explain the world from the point of view of Western hegemonic culture. Such a posture would block the thinking of the subaltern culture, which is peripheral, preventing the emergence of the heterogeneity of the "Other."⁵⁸ The consequence is that the "Other" ends up being constituted as a shadow of itself, where the subordinate culture cannot "speak" but "is spoken" through the voice of the central culture, and thus cannot express the reality of a way of life that occurs in non-European or non-Anglo-American socio-geographical spaces.

This implies that to understand anthropophagic thought, it would be necessary to adopt "the subaltern's point of view," the "savage thought"—*la pensée sauvage*—that Anthropophagy aimed to rescue, that is, the myth as magical thought. Lévi-Strauss argues that primitive magical thinking cannot be understood if we reduce it

> to a moment or stage of technical and scientific evolution. . . . Magical thinking is not a debut, a beginning, an outline, a part of a whole not yet accomplished; it forms a well-articulated System; independent, at this point, of this other system that constitutes science, except for the formal analogy that brings them together and that makes the first a kind of metaphorical expression of the second.⁵⁹

Savage thought is not a primitive form of scientific thinking. For this study, the main aspect that differentiates savage thinking from civilized thinking is the *denial of binary thinking*, of logical rationalism, which was characterized by the dialectical relations of cause and effect of Cartesian determinism. The speaker's perspective is no longer unidirectional, of the subject over the object; but multidirectional, disappearing the passive object, which is now heard and impacts as subject. Instead of binary thinking, the use of "Amerindian perspectivism" is proposed, according to which "Amerindian ontological regimes diverge from those more widespread in the West precisely with regard to the inverse semiotic functions attributed to body and soul,"⁶⁰ thus subverting also the related binaries, such as the universal and the particular, fact and value, animality and humanity, nature and culture.

In other words, the anthropophagic ritual allows the "Other" to be assimilated into the "Self," causing both to lose their individual identity.

Anthropophagy therefore promotes a *dissociation* from the Self, through the incorporation of the Other, where both lose their individuality and autonomy.[61] The *dissociation* process moves from the *individual* unconscious to the *collective*, where indigenous thought introduces the ritual element of the myth. As the duality between the self and the other disappears, the concept of dichotomy also disappears. The result is that binary thinking is replaced by *pluralist perspectivist thinking*, which allows the manifestation of multiple points of view attributed to all living beings. In this respect, several scholars agree: According to Cocco, Anthropophagy is an irreducible theory of multiplicities;[62] according to Clastres, "the logic of savage societies is a logic of the centrifugal, a logic of the multiple. The savages want the multiplication of the multiple";[63] and in the words of Alexandre Nodari, "the indigenous issue is to move from the two to the multiple, both in content and in form."[64]

This type of thinking when aimed at the carnivalization of life brought a surrealist dimension to anthropophagic art. When reading the Anthropophagous Manifesto (Appendix 1), one is confronted with a plurality of binary theoretical references, confronting Marxist materialism with Freudian psychoanalysis, the views of the "savage" from the perspective of Rousseau or Montaigne, the anthropological ideas of Levy-Bruhl and the technological philosophies of Keyserling. Such juxtapositions are pure surrealism, and their plurality asserts a carnivalized worldview that goes against any orthodoxy.

Anthropophagic Spacetime

Like other modernist movements, surrealism addressed new paradigms found in our view of reality. Indirectly, the surrealists acknowledged that the aberrations of time and space that are experienced when we dream are more in line with the counterintuitive reality posited in the new findings in science. Dream time does not obey the linearity of chronological time, and dream space does not conform to Euclid's axioms. Dreams also violate the laws of causality. Surrealist art approached the unconscious to celebrate the power of imagination. Their images conjure up the distortion of common elements found in nature, as well as the juxtaposition in space of unlikely things—elements and objects—with the abrogation of linear time. From the melting clocks of Dalí to the enigmatic paintings of de Chirico, a new conception of time is internalized. Dalí's *Christ of Saint John of the Cross* or Magritte's *The Glasshouse* approach, in a different, original way, the concept of a single frame of reference explored by the cubists; *Melancholy and Mystery of a Street*, by Giorgio de Chirico, violates traditional perspective by exaggerating the depth of the landscape. Each surrealist artwork can approach, through images, all the counterintuitive aspects of the modern conceptualization of reality.

European primitivism meant going back in time in search for the primeval origins of expression; or outward in space, in its curiosity concerning geographically distant primitive civilizations, particularly the ones from Africa and Oceania. In Latin America, a search for the elusive and mythical roots of inspiration progressed beyond the preoccupation with preindustrial or tribal societies. In Brazil, it evolved mainly into two models: one involving the outreach to geographical locations in the country densely impacted with legends; and another, which sought to see the mechanisms of modern society and everyday life as contemporary counterparts of ancient ritual, since the mestizo artists coexisted simultaneously—at least theoretically—with the primitive Amerindians in the same point of history. As modernist manifestations, both European and Brazilian primitivism redefined the coordinates of time and space, in correspondence with the discoveries of relativity in science.

Considering that Brazilian primitivism is focused on the collective myth replacing the individual dream of European surrealism, some scholars have used a Nietzschean approach to characterize the new coordinates of time and space as "the *intempestive* (or *untimely*) and *deterritorialized*."[65] Brazilian primitivism is usually not localized, due to the vastness of the territory. Artistic representations of the Amerindian are nonspecific, because the Tupi people that inhabited most of Brazil were divided into numerous tribes that despite speaking a common language, did not display a unified identity. Through hierophanies, the Amerindian creates his sacred space with a nonlocalized geography, something analogous to the establishment of the "Arcadia" during the Renaissance. In this sense, the *locus* of anthropophagic ideas is *deterritorialized*.

The *intempestive* or *untimely* means something that is at the same time *on our time*, *counter to our time*, and *for a time to come*, something that can be applied for example to the Caraib Revolution mentioned in the Anthropophagous Manifesto. It is a concept that comes from the interpretation by Deleuze and Guattari of a formulation by Nietzsche. According to them, "there is no act of creation that is not transhistorical and does not come up from behind or proceed by way of a liberated line. Nietzsche opposes history not to the eternal but to the subhistorical or superhistorical: the Untimely . . . "[66]

Derived from the *intempestive* or *untimely* is one of the most fascinating aspects of the Anthropophagous Manifesto: the reversal of chronology through a negation of history. For Oswald de Andrade, there is a chronology of ideas that superseded the chronology of dates.⁶⁷ In its glorification of the primitive, the denial of logic discourse is accompanied by the abrogation of the linearity of the arrow of time: "Down with the histories of Man that begin at Cape Finisterre. The undated world. Unrubrified," is proclaimed in the Manifesto.⁶⁸ In its critique of memory, the text exalts the personal experience for the achievement of wisdom, in detriment to memories that can be viewed as mental crutches. Memories and history are impositions characterized by European classifications of events and hierarchy of people.⁶⁹ The negation of collective history and individual memory became a *sine qua non* condition for the achievement of intellectual, artistic, and spiritual independence.

> Anthropophagy had at its core the reinvention of relations with the past. In this movement, more than the 'historical man'—of eschatological time and the progress of civilizations—created by the science of history itself, the interest was about the "undated man," a spectral figure associated with a remote past that remained as a wonder to the impasses and paradoxes of the historical world, particularly through the "disappeared matriarchal structures." The 'undated' allowed access to another past, another time.⁷⁰

Therefore, the temporality that appears in the Anthropophagous Manifesto is that of an "undated world," which does not mean "with no history," but an undated history. For Viveiros de Castro, this conception of time is defined by the anthropophagic ritual itself:

> in the Tupinambá dialogue [. . .] the present is the time of justification, that is, of revenge: of the affirmation of time. The duet and the duel between captive and killer, indissolubly associating the two faces of the warrior, who respond and listen to each other—the questions and answers are interchangeable—is what makes a relationship between past and future possible. . . . Far from being a device of an original integrity, and thus of 'denial of becoming,' the revenge complex, through this verbal agonism, produced *time*: the rite was the great Present.⁷¹

In short, the anthropophagic rite renews and founds time at each meeting between the captive and the cannibal killer. Summing up, as modernist manifestations, both European and Brazilian primitivism redefined the coordinates of time and space. The new perspectives "prospered under freshly colored banners of relativity in both science and art, where a new sense of time fostered illuminations available only through simultaneous projection, where the artists of visual arts set the stage."⁷² Yet, the conceptualization of time acquired new colors in music, which is after all an art that unfolds in time.

In the Overture of his book *The Raw and the Cooked*, Lévi-Strauss compares myth and music with respects to the temporality of human experience: "Both, indeed, are instruments for the obliteration of time."[73] In this view, music and myth require a natural diachronic dimension in order to exist since both take place in time, however simultaneously they transform "time into its own enclosed synchronic form."[74] Through its conception of the past as a timeless model, the Anthropophagic Manifesto accomplished the transformation of history into a myth.

Anthropophagy manages to juxtapose impulsive and incoherent aspects, such as the swirling rhetoric of modern life defended by the Futurists in opposition to the Dadaist's denial of all artistic and literary value of the past, so that the excitement about the future changes the understanding of the past. Anthropophagy thus proposes a transhistorical, paradoxical treatment, where the present precedes and at the same time succeeds precolonial Brazil in the creation of a utopian future, where "time without memory of a myth plunges into the hopeful time of a utopia that has yet to be accomplished."[75]

In other words, the Anthropophagic Manifesto promotes the pairing of Brazil's precolonial past with the avant-garde utopias of the future. The statement "we already had communism. We already had the surrealist language" in our Golden Age, suggests an historic inversion, where the matriarchy of the primitive would lead to the decline of capitalism to produce a new Golden Age. The victory of technology would then allow the new man a social overcoming that would free him for the exercise of leisure, spontaneity and primitive joy, in other words, the communism that was already present in the primitive society of the Amerindian.

The historic inversion allows us to speculate a deeper meaning in Villa-Lobos's habit to predate his later compositions, which, according to a number of critics, streamed from his desire to project the image of a more innovative composer in an era that praised originality over everything else.[76] The same can be said about Giorgio de Chirico, one of the most influential precursors of surrealism, who also developed the habit to predate a number of his works. Leonard Shlain noted that de Chirico's goal was "to overthrow the tyranny of the Western idea of absolute time [where] these guerilla-style attacks by a lone artist can be interpreted as a hit-and-run terrorist assault upon the domination and inflexibility of this invariant concept."[77]

All the processes described above imply that anthropophagic surrealism is characterized by a reshuffling of history based on a reassessment of memory, combined with the juxtaposition of conflicting materials through the manipulation of both time and space that provides a new set of coordinates.

Musical Surrealism

Considering that surrealism had such a pivotal impact in the development of cultural anthropophagy in Brazil, Villa-Lobos as the main representative in the music field was not immune to this influence. Anthropophagy complemented the expression of subconsciousness explored in surrealism with the aggressiveness of the Dada movement, the reduction to geometric forms of cubism, the "imagination without strings"[78] of futurism and other stimuli. These were reflected in Villa-Lobos's rhetoric: Cubism appears in the clipping of music materials, futurism appears in the use of sound blocks, Dadaism appears in the clash of his harmonic language, and surrealism appears in the juxtaposition of textures, as demonstrated below. All these multiple influences were encompassed under the umbrella of primitivism, a mixture of ingenuity and purity, of instinctive rebellion and mythical elaboration that constituted the historic fountain of Brazilian culture.

In an interview with the magazine *Newsweek*, Villa-Lobos classified himself as an "atonal neo-primitive."[79] However, contrasting with the prehistorical setting of *The Rite of Spring*, Villa-Lobos's landscape is unspoiled and idyllic, the *locus* where natural elements coexist with mythical creatures. The mythological associations of the Amerindian universe within the monumental landscape of the Amazon region, produced a sacred space where events take place in a mythical, atemporal time, as exemplified by *Uirapuru* and *Amazonas*. Both works reveal the "wonderful nature" described in the colonial literature of the time, combined with the Amerindian legends that the composer utilized for the program of these symphonic poems, which are also considered ballets.

> Villa-Lobos's musical landscape constructed an Edenic vision of Brazilian nature by expanding the sounds evoking nature including a wider range of forest sounds, animals, monsters, natural and supernatural beings, and by using Indian-like legends that reframed the identification of the Indian with nature and installed an atemporal mythical time.[80]

The exuberant orchestration, the use of leitmotifs, the dense texture, and the structure composed of individual cut-out sections give an epic aspect to these symphonic poems, where "the cumulative meaning of the recurring themes articulated within nonfunctional harmony creates a new kind of discourse that concurs to the installment of mythical time."[81] The use of rhythmic ostinatos that resemble the use of the indigenous drums are references to the concept of "eternal return," which Mircea Eliade attributes to primitive civilizations, and is another manifestation of mythic atemporality.[82]

Villa-Lobos conveys this dim mythological world above all through the manipulation of textures, which became a trademark of his compositional method. In doing so, he does not hesitate to juxtapose contradictory materials in the various layers of the texture, producing a disorientation of the auditory sense not unlike the bizarre juxtapositions in surrealist paintings.[83] This demonstrates that surrealism appears not only in the mythical spirit of the compositions, but is an integral part of Villa-Lobos's compositional style. The manipulation of textures became his trademark, just as the exploration of rhythm is so emblematic in the *Rite of Spring*, that it practically defined Stravinsky's primitivism. This allows us to conjecture that in a similar way, surrealism is the basic aesthetic that characterizes Villa-Lobos's modernist style.

A detail that often goes unnoticed is the possibility of a more somber and Freudian reading of Villa-Lobos's Amazonian symphonic poems. According to Hal Foster's view, surrealism has a dark side related to a compulsion to repeat and an impulse to death.[84] In *Uirapuru*, the arrow of the Amerindian huntress allows the bird to become the object of desire in the form of the handsome Amerindian, while the arrow can be interpreted as a phallic symbol. Upon being mortally wounded by another arrow emitted by the malicious savage, which is a character of the opposite sex, a mortal process leading to the final transfiguration goes back once again to Wagner.[85] In *Amazonas*, the death of the sensual Amerindian virgin who "dives into the abysm of her own desire" can be viewed as a representation of repressed sexuality. In both compositions, the drive toward death is prepared by sections that display a compulsion toward repetition through the use of ostinatos. Those ostinatos feature the use of percussion reminiscent of carnival drums, and they reflect the statement of Oswald de Andrade in a lecture given in 1923 at the Sorbonne, when he said that "one could never feel as intensively the suggestive encounter of the drum of the negro and the indigenous singing in the atmosphere of Paris. These ethnic forces are in full modernity."[86]

The transference of Wagner to the Brazilian jungle in both occasions is as parodic as the construction of the Amazon Theater, an opera theater that is considered a "jewel in the heart of the Amazon rainforest,"[87] and inspired Werner Herzog's movie *Fitzcarraldo*. The carnivalization of Wagner, which is a surrealist manifestation, had also been evident in the Brazilwood Manifesto, where Oswald de Andrade wrote:

> Carnival in Rio is the religious event of the race. Brazilwood. Wagner submerges before *Botafogo's cordões*. Barbarian and ours. The rich ethnic background. Vegetable richness. The ore. The kitchen. *Vatapá*, gold and dance.[88]

When Oswald de Andrade wrote that Brazil's surrealism preceded the European, the time reversal allegorically insinuated was already a reality in Villa-Lobos' aesthetic. In chapter 3 it is demonstrated that the Brazilian composer produced in *Polichinelo* the surrealist juxtaposition of a nursery song and a carnival song that praises drunkenness. The composition is a premature example of the incidence of surrealism in Villa-Lobos, occurring half a dozen years before the official formulation of the movement in André Breton's first manifesto, and ten years before the launch of the Anthropophagous Manifesto. At the other end of the spectrum is Villa-Lobos's *Suite Sugestiva (Cinemas)*—Suggestive Suite—written in 1929 during the composer's second stay in Paris, and premiered in the same year of the publication of the Second Surrealist Manifesto.

The *Suite Sugestiva*

The *Suite Sugestiva* is a composition in seven movements that exhibits unique characteristics within the composer's output, and also represents his most conspicuous foray into the field of surrealist aesthetics, where the aspect of carnivalization appears quite explicitly. It reflects both the composer's taste for cinema, as well as the advent of surrealist films that were appearing in France in the 1920s. The instrumentation includes single winds, a trumpet, a trombone, percussion, piano, celesta and a string quartet formed by violin, viola, cello, and double bass. This unique formation appears not only as a reminder of the small film orchestras with which Villa-Lobos worked during his youth, but also the new original chamber formations characteristic of the time, such as Schoenberg's Pierrot ensemble and Stravinsky's L'Histoire ensemble. In addition to the unique instrumentation, the composer's mastery in dealing with the timbres is observed, expanding the performance techniques of the instruments and obtaining magnificent sound effects with economy of resources.

The seven movements of the suite are framed by the opening and the finale, while the inner movements can be grouped in opposite pairs according to their theatrical nature: the third movement represents a comedy while the fourth represents a drama; the fifth movement is comical while the sixth is tragic:

1. Overture de L'Homme Tell
2. Prelude, Choral et Funèbre (cine journal, text by Oswald de Andrade)
3. Croche-pied au Flic (comédie, text by Oswald de Andrade)
4. Le Recit de Peureux (drame, text by Oswald de Andrade)

5. Charlot Aviateur (comique, text by René Chalup)
6. L'Enfant et le Youroupari (tragédie, text by Manuel Bandeira)
7. La Marche Finale

The suite also includes two singers: a soprano and a baritone. The texts are by Oswald de Andrade, the founder of the Anthropophagy movement in Brazil, Manuel Bandeira, another prominent Brazilian modernist poet, and René Chalup, the only French representative. Chalup was a poet and music critic, whose father was one of the administrators of *Salle Gaveau*, the concert hall where Villa-Lobos presented his works for the first time to the Parisian public.

The verses by Oswald de Andrade were originally written in Portuguese, and their translation into French is problematic. The challenge resides in Oswald's style, whose poems are marked by informal expressions, synthesis (his texts are truly aphoristic miniatures), telegraphic language, as well as broken, fragmented, and subliminal syntax. His poems are taken from the poetry book *Pau-Brasil* (Brazilwood, 1925),[89] a byproduct of his manifesto of the same name published in the previous year. One can argue that the incorporation of the translated poems into the *Suite Sugestiva* constitutes the ultimate act of surreal barbarism, equivalent to bringing a savage Amerindian from the depths of the Amazonian region to attend a performance at the Opera Garnier during the Belle Époque.[90]

The connection of the *Suite Sugestiva* with surrealism through an association with cinema is an important expression of the synesthetic relation of the senses that was intensively explored by artists in the beginning of the twentieth century. According to Steven Kovács, surrealism is the first literary and artistic movement to become seriously associated with cinema.[91] The advent of surrealism coincided with the birth of motion pictures, and the artists who took part in the movement were not only among the first generation to grow up with films as a part of their daily lives, but also a number of visual artists such as Dalí, Duchamp, and Léger ventured into the new medium. Cinema allowed surrealist artists to explore the boundaries between fantasy and reality within the confines of time and space. In this respect, films were the most palpable way to conjure up images and situations that were close to dreams or the unconscious states of mind, an idea articulated in Buñuel's statement that "the film is like an involuntary imitation of the dream . . . cinema seems to have been invented to express the life of the subconscious."[92]

The *Overture de L'Homme Tell* is a parody of Rossini's *William Tell Overture*, and it is the longest movement of the suite. Villa-Lobos later expanded the orchestration and published the work separately for possible execution independently of the suite. The element of parody that Villa-Lobos incorporated represents the Dada spirit to satirize traditional conventions of opera as a high art, the idea "to juggle away, to parody, and to ridicule all 'accepted ideas,' all forms of social activity."[93] The Brazilian musicologist Mário de Andrade characterized the Suite as "a joke, quite comical at times, with which the great musician diverted from the worlds of exaltation in which he lives."[94]

Villa-Lobos maintains the same structure in four sections of Rossini's overture and includes melodic quotations and clearly recognizable orchestral gestures, which are brought to a soundscape of non-tonal orientation. The first section keeps the main musical gestures and the meter of the opera overture; Rossini's storm scene corresponds to a section where the theme is represented by metals and ends with a trombone cadence; the *ranz des vaches* is replaced by a section reminiscent of the Brazilian *modinha* genre, a type of sentimental love song, maintaining the timbre of the oboe for the solo, accompanied by arpeggiated figures by the clarinet; and the emblematic final section emulates the famous string *saltando* of William Tell, as shown in the figure below. As a result, the *Overture de L'Homme Tell* is an intelligent and original parody of the *William Tell Overture*, through its avoidance of processes of hybridization or stylization of themes.

Although written by one of the most prominent Italian composers, *William Tell* is an opera in French, written within the conventions of "grand opera." Within the silent film tradition that used small orchestras in Rio de Janeiro, the beginning of the musical cinematographic programs invariably started with this overture, "and the musicians eased the work by parodying that masterpiece."[95] Its inclusion in the *Suite Sugestiva* curiously prophesies its popularity in cartoons and the Lone Ranger movies.

Figure 9.3. Comparison of the last section of Rossini's *William Tell Overture* and Villa-Lobos's *Overture de L'Homme Tell*.
Created by the author.

The cinema program used to present next the "cine journal," which highlighted the most important news of the time for the audience. In the suite, the second movement received the title *Prelude, Choral et Funèbre*, a clear nod to César Franck, composer of works such as *Prelude, Chorale and Fugue*; *Prelude, Aria and Finale* and *Prelude, Fugue and Variation*. Villa-Lobos's joke is to give such an eminent title for an aphoristic movement of just a little over one minute of duration, instead of a composition with three contrasting sections.[96]

However, the most surreal aspect of the movement is not the title pun, but a parody of Schoenberg. The movement is written aphoristically, a miniature for chamber ensemble where the female singer is expected to deliver the text through the use of *sprechstimme*, in a clear reference to *Pierrot Lunaire*.[97] The latter was premiered in Paris in December 1921, conducted by Darius Milhaud, who lived in Brazil from 1917 to 1919, and interacted with Villa-Lobos in a number of occasions. In December 1927, Schoenberg himself conducted *Pierrot Lunaire* in Paris, and Villa-Lobos, who was then living in France's capital, certainly took interest in the music. The orchestration of the second movement reminds one of the Pierrot ensemble, with minimal intervention of the brass, used only to articulate the form. The flute carries the melody accompanied by the waltz motion of the strings, while the percussion is written in quadruple meter through hemiolas.

Ironically, the characteristics of Oswald de Andrade's poetry that make it impossible to translate, are also responsible for a strong plastic quality that brings it closer to a cinematographic language quite appropriate for the suite. According to Haroldo de Campos, Oswald de Andrade "inaugurated in our literature the appropriation of cinematographic procedures with the intention of composing discontinuous, simultaneous and fragmented images."[98] The lyrics of the second movement of the suite come from the section of the poetry book *Pau-Brasil* called *Roteiro de Minas* (Minas Route), and is titled *Funeral Procession*, although the title in the suite was replaced for *Prelude, Choral et Funèbre*.

Procissão do enterro	Prelude, Choral et Funèbre	Funeral Procession
A Veronica estende os braços	Veronique étend les bras	Veronica extends her arms
E canta	Pour roucouler	And sings
O pálio parou	Le dais stoppe	The canopy stopped
Todos escutam	Le peuple en bave	Everybody listens
A voz na noite	De cette voix dans la nuit	The voice in the night
Cheia de ladeiras acesas	Aux pavés luisants	Full of illuminated slopes

What appears obscure in the French translation is that the text addresses not a common funeral, but the procession of the Lord's burial in state Minas Gerais, which takes place during the Holy Week holiday. Here lies the justification for the funeral nature of the title. The poem captures the Brazilian religious tradition, according to which the procession stages a biblical passage as if it is happening at that moment, and within the Minas Gerais scenario. In other words, a reinterpretation of the myth occurs: the procession became a mythological ritual created in that part of the country, and this rite is a localized theatrical interpretation of a second myth, a catholic one. Veronica is actually a person who identifies with the character (Jesus) by extending her arms to show the shroud on which Jesus' face appears, and then sings the disturbing motet "O vos omnes." As part of the procession, a parade of biblical figures follows, and this is described in the subsequent poem of Andrade's book, which was not used by the composer in the suite.[99]

A number of authors have demonstrated that the poems of *Roteiro de Minas* describe the interior of Brazil as a mythical territory, because of the strong remnants of colonial culture during the country's gestation period. These remnants produced a collective unconsciousness intended to found a surreal Brazil, endowed with its own culture and tradition.[100] The nocturnal landscape described in the poem is identified with nature, and Veronica's voice that enacts the myth takes over the poem's ambience, curiously capturing the myth reincarnated in popular culture, extending through the nature represented by the night. Villa-Lobos seizes this image masterfully in an expressionist language that recalls the nocturnal atmosphere illuminated by Pierrot's moon. An abridged recapitulation at the end of the movement reminds similar procedures in some of *Pierrot Lunaire*'s numbers.

The third movement of the suite is the most picturesque of all, formed by only thirteen measures, where three mechanical metronomes pulsate simultaneously in two, three, and five beats per bar (the metronome in duple meter is the only one asked to have the bell on in the downbeats). The dialogue in the poem is distributed between the two solo singers, where the soprano (verses one and three) stands for a black man and the baritone (verse 2) represents a Portuguese policeman.

O capoeira[101]	Croches-Pied au flic	The capoeira fighter
Qué apanhá sordado?	Tu veux un beignet salaud?	Do you want to get beaten?
O quê?	De quoi?	Pardon?
Qué apanhá?	Tu veux un beignet?	Want a beating?
Pernas e cabeças na calçada	Guibolles et têtes sur le trottoir	Legs and heads on the sidewalk

In order to understand this movement, it is necessary to know a little about the history of Brazil, rediscovered by Oswald de Andrade. This poem is part of the book section related to the colonization of the country, while the previous poem is part of the group that describes the itinerary of the trip around the state Minas Gerais. The theme highlighted in this poem is the exploitation and violence suffered by African slaves during the colonization period. The dialogue in *Capoeira* appears in the first three verses, while the last verse describes the result of the confrontation, where the absence of a verb stands out. The dialogue highlights the voice of the negro who challenges the State represented in the figure of the Portuguese soldier, where the former uses the blows of the African martial art to defend—through attack—his body, and, above all, his freedom.

Despite the sociopolitical character of the poem, this is poetry of ironic and parodic tone, because in the original language it imitates the wrong colloquial way of speaking of the common man, by incorporating stylized grammatical errors, which are completely lost in translation. In the original poem, this procedure conveys a mocking and comedic tone to the text, loading it with humor, one of Oswald de Andrade's trademarks. The critical and irreverent instinct of the poem is translated through the use of metronomes as musical instruments, reinforcing the idea that this type of poem-joke was aimed not only at laughter, but also at reflections on a social problem.

Adopting a syntax made by clipping, collage, and montage, the poem materializes the capoeira fight through the confrontation of the speech between the negro and the white man. The abrupt and unexpected nature of the scene is reflected in the poem's language, which employs the sudden cut, the velocity of motion, the brevity of the action, and the fragmented nature of the described image, which looks like a cinematic shot. The concept of poetry is shaken, through the absence of verses and contamination by prose, cubist imagery, and cinema, a "capoeira strike" against traditional poetry. Analogously, Villa-Lobos attacks traditional music by eliminating melody and using exclusively noise produced by metronomes in confronting meters. It is his response to the bizarre assemblages of ordinary objects found in surrealist visual artworks.

In the poem, the absence of a description of the struggle forms an eloquent void between the third and the last verses. Villa-Lobos fills that silence with noise, by asking the strings to emit a sound by skimming the hairs of the bows on the back of the instruments, thus giving the impression of broken wood—equivalent to broken bones. This happens right before the last verse, when the soprano becomes the narrator, describing the final static image: legs and heads on the sidewalk. It is an onomatopoeic artifice used for word painting: The fight is represented in just two hits of the strings representing the capoeira strokes that cause the rupture of the body.

In the last measure, the metronomes stop and the orchestra's instruments minus woodwinds produce a downward motion, illustrating the falling of a body. During this motion, the strings perform aggressive pizzicati against the percussion, ending on a low C. The protagonists are fragmented like the poetry and the music: shrapnel of bodies—legs and heads—lying on the floor. The maximum brevity coupled with a minimum use of resources in a soundscape that converges into silence constitutes a parody closer to Webern than Schoenberg.

The fourth movement introduces the dramatic suspense of a thriller. The text addresses a specific type of ghost that is part of the mythological vocabulary of black slaves in Brazil: a specter that is the haunting and frightening image of the soul of a dead person, a character that was frequently part of scary stories among the slaves on colonial farms. Such phenomenon has been described in Freud's essay "The Uncanny" as a situation that arises from objects and scenes that cause terror. It results from the sentiment of the double, from different forms of superstition, from people to whom we attribute malicious intentions, or from the effect linked to magical practices such as macumba[102] in Brazil.

O medroso	Le Récit du Peureux	The fearful
A assombração apagou a candeia	Le spectre souffla la bougie	The specter put out the lamp
Depois no escuro veio a mão	Puis dans la noir nuit la main	Then in the dark came the hand
Pertinho dele	Sur lui	Close to him
Ver se o coração ainda batia	Pour voir si son cœur battait encore	To see if the heart was still beating

Villa-Lobos's music parodies the soundtrack of horror movies with scary sounds reminiscent of the romantic conventions of fear that pervades a number of works, particularly the last movement of Berlioz's *Symphonie Fantastique*, the "Dream of a Witches Sabbath." Effects include the use of special techniques such as flutter-tonguing, expressionist leaps, glissandi, chromatism of the strings in dynamic oscillations, and percussion effects. The music includes jump scares produced by sudden attacks of dissonant chords in stressed fortissimo emitted after an atmosphere of eerie sounds is created.

The soprano soloist sings almost parlando: Most of the time the rhythms are written over a single pitch, G above middle C. Within the nocturnal landscape, Villa-Lobos incorporates onomatopoeia to represent sounds of the night, similar to the ones used to represent the nocturnal soundscape of the Brazilian jungle in *Uirapuru*, which are part of the personal sonorous iconography of the composer.

Figure 9.4. The nocturnal ambience of the 4th movement is conveyed through figurations on the various instruments (mm. 3–4). Compare it with the nocturnal atmosphere in *Uirapuru* (mm. 134–143). The strings have been omitted in the example above, which was based on the original manuscript in the Villa-Lobos Museum. The lack of consistency in the flute part might be due to accidental mistakes.
Created by the author.

The two subsequent movements form a pair of dualistic oppositions between the comic and the tragic, using lyrics by two poets whose verses were widely employed by musicians.[103] René Chalup is the only French author in the *Suite Sugestiva*. His text in the fifth movement invokes the figure of "The Tramp" immortalized by Charlie Chaplin, known as Charlot in France, and considered the most important picaresque character of the twentieth century. Today, most people do not remember that Chaplin was worshiped in France more than in any other country. As early as 1921, his biographer Louis Delluc positioned him as one of the most famous Frenchmen of all time, and a rumor circulated that Chaplin was born in France and not in England. The fever led the renowned poet Blaise Cendrars to argue poetically that Charlot was a Frenchman who was born on the battlefront and that thanks to him the French defeated the Germans in the First World War.[104] This makes Charlot one of the greatest examples of cultural cannibalization outside Brazil.

By summoning the figure of Charlot, Villa-Lobos brings to the *Suite Sugestiva* the greatest myth of cinema at the time, a myth appropriated even by French surrealist cinema, as the figure of Charlot introduces and concludes Ferdinand Léger's *Ballet Méchanique* (the opening credits show a cubist figure of Charlot with the phrase "Charlot présente le ballet mécanique"). René Chalup's poem relates to Chaplin's film "The Kid," his first full-length silent masterpiece. It takes us to the poetic universe of the child, connecting with the subsequent movement, which depicts the fate of a boy attacked by the Jurupari, a malevolent spirit of Amerindian mythology. The juxtaposition of the tragic and the comic under the guise of the myth provides another layer within the surrealistic thread, exemplifying Bréton's assertion that surrealism is a "method of creating a collective myth."[105] The lyrics of the fifth movement are as follows:

Charlot aviateur	Charlot aviator
Pour l'anniversaire du Kid,	For the Kid's birthday
Charlot lui a fabriqué	Charlot built him
en secret un beau jouet:	secretly a beautiful toy:
un avion fait de manches en balai,	a plane made of broomsticks,
de caisses en conserves	boxes of can
et de bouts de ficelles,	and pieces of strings,
les ailes taillées dans le vieilles	the wings carved with old
paires des drap hors d'usage.	pairs of discarded sheets.
À cause du régime sec	Due to the Prohibition
qui interdit l'importation du Champagne	which forbids the import of Champagne
Charlot a baptisé l'avion	Charlot christened the plane
avec un ice-cream soda	with an ice-cream soda
à la salse pareille acheté	dressed with a sauce purchased
chez Herbert Smith	at Herbert Smith's,
le pharmacien du coin	the pharmacist at the corner
et il lui a donné le nom	and gave it the name
de "El espiritu de los Angeles"	of "The spirit of Los Angeles"
(en français: L'Esprit des Anges).	(in French: L'Esprit des Anges).
Or voilà qu'à l'orient	Suddenly, from the east
une grande bourrasque est née,	a great flurry is born,
issue des coufins de l'horizon,	coming from the ends of the horizon,

Mystérieusement soufflée	mysteriously blown
de cette même joue du globe	from the same part of the globe
que les caravelles de Colomb	as Columbus's caravels
de l'historique "Fleur-de-Mai."	of the historic "Mayflower."
Puis le vent s'effémina,	Then the wind subsides,
dégénéra en brise minaudière,	converted into a soft breeze,
déposa avec une politesse mandarine	and the "Spirit of Los Angeles"
très doucement "L'Esprit des Anges"	softly lands with politeness
sur le rivage chinois,	onto the Chinese shore,
où des douaniers à lunettes,	where customs officers with glasses,
lettrés et cérémonieux	literate and formal,
leur demadèrent leur âge,	ask for their ages,
et s'ils ne se livraient pas à	and question whether they've been involved
une contre-bande illicite.	with illegal contraband.
Comment Charlot pris	Charlot, who is received
pour un ambassadeur du Ciel,	as an ambassador from heaven,
épousa la femme divorcée	marries the divorced wife
du Président de la Républicaine de Chine.	of the president of the Republic of China.
Et comment le Kid pénétra	And how the Kid enters
au cœur de la Pagode sacrée,	in the heart of the Sacred Pagoda,
en se faisant passer	pretending to be
pour un Grand-Prêtre macrobite	a miniature High Priest
fera l'objet d'un prochain episode.	will be the subject of a next episode.

Villa-Lobos sets this longer poem to music using just a trio of voice, piccolo, and double bass, investing a comical character to the instrumentation by combining the highest and lowest instruments of the small orchestra. The two instruments subliminally represent the relationship of the two characters, Charlot and the child. The introductory section polarizes the interval of perfect fourth (C-F) over several octaves, by making the open fifth string of the bass support an F trill of the piccolo in its highest register. The first strophe of the poem describes the gift that Charlot built for the child, a plane he named "Spirit of Los Angeles," making a poetic association of the child with angels. Not being able to baptize the plane with champagne due to the American Prohibition, Charlot baptizes it with an ice-cream soda.

The poetic anecdote is reflected in the music through parody, as Villa-Lobos practically reverses the role of the two instruments: The piccolo performs a moderate movement in its low register while the bass intones a virtuosic parody of the popular Brazilian chorinho[106] "Apanhei-te, cavaquinho," famous for the swing of its light sixteenth notes.

Figure 9.5. **Surrealist juxtaposition of a quotation in the lower voice (the choro Apanhei-te, Cavaquinho by Ernesto Nazareth) accompanied by the flute, while the soprano sings the lyrics of the poem.**
Created by the author.

Apanhei-te, cavaquinho is a chorinho or "Brazilian tango" written in polka style by Ernesto Nazareth, a composer from Rio de Janeiro who worked as film pianist in his hometown, and it is frequently referred to as the "Scott Joplin of Brazil." It is one of his most popular works, and it was quoted by Darius Milhaud in *Le Bœuf sur le toit*. Cavaquinho is a small Portuguese instrument of the guitar family, which is imitated by the left hand of the accompaniment in the piano chorinho, while the right hand carries the famous melody used by Villa-Lobos. In Nazareth's composition, the effect is that of a flute playing the melody accompanied by the cavaquinho in the left hand. Villa-Lobos produces a parody through inversion, by transferring the melody to the double bass parodying the flute in Nazareth, and in doing so produces a parody of another parody, a surrealist joke of the highest subtlety. It is interesting to note that the title *Apanhei-te, cavaquinho* actually corresponds to a Brazilian jargon expression that means to catch someone in the act of committing something illegal.

This section ends with an instrumental bridge in slower tempo, which uses bass harmonics to elevate its range above the flute in another musical pun. The polarized interval of perfect fourth (C-F) returns to complete the first section, giving way to the second strophe, which describes "the orient," with its exotic appeal explored by modernist artists. The composer uses multiple techniques of word painting to convey the text, such as flutter tonguing and *sul ponticello* playing. A quasi-imitation in the interval of perfect fourth between the two instruments prepares the next section when the flurry subsides. Other rhythmic, harmonic, and instrumental expanded procedures such as harmonic arpeggios, battuto string technique, and multiple stops contribute to further illustrate the lyrics, and the movement ends with an abridged recapitulation of *Apanhei-te, cavaquinho*. At the end, the composer asks the bass to perform tremolo vibrato in multiple stops simultaneously with pizzicato, another expression of the exploration of virtuosity.

The sixth movement has a tragic tone by invoking the character of the Jurupari, a malevolent being from Amerindian mythology, which the Jesuit colonizers have compared with Satan. The typical characteristics of Manuel Bandeira's poetry are present in the lyrics: verses of narrative character, the absence of rhymes, and the simplistic language.

L'enfant et le Youroupari	The Child and the Jurupari
Une femme et son fils	A woman and her son
Dormaient dans un humac	Sleep in a hammock
Le Youroupari retira	The Jurupari takes
l'enfant des bras de sa mère	The child from the mother's arms
et le dèposa sous le hamac.	and put it under the hammock.
Puis il appela	Then he calls the mother
Avec la voix du petit:	With the voice of the little one:
Maman! Maman!	Mom! Mom!
Regarde sous le hamac	Look under the hammock
Le Youroupari!	The Jurupari!
La femme saiset un baton	The woman grabs a stick
Et tapa sur son fils	And hits her son
Alors le Youroupari	While the Jurupari
Sauta de rire	With its evil laughter
Et s'éloigna en criant:	Walks away shouting:
Jel'ai eue! Jel'ai eue!	I've caught him! I've caught him!

The poem was written specifically at Villa-Lobos's request.[107] The five-measure introduction sets the tone in typical Villalobian fashion, starting with accented notes in fortissimo and ending softly to prepare the musical narrative of the poem. The dramatic atmosphere connects in the distance with the last measure of the movement through the notes A-B-C performed by the piano. The first stanza of the poem is set to music through tone painting: The oboe produces a wavelike motion imitating the movement of the hammock, while cellos and basses replicate through onomatopoeia the noise produced by the hammock: The instrumentalists are asked to perform between the bridge and the string holder, a procedure also used in *Amazonas* (see Figure 6.5). The latter and the *Suite Sugestiva* were premiered in the same year.

Figure 9.6. Illustration of the use of pictorialism in the *Suite Sugestiva* (5th movement, mm. 6–7). The oboe line expresses the wave-like movement of a hammock while cellos and basses imitate the noise produced by the hammock. The remaining voices play sustained notes that have been omitted.
Created by the author.

The eerie atmosphere is broken by the dramatic appearance of the Jurupari, highlighted through an ascending motion in arpeggiated crescendo by piano, celesta, and flute, leading to two dissonant accented chords on tutti fortissimo. This is followed by a descending chromatic motion of trills performed by strings and celesta, whose effect is remarkable. The second strophe starts with a return to the atmosphere of the beginning, where the oboe line representing the hammock is substituted by a muted trumpet. As the Jurupari starts to scream, imitating the voice of the child, the music is transformed into a rhythmic ostinato, which remains almost until the end of the piece. A motion in triplets of piano and bass makes a clear reference to Schubert's *Erlkönig*, while the remaining strings perform tremolo vibrato sul ponticello. Jurupari's diabolic laughter is emulated through a descending line in staccato fortissimo by strings and woodwinds, and another reference to *Erlkönig* appears close to the end, as the motion in triplets subsides with a diminuendo and written ritardando (the triplets become eighth notes, ending on a long note). A dramatic and long silence prepares the last sound of the piece, a cluster of the lowest A-B-C notes of the piano, coupled with the open fifth string of the bass and a soft hit of the tam-tam, a faint scream floating in the air.

276   Chapter Nine

The last movement arrives with a sonorous pun, enhanced by the composer's request to start immediately and without a break from the previous movement. Woodwinds, brass, and strings attack in octaves the four-measure introduction of "Stars and Stripes Forever," another unexpected, illogical juxtaposition. John Philip Sousa was known in France through his participation at the Paris Exhibition of 1900, when he marched with his band through the streets in Paris to the Arc de Triomphe, one of the few parades that the band marched under Sousa's tenure.

Figure 9.7. Comparison of the beginning of *Stars and Stripes Forever* by John Phillip Sousa (top staff) and its citation in the last movement of the *Suite Sugestiva* (lower staff). Created by the author.

From this moment on, the composer starts a process of deconstruction, by introducing the element of chance in the next five measures of the score (mm. 5–9). Percussion with celesta plus clarinet and bassoon, followed by flute and strings, are asked to perform random pitches over a predetermined rhythm scheme, constituting an unusual case of controlled improvisation in an orchestral work, a sort of instrumental *sprechstimme*. The notation is quite loose and has just the goal of provide a decomposition of the music.

The process has an analogy with the automatism and the spirit of spontaneity sought by surrealist artists. In this case, the combination of random pitches and multiple rhythmic formulas create a cacophony that produces the collapse of the work. Some authors saw in this process an allegory of the disintegration of the American economy in the Wall Street crash of 1929 that led to the Great Depression.[108] Under this perspective, the suite suggests a route that begins in France, with a parody of grand opera, and ends in the United States, in a parody of one of the most famous patriotic martial hymns of the country. It is the same itinerary traveled by Villa-Lobos, which goes from Josephine Baker to Carmen Miranda.

The composition ends with the insistent repetition of the "um-pah rhythm" of the march performed by the strings, in a gradual and continuous diminuendo toward silence. This ending brings up a recollection of Stravinsky's *L'Histoire du Soldat*, which concludes with the deconstruction of the "Triumphal March of the Devil." Stravinsky's work was fully staged by Diaghilev in 1924 in Paris, during Villa-Lobos's first period France. In this way, the suite also represents an itinerary from Schoenberg in the *Prelude*, *Choral et Funèbre*, to Stravinsky in the not-so-grand finale. The inventiveness of the work, its degree of experimentalism, the use of external references with quotes from established works inserted in a post-tonal environment, and the use of unusual combinations involving emblematic gestures of well-known musical genres, make the *Suite Sugestiva* a visionary work that is the culmination of Villa-Lobos's surrealist writing.

Conclusion

While the anthropophagic style is dominant in the aesthetics of Villa-Lobos and the Brazilian modernists linked to the movement, among the various influences, surrealism emerged as the prevailing aesthetic, however adapted to the Brazilian tropical scenario. Within the multiple ingredients, the element of parody stands out through its Dada origins, and it was incorporated via the carnivalization of surrealism.

One of the most striking links between surrealism and anthropophagy is found in their relation with primitivism. The meeting point of the two movements is found in the exploration of myth, the pursue of the magical in the quest to evoke the "ultimate other":

> If myth is similar to dreams and poetry, then, it too can reveal facets of the exterior world that are obscured by modern humanity's instrumental, utilitarian relation with its surroundings. The surrealists found support for their detection of this similarity in the findings of psychoanalysis, and so myth fit with surrealism's early preoccupations.[109]

The intersection of myth and surrealism does not rest in the narrative aspect of the myth, but in its representation of the collective unconscious. This deserves an explanation. For Brazilian modernists, the exploration of the myth was something very natural, because these artists identified themselves as mestizos. This in itself constitutes the anthropological myth of the Brazilian race being the product of the mixture of the indigenous, African slaves and white races of the Portuguese colonizers. In the rediscovery of original Brazilian art and its hybridization with modern art via anthropophagy, it was the mythological nature of Brazilian art that appealed to the artists' sensitivity.

The hybridization of the Brazilian with the foreign and of the primitive with the modern created a productive tension between historical chronology and the timelessness of the myth. In Brazil, the myth expressed in the works of art was a representation of the collective unconscious, different from the expression of the Freudian subconscious that appeared in the initial phase of surrealism in France. Thus, the myth served as a model for the creation of an art that sought to escape from the limitations of art as a solitary pursue of aesthetic value, to become an expression of social collectivity. With the perspective of time, Villa-Lobos's music is seen today not through the exotic use of folklore and legends, but as the embodiment of the collective imagery of Brazilian society, which saw in his music the image of Brazil as a country of great potential displaying an exuberant nature.

Oswald de Andrade was more correct than he imagined when he stated poetically that surrealism in Brazil preceded its official promulgation in Europe. Some of the basic ideas expressed in the Anthropophagic Manifesto were prophetic in relation to what happened to the surrealist movement, especially after the Second World War.

When Breton departed from Europe to New York in 1941, he traveled with Claude Lévi-Strauss, the structuralist anthropologist who lived in Brazil studying indigenous myths. This helped spark his interest in further exploring mythological themes as well as magical and symbolic languages. After the war, Breton defined surrealist poetry as "something akin to an occult operation, claiming surrealism to be the culmination of a repressed counter-tradition of magic art."[110] Like the Brazilian anthropophagy formulated previously, Breton started to attempt "to reconcile Surrealism as a method of creating a collective myth with the much more general movement involving the liberation of man."[111] Although mythology was already present in previous artworks, the goal of using surrealism as an aesthetic that could transform personal myths into collective myths to promote a transformation of the world was a new attitude for the surrealists. In this, they were preceded by the Brazilian cannibal artists, for whom Oswald de Andrade had already instigated toward the "Caraib Revolution," one that would lead to the creation of a new myth for modern times. The surrealists used the same idea in the postwar period to redefine the artist's role as a magician, and the purpose of art as a means of self-knowledge, transformation of the world, and enlightenment of knowledge.

Furthermore, Oswald de Andrade's "Caraib Revolution" intended to transform "taboo into a totem," which means a return to a matriarchal society, where intuitive values would replace the decadent bourgeois patriarchal society. This aspect also resonated with Breton, who proposed to counter the crises of contemporary culture with a revaluation of the feminine: "Let art resolutely yield the passing lane to the supposedly 'irrational' feminine, let it fiercely make enemies of all that which, having the effrontery to present itself as sure and solid, bears in reality the mark of that masculine intransigence which, in the field of human relations at the international level, shows well enough today what it is capable of."[112] The explorations of the feminine in the realm of the myth were characteristic of a number of surreal works post–World War II, and were already present in Villa-Lobos's compositions such as *Uirapuru* and *Amazonas*.

The traced path demonstrates the prevalence of a dominant aesthetic—surrealism—in an important period of Villa-Lobos's artistic evolution. According to Paulo de Tarso Salles, the *Suite Sugestiva* marks the heyday of Villa-Lobos's modernist writing, but also his farewell to this terrain of greater experimentation.[113] The current study opens the door for subsequent research that will address the remaining internal stimuli assimilated through anthropophagy in the music of the Brazilian composer beyond the Amerindian influence. In the same way that anthropophagy deals with the assimilation of the "foreign other," it also applies to the internal assimilation of the Brazilian culture, which traditionally is related with the process of racial miscegenation, where the Afro-Brazilian influence is particularly remarkable. The above analysis of the *Suite Sugestiva* touches briefly on this topic.

Brazilian modernism had to deal with the scars from the previous century, when intellectuals believed that miscegenation was to a great extent the cause for the country's backwardness. This generated a desire in the elites for a process of "racial whitening" that has been the subject of research of numerous scholars. Throughout the years, music remained essential for the establishment of a Brazilian national identity, and the Afro-Brazilian influence has had a primordial role, after all "more than 50 percent of Brazilians are of African ancestry—the largest of African descent outside Nigeria, due to Brazil's large-scale importation of slaves (nine times more than were brought to mainland North America)."[114]

During the inception of modernism in the country in the 1920s, racist views persisted and were manifested in popular entertainment. Against this backdrop, modernism sought to awaken an interest in the popular culture and folk traditions. Since the beginning of the movement, Villa-Lobos already incorporated the Afro influence in his music through anthropophagy.[115] Together with other anthropophagite artists, his work allowed for a new perception in which racial miscegenation was seen as a positive force and not a sign of inferiority, which later led to the view that Afro-Brazilian cultural manifestations were proof of the nation's "racial democracy," however ambivalent this concept might be. During the first government of Vargas (1930–1945), Afro-Brazilian culture became a national symbol that included the exaltation of samba as the national rhythm of the nation.

For a more comprehensive analysis of Villa-Lobos and modernism, it would remain to make a deeper assessment of a whole body of musical literature that he produced in the 1920s, especially the *Chôros*, which need to be reevaluated within the surrealist and anthropophagic perspectives. After his second sojourn in Paris, from 1930 on Villa-Lobos was back in Brazil and began to write a great deal of patriotic and educational music. As far as the Anthropophagy movement, it became dormant, waiting to be rediscovered or emerging with more intensity in some of his later compositions. To paraphrase Subirats, as usually happens with myths, anthropophagy—those collective dreams, those protests in the form of savage images, carnival sounds and poetic expressions—have metamorphosed into stars, which are hanging in the firmament.

Notes

1. https://youtu.be/wNq3hPhtsSc.
2. See aphorism 24 in Appendix 1 for further information about this opera.
3. *Paraty* was the brand name of the most popular sugar cane brandy in Brazil at the time.
4. Severa was described as a Portuguese woman dressed in character, wearing a headscarf and a beautiful red and green dress with the emblem of the club on the front. The soccer team Portuguesa de Desportos was highly competitive and stood out exactly for being Portuguese in the middle of the Brazilian teams. Severa was based on Maria Severa, the singer-owner of the most renowned fado establishment in Lisbon. Fado is the most typical Portuguese musical genre.
5. Breton defined *surrealism* as a philosophy "based on the belief in the superior reality of certain forms of previously neglected associations, in the omnipotence of dream, in the disinterested play of thought. It tends to ruin once and for all other psychic mechanisms and to substitute itself for them in solving all the principal problems of life." André Breton, *Manifestoes*, 26.
6. See Nunes, *A Utopia Antropofágica*, 9.
7. Ibid., 10.
8. André Breton, *Manifestoes*, 26.
9. Kenneth David Jackson, "Vanguardist Prose in Oswald de Andrade," 24.
10. Mário de Andrade, *Poesias Completas*, 59.
11. Cinzia Sartini-Blum, "Incorporating the Exotic," 152.
12. Oswald the Andrade met Picabia in Paris in 1923.
13. Kenneth David Jackson, "Three Glad Races," 91.
14. Eduardo Subirats, *A Penúltima Visão do Paraíso*, 87–88.

15. Virginie Pouzet-Duzer, "Dada, Surrealism, Antropofagia," 86.
16. Allen S. Weiss, *Perverse Desire and the Ambiguous Icon*, 35.
17. Breton, *Manifestoes of Surrealism*, 12.
18. A more detailed discussion of this point appears in the commentary of the Anthropophagous Manifesto in Appendix 1.
19. In his second Manifesto of Surrealism, Breton wrote that "the simplest surrealist act consists of dashing down the street, pistol in hand, and firing blindly, as fast as you can pull the trigger, into the crowd."
20. See Appendix 1, aphorism 11.
21. Oswald de Andrade, "Péret / *Cunhambebinho*," [pseud. of Oswald de Andrade], in *Revista de Antropofagia do Diário de São Paulo*, March 17, 1929.
22. Abaporu is the equivalent of "Anthropophagous" in the Tupi-Guarani language.
23. Michele Greet, "Devouring Surrealism: Tarcila do Amaral's Abaporu," 5. The painter recalled later: "[the Abaporu] a solitary, monstrous figure, immense feet, seated on a green plain, his bent arm resting on his knee, his hand supporting the featherweight of his tiny head. In front of a cactus exploding into an absurd flower. [. . .] Only then did I realize that I myself had created subconscious images, suggested by stories I had heard as a child. [. . .] The house is haunted, the voice from above screaming from the ceiling of the room, open in the corner, 'I fall,' and dropping one foot (which seemed immense to me); I fall,' another foot fell, and then the hand, another hand and the whole body, to the horror of terrified children." See Kathleen Santini, "Depois do Surrealismo, Só a Antropofagia," 285.
24. Willy Corrêa de Oliveira, *Com Villa-Lobos*, 94 and 99. The italics were added for emphasis. Willy Corrêa de Oliveira is a contemporary composer, and in this text, he seems to refer poetically to the psychological spontaneity in Villa-Lobos's compositional process. Villa-Lobos stated that "[In Choros I] had no fixed formulas for the use of the themes. I use them for the development of atmosphere as I feel the need. I never repeat themes merely for the pleasure of repetition or to create 'cyclic' music. . . . My artistic creed is *la liberté absolue*. When I write, it is according to the style of Villa-Lobos." Simon Wright, *Villa-Lobos*, 67.
25. Raymond Cogniat, 'La vie artistique: Deux peintres brésiliens: Mme Tarsila, M Monteiro,' *Revue de l'Amérique Latine* 16, no. 80, 1 August 1928, 158, as quoted in Michele Greet, *Devouring Surrealism*, 8.
26. Furthermore, the incidence of surrealism in Villa-Lobos was already mentioned on chapter 4, when it was observed that the seven-note generator motif of Uirapuru's theme can be considered an *objet-trouvé* (ready-made), a term introduced by Marcel Duchamp in 1915 that represents a practice widely adopted by Dadaism and surrealism.
27. Michele Greet, *Devouring Surrealism*, 23.
28. *The Raw and the Cooked* is the title of the first volume of Lévi-Strauss's *Mythologiques*, considered his magnum opus. In the book, he expands the idea of the structure of myths being revealed like musical scores, since both music and myth transcend the plane of articulate language.

29. David Kozel, "A Musical Analysis of Mythical Thought in the Work of Claude Lévi-Strauss," 64.

30. Pandora Hopkins, "The Homology of Music and Myth," 253.

31. Pouzet-Duzer, *Dada, Surrealism, Antropofagia*, 85.

32. Mikhail Mikhailovitch Bakhtin, *A cultura popular na Idade Média e no Renascimento: o contexto de François Rabelais* (São Paulo: Hucitec, 1999).

33. Bakhtin, *A Cultura Popular*, 9.

34. David P. Appleby, *Heitor Villa-Lobos*, 77. Another episode that has been widely publicized was the scandalous participation of Villa-Lobos in the Modern Art Week of 1922. During the festival, there were occasional conflicts resulting from the reception of the composer's music by the audience, and one incident in particular drew the attention of the press. During one of the performances, the composer entered the stage dressed in a tuxedo, but wearing a slipper on his bandaged foot while carrying an umbrella as a walking stick. The audience's reaction included intense boos, deriding the composer's posture as a modernist manifestation that was disrespectful to the music. The real cause of the incident was a "gross manifestation of uric acid," which caused Villa-Lobos to travel from Rio de Janeiro to São Paulo with a limp. Other accounts mention an ingrown toenail, but the episode was distorted and became known as a legendary manifestation of outlandish behavior.

35. In the case of the Caraib Revolution (see Appendix 1, aphorism 11), it is not to be excluded is the possibility that Oswald de Andrade advocated for it in a self-deprecating, mocking tone of proclamation, something that would be equivalent to a "Hillbilly Revolution" in the United States.

36. Anthropophagous Manifesto, aphorism 24 (see Appendix 1).

37. Villa-Lobos's detractors say that those false Amerindians are the ones that appear in Villa-Lobos's music, due to the unlikely veracity of his stories about his trips to the Brazilian jungle to collect original Amerindian music.

38. *Baianas* are women of African descent who work as street vendors. Originally from the state of Bahia the main port of entrance for African slaves, *baianas* wear a full-length skirt and a decorated turban on their heads.

39. Ermelinda A. Paz, *Villa-Lobos e a Musica Popular Brasileira: Uma Visão sem Preconceito* (São Paulo: Editora Tipografia Musical, 2019): 53.

40. The first carnival march in history is considered to be "Ó Abre Alas," written by Chiquinha Gonzaga in 1899. Gonzaga was also a prominent composer of choros.

41. https://youtu.be/FL8x2ozWJVs.

42. The swarming ants in Dalí's paintings are said to be "references to death and decay, and are reminders of human mortality and impermanence. They are also said to represent overwhelming sexual desire." See https://www.thedaliuniverse.com/en/symbol-dali-ants.

43. Mocotó is a Brazilian dish made from rich and nutritious ingredients: boiled legs of bovines without hulls or ends. The song originally belonged to a Portuguese musical burlesque staged in Brazil in 1915 and was adapted three years later for the carnival in Rio.

44. https://youtu.be/37y_xH3ujos.

45. Nanica is the most common among the numerous types of bananas in Brazil.

46. Ironically, the Portuguese lyrics unintentionally announce the death of the surrealist movement. The gradual disappearance of surrealism has a lot to do with the existentialist asceticism that permeated French philosophy in the 1940s. Existentialist aesthetics were based on action and pragmatism, where artistic activity and artworks were supposed to reveal the world to others, therefore, conflicting with the idea of art for art's sake. While revolutionary, surrealism was closed in upon itself, with its journey inward, something that existentialists could not tolerate.

47. Brazil's last emperor Pedro II was nicknamed Pedro Banana by the press, and bananas were frequently used to represent Brazil. For example, a banana tree appears prominently in the background of the painting *Antropofagia* (Anthropophagy) by Tarsila do Amaral.

48. https://youtu.be/Ou_N7ajW96I. This song was a parody of the American song "Yes, We Have No Bananas" (1923) by Frank Silver and Irving Cohn. It was a critical response to the predominance of USA culture in the Americas, which resulted from the Good Neighbor Policy implemented by the United States. The carnivalization of national life is a stereotype built especially during World War II, when Brazilian dictator Getúlio Vargas, in a political maneuver to bargain advantages for Brazil in negotiations with the United States, entered the war with the Allies. At that time, the US Secretary of State encouraged the production of several films and cartoons that exalted Brazil, bringing artists such as Carmen Miranda, Dorival Caymmi, and composer Ary Barroso to Hollywood. This was an attempt to seduce Brazilians through the Good Neighbor Policy. The result was the construction of the stereotype of a tropical, sensual paradise, which takes nothing seriously, despite its own ailments. Characters such as Zé Carioca by Walt Disney were produced, and Carmen Miranda had her talent recognized and projected worldwide. In one of her films, she sings *The Lady in the Tutti Frutti Hat* as she arrives in an ox cart full of bananas. The fruit is treated as a phallic symbol, as in the carnival march *Yes, Nós Temos Bananas*, portraying an agricultural country that produced cotton, bananas, coffee, and mate tea, which was a fact at the time.

49. Stephanie Dennison and Lisa Shaw, *Popular Cinema in Brazil: 1930–2001* (Manchester: Manchester University Press, 2004): 51.

50. https://youtu.be/ojo3I59Gn6c.

51. Bahia's capital, Salvador, was Brazil's main port of entry for African slaves during the previous century.

52. Lisa Shaw, "'What Does the Baiana Have? Josephine Baker and the Performance of Afro-Brazilian Female Subjectivity on Stage," 91.

53. For more details about the connection between Carmen Miranda and Josephine Baker during this occasion, see Lisa Shaw, *Tropical Travels: Brazilian Popular Performance, Transnational Encounters, and the Construction of Race* (Austin: University of Texas Press, 2018).

54. Ermelinda Paz (2019), 51–69.

55. Breton, *Manifestoes*, 14.
56. Anthropophagous Manifesto, aphorism 25 (see Appendix 1).
57. Alejo Carpentier, "De lo real maravilloso americano," in *Tientos y Diferencias*, 96–112 (Montevideo: Arca, 1967). https://www.literatura.us/alejo/deloreal.html.
58. This topic is compellingly raised in the classic essay "Can the Subaltern Speak?" See Gayatri Chakravorty Spivak, "Can the Subaltern Speak?" in *Marxism and the Interpretation of Culture*, ed. Cary Nelson and Lawrence Grossberg (Basingstoke: Macmillan, 1988), 271–313.
59. Claude Lévi-Strauss, *O pensamento selvagem*, 28.
60. Eduardo Viveiros de Castro, *Metafísicas canibais: elementos para uma antropologia pós-estrutural*, 36–37.
61. "To create something new there has to be a 'becoming-Other,' taking a point of view as self-metamorphosis. This different metaphysics . . . requires a different theory of knowledge: not one based on the fixed and hierarchical nature of positions such as subject and object but one in which subjects interrelate and therefore may devour each other. [. . .] For standard modern thought [meaning, "standard civilized thought"], there is only *one nature* or world for *various different cultures* or 'worldviews,' while for Amerindian thought there are *multiple natures* and worlds for *one single culture* or 'worldview.' Modernity sees difference in *culture*, in the proliferation of souls (in the sense that the body is a common measure of all existing souls); the latter sees difference in *nature*, in the proliferation of bodies (in the sense that all share a single soul with no particularized being). From this perspectivist standpoint, the subject is simply a position that may be occupied by any existing thing, which means that anything may be a subject—so everything may be human [the Amerindian view is anthropomorphic]. . . . Among different Amerindian cosmologies, cannibal spirits or soul eaters populate the cosmos. Note that the Amerindian notion of the soul is actually corporeal: souls have bodies and may be eaten, but, for that very reason, they too may devour others." See Sztutman, "The (Re)turn of the Anthropophagites," 214–15.
62. Giuseppe Cocco, *Mundobraz: o devir-mundo do brasil e o devir-brasil do mundo*, 236.
63. Pierre Clastres, *Arqueologia da violência: Pesquisas de Antropologia Política*, 248.
64. Alexande Nodari e Maria Carolina de Almeida Amaral. "A Questão (Indígena) do Manifesto Antropófago," 2463.
65. See, for example, Murilo Duarte Costa Corrêa. "O Intempestivo e o Desterritorializado: Oswald de Andrade e o Lugar das Idéias no Brasil."
66. Craig Lundy provides a critique of this conceptualization. See Craig Lundy, "Deleuze's Untimely: Uses and Abuses in the Appropriation of Nietzsche," 202.
67. Oswald de Andrade, *A Crise da Filosofia Messiânica*, 79.
68. See Appendix 1, aphorism 28.
69. "Down with Memory as a source of custom. The renewal of personal experience." Ibid., aphorism 44.
70. Mauro Franco, "O Passado Manifesto," 182.

71. Viveiros de Castro, Eduardo. "O mármore e a murta," 238 and 240.
72. Glenn Watkins, *Pyramids*, 5.
73. Claude Lévi-Strauss, *The Raw and the Cooked*, 16.
74. Kozel, *Music Analysis*, 71.
75. Nunes, *Antropofagia e Vanguarda*, 325. As the Brazilian musicologist Mario de Andrade stated: "we are the primitives of a new era."
76. To date, a comprehensive study that surveys the composer's predated works has not yet been produced. However, new studies have gradually illuminated Villa-Lobos's compositional process and the creation of new works from the remodeling of previously written compositions, such as the commented study score of *Uirapuru* produced by Manoel Corrêa do Lago and Guilherme Bernstein. See Manoel Corrêa do Lago and Guilherme Bernstein, *Uirapuru: Partitura de estudo comentada*.
77. Leonard Shlain, *Art and Physics: Parallel Visions in Space, Time and Light* (New York: Harper Collins Publishers, 1991), 228.
78. Imagination without strings (*L'immaginazione senza fili*) is an expression that Marinetti created through an article published in 1913, four years after the publication of his manifesto of futurism. In it, Marinetti describes the impact of the great discoveries of science upon the human psyche, and how this should be reflected in art.
79. Bush, "Heitor Villa-Lobos," 21.
80. Maria Alice Volpe, *Indianismo and Landscape in the Brazilian Age of Progress: Art Music from Carlos Gomes to Villa-Lobos, 1870s–1930s*, Austin: UMI Research Press, 2001, 290.
81. Ibid., 318.
82. See Mircea Eliade, *The Myth of the Eternal Return: Cosmos and History*. New York: Harper, 1959.
83. See, for example, the description of the nocturnal atmosphere achieved in Uirapuru (Figure 5.8).
84. See Hal Foster, *Compulsive Beauty*, Cambridge: MIT Press, 1993.
85. This is a reference to Isolde's transfiguration at the end of Wagner's opera *Tristan and Isolde*. It represents the ultimate consummation, or union, in death, as Isolde sinks onto Tristan's body, mystically united with him at last.
86. Oswald de Andrade, "L'effort intellectuel du Brésil contemporain," 207 (Lecture at Sorbonne).
87. The Amazon Theater was inaugurated in 1896, one decade after Villa-Lobos's birth.
88. Oswald de Andrade, "Manifesto of Pau-Brasil Poetry," 184. Botafogo's cordões refers to the carnival rows in the neighborhood *Botafogo* in Rio de Janeiro. Vatapá is a typical Afro-Brazilian dish.
89. The book was published by Sans Pareil in France. It is dedicated to Blaise Cendrars "on the occasion of the discovery of Brasil," or more appropriately, on the occasion of the rediscovery of Brazil by Oswald de Andrade. In the preface of the edition, the historian Paulo Prado writes that it was in the French capital—navel of world—that Andrade "discovered, dazzled, his own land." The book starts with a

section with the title "*Falação*," where a different version/summary of the Brazilwood Manifesto is presented. Oswald de Andrade, *Pau Brasil* (Paris: Sans Pareil, 1925).

90. In 2010, the French scholar Antoine Chareyre published for the first time an edition in French of Oswald de Andrade's *Pau Brasil* poetry book (the first translation in Spanish dates from 2008). Oswald de Andrade, *Bois Brésil: poésie et manifeste* (Paris: Éditions de la Différence, 2010). The translation of the three poems used in the *Suite Sugestiva* are different from the ones used by Villa-Lobos and are transcribed below for comparison (they appear respectively on pages 209, 121, and 119 of the publication). The book in bilingual translation includes a preface and translator's notes, in addition to illustrations by Tarsila do Amaral.

Procession d'enterrement	*Le capoeira*	*Le froussard*
La Véronique étend les bras	- T'veux t'battr' soldat?	Le spectre éteignit la bougie
Et chante	- Quoi?	Puis dans l'obscurité il approcha la main
Le dais s'est arrêté	- T'veux t'battr'?	Tout près de lui
Tous écoutent	Jambes et têtes sur le pavé	Pour voir si son cœur battait encore
La voix dans la nuit		
Toute de ruelles allumées		

91. Steven Kovács, *From Enchantment to Rage: The Story of Surrealist Cinema*, Cranbury, NJ: Associated University Presses, 1980, 15.

92. Luis Buñuel, "Poetry and Cinema," 107.

93. Quote by M. Emile Bouvier taken from John G. Frey, "From Dada to Surrealism," 12.

94. Donatello Grieco, *Roteiro de Villa-Lobos*, 76.

95. *Villa-Lobos: Sua Obra*, 2nd edition, 226.

96. César Franck is a known influence in Villa-Lobos's early compositions, particularly through Franck's student Vincent D'Indy. During his youth, Villa-Lobos studied D'Indy's *Cours de Composition Musicale*.

97. Villa-Lobos indicated "*Parlez (sans emphase)*" in the score and notated only the melodic gestures accompanying the rhythmic figures.

98. Tânia Veiga Judar, "O livro-objeto Pau Brasil," 97.

99. See Paula Albiero Marconi de Lima, "O Sujeito do Pau-Brasil," 120–21.

100. Alfredo Bosi stated that Brazilian artists saw the country as "a huge, proteinaceous myth whose Amazonian totems would be the seminal symbols. Tarsila's strong and beautiful anthropophagic images, Oswald's manifestos and Mário de Andrade's [and we could certainly include here Villa-Lobos's music] could not have been born but from the minds of artists who imagined ludically and surreally their country." Alfredo Bosi, "Moderno e Modernista na Literatura Brasileira," 216.

101. Capoeira is a martial art created by African slaves in Brazil to help them defend against slavery. It combines elements of dance, acrobatics, and music.

102. Macumba is a type of voodoo typical of Brazil.

103. According to Vasco Mariz, fifty-four poems by Manuel Bandeira were set to music in ninety-two songs, of which fifteen were by Villa-Lobos, his first musical partner (Vasco Mariz, *A canção brasileira de câmara*, 41). This makes Bandeira the poet with most lyrics set to music of his generation. Chalup's inventory contains at least eighty-three poems put to music by twenty-seven composers, according to Wikipedia.

104. Cendrars frequented in Paris the same intellectual circle as Villa-Lobos, and was introduced to him at the studio of Tarsila do Amaral.

105. Kristoffer Noheden, *Surrealism, Cinema, and the Search for a New Myth*, 14.

106. A chorinho is an instrumental pop composition from the urban folklore of Rio de Janeiro. The genre had a major influence on Villa-Lobos's formation. During the 1920s, the composer wrote a series of approximately fifteen *chôros*, which are considered among his top masterpieces.

107. It was not possible to find this poem in any collection of Manuel Bandeira's poems. Most likely the poem was originally written in French, since Bandeira was fluent in this idiom.

108. Joel Albuquerque, "Suite Sugestiva de Villa-Lobos: paródia, ruido e acaso," 10.

109. Noheden, *Surrealism*, 13.

110. Ibid., 12.

111. Breton apud Jacqueline Chénieux-Gendron, *Surrealism*, 106.

112. André Breton, *Arcanum 17: With Apertures, Grafted to the End*, 81.

113. Salles, *Villa-Lobos*, 92.

114. Thomas E. Skidmore, *Brazil: Five Centuries of Change*, 5.

115. See Juliana Ripke da Costa, "Tópicas Afro-Brasileiras como Tradição Inventada na Música Brasileira do Século XX," 114–20.

APPENDIX ONE

~

The Anthropophagous Manifesto
An Annotated Translation

Almost a century after its publication, the Anthropophagous Manifesto, or Cannibalist Manifesto, remains the most influential document to arise from the modernist movement in Brazil. According to Viveiro de Castro, "The Oswaldian Anthropophagy is the most original metacultural reflection produced in Latin America to date. It throws the (Amer)Indians into the future and into the ecumenum; it was not a theory of nationalism, of going back to the roots, of (Amer)Indianism. It was and is a truly revolutionary theory."[1] For Augusto de Campos, anthropophagy is "the only original Brazilian philosophy and, in some respects, the most radical of the artistic movements ever produced in Brazil."[2] The manifesto was published in the first number of the *Revista de Antropofagia* in 1928, an ephemeral magazine that became soon neglected. The concept of cultural cannibalism resurfaced periodically in later years in Brazil; however, translations started to appear only half a century after the initial publication. Ultimately, it acquired international fame as a relevant theory in the field of postcolonial studies in the postmodern era, and today cultural cannibalism is regarded as an influential theory that migrates to other fields.

The language of the manifesto, which is structured as a series of aphorisms, reflects the lyric impulse of the author, a poet, to produce an aesthetic creation in the form of a manifesto. The text includes jokes, metaphorical syntheses, provocative aphorisms, profound insights, and the use of allegory. It interweaves literature, art, history, philosophy, anthropology, psychology, economics, and politics, approaching different themes and personalities from Brazilian and European culture, from different times and places, taking the reader on a ride to unexpected destinations. It is also a profound work that contains substantial coherence and depth, yet its playful, elusive style has confounded a number of scholars. The manifesto elicits a continuously evolving interpretation that requires familiarity with history, linguistics, and a variety of other topics addressed in the text.

The paragraph above explains why an English translation is a difficult task. The original publication of the Manifesto in 1928 used an old orthography that has been substantially modified since then, and certain idiomatic expressions are challenging to translate. Oswald de Andrade manipulates the language in a way that allows for multiple interpretations, and occasionally there are words that do not exist in Portuguese, or they could be the product of typographical errors. The current translation is based mainly on two previous versions: The first is by Hélio Oiticica, who was a prominent Tropicalist visual artist, therefore a direct descendant from the Anthropophagic Movement. His translation has the title *Anthropophagic Manifesto* and dates from 1972. The second version is by Leslie Bary, a scholar who gave it the title *Cannibalist Manifesto*, and published it originally in the *Latin American Literary Review* in 1991.[3]

The discourse of the Anthropophagous Manifesto is notable for its rejection of reason and logic. The text displays no sense of continuity; its language flows through a series of fragmentary and apparently disconnected statements that break with the logical, linear discourse of the past in an attempt to communicate ideas within a structure where sequential and logical arguments are eschewed. The frequent omission of verbs, the occurrence of gaps in the middle of sentences due to the manipulation of grammar, and an odd punctuation imply that the structure reflects metaphorically the way of thinking of the Amerindian, the *pensée sauvage*, which is at the same time mystical, collective, and pre-logical. Such a thought structure resists categorization or segmentation, and through the rejection of logical discourse it opens the possibility for a mystical belief "in signs, in sextants and in the stars" (aphorism 45). In doing so, the author to some degree re-creates in the manifesto the aural language of the Amerindian.

The visual aspect of the original version published in the *Revista de Antropofagia* in 1928 presents the reproduction of a drawing based on Tarsila do Amaral's *Abaporu* on the first page. The drawing is followed by each aphorism separated from the next by a horizontal line, demarcating a certain rhythm; the lines also mimic the layout of a restaurant menu, most appropriate for an *Anthropophagous Manifesto*. For this and other insights, we are indebted to the work of Beatriz Azevedo, who characterized the manifesto as a "savage palimpsest."[4]

The poetic prose style of the manifesto has been compared to the symbolist aesthetic of Arthur Rimbaud's 1873 work *Une saison en enfer* (*A Season in Hell*). The radical contents combine references to a multiplicity of topics ranging from psychoanalysis (Freud) to philosophy (Rousseau), from primitivism to Marxism, and many more. Furthermore, the sort of irrational bricolage displayed in the Manifesto would become one of the main features of the cultural production of the country. This justifies the contention that a proto-surrealism was already present in Brazilian aesthetics prior to being imported from Europe, revealing another dimension of the possibilities of Cultural Cannibalism. Instead of dominating Brazilian culture, European surrealism was ultimately devoured by the rejection of logic already present in the Brazilian art of the time. Primitivism, futurism, surrealism, and all the modernist manifestations in Europe were ultimately cannibalized into Brazilian artworks, which stand out independently as products that carry their own merit and originality.

Through the features described above, the Anthropophagous Manifesto becomes a metaphor for its contents: "It is simultaneously a concept—Cultural Anthropophagy—a *Weltanschauung*, or worldview, and its own aesthetic incarnation. After all, it is in the body of the text that the author practices his own theory, transforming the taboo (Anthropophagy) into totem (the Manifesto)."[5]

Oswald de Andrade (1890–1954)

Like Villa-Lobos, Oswald de Andrade was born in the historical moment that saw the abolishment of slavery and the proclamation of Brazil as a republic. A native of São Paulo, he started his career as a journalist and later took a degree in law. Although he never practiced, his legal knowledge is apparent in the manifesto. It was through his multiple trips to Europe—particularly Paris—that he realized that "the primitivism that appeared in France as exoticism was for us in Brazil genuine primitivism."[6] In other words, the valorization of the cannibal by the European was rather artificial, because the primitive world is far removed from that civilization. But the allegory that Oswald de Andrade created based on the Amerindian is essentially the incorporation and transformation of his own natural origins, rooted in the New World.[7]

Through his trips abroad as well as around Brazil, he participated together with other artists in a process of rediscovering his homeland, which enabled him to assess the true value of the national culture. Of particular importance was his journey to Minas Gerais in 1924, known as the "modernist caravan," during which he was accompanied by Tarsila do Amaral, the Swiss poet Blaise Cendrars, and others. This trip helped him formulate the "Brazilwood Manifesto" in the same year, as well as a homonymous volume of poetry published in France, which furnished materials that Villa-Lobos would incorporate in his *Suite Sugestiva* (1929). In 1926 Andrade formally married Tarsila, a marriage that lasted for approximately four years. His personal life remained intense: Altogether he officially married five times, though he also had numerous extramarital affairs. His vision of the women's role in the philosophy of matriarchy stated in the Anthropophagous Manifesto caused controversy among scholars: While Antônio Cândido considered him a feminist, Beth Joan Vinkler thinks the opposite.[8]

Oswald divorced Tarsila in 1929, the year following the publication of the Anthropophagous Manifesto, and abandoned his artistic endeavors—even disowning his previous productions—in order to dedicate himself to political militancy within the Communist Party. Yet his communism remained anthropophagic, with the utopic goal of establishing an equalitarian society and ending the exploitation of men. After his rupture with the party in 1945, he passionately devoted himself to philosophy, and in 1950 he applied unsuccessfully for a professorship in philosophy at the Faculdade de Filosofia, Ciencias e Letras of São Paulo University. His thesis, "A Crise da Filosofia Messiânica" (The Crisis of Messianic Philosophy), was essentially a philosophical extension of his ideas about cultural anthropophagy. Throughout his career, in his novels, romances, poetry, theater plays, essays, and lectures, he remained faithful to his anthropophagic ideas, and thus his multiple statements on the topic on various occasions help to elucidate the theory as initially conceived in the Anthropophagous Manifesto.

It is worth pointing out that although Oswald de Andrade remains one of the most influential artists Brazil ever produced, as a poet and writer he was not accepted at the Academia Brasileira de Letras; as a philosopher, he did not earn a professorship in philosophy at the Universidade de São Paulo (because he took his degree in law); and as a militant communist, he ended up breaking up with the party. He dissolved relationships with former friends such as Mário de Andrade and Paulo Prado, was arrested by the police in Rio de Janeiro for threatening a former poet friend, and he had a criminal record as a subversive. At the end of his life, he was discouraged by the repeated rejection of his ideas, the lack of a readership for his publications, and his failure to achieve recognition.

Nevertheless, Oswald de Andrade excelled in literature as a poet and author of novels, romances, essays, manifestos, and dramas, and he did become a full professor of Brazilian literature at the Universidade de São Paulo, the most prestigious university in Brazil. He displayed interest not only in literature and philosophy, but also in the visual arts and music, even publishing a work called *Cântico dos Cânticos for Flute and Guitar*, dedicated to his future wife Maria Antonieta D'Aikmin. The deceptive title hides the fact that the work is a poem, and not a musical composition.

For Andrade, artists are "hypersensitive seismographs of the physical deviations of the mass; they are avant-garde and hyper-aesthetic beings."[9] Visionary artists, like seismographs, are able to alert the members of society that a conceptual shift is about to occur in the thought system used to perceive the world. As a poet, he understood that words were the most powerful weapons, and enabled the artist to subdue nature. Therefore, he viewed the artist as a precursor who has the sensibility to introduce radical innovations and in doing so anticipates scientific revisions of reality.

Yet, he could not have realized the extent of his prophetic ideas. For example, in an interview given in 1950, he stated: "We need . . . to *desvespucize* and *decolombize* America and *decabralize* Brazil (the great date of the anthropophagous: October 11th, that is, the last day of America without Columbus). The (Amer)Indians were very serene, absolutely *ametaphysical*. They didn't suffer from psychosis like we all do today."[10] The terms *desvespucization* (from Amerigo Vespucci, the navigator from whose name the term "America" is derived); *decolombization* (from Christopher Colombus, the "discoverer of America"), and *decabralization* (from Pedro Álvares Cabral, the "discoverer of Brazil") were nothing less than a call to "cancel culture" that happened decades before its real affirmation in our time.[11]

Manifesto Antropófago

Só a antropofagia nos une. Socialmente. Economicamente. Filosoficamente. (1)

Única lei do mundo. Expressão mascarada de todos os individualismos, de todos os coletivismos. De todas as religiões. De todos os tratados de paz. (2)

Tupi, or not tupi that is the question. (3)

Contra todas as catequeses. E contra a mãe dos Gracos. (4)

Só me interessa o que não é meu. Lei do homem. Lei do antropófago. (5)

Estamos fatigados de todos os maridos católicos suspeitosos postos em drama. Freud acabou com o enigma mulher e com outros sustos da psicologia impressa. (6)

O que atropelava a verdade era a roupa, o impermeável entre o mundo interior e o mundo exterior. A reação contra o homem vestido. O cinema americano informará. (7)

Filhos do sol, mãe dos viventes. Encontrados e amados ferozmente, com toda a hipocrisia da saudade, pelos imigrados, pelos traficados e pelos touristes. No país da cobra grande. (8)

Foi porque nunca tivemos gramáticas, nem coleções de velhos vegetais. E nunca soubemos o que era urbano, suburbano, fronteiriço e continental. Preguiçosos no mapa-múndi do Brasil. (9)

Uma consciência participante, uma rítmica religiosa.

Contra todos os importadores de consciência enlatada. A existência palpável da vida. E a mentalidade pré-lógica para o Sr. Lévy-Bruhl estudar. (10)

Queremos a Revolução Caraíba. Maior que a Revolução Francesa. A unificação de todas as revoltas eficazes na direção do homem. Sem nós a Europa não teria sequer a sua pobre declaração dos direitos do homem.

A idade de ouro anunciada pela América. A idade de ouro. E todas as girls. (11)

Filiação. O contato com o Brasil Caraíba. *Où Villegaignon print [prit] terre*.[12] Montaigne. O homem natural. Rousseau. Da Revolução Francesa ao Romantismo, à Revolução Bolchevista, à Revolução Surrealista e ao bárbaro tecnizado de Keyserling. Caminhamos. (12)

Nunca fomos catequizados. Vivemos através de um direito sonâmbulo. Fizemos Cristo nascer na Bahia. Ou em Belém do Pará. (13)

Mas nunca admitimos o nascimento da lógica entre nós. (14)

Contra o Padre Vieira. Autor do nosso primeiro empréstimo, para ganhar comissão. O rei-analfabeto dissera-lhe: ponha isso no papel mas sem muita lábia. Fez-se o empréstimo. Gravou-se o açúcar brasileiro. Vieira deixou o dinheiro em Portugal e nos trouxe a lábia. (15)

O espírito recusa-se a conceber o espírito sem o corpo. O antropomorfismo. Necessidade da vacina antropofágica. Para o equilíbrio contra as religiões de meridiano. E as inquisições exteriores. (16)

Só podemos atender ao mundo orecular.¹³ (17)

Tínhamos a justiça codificação da vingança. A ciência codificação da Magia. Antropofagia. A transformação permanente do Tabu em totem. (18)

Contra o mundo reversível e as idéias objetivadas. Cadaverizadas. O stop do pensamento que é dinâmico. O indivíduo vítima do sistema. Fonte das injustiças clássicas. Das injustiças românticas. E o esquecimento das conquistas interiores. (19)

Roteiros. Roteiros. Roteiros. Roteiros. Roteiros. Roteiros. Roteiros. (20)

O instinto Caraíba. (21)

Morte e vida das hipóteses. Da equação *eu* parte do *Cosmos* ao axioma *Cosmos* parte do *eu*. Subsistência. Conhecimento. Antropofagia. (22)

Contra as elites vegetais. Em comunicação com o solo. (23)

Nunca fomos catequizados. Fizemos foi Carnaval. O índio vestido de senador do Império. Fingindo de Pitt. Ou figurando nas óperas de Alencar cheio de bons sentimentos portugueses. (24)

Já tínhamos o comunismo. Já tínhamos a língua surrealista. A idade de ouro.
Catiti Catiti
Imara Notiá
Notiá Imara
Ipeju. (25)

A magia e a vida. Tínhamos a relação e a distribuição dos bens físicos, dos bens morais, dos bens dignários. E sabíamos transpor o mistério e a morte com o auxílio de algumas formas gramaticais. (26)

Perguntei a um homem o que era o Direito. Ele me respondeu que era a garantia do exercício da possibilidade. Esse homem chamava-se Galli Mathias. Comi-o.

Só não há determinismo onde há mistério. Mas que temos nós com isso? (27)

Contra as histórias do homem, que começam no Cabo Finisterra. O mundo não datado. Não rubricado. Sem Napoleão. Sem César. (28)

A fixação do progresso por meio de catálogos e aparelhos de televisão. Só a maquinaria. E os transfusores de sangue. (29)

Contra as sublimações antagônicas. Trazidas nas caravelas. (30)

Contra a verdade dos povos missionários, definida pela sagacidade de um antropófago, o Visconde de Cairu:—É mentira muitas vezes repetida. (31)

Mas não foram cruzados que vieram. Foram fugitivos de uma civilização que estamos comendo, porque somos fortes e vingativos como o Jabuti. (32)

Se Deus é a consciência do Universo Incriado, Guaraci é a mãe dos viventes. Jaci é a mãe dos vegetais. (33)

Não tivemos especulação. Mas tínhamos adivinhação. Tínhamos Política que é a ciência da distribuição. E um sistema social-planetário. (34)

As migrações. A fuga dos estados tediosos. Contra as escleroses urbanas. Contra os Conservatórios e o tédio especulativo. (35)

De William James a Voronoff. A transfiguração do Tabu em totem. Antropofagia. (36)

O pater famílias e a criação da Moral da Cegonha: Ignorância real das coisas + falta de imaginação + sentimento de autoridade ante a prole curiosa. (37)

É preciso partir de um profundo ateísmo para se chegar à idéia de Deus. Mas o caraíba não precisava. Porque tinha Guaraci. (38)

O objetivo criado reage como os Anjos da Queda. Depois Moisés diverga. Que temos nós com isso? (39)

Antes dos portugueses descobrirem o Brasil, o Brasil tinha descoberto a felicidade. (40)

Contra o índio de tocheiro. O índio filho de Maria, afilhado de Catarina de Médicis e genro de D. Antônio de Mariz. (41)

A alegria é a prova dos nove. (42)

No matriarcado de Pindorama. (43)

Contra a Memória fonte do costume. A experiência pessoal renovada. (44)

Somos concretistas. As idéias tomam conta, reagem, queimam gente nas praças públicas. Suprimamos as idéias e as outras paralisias. Pelos roteiros. Acreditar nos sinais, acreditar nos instrumentos e nas estrelas. (45)

Contra Goethe, a mãe dos Gracos, e a Corte de D. João VI. (46)

A alegria é a prova dos nove. (47)

A luta entre o que se chamaria Incriado e a Criatura—ilustrada pela contradição permanente do homem e o seu Tabu. O amor cotidiano e o modus-vivendi capitalista. Antropofagia. Absorção do inimigo sacro. Para transformá-lo em totem. A humana aventura. A terrena finalidade. Porém, só as puras elites conseguiram realizar a antropofagia carnal, que traz em si o mais alto sentido da vida e evita todos os males identificados por Freud, males catequistas. O que se dá não é uma sublimação do instinto sexual. É a escala termométrica do instinto antropofágico. De carnal, ele se torna eletivo e cria a amizade. Afetivo, o amor. Especulativo, a ciência. Desvia-se e transfere-se. Chegamos ao aviltamento. A baixa antropofagia aglomerada nos pecados de catecismo—a inveja, a usura, a calúnia, o assassinato. Peste dos chamados povos cultos e cristianizados, é contra ela que estamos agindo. Antropófagos. (48)

Contra Anchieta cantando as onze mil virgens do céu, na terra de Iracema,—o patriarca João Ramalho fundador de São Paulo. (49)

A nossa independência ainda não foi proclamada. Frase típica de D. João VI:—Meu filho, põe essa coroa na tua cabeça, antes que algum aventureiro o faça! Expulsamos a dinastia. É preciso expulsar o espírito bragantino, as ordenações e o rapé de Maria da Fonte. (50)

Contra a realidade social, vestida e opressora, cadastrada por Freud—a realidade sem complexos, sem loucura, sem prostituições e sem penitenciárias do matriarcado de Pindorama (51)

> Oswald de Andrade
> Em Piratininga.
> Ano 374 da Deglutição do Bispo Sardinha.
> (*Revista de Antropofagia*, Ano I, No. 1, maio de 1928)

Anthropophagous Manifesto

Only anthropophagy unites us. Socially. Economically. Philosophically. (1)

The only law in the world. The masked expression of all individualisms, of all collectivisms. Of all religions. Of all peace treaties. (2)

Tupi, or not tupi that is the question. (3)

Down with all catechisms. And down with the Gracchi's mother. (4)

I'm only interested in what's not mine. Man's law. Law of the cannibal. (5)

We are weary of all suspicious catholic husbands thrown into drama.[14] Freud did away with the feminine mystique and other horrors of printed psychology. (6)

What collided with truth was clothing, the impermeable barrier placed between the inner and outer worlds. The reaction against the dressed man. American cinema will inform it. (7)

Children of the sun, mother of the living. Ferociously found and loved, with all the hypocrisy of *saudade*,[15] by the immigrants, by the trafficked victims and by the *touristes*.[16] In the country of the big snake. (8)

It was because we never had grammars nor collections of old plants. And we never knew what urban, suburban, frontier and continental were. Lazy on the *mappa mundi* of Brazil. (9)

A participating consciousness, a religious rhythm. (10)

Down with all importers of canned conscience. The palpable existence of life. And the pre-logical mentality for Mr. Lévy-Bruhl to study. (11)

We want the Caraib Revolution. Bigger than the French Revolution. The unification of all effective revolts in the direction of man. Without us, Europe would not even have its poor Declaration of the Rights of the Man and of the Citizen.

The Golden Age heralded by America. The Golden Age. And all the *girls*. (12)

Origins. Contact with Caraib Brazil. *Où Villegaignon print [prit]*[17] *terre*. Montaigne. The natural man. Rousseau. From the French Revolution to Romanticism, to the Bolshevik Revolution, to the Surrealist Revolution and Keyserling's technicized barbarian. We march.

We were never catechized. We live by a somnambulist legal right. We made Christ to be born in Bahia. Or in *Belém do Pará*. (13)

But we never allowed the birth of logic among us. (14)

Down with Father Vieira. Author of our first loan, to earn a commission. The illiterate king had told him: put that down on paper, but without too much smooth talk. The loan materialized. Brazilian sugar was signed away. Vieira left the money in Portugal and brought us the smooth talk. (15)

The spirit refuses to conceive a spirit without a body. Anthropomorphism. The need for the anthropophagic vaccine. To achieve the balance against the meridian religions. And the exterior inquisitions. (16)

We can only attend to the auricular world. (17)

We used to have a justice system that codified vengeance. Science as codification of Magic. Anthropophagy. The permanent transformation of Taboo into totem. (18)

Down with the reversible world and the objectified ideas. Cadaverized. The *stop* of thinking that is dynamic. The individual as victim of the system. Source of classic injustices. Of the romantic injustices. And the oblivion of the inner achievements. (19)

Itineraries. Itineraries. Itineraries. Itineraries. Itineraries. Itineraries. Itineraries. (20)

The Caraib instinct. (21)

Death and life of all hypotheses. From the equation "Self as part of the Cosmos" to the axiom "Cosmos, part of the Self." Subsistence. Knowledge. Anthropophagy. (22)

Down with the vegetable elites. In communication with the soil. (23)

We were never catechized. Instead, we produced Carnival. The Amerindian in costume of senator of the Empire. Pretending to be Pitt. Or appearing in Alencar's operas full of polite Portuguese feelings. (24)

We already had communism. We already had the surrealist language. The golden age.
Catiti Catiti
Imara Notiá
Notiá Imara
Ipeju. (25)

Magic and life. We used to have the listing and allocation of tangible goods, moral goods, and *dignary* goods.[18] And we knew how to transpose mystery and death with the help of a few grammatical forms. (26)

I asked a man the meaning of Law. He replied that it was the guarantee of the exercise of possibility. That man's name was Galli Mathias. I ate him. (27)

Only where mystery dwells there is no determinism. But what do we have to do with it? (28)

Down with the histories of Man, which begin at Cape Finisterre. The undated world. Unrubrified.[19] Without Napoleon. Without Caesar. (29)

The determination of progress through catalogues and television sets. Only machinery. And blood transfusers. (30)

Against the antagonistic sublimations. Brought in the caravels. (31)

Down with the truth of the missionary peoples, defined by the sagacity of an anthropophagous, the Viscount of Cairu:—It's a lie often repeated. (32)

But those who came weren't crusaders. They were fugitives from a civilization we're eating, because we're strong and vindictive like the Tortoise. (33)

If God is the conscience of the *Increated* Universe, Guaraci is the mother of the living. Jaci is the mother of the plants. (34)

We had no speculation. But we had divination. We had Politics, which is the science of distribution. And a social system in harmony with the universe. (35)

The migrations. The flight from tedious states. Down with the urban sclerosis. Down with the Conservatories and speculative tedium. (36)

From William James to Voronoff. The transfiguration of Taboo into totem. Anthropophagy. (37)

The paterfamilias and the creation of the Morality of the Stork: Real ignorance of things + lack of imagination + sense of authority towards the curious offspring.

One must depart from a profound atheism in order to arrive at the idea of God. However, the Caraib didn't need to. Because he had Guaraci. (38)

The established objective reacts like the Fallen Angels. Next, Moses divagates. What do we have with it? (39)

Before the Portuguese discovered Brazil, Brazil had discovered happiness. (40)

Down with the torchbearer Amerindian. The Amerindian son of Mary, godson of Catherine de' Médici and son-in-law of D. Antônio de Mariz. (41)

Joy is the ultimate proof. (42)

In the matriarchy of Pindorama. (43)

Down with Memory as source of habit. Personal experience renewed. (44)

We are concretists. Ideas take hold, react, and burn people in public squares. Let's get rid of ideas and other paralysis. By means of itineraries. Let's believe in signs, in sextants and in the stars. (45)

Down with Goethe, the Gracchi's mother, and the court of D. João VI. (46)

Joy is the ultimate proof. (47)

The struggle between what would be called the *Increated* and the *Creature*—illustrated by the permanent contradiction of Man and his Taboo. Mundane love and the capitalist way of life. Anthropophagy. Absorption of the sacred enemy. To transform him into a totem. The human adventure. The earthly purpose. However, only the pure elites managed to carry out carnal anthropophagy, which carries within itself the highest meaning of life and avoids all the evils identified by Freud, evils of catechism. What happens is not a sublimation of the sexual instinct. It is the thermometric scale of the anthropophagic instinct. Carnal at first, it becomes elective, creating friendship. When affective, it creates love. When speculative, it creates science. It takes detours and moves around. We arrive at degradation. The low anthropophagy clustered in the sins of catechism—envy, usury, slander, murder. We are acting against this plague of the supposedly cultured and Christianized peoples. Anthropophagi. (48)

Against Anchieta singing about the eleven thousand virgins of Heaven, in the land of Iracema—the patriarch João Ramalho, founder of São Paulo. (49)

Our independence has not yet been proclaimed. A typical expression of D. João VI:—My son, put this crown on your head, before some adventurer puts it on his! We expelled the dynasty. It remains to expel the Bragantine spirit, the ordinations[20] and Maria da Fonte's snuff box.

(50)

Against the dressed and oppressive social reality registered by Freud—the reality without complexes, without madness, without prostitution and penitentiaries of the matriarchy of Pindorama.

(51)

> Oswald de Andrade
> In Piratininga,
> in the 374th year of the swallowing of Bishop Sardinha
> (*Revista de Antropofagia*, Year I, No. I, May of 1928)

Explanatory Notes

(1) Only anthropophagy unites us. Socially. Economically. Philosophically.

This aphorism summarizes the essence of anthropophagy as the seminal movement of Brazilian modernism. The manifesto starts with a witty parody of the last line of the Communist Manifesto written by Marx and Engels, the famous slogan which declares "Working Men of All Countries, Unite!" (Oswald de Andrade was Marxist and would later join the communist party in Brazil). Cannibalism stands as the common denominator of modernism, a process of swallowing up external and internal cultures in the construction of a national identity characterized by hybrid features. In addition, it opens the door for anthropophagy to migrate to other spheres beyond art and culture, with social, economic and philosophical ramifications. The later, in particular, was retaken by Oswald de Andrade in the 1940s and 1950s, particularly though his thesis "The Crisis of the Messianic Philosophy."[21]

(2) The only law in the world. The masked expression of all individualisms, of all collectivisms. Of all religions. Of all peace treaties.

It is remarkable that with his background in law, Oswald de Andrade immediately declares that cannibalism is "the only valid law," giving it universal character and expanding its application to areas beyond the ones indicated in the previous aphorism: politics and religion. There are at least two main aspects that make anthropophagy a universal law. The first is the ritual of the Eucharist. Brazil is the largest catholic country in the world, and the

Eucharist is the supreme anthropophagic ritual because it transubstantiates the body and blood of Christ into bread and wine, so that they can be consumed by believers in reenactment of the central covenant of the Christian religion. An important corollary, clarified by Andrade a few months after the publication of the manifesto, is that all religions have adopted in one way or another the cannibalistic idea of holy communion. The Amerindians practiced it with real human flesh. Catholicism simply plastered over this natural tendency by introducing a symbolic ritual.[22]

The second universal feature of anthropophagy is its Darwinian conception of life as a dog-eat-dog struggle for existence. Indeed, according to Freud, even the sexual desire that motivates human reproduction is essentially a disguised appetite for human flesh. What Brazil had to do in order to achieve moral liberation was to give religious expression to the latent, cannibalistic sexual drive of its people. In sum, since life is essentially "devouring," anthropophagy encompasses all areas of our existence: the social, the economic, and the philosophical, as stated in the previous aphorism, as well as the political and religion spheres of our existence.

(3) *Tupi, or not tupi that is the question.*

The Tupi people were one of the most numerous of Brazil's indigenous peoples before colonization. They inhabited almost all of Brazil's coast when the Portuguese arrived in 1500, and their practice of cannibalism ensured their perception as savages. To a great extent, this is the motto that led to the creation of the manifesto, and therefore is considered by many the slogan that defines the anthropophagic movement: the dilemma between returning to the roots of the native Amerindian aesthetic or embracing the Western European aesthetic of the colonizers. The existential problem is ultimately solved: the final rejection of the colonial values of the European as well as the erasure of the inferiority complex of the colonized can only be achieved through identification with the cannibalistic Amerindian, on the premise that the eating of human flesh is the most extreme form of opposition to the morality of Western civilization. Yet there is a central aspect to Andrade's play on words: the replacement of the Shakespearean metaphysical abstraction of the verb "to be" by the ontological concreteness of the noun "tupi."

(4) Down with all catechisms. And down with the Gracchi's mother.

This is a call against colonization, and specifically the imposition of a new culture on the colonized. Catechetical instruction in the catholic faith is derided as a false form of benevolence used by the Portuguese as an instrument to dominate the indigenous population of Brazil. The allusion to Cornelia, a Roman widow of the second century BCE who dedicated herself to ensuring that her sons, the Gracchi brothers, received a Greek education from Greek tutors, is another instance of embracing and submitting to a foreign culture. Thus the indictment of Cornelia here is a rare instance in the manifesto where the female role is viewed under a negative light, since at its heart the manifesto pleads for a matriarchal society.

(5) I'm only interested in what's not mine. Man's law. Law of the cannibal.

Emphasizing the violent aspect of anthropophagy, Andrade affirms that the cannibal is only interested in absorbing the qualities of the enemy, and this is an invariable and assertive law. The interest in the alterity is the central thought of anthropophagy, where Viveiros de Castro observes that "it is the exchange, and not identity, the fundamental value to be affirmed."[23] In other words, differently from the European, the Amerindian is not interested to impose his identity over the other, or suppress their identity while imposing his. The Amerindian wants to update his identity in relation with the identity of "the other," and in the process transforms his own identity.

(6) We are weary of all suspicious catholic husbands thrown into drama. Freud did away with the feminine mystique and other horrors of printed psychology.

Marriage as one of the cornerstones of catholic morality has been dismantled by the new scientific studies on sexuality developed mainly by Freud. Besides morality plays, the author might be referring to American cinema, a space of transgression and transformation of values at the time. He speaks more specifically of the fact that cinema shows women who are eroticized and wearing little clothing.

(7) What collided with truth was clothing, the impermeable barrier placed between the inner and outer worlds. The reaction against the dressed man. American cinema will inform it.

This is a validation of Amerindian primitivism as the most genuine expression of authenticity and artistic truth, represented by the naked Amerindian. The civilized man does not have access to this ideal because the use of waterproof clothing separates his inner world from the outer world, something that does not happen with the Amerindian. Clothes in anthropophagy represent work, catechism, and all the abominable remnants of civilization that are of no use to the primitive figure of the naked natural man. The matrix of capitalism is found in clothing and the dignification of man through work. This is what distinguishes civilized society from the anthropophagic utopia, which is characterized by the dignification of man through leisure, the ludic spirit.

The inversion of the hierarchy of contact between the dominant culture of the colonizer and the dominated culture of the savage through the metaphor of clothing can be illustrated by the poem "Erro de português" (Portuguese Mistake), written by Oswald de Andrade in 1927:[24]

Quando o português chegou	When the Portuguese arrived
debaixo duma bruta chuva	under pouring rain
vestiu o indio	he dressed the (Amer)Indian
que pena!	what a shame!
fosse uma manhã de sol	if it was a sunny morning
o indio tinha despido o português	the (Amer)Indian would have had undressed the Portuguese

Westerns were the most popular Hollywood film genre from the early twentieth century through the 1960s. Andrade is probably referring to westerns produced during the silent film era (1894–1927), which frequently depicted conflicts between natives and North American colonizers. However, in the current context, the allusion is made in a jocular sense, bringing humor to the text in the same way as the later allusion to the "girls" in aphorism 11 does.

(8) Children of the sun, mother of the living. Ferociously found and loved, with all the hypocrisy of *saudade*, by the immigrants, by the trafficked victims and by the *touristes*. In the country of the big snake.

Andrade describes Brazilian Amerindians as children of the sun, a female divinity—and this is important due to his defense of matriarchy over patriarchy—who were found by the colonizers, by the immigrants, by the negroes who were trafficked as slaves, and by the tourists, to whom they became a source of entertainment. The colonizers not only imposed themselves, but also fiercely loved the Amerindian women, meaning, through rape. Andrade uses the French word for "tourists" (*touristes*) in order to underline their status as foreigners.

Even stronger is the effect achieved by the use of the word *saudade*, which encapsulates a feeling of longing, melancholy, or nostalgia, a word that exists only in the Portuguese language to define an untranslatable emotion. In mentioning the "hypocrisy of *saudade*," the author is evoking once again the paternalistic attitude of the foreigner in Brazilian lands, "the country of the big snake." In Amazonian indigenous mythology, the "big snake" is a spirit of the waters; it was the subject of a long anthropophagic poem, *Cobra norato* (1931), by Raul Bopp (1898–1984), one of the prominent poets of the anthropophagic movement.

Another possibility is that through the "hypocrisy of *saudade*" the author is making a specific reference to the plot of the novel *Iracema* by the prominent romantic writer José de Alencar. A landmark in Brazilian literature, *Iracema* features the themes and literary style that go against the modernism that Oswald de Andrade pursues. In the present case, Iracema is a young Amerindian woman who falls in love with a Portuguese immigrant and abandons her tribe for him, however later feels remorse and longing (*saudade*) for her family when they were decimated by the colonizers.

(9) It was because we never had grammars nor collections of old plants. And we never knew what urban, suburban, frontier and continental were. Lazy on the *mappa mundi* of Brazil.

A participating consciousness, a religious rhythm.

This aphorism lists multiple characteristics of the Brazilian as a primitive man and claims that the Amerindian's coexistence with nature is more authentic than the sterile botanical categorizations imposed by civilized Europe. Rather, instinct should be praised above the formal study of grammars and treatises, or a more systematic form of education. Frivolous matters such as the categorization or labeling of plants are trivial to someone who is living alongside those plants.

Andrade concedes that the Amerindian is inherently lazy and indolent. In contrast to the work ethic present in a consumer society, the primitive society of the Amerindian does not require that individuals continue to work after their basic necessities have been satisfied. This attitude toward work is viewed in a positive light, and was thoroughly explored by Mário de Andrade in his magnum opus *Macunaíma*. Laziness can be seen as a symbol of resistance against an economic system that did not serve the needs of the original Brazilian people,[25] to whom the country was not divided in urban, suburban, frontier and continental. The manifesto proclaims "uma consciência participante, uma rítmica religiosa," meaning that the consciousness of the Amerindian is more real—something that is clarified later in aphorism 16—and his religion is rhythmic, comparable to the religion of African American slaves, which incorporates the rituals of *macumba* and *candomblé*, elements intrinsically rhythmic. This is one of the few subtle allusions to the Afro influence present in the manifesto.

(10) Down with all importers of canned conscience. The palpable existence of life. And the pre-logical mentality for Mr. Lévy-Bruhl to study.

To clarify the superiority of a participative consciousness, Andrade juxtaposes this concept against European consciousness, which is fabricated and therefore not genuine. An important inherent feature of the Amerindian consciousness is the pre-logical kind of thinking theorized by the anthropologist Lucien Lévy-Bruhl (1857–1939), who studied the primitive mind and posited the existence of two basic mindsets in humankind, the "primitive" and the "modern." According to Lévy-Bruhl, the primitive mind is mystical, collective, and pre-logical. However, this aphorism is against theorization, and in essence promotes the concreteness of the body ("the palpable existence of life"), without entering into metaphysical digressions, which are left for intellectuals such as Lévy-Bruhl to study.

(11) We want the Caraib Revolution. Bigger than the French Revolution. The unification of all effective revolts in the direction of man. Without us, Europe would not even have its poor Declaration of the Rights of the Man and of the Citizen.
The Golden Age heralded by America. The Golden Age. And all the *girls*.

Andrade wants to instigate a major revolution (the "Caraib Revolution" means a revolt among the Caraibs, essentially the Amerindians of the sixteenth century who spoke the Tupi language[26]), claiming that it would be even more important than the French Revolution, considered a cornerstone in the history of Western civilization, for promoting some of our most fundamental values, expressed in the slogan "freedom, equality, and brotherhood." In this call to arms, Andrade promotes a geographic inversion, claiming that the Declaration of the Rights of Man and of the Citizen, the seminal document produced by the French Revolution, is actually a Brazilian product instead of a French import, the result of this ultimate revolution, one that consists in the "unification of all effective revolts in the direction of man."

The scholar Benedito Nunes described the Caraib Revolution in the following terms:

The Caraib Revolution... would lead us from the historical to the transhistorical, from the chronology of civilization to the time of the primeval life it re-established, and would consummate an anti-colonial reaction, swallower of imperialisms. This anti-colonial reaction would happen in the form of an imaginary tribal revenge, which ritualized the romantic violence of individual rebellion.[27]

According to Mário Chamie, the main goals of the Caraib Revolution are: a) to promote "possession" instead of "property" (a Marxist proposition); b) to superimpose the savage over the civilized; c) to replace the metaphysical abstraction of the verb "to be" by the ontological concreteness of the noun "Tupi" ("Tupi or not Tupi, that is the question"); d) and, above all, to transform the taboos of literate culture into totems of a primitive culture, free from neurosis and other catholic diseases, diagnosed but not extirpated by Freud.[28]

As a corollary, Andrade promotes a temporal inversion, suggesting that the ultimate goal of the Caraib Revolution is the return of the "Golden Age," which according to him was born in America. The motif of the so-called golden age appeared originally in Greek mythology, which describes the decline of the golden race of humanity over five stages: golden, silver, bronze, heroic, and the current iron stage. The golden age is a period of primordial peace, harmony, stability, and prosperity; people did not have to work to feed themselves, for the earth provided food in abundance. Andrade posits that instead of being a product of Greek mythology, the golden age is a period in the indeterminate past of the indigenous inhabitants of Brazil, a period that can be recaptured through the Caraib Revolution. He ends the paragraph with a jest: after talking about the French Revolution, he uses the term "girls" in English to allude to the Golden Age as a time of moral liberation, symbolized by sexual freedom, as if shouting, "We want all the girls!"

(12) Origins. Contact with Caraib Brazil. *Où Villegaignon print terre.* Montaigne. The natural man. Rousseau. From the French Revolution to Romanticism, to the Bolshevik Revolution, to the Surrealist Revolution and Keyserling's technicized barbarian. We march.

Building on the previous aphorism, this one describes an inversion of values in order to demonstrate that the Americas would have been the true source of major historical events, the root of the main Western ideas and political structures present in Europe. Hence the strategic quotes from events and authors with a more or less evident relationship with the discovery of the New World.

The history of "Brazil"—the name of the country is not indigenous, but derives from the name the Portuguese gave to a species of tree that was used to produce a dye—started when the Portuguese made contact with the Amerindians in 1500, eight years after the arrival of Christopher Columbus in the New World. In between the two discoveries, Portugal and Spain signed the Treaty of Tordesillas, which provided for the division of the new lands and those yet to be discovered, thus protecting the interests of both nations. Yet the hegemony of Portugal over Brazil was challenged by other nations that sought to compete against the Iberian maritime expansion. English pirates and corsairs, as well as French and Dutch invaders, threatened Portuguese rule in colonial territory. Throughout the sixteenth century and the beginning of the seventeenth, they competed for power by invading the colony or trading goods. For the purposes of this manifesto, the French invasion is the most relevant, because France was the center of modernism when the manifesto was written, and a country that Andrade, as an intellectual, had the opportunity to visit on several occasions.

During the first decades of the colonial period, the French were constantly conducting "illegal" commerce in Brazil, exploiting the brazilwood trade and establishing alliances with Amerindian tribes, particularly the Tupinambá tribe. In response to the religious persecution of Protestants in France, influential leaders of the Huguenots (French Calvinists) attempted to transform the region of present-day Rio de Janeiro into a Huguenot stronghold. This region, known as Antarctic France, is referred to as "où Villegaignon print [prit] terre" (the place where Villegaignon landed) since this colonialist and military expansionist project started in 1555 under the command of Nicolas Durand de Villegaignon (1510–1571).[29] Villegaignon was a typical Renaissance man, a mixture of soldier, scientist, explorer, adventurer, and entrepreneur.

Villegaignon returned to France in 1559, taking with him three Brazilian Amerindians from the Tupinambá tribe. In 1562, these natives were able to meet Michel de Montaigne (1533–1592), the famous French philosopher of the Renaissance. In his essay "Of Cannibals" (1580), Montaigne showed an original vision by considering the Amerindians superior to the Europeans, who with their bloody conquest of the New World and their internal wars proved themselves the true barbarians. In contrast, the Amerindians demonstrate personal dignity and a sense of beauty that characterize a genuine fidelity to their human nature. Montaigne thus provided an early example of the European primitivist point of view, through an example of cultural relativism and tolerance that was unusual for the time: the belief in the superiority of Amerindian values over barbarian European practices.

The best-known European celebration of the primitive man is Rousseau's conception of the natural man—a savage man, a loner and self-sufficient, who kills only for self-preservation. In his *Discourse on the Origin and Basis of Inequality among Men* (1775), Rousseau presented the Romantic concept of the "noble savage." This figure, possessed of "natural rights," would help to shape a series of revolutions that sought to define and establish the idea of liberty and related concepts. Thus there is a direct lineage leading from the Amerindian savages whom Europeans encountered to the French Revolution, which set the stage for the spread of Romanticism; the Bolshevik Revolution (Andrade was a Marxist and later joined the Communist party in Brazil); and the Surrealist Revolution, which was not a political revolution but a poetic-political technique of destroying the superficial and repressive psychic layer of civilization for the vital eruption of instincts, the unconscious, the primitive, and the repressed, standing at the core of cannibal aesthetics.

The evolution traced by Andrade ends with Hermann von Keyserling (1880–1946), a spiritualist and a writer with a sweeping, associative style, rather than a deductive and logical one. His extensive travels gave him insights into other cultures, particularly those of the Far East; he also foresaw the ascension of Latin America as a world power. From Keyserling, Andrade borrowed the idea of the "technicized barbarian," casting this figure as the ultimate stage in the evolution of primitive man and giving him a positive valence.

For Keyserling, the technicized barbarian was a despicable figure, a point that comes across in his invention of the term "chauffeur-type" to describe the modern American man:

> The chauffeur is primitive man made technical. Technical endowment is closely related to the savage's gift of orientation, the technical as such is self-evident. . . . A mass age is emerging all over the globe. . . . To-day all the old culture on the face of the earth is perishing because the new, determined type of man disavows it. . . . How is it possible for any man . . . who hearkens back enthusiastically to classical times . . . honestly to believe that, in comparison with any Bolshevist leader of consequence he represents any force whatsoever?"[30]

The description above seems quite distant from what one would expect of the "technicized barbarian" cited by Andrade.[31] Due to Keyserling's diffuse writing style, it is difficult to determine whether Andrade adopted Keyserling's ideas or created his own associative interpretation of them. It seems more likely that Andrade adapted the concept of the "technicized barbarian" from Keyserling's *Le mond qui nait*, where this figure is described not as the primitive redeemer of the half-dead West, but rather as the end result of technology's destructive potential. Since technology is universal and does not belong to any culture, according to Keyserling, it establishes progress as an overwhelming and deadly conception of time. Unlike Keyserling, however, Andrade saw the barbarian as a creator of culture because of his vitality. What Keyserling saw as a symptom of decadence was for Andrade a sign of redemption. Thus, in Andrade's hands, the phrase borrowed from Keyserling posits that the ultimate product of the Caraib Revolution would be the humanization of technology and the liberation of its creative potential, which has been repressed in industrialized society. The process would allow Latin America, and especially Brazil, to become a world leader for the cultural renewal of all humanity.

(13) We were never catechized. We live by a somnambulist legal right. We made Christ to be born in Bahia. Or in *Belém do Pará*.

The Brazilian population, represented by the Amerindian, was never successfully catechized by the Portuguese invaders, despite persistent attempts by the Jesuits.[32] This is one of the reasons why the colonizers turned to the African slave trade as a source of labor. Here Andrade seems to criticize the legal system of his country. He considers the system "somnambulant," in the sense that the laws are mere mechanical artifacts that are imposed by inertia and do not reflect the real needs of society. It should be noted that according to aphorism 11, it is exactly this somnambulist legal system that provided the basis for the declaration of human rights that the author considers poor, and in a geographical inversion was transported from Brazil to Europe.

A similar geographic deterritorialization happens when Andrade locates the birth of Christ in Bahia, the main market for African slaves. While the Manifesto has at its heart the glorification of the Amerindian as the primitive being responsible for Brazilian culture, here is a rare exception where African influence is manifest. The author quotes a popular maxixe[33] from 1927 titled *Cristo Nasceu na Bahia* (Christ was born in Bahia),[34] whose first stanza reads:

Dizem que Cristo nasceu em Belém	They say that Christ was born in Bethlehem
A história se enganou	History was wrong
Cristo nasceu na Bahia, meu bem	Christ was born in Bahia, my dear
E o baiano[35] criou	And the Bahian created

To the north of Bahia state is the state of Pará, whose capital is the city Belém (Bethlehem), and Andrade seizes the opportunity to add a pun to his aphorism. The incorporation of popular or folk elements into the Manifesto is characteristic of the time and goes back to the Brazilwood Manifesto. The most important feature in this aphorism, however, is the rare presence of the African primitivist element in the Anthropophagous Manifesto. As Azevedo writes,

> Throughout the theme of the Manifesto, clearly more focused on the Amerindian presence in Brazil, this aphorism stands out for the movement that shifts this indigenous origin ("We were never catechized") to the Afro-Brazilian universe ("We made Christ born in Bahia"), in an interesting and double relationship that reinvents the paradigms of Jesuit colonization: as if it wasn't enough that the unstable and unreliable savages did not accept catechization in the tribes, on top of that they also end up dislocating the geography of Christian history, making Christ be born in the state with the largest black population in Brazil.[36]

(14) But we never allowed the birth of logic among us.

A typical characteristic of the "savage thought" of the Amerindian is the absence of the use of logic, which goes against the main characteristic of the civilized thought of the civilized man. Logical thinking is frequently associated with Cartesian rationalism and the use of pure deduction in order to reach truth. The scientific method, the deterministic laws of cause and effect, and the use of reason instead of intuition are all characteristic of logical thinking. One element of primitivism's reaction against traditional European values was the valorization of the intuitive and pre-logical kind of thinking that was claimed to have the potential to reach the real essence of truth, which could not be achieved through the use of logic. The anthropologist Lucien Lévy-Bruhl, previously mentioned in the manifesto (aphorism 10), posited the existence of two types of mind: the primitive and the modern. The primitive mind does not differentiate the supernatural from reality and uses "mystical participation" to manipulate the world. The primitive mind does not address contradictions. The modern mind uses reflection and logic to draw conclusions.

For the purposes of this study, it is relevant to mention also the work of two other anthropologists: Claude Lévi-Strauss (1908–2009) and Eduardo Viveiros de Castro (b. 1951). Educated in France, Lévi-Strauss served as a university professor in São Paulo during the late 1930s. His study of the Amerindians formed the basis of his book *The Savage Mind*, in which, like

Lévy-Bruhl, he too argued for the existence of two modes of thought: mythical thought and modern scientific inquiry.[37] For Lévi-Strauss, however, both scientific and mythical thought should be understood as valid systems; one does not supersede the other. They are two autonomous ways of thinking, rather than two stages in the evolution of thought. Viveiros de Castro clarifies this aspect: the "'savage mind' is not 'savage' or 'primitive' thinking (as opposed to 'Western thinking'), but thinking in its primeval state, that is, human thinking in its free exercise, an exercise not yet domesticated with a view to obtaining some kind of profit."[38]

(15) Down with Father Vieira. Author of our first loan, to earn a commission. The illiterate king had told him: put that down on paper, but without too much smooth talk. The loan materialized. Brazilian sugar was signed away. Vieira left the money in Portugal and brought us the smooth talk.

The Jesuit priest Antonio Vieira (1608–1697)[39] is considered the main representative of Baroque literature in Brazil; his formal and elegant rhetoric was diametrically opposite to the poetic idiom that Andrade envisioned for Brazil. Vieira had a major role in diplomatic negotiations on behalf of Dom João IV, the king who liberated Portugal from Habsburg Spain and restored it as an independent kingdom. He devoted himself to the evangelization of the Amerindians while opposing their enslavement. He was deeply involved in the political-economic machinations behind the exploitation of sugar—a new commodity during the colonial period—in the state of Maranhão. But the venture only benefited the Portuguese metropolis, while leaving the colony in complete misery. In this aphorism, Andrade violently criticizes Father Vieira as the corrupt servant of an illiterate king who used the power of his rhetoric to benefit the colonizer. He used in Portuguese the word *lábia*, which is a slang term that means smooth talk. It is no wonder that Father Vieira was considered "the Brazilian Judas."

(16) The spirit refuses to conceive a spirit without a body. Anthropomorphism. The need for the anthropophagic vaccine. To achieve the balance against the meridian religions. And the exterior inquisitions.

In the eternal tension between body and soul, the anthropophagic movement is conceived as a movement where the body prevails over the spirit and form prevails over content. Anthropomorphism is a thought process characteristic of the Amerindian that legitimizes the anthropophagic movement by attributing to gods, natural phenomena, or supernatural creatures behaviors and thoughts characteristic of human beings. It is a thought process that gives "body" to ideas and should prevail over purely amorphous spiritual beliefs.

Anthropophagy's "cult of the body" functions as an immunization against the "meridian religions," the religions that preach "doctrines of salvation," particularly catholicism, since Brazil is the largest catholic country in the world. Perhaps Andrade calls them meridian religions because he metaphorically conceives of meridians as dividing lines between body and soul that run contrary to anthropophagy's cult of the body. According to the Christian faith, we are redeemed from our prior condition of "slavery to sin" by Christ's death on the cross. Against this doctrine, Andrade dialogues with Nietzsche by rejecting the presupposed sinfulness and dejection of our existence, as well as the eternal, unrepayable debt to the Redeemer.

The Christian doctrine of sin engenders feelings of impotence, guilt, and damnation as characteristic of our lives on earth, which serve as preparation for an eternal, otherworldly existence. The disavowal of passions, particularly sexual desire, denigrates man's general state of vitality, turning Christianity into an anti-life religion. Through inquisition or catechization, religion kills the devouring instinct of the natural man, something that can only be overcome through an anthropophagic vaccine, a Nietzschean view of life.

(17) We can only attend to the auricular world.

The dichotomy between the senses of sight and hearing can be traced back to mystical theories such as sacred geometry. In geometry, ruler and compass are the two essential tools. The ruler corresponds to the sense of vision, while hearing corresponds to the compass. As a phallic symbol, the ruler is linked to the male, the sense of sight, and the use of logic—"seeing is believing." The compass corresponds to the feminine, with its ability to draw curves—the circle is the symbol of the ovary—and is associated with the sense of hearing. Anthropophagy goes against the patriarchal instinct, positioning itself on the side of the female and the auditory sense, which is much more intuitive. After all, knowledge obtained through hearing is not knowledge acquired through something experienced in time/space, but knowledge gained by hearsay. Metaphorically, Andrade is stating that for the poet, the ludic value reigns over the realm of logic, therefore denying the importance of the world of facts.

(18) We used to have a justice system that codified vengeance. Science as codification of Magic. Anthropophagy. The permanent transformation of Taboo into totem.

This paragraph summarizes three essential aspects of Anthropophagy: the sense of justice as a code of vengeance; mythical thought replacing logical thinking; and the triumph of the matriarchal system. Let's examine the three separately.

a) Concerning the definition of justice as the codification of vengeance, the anthropologists Viveiros de Castro and Carneiro da Cunha explain how this can be understood. According to them, for the Tupi Amerindian,

> the cycle of life and posthumous fate are both organized around revenge. A man is born as a future avenger. The mother smears the breasts with the enemy's blood for the child to taste. . . . Finally, the breaking of the skull of the first enemy will allow access to the full condition of Man: the first revenge, the first renaming, the first access to a fertile woman, toward a true marriage, the first paternity. Every child was the son of a killer, and the women would reject anyone who was not a killer.[40]

Another central aspect of the code of vengeance of the Brazilian Amerindian is that the prisoner saw in death itself his only form of revenge/identity affirmation. This is because the captives assumed that through their death and devouring, they were already avenged of those who would kill them, because this was part of the cycle advocated by the Code of Vengeance: the victim had already killed and eaten many enemies and, in addition, would be avenged by his own living relatives. A complicity is formed between victims and executioners, which guaranteed the constitution of the Tupi (cultural) identity and its perpetuation.

Benedito Nunes corroborates this view: "The absorption of the flesh of another killed in battle was anthropophagy, the ingestion of the enemy called 'sacred.' . . . the one who had virtues to be exploited. The ingestion of human flesh was, then, at the same time an act of revenge and of appropriation of the faculties of the courageous enemy. This ingestion provided, therefore, a magical continuity of the spoils consumed."[41] In the anthropophagous rite there is a fundamental dialogue that haunted the Jesuit missionaries, namely the dialogue held between the prisoner and his future murderer: he who will be eaten affirms that he will be avenged by his tribe, in the same way that he has already eaten others from this tribe that is now avenging their ancestors. This is not a process of transcendence; it is a simple statement about past and future, which ensures the temporal, cyclical permanence of both tribes.[42]

b) The phrase "science as codification of Magic" means that magic should be raised to the same level of (or above) science, and the mythical thought of the savage should be raised above logical thinking. Magic or divination is a way to refer to the mythical thought of the primitive man. Going back to the two types of thought as defined by Claude Lévi-Strauss in *The Savage Mind*, the "science of the concrete" (or mythical thought) and modern scientific inquiry are two autonomous ways of thinking, rather than two evolutionary stages, and therefore magic should not be considered primitive science. Mythical thought is based on observation "of the sensible world in sensible terms," producing a sort of intellectual "bricolage."[43] If scientific thought is represented by the engineer who asks a question and tries to design an optimal or complete solution, savage thought resembles the bricoleur, who constructs things using whatever materials are at hand.

c) The transformation of taboo into totem is the ultimate goal of the anthropophagic utopia conceived by Andrade: it represents the transformation of a patriarchal society into a matriarchal society, according to which the removal of authority imposed by "paternal" tradition inherited from the European continent—that is, the act of parricide—is the only solution capable of ending the domination imposed for centuries on national art. Only the break with the father figure could enable Brazilian artistic production to become the product of a truly autonomous conscience.

Andrade's theory is based on his unorthodox interpretation of Freud's *Totem and Taboo* (1913).[44] Freud's theory is complex, and Andrade's interpretation produces the transgressive radicality of the "anthropophagic conscience," destined to overcome the "external resistance" of patriarchal values and to inaugurate the new "ethical conscience" of a future matriarchal society.[45] In short, the process consists in the transformation of the taboos of civilized culture into totems of a primitive culture, free from neurosis and other "catholic diseases" diagnosed but not extirpated by Freud. According to Benedito Nunes,

> The transformation of taboo into totem, the essence of this ritual [the anthropophagic ritual], was taken by our author [Oswald de Andrade] from *Totem and Taboo*, where Freud, in order to explain the passage from the natural to the social state, from Nature to Culture, established the mythical hypothesis of cannibalistic parricide. After the murder and devouring of the tyrannical father, leader of the horde, by the rebellious children, came the interiorization of the paternal authority, as a collective Superego that prohibits incest. Compelled to expiate that crime, humanity keeps repeating this anthropophagic devouring, transforming the taboo into a totem, the fateful parricide.[46]

Patriarchy is represented by the bourgeois and capitalist society of the colonizer, centered on the dominator's right to property, on usury, on the family hierarchy, on the vices of the civilized man, in logical and metaphysical speculations, and in the repression of our instincts and of sexual freedom. From Andrade's perspective, patriarchy is a taboo embedded in the course of history. Matriarchy, on the other hand, is identified with the arrival of a new golden age, whose revolutionary values would promote the replacement of civilized man's right of property by primitive man's right of possession, the overcoming of usury and business through idleness, the ending of the centralizing and authoritarian powers promoted through the advent of a communal life open to life's pleasures, dictated by an uncensored individual libido. Matriarchy would unravel the patriarchal taboo of history, transforming it into a totem of a blissful new era. This transformation would be a product of the Caraib Revolution, produced by the technicized barbarian of our times, a natural/primitive man not yet contaminated by the degradations imposed by Western civilization.

(19) Down with the reversible world and the objectified ideas. Cadaverized. The *stop* of thinking that is dynamic. The individual as victim of the system. Source of classic injustices. Of the romantic injustices. And the oblivion of the inner achievements.

Once again, the author positions himself against colonialism, which brought objectified ideas that allowed the European colonizer to attack the basic elements of the Brazilian primitive culture: nudity, polygamy, nomadism, and the ritual of cannibalism. Catechism is viewed as a retrograde process that victimizes the individual and stops the dynamism of free thought, constantly in movement, and Andrade demonstrates it in the style of this aphorism, where the sentences are abruptly terminated by periods that interrupt the continuity of the thought process. He even incorporates a word in English—"stop"—to boost the roughness of the sentence. The multiple injustices brought by the colonial system promoted the ostracism of the inner achievements that the author wants to rescue, the achievements that include all the positive traits of the native primitivism of the country.

(20) Itineraries. Itineraries. Itineraries. Itineraries. Itineraries. Itineraries. Itineraries.

This sevenfold repetition of the word "itineraries," separated by periods in the telegraphic writing style used in the previous aphorism, functions like an adage that instils a poetic rhythm in the narrative. By juxtaposing this aphorism with the previous one, the poet points out the need for a dynamic route for the anthropophagic process, since anthropophagic thought is free and dynamic.

(21) The Caraib instinct.

The Caraib instinct referred to is the cannibal instinct; the word "cannibal" itself is derived from "Caraib," as is the name of the Caribbean Sea. According to Raquel R. Souza, Andrade's use of the term *Caraib* in this context designates both the indigenous community in the northern region of Brazil with whom the Portuguese colonizers first established contact, as well as the large linguistic family to which the tribes found in the south of the colony also belong.[47] However, the initial encounter of the European colonizer with the American cannibal was limited to the Caraibs, indigenous people who lived in the islands of the Caribbean, where Columbus landed on his four voyages. Soon afterward, the name "cannibal" given to the *Caraib* (Caribbean) was applied to Amerindians throughout South America, including Brazil, while the term "cannibalism" came to be understood as the specific act of eating human flesh.

Adding to the confusion is the fact that the European colonizers were sometimes called "karaiba." According to Viveiros de Castro, "it is worth noting that the Europeans, called *Karaiba*, as such characters were initially treated, ended up bringing to the Amerindians the exact opposite of what the *Karaiba* promised: instead of migratory wandering, forced settlement; in place of long life and effortless abundance, death from epidemics and slave labor; in place of victory over enemies, prohibition of war and cannibalism; in place of marital freedom, new restrictions."[48]

The main consequence of the above is that the central concept of the anthropophagic movement, that of cannibalism, is essentially a deterritorialized concept, while the author seems to be referring to instinct as the feature that would transfer from the Amerindian to Keyserling's technicized barbarian (see aphorism 12).

(22) Death and life of all hypotheses. From the equation "Self as part of the Cosmos" to the axiom "Cosmos, part of the Self." Subsistence. Knowledge. Anthropophagy.

Anthropophagy represents a process of communion of the individual with the universe (the cosmos) that ensures the individual's survival and the acquisition of knowledge. In other words, the author presents anthropophagy as an animistic conception of the universe.

(23) Down with the vegetable elites. In communication with the soil.

The phrase "vegetable elites" refers to the intellectuals whose critical incapacity leads to the perpetuation of the European canon. Vegetables are understood as living beings without mobility, which is to say, without the critical capacity that fosters change. Communication with the earth is equated with the search for a national identity.

(24) We were never catechized. Instead, we produced Carnival. The Amerindian in the costume of the senator of the Empire. Pretending to be Pitt. Or appearing in Alencar's operas full of polite Portuguese feelings.

Despite the efforts of the Jesuits, the Brazilians were never catechized. Instead, they transformed a catholic religious holiday—carnival—into an orgiastic party, where one can see the Amerindian in the most transgressive light: pretending to be a politician of the monarchy; dressed up as William Pitt (1759–1806), prime minister of Britain and influential in the colonization of India; or dressed up as an opera character of the Romantic era. In the latter case, the author specifically refers to the opera *Il Guarany* (1870) by Carlos Gomes (1836–1896), a composition based on the homonymous novel by José de Alencar (1829–1877), arguably the most influential Brazilian Romantic novelist of the nineteenth century, and a major exponent of the literary tradition known as "Indianism." The typical Amerindian character in the opera is the "noble savage," the catechized native that Andrade repudiates—the acculturated, domesticated, and catechized Amerindian. Written in Italian rather than Portuguese, *Il Guarany* represents the art of the colonizer that has the basic ingredients that the anthropophagic movement attempts to counteract.

(25) We already had communism. We already had the surrealist language. The golden age.
Catiti Catiti
Imara Notiá
Notiá Imara
Ipeju.

The reversal of history in the negation of chronological time is a primordial characteristic of primitive thought. In this aphorism the author indicates that communism was already present in the golden age of Brazil, the age that preceded the colonization of the country and the age toward which the country is again marching. This progress toward the golden age can also be viewed as a reversal of time, or—more precisely—as an expression of the "eternal return" for the primitive man, as conceived in different yet nevertheless similar ways by Nietzsche, Mercia Eliade, Lévi-Strauss, Bergson, and others.

The idea of the eternal return is essentially a belief that one is able to become contemporary with, or return to, the "mythical age"—the time when the events described in one's myths occurred. In Nietzsche's philosophy, the eternal return frames human existence as a series of endless repeating cycles—"all events in the world repeat themselves in the same sequence through an eternal series of cycles."[49] It is thanks to the negation of chronological time that Andrade can credit the Brazilian Amerindian as the precursor of communism, surrealism, the Declaration of Rights of the Man and Citizen, and other elements present in the Manifesto.

The author concludes this aphorism by quoting transliterated verses of an excerpt from an Amerindian poem that appeared in Portuguese translation in a book by Couto de Magalhães as a "New Moon Invocation Chant."[50] The lines can be translated as "New Moon, O New Moon, blow memories of me on *fulano*."[51] According to Couto de Magalhães (1836–1898), Cairê, the full moon, and Catiti, the new moon, were distinct beings for the Tupi tribes, configuring themselves as helpers of Rudah, the god of love; "they had invocations similar to those that were sung to that god, and for the same purpose of bringing lovers home through the power of nostalgia (*saudade*)."[52]

(26) Magic and life. We used to have the listing and allocation of tangible goods, moral goods, and *dignary* goods.[53] And we knew how to transpose mystery and death with the help of a few grammatical forms.

In the exaltation of magic and life, the author favors the ludic, the magical, and the non-logical primitivist thinking, which is more effective in addressing the mysteries of our existence—the idea of life and death—through a poetic and symbolic language deprived of a sophisticated grammar. Continuing one of the themes of the previous aphorism, he once again indirectly mentions the communist differentiation between possession and ownership (distribution of physical assets), using specific legal terms for the various types of assets, and expands the idea of possession to include tangible, moral and *dignary* goods (goods provided by the Portuguese monarch).

(27) I asked a man the meaning of Law. He replied that it was the guarantee of the exercise of possibility. That man's name was Galli Mathias. I ate him.
Only where mystery dwells there is no determinism. But what do we have to do with it?

With a background in law, Oswald de Andrade criticizes the imported concept of a legal system as a confusing and misleading notion by presenting a definition and attributing it to a certain person called "Galli Mathias." In fact, *galimathias* is a French term that means "a confusing unintelligible affair." The aphorism ends with a cannibal joke: "I ate him."[54]

Determinism is another way to define logical thinking, a process based on the concept of cause and effect. Determinism kills the beauty of the mystery of our existence, but this seems to be irrelevant, because based on the course of the manifesto so far, this is obvious ("what do we have to do with it?").

(28) Down with the histories of Man, which begin at Cape Finisterre. The undated world. Unrubrified. Without Napoleon. Without Caesar.

Cape Finisterre is so named because it comes from *"finis terrae,"* the end of the earth in Latin, the location where in Roman times it was believed to be an end of the known world. It is sometimes, like the present case, said to be the westernmost point of the Iberian Peninsula. In this context, Cape Finisterre as the location where history began alludes to the cycle of Portuguese overseas discoveries initiated in 1421 under the command of Infante Dom Henrique, son of Dom João I, which culminated in the discovery of Brazil in 1500. The geographical feature mentioned by the author is the well-known Ponta de Sagres, a cape formed by high rocks and a desolate place of tragic beauty from which the first Portuguese oceanic expeditions would have sailed to start the expansion of the European man; in fact, the expeditions led by Infante Dom Henrique departed from Vila de Lagos, located about thirty kilometers east of Ponta de Sagres, in the Algarve region.

The aphorism positions anthropophagy against chronological history, favoring a non-historical, non-sequential, "undated" concept of time, and denies renowned historical symbols of colonizers such as Napoleon and Julius Cesar. In an article titled "Os erros de Marx" (Marx's mistakes), Oswald argues that "the 'historical man' is an artificial creation who cannot preside over any serious psychological research. Historical determinism is the anecdote of biological determinism. Often poorly told."[55] A non-rubricated world is an *ahistorical* world, basically the same concept as the undated world—in Oswald's own words, a world "without the calendars and leaflets that place trivial life in the microscopic time asserted by Heidegger."[56]

(29) The determination of progress through catalogues and television sets. Only machinery. And blood transfusers.

This aphorism expresses the author's interest in contemporary technological developments, such as the television, machines, and blood transfusion techniques. Andrade connects the technicized world with his new version of the natural man, the "technicized barbarian" that he borrowed from Keyserling (see aphorism 12).

(30) Against the antagonistic sublimations. Brought in the caravels.

The "antagonistic sublimations" refer mainly to the catholic religion brought through the Jesuits in the Portuguese caravels. It can also refer to metaphysics, which the author attacked in the *Revista de Antropofagia* under the pseudonym "Freuderico," a combination of Freud and Frederick ("Frederico" in Portuguese, in reference to Nietzsche or Engels).

(31) Down with the truth of the missionary peoples, defined by the sagacity of an anthropophagous, the Viscount of Cairu: —It's a lie often repeated.

This aphorism refers to José da Silva Lisboa (1756–1835), a liberal economist who received the title of Viscount of Cairu. He had an important role in Brazilian history, by promoting economic reforms and participating in the process of political independence. Here the author gives him the status of anthropophagite because the viscount seems to have helped expose the hypocrisy of the catechizing Jesuits, who kept telling lies. Oswald de Andrade makes a reference to a quote attributed to Vladimir Lenin: "A lie told often enough becomes the truth."

(32) But those who came weren't crusaders. They were fugitives from a civilization we're eating, because we're strong and vindictive like the Tortoise.

The Brazilian colonizers were not nobles like the crusader knights of medieval Europe, but fugitives, renegades, and the scum of the European nations. The reaction of the Brazilian Amerindian was to eat the colonizer, which Andrade metaphorically associates with the legend of the revengeful tortoise, a Tupi Amerindian myth that appears in Couto de Magalhães's book *The Savage*.[57] The tortoise is considered a cunning animal in Amerindian folklore.

(33) If God is the conscience of the *Increated* Universe, Guaraci is the mother of the living. Jaci is the mother of the plants.

In this aphorism, the author does not seem to be using the term "Increated" in the sense of "not yet created," therefore it is italicized in the translation. It seems he is referring to a concept established by the late antique Roman philosopher Boethius, in his work *De trinitate*. According to Boethius, the divine substance (God) is pure form, form without matter, perfectly one and simple, and it is this simplicity that allows us to affirm that God "is that which is" (*est id quod est*), which is taken here to mean essence or total form, for in God form and essence are one. Since the universe is eternal, and not something that came to be at a certain time, God would be the universe's awareness of itself. Andrade juxtaposes this metaphysical conception with the pure animistic view of the Amerindian: Guaracy, as the god of the sun (mother of man and the living beings), and Jacy, as the god of the moon (mother of the plants). In this particular aphorism, Oswald de Andrade does not render a value judgment indicating that the position of the Amerindian is superior to the metaphysical one, but we can assume that this is what he intends.

Assuming that the above interpretation is correct, one should note that there is an equivalency in the way Boethius addresses the Holy Trinity in the work *De trinitate*, and the Amerindian conception in their mythology: the Holy Trinity for the Amerindian is formed by the two female goddesses Guaracy and Jacy along with the male god Rudah, who is not mentioned in the above aphorism. Rudah is the god of love and reproduction, responsible for the full moon (Cairê) and the new moon (Catití).[58]

(34) We had no speculation. But we had divination. We had Politics, which is the science of distribution. And a social system in harmony with the universe.

The author describes some of the most important characteristics of the primitive Amerindian: the absence of material property and greed, with its explicit criticism of societies driven by profit; the use of intuition in the form of divination; the Amerindian politics that were based on the communist concept of distribution; and a non-hierarchical society that he calls "a social system in harmony with the universe" (literally, a "social-planetary system").

(35) The migrations. The flight from tedious states. Down with the urban sclerosis. Down with the Conservatories and speculative tedium.

By "migrations" the author might be referring either to the mobility and free circulation of ideas, which provide an escape from the tedious values of the civilized society, or to the nomadic spirit of the Amerindian, which is the source of the geographic deterritorialization of cannibalism (see aphorism 21). The migrations constitute an escape against all the evils of the civilized man: the urban structures, the conservatories (understood as repositories of knowledge or as greenhouses) and the use of logical thinking, based on tedious speculations.

(36) From William James to Voronoff. The transfiguration of Taboo into totem. Anthropophagy.

William James (1842–1910) was an American philosopher, historian, and psychologist, considered one of the fathers of pragmatism. He participated in the Thayer Expedition to Brazil in 1865–66,[59] when he was a 23 years old student at Harvard. Serge Voronoff (1866-1951) was a French surgeon of Russian descent and representative of biological pragmatism who visited Brazil in 1928,[60] the year in which the Anthropophagous Manifesto was published. He was renowned for his studies on rejuvenation.

The presence of the two renowned thinkers/scientists who came to Brazil might be related to Oswald de Andrade's interest in contemporary matters, from technology to philosophy. Benedito Nunes argues that anthropophagy as a religion can be viewed as a pragmatic instrument of adaptation to life, and in this sense can be connected with the biological pragmatism of the two scientists above, by producing the transfiguration of the taboo into totem.[61]

(37) The paterfamilias and the creation of the Morality of the Stork: Real ignorance of things + lack of imagination + sense of authority towards the curious offspring.

Oswald de Andrade proceeds with a mathematical formula that is essentially a criticism of patriarchy. The criticism is a combination of the concepts of the *pater familias* (the patriarch, the oldest living male in a household) and the stork (the "morality of the stork" is the puritan and shamed view of sex), both representing ignorance about reality. The formula adds the lack of imagination of the colonizer and the autocratic authority of the father over the extended family to sum up all the flaws of the patriarchal society.

(38) One must depart from a profound atheism in order to arrive at the idea of God. However, the Caraib didn't need to. Because he had Guaraci.

A genuine religiosity for the civilized man can only be the product of a long and paradoxical journey: profound spiritualism as the product of an insightful atheism. Yet the natural man achieves the same result with a short cut: animism, symbolized by the figure of Guaraci, goddess of the sun.

(39) The established objective reacts like the Fallen Angels. Next, Moses divagates. What do we have to do with it?

The goal of the formulation of the anthropophagic movement is a reaction against civilized religion, symbolized by the fallen angels of Genesis and Moses's ten commandments. Such fundamental doctrines of the Judaic and Christian religions are not really relevant ("what do we have to do with it?").

(40) Before the Portuguese discovered Brazil, Brazil had discovered happiness.

In an exaltation of primitivism, the author states that joy—the ultimate goal of life—was existent in the country before its colonization. Much later, in a reflection on his anthropophagic ideas, Andrade wrote that matriarchy "has presided over the peaceful happiness of marginal peoples, ahistorical peoples, peoples whose purpose is nothing more than to live without getting involved with conquerors, owners of the world, and makers of empires."[62] The ultimate goal of happiness is emphasized several times in the manifesto (see aphorisms 42 and 47).

(41) Down with the torchbearer Amerindian. The Amerindian son of Mary, godson of Catherine de' Médici, and son-in-law of D. Antônio de Mariz.

This is a criticism of Romantic Indianism, the nineteenth-century literary movement that explored the image of the noble savage, the docile and catechized Amerindian. His image is evoked through a recollection of Peri, the main character of the renowned novel O Guarany by José de Alencar (see aphorism 24). Peri, the torchbearer Amerindian, is Maria's son (Maria, the name of Christ's mother, is also a typical Portuguese catholic name);[63] godson of Catherine de' Medici (1519–89), queen of France and one of the most powerful women in sixteenth-century Europe; and the son-in-law of D. Antônio de Maris (1536–84), a character in Alencar's book based on a real Portuguese nobleman who was one of the founders of Rio de Janeiro.

Andrade demonstrates creativity and historical accuracy by establishing relationships among contemporary characters, mixing fiction and reality—a sort of precursor to magical realism in literature. He deterritorializes Peri, the Brazilian Amerindian, connecting him with the Portuguese and French colonizers who were simultaneously present in Brazil. And he does so by creating a plausible chronology: D. Antônio de Maris was a contemporary of his French counterparts, Catherine de' Medici was related to Villegaignon (the latter was sponsored by Catherine's husband on his trip to Brazil), and Montaigne, who is not mentioned in this aphorism, was a prominent figure at the court during the latter part of Catherine's reign as queen.

(42) Joy is the ultimate proof.

This aphorism has fallen victim to numerous errors of translation. In the original form of the manifesto in Portuguese, the author refers to a method for detecting arithmetical errors known as the "proof of nines" (casting out nines) to express the thought that joy is the ultimate goal of life.

According to Jorge Schwartz, Oswaldian anthropophagy proposes the carnivalization of life, "a burlesque sense of the world, which ends up subverting everything. *Irony, humor and parodic dimension* represent a carnivalized interpretation of life."[64] This is one side of the happiness that permeates the thought of the Manifesto. However, there is another perhaps more important philosophical aspect that connects anthropophagy with happiness, something that is found in the philosophy of Bergson, according to whom happiness is a sign that life worked, that it was worth it, making happiness the ultimate goal of life:

> Philosophers who have speculated on the meaning of life and the destiny of man have not observed well that nature itself has taken the trouble to inform us about it: it warns us by means of a precise sign that our destiny has been reached. That sign is happiness. I'm talking about happiness, not pleasure. Pleasure is nothing more than a device imagined by nature to obtain the conservation of life from living: it does not indicate the direction in which life is launched. But happiness always announces that life has won, that it has gained ground, that it has conquered a victory: every great happiness has a touch of triumph.[65]

The essence of Bergson's proposal is that life is a true source of joy (happiness) when we let ourselves be guided by the intuitive knowledge that gives us the enjoyment of a reality that we do not grasp through intellectual understanding.

(43) In the matriarchy of Pindorama.

Pindorama is the name given to Brazil in the Tupi-Guarani language, meaning "land of palms," the territory where matriarchy prevailed in the "totemization of the taboo" (see aphorism 18), a "matriarchal conception of the world without God."[66] By using the term Pindorama instead of Brazil, Oswald de Andrade *deterritorializes* the loco where the anthropophagic ideas take place.

(44) Down with Memory as source of habit. Personal experience renewed.

This aphorism contrasts memory with "renewed personal experience." Memory as the source of custom is viewed in the same way as conceived by

Marcel Proust in *In Search of Lost Time*, a consideration of how time slips through our fingers. Within this perspective, memory remains an element of unchanging purpose in the transformation of the eternal present, which according to Andrade is a property of the taboo.[67] The renewal of personal experience corresponds to the "totemization" of life, turning life into a permanent devouring process.

(45) We are concretists. Ideas take hold, react, and burn people in public squares. Let's get rid of ideas and other paralysis. By means of itineraries. Let's believe in signs, in sextants, and in the stars.

The characterization of anthropophagy as concretist implies a materialist view of life as opposed to an idealistic conception: the prevalence of the body over the spirit, experience over speculative theories.[68] The author rails against the evils of idealism, favoring life itineraries guided by instincts, magical signals, scientific instruments, or the stars. Despite the negation of idealism and spiritualism, Andrade incorporates the ludic, the magical, and the artistic as life-affirming elements.

(46) Down with Goethe, the Gracchi's mother, and the court of D. João VI.

The modernism associated with anthropophagy is contrasted with the negation of traditional Romantic poetry as represented by Goethe; with the catechism symbolized by Cornelia, responsible for the systematic education of the Gracchi brothers; and with the colonialism represented by the monarchy of the court of D. João VI, the Portuguese king who fled to Brazil in 1808 to escape the Napoleonic advance in Europe.

(47) Joy is the ultimate proof.

An emphatic reiteration of aphorism 42.

(48) The struggle between what would be called the *Increated* and the *Creature*—illustrated by the permanent contradiction of Man and his Taboo. Everyday love and the capitalist way of life. Anthropophagy. Absorption of the sacred enemy. To transform him into a totem. The human adventure. The earthly purpose. However, only the pure elites managed to carry out carnal anthropophagy, which carries within itself the highest meaning of life and avoids all the evils identified by Freud, evils of catechism. What happens is not a sublimation of the sexual instinct. It is the thermometric scale of the anthropophagic instinct. Carnal at first, it becomes elective, creating

friendship. When affective, it creates love. When speculative, it creates science. It takes detours and moves around. We arrive at degradation. The low anthropophagy clustered in the sins of catechism—envy, usury, slander, murder. We are acting against this plague of the supposedly cultured and Christianized peoples. Anthropophagi.

No author seems to have made a connection between the concepts of the *"Increated"* and the *"Creature"* as deriving from Boethius (see aphorism 33). Yet, this seems to be the source for Oswald de Andrade's coinage in Portuguese of the noun *Incriado*. The idea posited by Boethius in *De trinitate* is that in God there is an identity between being and form that cannot occur in the Creature (man). While in God there is an overlap between form and essence, in the Creature, essence is not part of the equation. The Creature is constituted only by matter and form, and as such it can only be considered an "image of the true form," which does not include the essence.

If the interpretation above is correct, the beginning of the aphorism can be explained as follows: the struggle between the Increated and the Creature is equivalent to the dialectical tension between the supposed Creator (the Portuguese "discoverer," the Increated, which is in fact a creator of nothing) and the Creature (the Caraib people, the Amerindian). This dialectic tension is equivalent to the tension between the Father and his children, the Taboo relationship presented in Freud's *Totem and Taboo*. As we know through the explanation given in aphorism 18, the *Increated* was never a real creator in its roots, since this type of creation is unilateral. Through parricide, in the dialectical movement of human relations, the creature becomes a creator in the course of the historical-temporal process.

According to Benedito Nunes, the thought that "it is necessary to start from a deep atheism to arrive at the idea of God" (see aphorism 38) is the culminating paradox of barbaric metaphysics, expressing the major struggle apparent in the manifesto, the one "between what would be called the *Increated* and the Creation."[69] The same contradiction is found between man and his taboo, mundane love and the capitalist way of life. They constitute dialectic opposites resolved by anthropophagy, which gives real meaning to life: the search for joy is the goal of the human adventure. The evils identified by Freud are essentially related to catechism, and should not be reduced to a problem of sublimation of the sexual instinct.[70] In proceeding with such a reductive interpretation (i.e., treating the sublimation of the sexual instinct as the root of the problem), carnal appetite is reduced to friendship; affection is confused with love, and speculation is confused with science. This is a distortion of the meaning of anthropophagy that ultimately reduces it to a sort of "low anthropophagy," which brings the same evils that the actual "high anthropophagy" aims to fight, namely envy, usury, slander, murder, and so on.

As a final observation on this longest of the aphorisms, when addressing the human adventure and the earthly purpose, Andrade is incorporating mythology into the collective spiritual development. The author stated in 1944: "Note that the masses have always tended toward the mythological in their spiritual development. Perhaps today a mystical door opens wide for them, in History, in the inflexible direction of earthly achievements."[71] This thought leads to the thesis presented in the current monograph, namely that the incorporation of mythology produces the carnivalization of surrealism in Brazilian art, as described in chapter 9.

(49) Against Anchieta singing about the eleven thousand virgins of Heaven, in the land of Iracema—the patriarch João Ramalho, founder of São Paulo.

Padre José de Anchieta (1534–1597), known as "the Apostle of Brazil," land of Iracema[72] was one of the most prominent Jesuits responsible for the catechization of the Brazilian Amerindians and was later canonized as a saint. Anchieta criticized the "inconstancy of the savage soul" of the Amerindian, reflected in his "inability" to acquire the discipline to adhere to the Christian program imposed by the Jesuits.

Expressing a negative view of the Jesuit, Oswald mentions the priest's puritan view of the virgins in heaven, in contrast with the positive figure of João Ramalho, a Portuguese colonizer who founded São Paulo. Ramalho married the Amerindian woman Bartira, daughter of the chief Tibiriçá, with whom he had nine children, in addition to enjoying dozens of other Amerindian women before, during, and after his marriage.

(50) Our independence has not yet been proclaimed. A typical expression of D. João VI:—My son, put this crown on your head, before some adventurer puts it on his! We expelled the dynasty. It remains to expel the Bragantine spirit, the ordinations,[73] and Maria da Fonte's snuff box.

The official date of Brazil's independence is September 7, 1822, when Dom Pedro I, son of the Portuguese monarch Dom João VI, proclaimed the country's liberation on the banks of the Ipiranga Brook, located in the city of São Paulo, with the words: "Independence or Death!" According to the legend, he was following his father's advice to crown himself before some adventurer took the initiative before him. Yet Andrade is stating that despite the declaration of political independence ending 322 years of colonial dominance of Portugal over Brazil, even after a century of political autonomy the "Bragantine spirit" still hung over the national territory.[74] In fact, this was the impulse that led artists and intellectuals to proclaim the need for the cultural independence of the country one century later, during the Modern Art Week of 1922.

As a lawyer, Oswald de Andrade also mentions two other examples of the Portuguese presence: the *ordenações*—legal norms imported from Portugal—and the snuff or *rapé* of Maria da Fonte.[75] She was a Portuguese peasant woman who led a rebellion in 1846 against the political and economic oppression of D. Maria da Glória, then queen of Portugal. The rebels demanded, among other things, that Portuguese agricultural products be placed on the domestic market, which at that time was dominated by English products. In fact, Maria da Fonte's uprising ended up strengthening the conservative forces of Portugal, making her a negative emblem of allegiance with the Portuguese tradition of absolutism and colonialism.[76]

(51) Against the dressed and oppressive social reality registered by Freud— the reality without complexes, without madness, without prostitution and penitentiaries of the matriarchy of Pindorama.

The author sums up the main ideas of the manifesto: a movement against colonialist oppression, in favor of the natural man, free of the evils of the civilized man—sexual complexes, madness, prostitution, and penitentiaries— that aims to rebuild the same matriarchal society found before the advent of the colonizer.

Oswald de Andrade lists Piratininga as the place where the document was signed. The Amerindian term designates the territory that would be known as São Paulo after the advent of the Jesuits. The date he gives is irreverent: instead of following the catholic calendar that started with Christ's birth, Andrade creates his own starting point using the date of the first official cannibal act against the Portuguese. This is when Pero Fernandes Sardinha (1496–1556), the first bishop of Brazil, was slaughtered and devoured by the Caeté Amerindians, one of the Tupi tribes, in the northeast of Brazil after a shipwreck. Curiously, the math seems to be wrong: Bishop Sardinha was eaten in 1556 and the manifesto was published in 1928—only 372 years, not 374 years, after the deglutition of the bishop. Metaphorically, the Manifesto is misplaced geographically (*deterritorialized*) and historically (*intempestive*, or *untimely*).

Final Considerations

Throughout the text, Andrade presents a number of aphorisms of different length, some of which can be elevated to the status of slogans, mottos, or adages, due to their brevity and power of expression.

Tupi or not tupi, that's the question. (3)

The first adage is powerful in its simplicity and directness. It has been considered the core of the entire manifesto, in the sense that it captures the essence of the anthropophagic impulse: the decisive question about the acceptance or denial of Brazilian origins, of the Caraib people—to be or not to be Brazilian, to possess and be possessed by this instinct or not, or simply to be assimilated by the Eurocentric culture so much in vogue at the time.

The transformation or transfiguration of Taboo into totem. (18, 36)

The second adage is also fundamental because it summarizes the essential process advocated by anthropophagy: the transformation of taboo into totem corresponds to the passage from a patriarchal to a matriarchal society, which is explained in aphorism 18 and developed in the author's thesis "The Crisis of Messianic Philosophy." In the messianic system, of Platonic origin, the myth of origin indicates the existence of a being responsible for dictating the course of civilization and acting as the nucleus of the entire messianic idea. From the Oswaldian perspective, every cultural construction originating from European systems of thought would be based on the principle of divine supremacy, producing a patriarchal society. Everything that is nature or culture, if it does not belong to biblical ideals, must be dominated or superimposed, be it the soil or the ideas. It is from this pillar that the seizure of territory and the deprivation of the subaltern people—the process of colonization—is carefully developed. For Andrade, private property, as a rule of coexistence for almost all of modern society based on the image of a single, dominant owner, comes from a European Christianity whose principle of life is the figure of a single, master god of all things. This represents the taboo side of the equation.

Before colonization, Brazil was not contaminated with the evils of the messianic system. The Amerindian society was matriarchal, based on the concept of the soil as common property and a classless state—in fact, the absence of a state. That ancestral society, essentially anthropophagous, had a philosophy based on countless myths that portray the origins of nature and its beings. Such philosophy was never as centralizing and dominating as the messianic philosophy, built on patriarchal and European bases. Thus, Oswald suggests a utopic march not toward a return to the primitive state, but a forward motion that will culminate with the arrival of a Golden Age ruled by the new technicized barbarian, producing an analogous condition similar to pre-colonial times. In order for this to be achieved, he advocates for a metaphysical operation:

> The metaphysical operation that is linked to the anthropophagic rite is that of transforming the taboo into a totem. From the opposite value, to the favorable value. Life is pure devouring. In this devouring that every minute threatens human existence, it is up to man to totemize the taboo. . . . While in its fundamental axiological scale, the man of the West elevated the categories of his knowledge to God, the supreme good, the primitive instituted his scale of values up to God, the supreme evil. In this there is a radical opposition of concepts that gives rise to a radical opposition of conduct. And everything is linked to the existence of two cultural hemispheres that divided history into Matriarchy and Patriarchy. That is the world of primitive man. This is the civilized one. That one produced an anthropophagic culture, this one a messianic culture.[77]

Itineraries. Itineraries. Itineraries. Itineraries. Itineraries. Itineraries. Itineraries. (20)

The third adage is unusual; it consists of a single word repeated seven times. Besides the explanation already given in the preceding notes, this staccato passage stands out because it represents a central idea of anthropophagic thought: savage thought. The a-logical *pensée sauvage* is not binary, like civilized determinism, which is based on the relations of cause and effect, a product of the dialectic of metaphysics.

While this idea is developed more completely in chapter 9, it is relevant to indicate that it refers to a new conception of time and space: the idea of *intempestive* (or *untimely*) *time* and *deterritorialized space*. As Alexandre Nodari points out, "the indigenous question is to move from the duple to the multiple, both in content and in form," because, as Beatriz Azevedo points out, 'with his aphoristic language, Oswald also goes from the 'double sense' to the multiple sense, from dual crossroads to the 'Itineraries. Itineraries. Itineraries. Itineraries. Itineraries. Itineraries. Itineraries.'"[78]

In other words, while the manifesto is notorious for expressing a long compilation of opposing elements—colonizer vs. colonized, *Incriated* vs. *Creature*, Anchieta vs. João Ramalho, clothed civilized man vs. naked natural man, patriarchal vs. matriarchal, Judeo-Catholic God vs. Amerindian mythology, logical vs. pre-logical thinking, auricular vs. visual, taboo vs. totem, self vs. cosmos, death vs. life, speculation vs. divination—we need to understand this dualistic or binary thought as characteristic of the civilized man. In contraposition, the governing way of thought embedded in the manifesto is pluralistic, hence "Itineraries. Itineraries. Itineraries. Itineraries. Itineraries. Itineraries. Itineraries" becomes an adage, a metaphorical expression of the Amerindian's way of thinking.

Joy is the ultimate proof. (42 and 47, repeated for emphasis)

In this statement, Andrade is emphasizing what can be considered a naive idea: life as a journey in search of happiness. This idea is a product of what the author used to call "the ludic constant," the sentiment that characterizes man's evolution. For him, "Man is the animal who lives between two great games—Love, where he wins, and Death, where he loses. Therefore, he invented the plastic arts, poetry, dance, music, theater, the circus and, finally, cinema."[79] In the search for happiness, the ludic constant is found in magical thinking, in community relations and in the links between the inner tradition of the Brazilian people and the search for happiness, as opposed to the rationalism of Europeans.

The ludic aspect of life was addressed by Freud in *Totem and Taboo* in a way that corresponds with Oswald de Andrade's conception:

> Only in one field has the omnipotence of thought been retained in our own civilization, namely in art. In art alone it still happens that man, consumed by his wishes, produces something similar to the gratification of these wishes, and this playing, thanks to artistic illusion, calls forth effects as if it were something real. We rightly speak of the magic of art and compare the artist with a magician. But this comparison is perhaps more important than it claims to be. Art, which certainly did not begin as art for art's sake, originally served tendencies which to-day have for the greater part ceased to exist. Among these we may suspect various magic intentions.[80]

Structure

The body of the manifesto presents ideas in a free structure that reflects the freedom of thought advocated by the author in the anthropophagic spirit. The apparently random sequence of ideas produces a juxtaposition of elements from the most varied fields of knowledge—anthropophagy, Brazil, colonization, the history of Western civilization, Amerindians, psychology, religion, anthropology, numerous historical revolutions, communism, law, patriarchalism, the matriarchy, and the independence of Brazil—and such juxtapositions recall the automatic writing technique of the surrealists.

Yet the periodic repetition of certain ideas, the repetition or echoing of certain expressions, as well as the placement of the four adages mentioned above, allows us to attempt to devise an inner structure for the text, analogous to a musical rondo, A-B-A-C-A:

A: The conceptualization of Anthropophagy. Aphorisms 1 – 10.

The Manifesto introduces anthropophagy as its unifying agent and proceeds to state its main features. As the Exposition, this section introduces the first adage (*Tupi or not Tupi*).

B: The Caraib Revolution. Aphorisms 11–21.

Aphorism 11 starts with "We want the Caraib Revolution" and aphorism 21 closes with "The Caraib instinct," framing this segment. This section introduces mainly the third adage (*Itineraries*), but also includes the first statement of the second adage (*transformation of taboo into totem*).

A: Return of the conceptualization of Anthropophagy. Aphorisms 22–36.

Note that this section is framed by two aphorisms (22 and 36) that end with the word "Anthropophagy." As a first recapitulation, it includes the second iteration of the second adage (*transformation of taboo into totem*).

C: A section of contrasts focused on matriarchy. Aphorisms 37–47.

The contrast starts with the introduction of a mathematical formula in aphorism 37, and ends with one of the adages of the manifesto: "Joy is the ultimate proof" (47). As the most contrastive section of text, it can be further subdivided in two halves—37–42 and 43–47—both of which end with the same adage about joy.

A: Conclusion. Aphorisms 48–51.

Although this section includes a smaller number of aphorisms, they are usually longer, particularly aphorism 48, producing the necessary balance among the various sections. It includes the final iteration of the second adage (*transformation of taboo into totem*).

Final Remarks

Despite the great variety of topics addressed, the manifesto presents a remarkable coherence of ideas. Due to his training as a lawyer, Andrade included numerous legal aspects, using on several occasions archaic terminology, as the laws changed over time. The manifesto presents many leitmotives that dialogue with each other, and thus it can be read as a musical score, horizontally and vertically. The message, while primitivist, uses a symbolist language and a surrealist writing method.

In addition to the concept of anthropophagy itself, the major themes discussed are as follows: colonialism and its evils (catechesis, the catholic religion, European rationalism, systematized education); the evolution of history, addressed particularly from the perspective of great revolutions; and the contributions of several outstanding personalities to the development of the anthropophagic theory (Freud, Marx, and European individuals from the most varied fields, such as Dom João VI, Father Vieira, Father Anchieta, João Ramalho, and others); geographic elements; and Amerindian mythology.

Introducing a revolutionary spirit of action, the manifesto displays a dialectic of opposites: European vs. Brazilian, local vs. cosmopolitan, catholicism vs. divination, rationalism vs. alogical thinking, clothed vs. nude, spirit vs. body, visual vs. auricular, taboo vs. totem, Increated vs. Creature, patriarchy vs. matriarchy, and many others. The presence of such a large number of dichotomies should not mask the fact that any reading of the manifesto must be pluralistic, reflecting the primitive man's a-logical way of thinking. As Beatriz Azevedo rightly remarks, the Manifesto is a "savage palimpsest."

While the influence of Montaigne, Freud, and to a lesser extent Marx, are clearly at the core of a critical reading of the manifesto, as many scholars have pointed out, the great absentee in the manifesto is the one who provided the most central philosophical influence on Andrade's thought: Friedrich Nietzsche. The German philosopher is credited with ideas relating to meridian religions (or doctrines of salvation), digestive images from his *Genealogy of Morals*, the idea of sexual sublimation, the conception of man with his anthropophagic instinct relating to his will to power, the juxtaposition of the dressed and civilized man with the naked man, the Dionysian valorization of the body, the denial of God and religion, and even a return to barbarism in the pursuit of happiness. One could say that Oswald's conception of the permanent transformation from taboo to totem—the conversion of a patriarchal society into a matriarchal society conquered in a golden age—corresponds to a Nietzschean reading of Freud, a step toward the Übermensch advocated in *Thus Spoke Zarathustra*.[81]

Andrade used to sign articles in the *Revista de Antropofagia* with the pseudonym Freuderico, which is a mixture of Freud with Friederich (Frederico in Portuguese, probably referring to Nietzsche). The German philosopher provides the bridge that connects the early manifestation of Andrade's anthropophagic ideas in the manifesto with his philosophical doctrine of the crisis of the messianic philosophy at the end of his life. This process in essence represents metaphorically the idea of "eternal return," which brings to the Anthropophagous Manifesto a mythological dimension.

Notes

1. Eduardo Viveiros de Castro, "Temos que criar um outro conceito de criação (2007)," interview with Pedro Cesarino and Sérgio Cohn, in *Eduardo Viveiros de Castro*, ed. Renato Sztutman, Coleção Encontros (Rio de Janeiro: Azougue, 2009), 168.

2. Augusto de Campos, "Revistas re-vistas: Os antropófagos," in Revista de Antropofagia (São Paulo: Metal Leve, 1975). In a similar statement, Antônio Candido wrote that oswaldian anthropophagy represents "the densest moment of modernist dialectics." Antônio Candido, *Literatura e Sociedade*, 164.

3. First version: Oswald de Andrade, "Anthropophagic Manifesto," transl. Hélio Oiticica, DanLarsen.art, accessed October 31, 2021, https://danelarsen.blogspot.com/2015/03/manifesto-antropofago-anthropophagic.html. Second version: Leslie Bary, "Oswald de Andrade's 'Cannibalist Manifesto,'" *Latin American Literary review* 19, no. 38 (Jul.–Dec. 1991): 35–47, https://www.jstor.org/stable/20119600 and https://writing.upenn.edu/library/Andrade_Cannibalistic_Manifesto.pdf.

4. Ana Beatriz Sampaio Soares Azevedo, "Antropofagia—palimpsesto selvagem" (Masters diss., Universidade de São Paulo, Brazil, 2012).

5. Ibid., 85.

6. Interview given to the newspaper *Correio paulistano* on June 26, 1949.

7. This idea has been criticized by a number of scholars such as Kimberle López, who considers artists like Oswald as tourists in their own land who assume the same position of the colonizer, because they are not as close to the Amerindian as they claim; their identification with the Amerindian is perfunctory. See Kimberle S. López, "Modernismo and the Ambivalence of the Postcolonial Experience," 25–38.

8. The feminist aspect of anthropophagy is categorically denied by Beth Joan Vinkler, who argues that its feminist orientation is imaginary. According to her, Oswald rewrote the meaning and identity of the female to serve his own goals. His anthropophagic discourse suppresses within itself the authentic Other: the female Other. See Beth Joan Vinkler, "The Anthropophagic Mother/Other," 105–11, https://www.jstor.org/stable/3513808.

9. Oswald de Andrade, "Nova escola literária," *O jornal* (Rio de Janeiro), May 18, 1928.

10. Oswald Andrade, *Os dentes do dragão* (São Paulo: Editora Globo, 1990), 182. Interview given to Milton Carneiro, *Letras e artes* (Rio de Janeiro), September 10, 1950.

11. According to Glen Watkins: "Columbus . . . was seized upon as the historical figure most susceptible to charges of multiple contemporary heresies—Eurocentrism, imperialism, elitism, and phallocentrism. Appropriately, the new perspective

argued for a recounting of the Spanish [and Portuguese] conquest of the Americas, of enforced Christianity, of the abuse and enslaving of Native Americans, and continued deception and pillage following the birth of a nation." Watkins, *Pyramids at the Louvre*, 460.

12. This sentence is likely to have a typographical error, where the word "*print*" is mistakenly replacing the French word "*prit*."

13. The term "orecular" has been questioned, because it does not exist in the Portuguese language. While most scholars think that this term is supposed to be "auricular," as related to the auditory sense, Hélio Oiticica raised the possibility of a misprint where the correct word would be "oracular." In this case, the word would be linked to the notion of oracle and the power of foresight. We opted for the traditional interpretation, which refers to aural traditions and the importance of hearing (ears) above vision (eyes).

14. The author seems to be referring to romantic plays where adultery frequently appears.

15. *Saudade* is a sad feeling connected with nostalgia; the term is not fully translatable in English or any other language.

16. The word *touristes* appears in French in the original.

17. As explained in note 12, this sentence is likely to have a typographical error, where the word "*print*" is mistakenly replacing the French word "*prit*."

18. This aphorism has also been translated as "We had relations and distribution of fiscal property, moral property, and honorific property." As a lawyer, the author is using Brazilian legal terminology, some of which is outdated and untranslatable. Tangible goods are goods that can be exchanged; moral goods are inherent to the person; and *dignary* goods are goods granted by the Portuguese king.

19. A legal term, which means "not initialed," in the sense of history written without being formally verified.

20. A legal term that refers to legal norms given by the royal monarchy to the colony.

21. Oswald de Andrade, "A Crise da Filosofia Messiânica," in *Do Pau-Brasil à Antropofagia e às Utopias*, 2nd ed. (Rio de Janeiro: Civilização Brasileira, 1970): 75–138.

22. Though this interpretation needs to be distinguished from St. Augustine's. In *Confessions*, Christ seemed to be calling from on high, saying, "I am the food of full-grown men. Grow and you shall feed on me. But you shall not change me into your own substance, as you do with the food of your body. Instead you shall be changed into me." See Maggie Kilgour, *From Communion to Cannibalism*, 51.

23. Eduardo Viveiros de Castro, "O mármore e a murta," in *A Inconstância da Alma Selvagem* (São Paulo: Cosac Naify, 2002): 206.

24. Oswald de Andrade, "Poesias reunidas," in *Obras Completas*, v. VII (Rio de Janeiro: Civilização Brasileira, 1974), 177.

25. Telê Porto Ancona Lopez, *Macunaíma: A margem e o texto* (São Paulo: HUCITEC, Secretaria de Cultura, Esporte e Turismo, 1974), 199. *Macunaíma*'s motto is

"que preguica!" ("what laziness!"). Gender and race-oriented approaches to literature and culture have demonstrated how marks of difference can be used by the oppressed as a means of resistance and empowerment.

26. The more specific meaning of "Caraib" will be elucidated in aphorism 21.

27. Benedito Nunes, "A Antropofagia ao Alcance de Todos," 28.

28. Mário Chamie, "Freud, Oswald de Andrade e Antropofagia," *A Fábrica do Futuro—Residência Criativa do Audiovisual*, Espaço de Aprendizado em Rede, Textos. http://sv2.fabricadofuturo.org.br/sitev1/index.php?pag=38&prog=130&id=144.

29. In 1557 a reformed pastor called Jean de Léry joined the Antarctic France with thirteen other Swiss protestants. Due to conflicts, these protestants had to leave the French colony and began to live among the Tupinambá Amerindians, who were cannibals. These few months spent in the intimacy of anthropophagi left a deep mark on Léry, torn between his admiration of savages and his rejection of paganism. Léry wrote an influential book called *Histoire d'un voyage fait en la terre de Brésil* (History of a Trip to the Land of Brazil), published in 1578, which praised the Amerindians. His writing conflicted directly with André Thevet, the chaplain of Villegaignon's fleet, who considered the Amerindians "the most cruel and inhuman people in all of America." Montaigne read Léry and probably drew from his work the inspiration for his chapter "Of Cannibals" (Book I of *Essays*, 1580), which was so influential for the creation of the Anthropophagous Manifesto. Antartic France lasted less than five years, ending in 1560 when the French were expelled by the Portuguese.

30. See Liam Brophy, "Hermann Keyserling, Knight of the Holy Ghost," *The Irish Monthly* 74, no. 879 (1946): 376–83, at 380, http://www.jstor.org/stable/20515547 (accessed September 7, 2021). The quote in question appeared in "America Set Free," published by Keyserling in 1929, slightly after the publication of the Anthropophagous Manifesto. The text is based on his 1927 tour to North America, where he propagated through lectures the ideas of his so-called School of Wisdom. In 1929 he also toured South America and was a guest of Andrade at his farm in Rio de Janeiro.

31. These ideas are based on Daniel Faria's article "As meditações americanas de Keyserling: Um cosmopolitismo nas incertezas do tempo," 905–23.

32. The Jesuits justified this point by referring to the Amerindian's "inconstant soul," which prevented them from being enslaved.

33. Maxixe is a genre of instrumental dance also known as Brazilian tango. Its origins are attributed to a combination of African and European elements, making the maxixe a precursor of both the samba and the lambada.

34. https://youtu.be/tT9e—ByZlk.

35. *Baiano* (male) and *baiana* (female) are the designations for people born in the state of Bahia.

36. Azevedo, "Antropofagia–palimpsesto selvagem," 115.

37. Lévi-Strauss's position is different from Lévy-Bruhl's: he makes clear that *"la pensée sauvage"* refers not to the discrete mind of any particular type of human, but rather to "untamed" human thought: "It is neither the mind of savages nor that of

primitive or archaic humanity, but rather mind in its untamed state as distinct from mind cultivated or domesticated for the purpose of yielding a return." Claude Lévi-Strauss, *The Savage Mind*, 219.

38. Carolina Cantarino and Rodrigo Cunha, Interview with Eduardo Viveiros de Castro, *Com Ciência*, May 10, 2009, https://www.comciencia.br/comciencia/handler.php?section=8&tipo=entrevista&edicao=46.

39. See João Batista Pereira, "O padre Antonio Vieira: Orador e profeta do V Imperio" (Masters diss., Universidade Estadual de Maringá, 2005), http://www.ppe.uem.br/SITE%20PPE%202010/dissertacoes/2005-Joao_Pereira.pdf.

40. Manuela Carneiro da Cunha and Eduardo Viveiros de Castro, "Vingança e temporalidade: Os Tupinambá," 61.

41. Benedito Nunes, "O Animal e o Primitivo: Os Outros de Nossa Cultura," *Ensaio* 14, supplement (Dec. 2007): 288, https://www.scielo.br/j/hcsm/a/G3cP8ZDj47v4RdhbPbRdwWp/?lang=pt&format=pdf.

42. Rodrigo Ornelas, "Oswald de Andrade, leitor de Nietzsche, genealogia, catequese e antropofagia," *Cad. Nietzsche* (Guarulhos / Porto Seguro) 41, no. 3 (2020): 220–34, https://doi.org/10.1590/2316-82422020v4103ro.

43. Claude Lévi-Strauss, *The Savage Mind* (Chicago: University of Chicago Press, 1967), chapter 1.

44. Sigmund Freud, *Totem and Taboo: Resemblances between the Psychic Lives of Savages and Neurotics* (London: Routledge, 1919).

45. Numerous articles provide a critical analysis and interpretation of the relationship between Freud's and Andrade's positions. See, for example, Alexandre Nodari, "A Transformação do Tabu em totem: Notas sobre um(a) formula antropofágica," 409–54; Pedro de Teixeira Castilho and Leo Bryan Lisboa, "O Mau Selvagem," A apropriação do Mito Freudiano de Totem e Tabu por Oswald de Andrade no 'Manifesto Antropófago,'" *Dossiê em tese* (Belo Horizonte) 23, no. 1: 119–32.

46. Benedito Nunes, "A antropofagia ao alcance de todos," 20. https://www.academia.edu/16417381/A_antropofagia_ao_alcance_de_todos_Benedito_Nunes.

47. Oswald de Andrade, "O Manifesto Antropófago," in *Vanguarda europeia e modernismo brasileiro: Apresentação e crítica dos principais manifestos vanguardistas*, 3.

48. Eduardo Viveiros de Castro, "O mármore e a murta," 213.

49. Gilles Deleuze suggested that Nietzsche's eternal return was not only a directive for ethical behavior, but also a radical understanding of the nature of time. As he put it, "The present must coexist with itself as past and yet to come. The synthetic relation of the moment to itself as present, past, and future grounds its relation to other moments. The eternal return is thus an answer to the problem of *passage* [between past and present, or present and future]." Gilles Deleuze, *Nietzsche and Philosophy*, 48.

50. "Lua Nova, ó Lua Nova, assopra em *Fulano* lembranças de mim." Couto de Magalhães, *O selvagem*, 147.

51. The word *fulano* is a colloquial expression difficult to translate into English. Essentially, it means a generic person, frequently translated as "so and so." Within

this context, it would mean "my beloved," so the sentence can be translated as "blow memories of me onto my beloved."

52. Couto de Magalhães, O Selvagem, 171.

53. Again, the author uses here Brazilian legal terminology, some of which is outdated and untranslatable.

54. As a curious fact, "Galimathias musicum" is a comic piece of music for orchestra with clavier and other obligato instruments written by Mozart in 1766 at the Hague, for the festivities at the coming of age of William V, Prince of Orange (March 8). Mozart was only ten years old at the time.

55. Oswald de Andrade, "A Psicologia Antropofágica," in Os dentes do dragão, 52.

56. Oswald de Andrade, "Mensagem ao antropófago desconhecido (da França Antárctica)," Travessia 3, no. 5 (1982): 63.

57. Couto de Magalhães, O selvagem (Belo Horizonte, Livraria Itatiaia, USP, 1975).

58. *Rudah, the God of Love* is the title of a symphonic poem/ballet by Villa-Lobos.

59. William James created the term *pluriverse*, meaning a world composed of many worlds. This term connects William James with anthropophagy, because it can be applied for example to Amerindian shamans when they experience "becoming Other." By visiting the world of the dead or entering different realms, they inhabit a *pluriverse*. "One can only learn or know to the extent that one takes up different perspectives, and that is a cannibal act." See: Renato Sztutman, "The (re)turn of the anthropophagites," 214.

60. The visit of Serge Voronoff to Brazil became legendary. The physician was famous for his curious glandular xenoimplants, which for the elderly represented hopes of rejuvenation. Among young people, however, it generated mockery and jokes, and even a 1929 carnival march by Lamartine Babo and João Rossi titled "Seu Voronoff," an informal way to address Mr. Voronoff. In the same year, the popular composer Noel Rosa wrote a samba with the title "Minha viola" (my guitar), which also mentions the Russian surgeon. Both were preceded by Eduardo Souto, who in 1926 wrote a samba titled *Voronoff*.

61. See Benedito Nunes, A antropofagia ao alcance de todos, 22.

62. Oswald de Andrade, "A Marcha das Utopias," 189.

63. Oswaldo Costa, one of the most prominent members of the Anthropophagic Movement, stated that "Anthropophagy has nothing to do with the romantic Amerindianism. To the Amerindian son of Mary, to the brother of the Most Holy [meaning, Christ], to the Amerindian degraded by catechism described by Couto de Magalhães, we oppose the cannibal who devoured catechism and told Hans Staden not to bother him, because it was so delicious. The naked Indian." Oswaldo Costa, "De Antropofagia," Revista de Antropofagia 2, no. 9 (August 15, 1929).

64. Oswald de Andrade, *Oswald de Andrade: Literatura Comentada, selections of texts, notes by Jorge Schwartz*, 2nd ed. (São Paulo: Nova Cultural, 1988), 18. The italics serve to emphasize the idea that the happiness advocated by Oswald de Andrade is related with the carnivalization of anthropophagy.

65. Henri Bergson, A energia espiritual, trans. Rosemary Costhek Abílio (São Paulo: Martins Fontes, 2009): 22. A more detailed explanation about this point can be found in Ferreira, "O Problema da Intuição Mística," 326–27. On page 323, the same article makes a reference to Bergson's philosophy in relation to the pragmatism of William James, connecting with another dimension of the Manifesto as it appears in aphorism 36.

66. Oswald de Andrade, A Marcha das Utopias, 144.

67. Oswald Andrade, "A psicologia antropofágica," in Os dentes do dragão, 53.

68. Concretism became later an aesthetic movement involving mostly Brazilian poetry through the group Noigandres, a team of poets who considered themselves anthropophagites. The group functioned approximately from 1952–1962, involving the brothers Haroldo and Augusto de Campos plus Décio Pignatari, with others joining later.

69. Benedito Nunes, A antropofagia ao alcance de todos, 22. The terms "Increated" and "Creation" are derived from Boethius's conception of the Holy Trinity, where he finds an immeasurable ontological difference between God, an "increated" and creator being, and the creation.

70. The contraposition of the anthropophagic instinct with the sexual instinct reflects the idea that sex is nothing more than a disguised appetite for human flesh.

71. Oswald de Andrade, "Meu testamento," 29.

72. Iracema is the title of another major literary novel by José de Alencar, about an Amerindian woman who marries a Portuguese colonizer. It is notable that Iracema, an Amerindian name that means "honey leaps," is also an anagram for the word America. The characterization of Brazil as the land of Iracema is another incidence of the deterritorialization of the anthropophagic ideas.

73. A legal term that refers to legal norms given by the royal monarchy to the colony.

74. "Bragantine" refers to the Portuguese dynasty of Bragança.

75. Rapé is a fine powder made from tobacco together with a mixture of tree bark, herbs, and other plants. When inhaled, rapé has curative and ritualistic effects.

76. Maria da Fonte and Cornelia, the mother of the Gracchi brothers are two female characters seen under a negative light in the Anthropophagous Manifesto.

77. Oswald de Andrade, Do Pau-Brasil à Antropofagia e às Utopias: manifestos, teses de concursos e ensaios, 77.

78. Alexandre Nodari and Maria Carolina de Almeida Amaral, "A questão (indígena) do Manifesto Antropófago," Revista direito e práxis 9, no. 4 (2018): 2461–502 at 2463, doi:10.1590/2179-8966/2018/37974.

79. Oswald de Andrade, "A Crise da Filosofia Messiânica," 126.

80. Sigmund Freud, Totem and Taboo, last paragraph of Chapter 3. The "playing" that Freud refers to in the paragraph has been also translated as the "ludic spirit," and is equivalent to the ludic constant that Oswald de Andrade is referring to.

81. Beatriz Azevedo has given a detailed account of the multiple manifestations of Nietzsche's influence in the Anthropophagous Manifesto. See Azevedo, Antropofagia–palimpsesto selvage, 167–69.

APPENDIX TWO

Glossary of Musical Terminology

Augurs chord: dissonant chord that appears two hundred and twelve times in the section "Augurs of Spring," the second section of Stravinsky's *Rite of Spring*. According to Robert Craft, a conductor who held a long-standing relationship with the composer, this chord serves as "motto chord" for the entire composition.[1]

FA.1.
Created by the author.

Complementary rhythm (simple and compound): resultant rhythm that is a combination of the different rhythms of multiple voices. The complementarity is simple when the resultant rhythm is formed by notes of a single duration; and compound when the resultant rhythm is a complex rhythmic figure that includes notes of different durations.

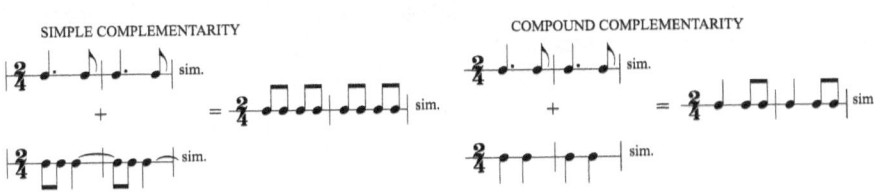

FA.2.
Created by the author.

First Webernian archetype: chord derived from the Tristan chord (the half-diminished chord) through the suppression of the interval of major third that appears in the middle written enharmonically as a diminished fourth (written as B—E flat). The major third is the only interval of the *Tristan chord* that appears in a tonal triad among the three intervals (tritone—major third—perfect fourth). With that, Webern reduces the superposition of three intervals to two, eliminating the one that could possibly have a tonal connotation, and leaving the two that are in dialectic opposition: the tritone and the perfect fourth.

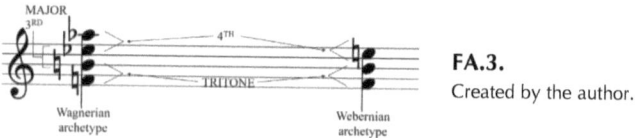

FA.3.
Created by the author.

An interesting characteristic of this chord is that the sequential repetition of its intervallic relationships produces the twelve notes of the chromatic scale without repetition, analogous to the circle of fifths:

FA.4.
Created by the author.

Foreground and Background textures: analogous to the concept of melody with accompaniment, the music of Villa-Lobos analyzed in this study is built in textural strata, where the layers obey a certain hierarchy. This allows us to determine which layers constitute the foreground and which ones constitute the background of the texture.

Golden Mean: The golden mean, also known as the Golden Section or Divine Proportion, is a mathematical concept that is typically traced back to the Greeks as an attempt to use geometry for practical and symbolic purposes in the search for the perfect aesthetic proportions. It is a ratio derived from the Fibonacci series that defines a recurring geometrical relationship as the irrational number phi (Ø), the ratio between a larger element and a smaller subset of that element (phi = 1.6180 . . .) Musicological studies found the presence of the golden mean in the works of many composers, including Mozart and Beethoven, though such occurrences don't seem to have happened consciously, as part of their compositional process. On the other hand, Villa-Lobos's contemporary Béla Bartók is known to have consciously explored the concept of the golden mean in the architecture of numerous of his compositions.

Polarization: process analogous to tonality, through which a certain note assumes the role of a polarized key center, analogous to the role of a tonic note or key. The difference is that in tonality the role of the tonic is a consequence of the harmonic series, while in polarization it is due to other reasons. For example, the positioning of the polarized key center symmetrically placed between the highest and lowest notes of a passage creates the perception of the key center not so much due to its gravitational power, but due to its strategic placement. This type of polarization appears in the initial theme of the bassoon in the *Rite of Spring* (Figure 4.4). See also *polarization by exclusion*.

Polarization by exclusion: process through which a certain note assumes the role of polarized center of a passage—analogous to the role of tonic—due to its noticeable absence during the passage. When this happens, the polarized center should appear prominently immediately after–or immediately before—the passage in question, in order to justify the polarization. Polarization by exclusion is a resource that provides an expansion of the concept of tonality through the idea of a "key center" that functions as a pole of attraction. However, in this case, the key center is not produced by its gravitational power, but by its absence as a key center in a certain passage. This creates an expectation fulfilled by the prominent appearance of the absent key center in the subsequent passage immediately after. Example: in Figure 6.13 (*Theme of the Sensual Dance of the Amerindian Girl*) the monophonic texture includes all the pitches of the chromatic scale except E, which becomes polarized by exclusion.

Polichinelo chord: chord that combines the black and white keys of the piano, producing a cluster effect.

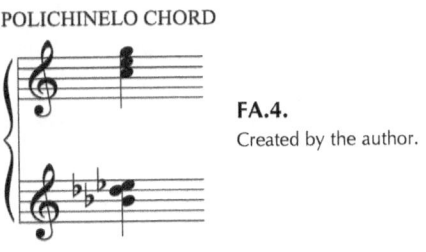

FA.4.
Created by the author.

Semitone sliding: process according to which certain notes of a chord in a passage "slide" to their neighboring notes, and therefore function as foreign or passing notes within the harmony that chord represents.

FA.6. In the example above, we can observe both semitone and whole-tone sliding in the upper voice of the lower stave.
Created by the author.

Sound bands: accumulation of multiple neighboring notes repeated very fast through tremolo, producing a sound effect where the notes are not perceived individually, but as a timbre. Sound bands are frequently produced in the piano, as a result of the fast alternation of both hands. See for example Figure 3.2.

Sound block: tone cluster produced by chords comprising a number of adjacent tones in a scale. According to the Merriam-Webster dictionary, a tone cluster is a combination of musical tones sounded together each of which is a scale degree apart from one or two neighboring tones in the group.

Sound stain: dissonant passage that corresponds to a gestural sonority perceived as a unity, where the individual notes are not distinguished individually, but just as part of the musical gesture. It is the aggregate effect that produces the perception of a stain in the texture. For example, the first musical gesture in Villa-Lobos's *Uirapuru* is a sound stain.

Structural metaphor: in the case of this study, a structural metaphor occurs when the musical notation of a passage is a metaphorical representation of the program of the composition, such as for example, the wavelike motion of a melodic line representing the waves of a river or the motion of the wind. A more sophisticate type of structural metaphor happens through the interaction of different layers of the texture, for example when something happening on the low register of the texture—that could be representing the depths of the ocean or a river–somehow reflects in the upper register, which could be representing metaphorically the surface of the water. See, for example, Figure 7.4 and Figure 7.6.

Tristan chord: chord that appears in the opening phrase of Richard Wagner's opera *Tristan and Isolde*, on the downbeat of the second measure. It is considered the most significant chord in Western music, mainly due to having provoked diverse analytical explanations under different ideological guises. According to Bryan Magee, "the first chord of Tristan, known simply as 'the Tristan chord' remains the most famous single chord in the history of music. It contains within itself not one but two dissonances, thus creating within the listener a double desire, agonizing in its intensity, for resolution. The chord to which it then moves resolves one of these dissonances but not the other, thus providing resolution—but-not-resolution."[2]

Tone painting: device used by composers to depict musically something found in nature, such as for example the use of wavelike motion to depict waves of the sea. This also applies to the employment of musical instruments imitating sounds found in nature, such as flutes imitating the sound of birds. *Tone painting* is slightly different from *word painting*, where composers attempt to illustrate musically the lyrics of a song or aria.

Vagrant chords: According to Schoenberg, vagrant chords are wandering, ambiguous harmonies. Several vagrant chords are chromatic transformations of major or minor triads. As a result of these transformations, two classes of vagrant chords are produced. The first one is characterized by the superposition of equal intervals: major seconds, minor thirds, major thirds, and perfect fourths leading respectively to the whole-tone chord, the diminished seventh chord, the augmented triad, and the chord built with perfect fourths, as examples. The *Tristan chord* belongs to the second class: harmonies that don't have equal intervallic construction, but allow for multiple possible interpretations. Depending on the enharmonic spelling of certain pitches, different resolutions are achieved. Both classes of vagrant chords provide easy access to distant tonalities, allow for multiple resolutions, and contribute to tonal instability, emancipating chords from tonal contexts.[3]

Notes

1. Vera Stravinsky and Robert Craft, *Stravinsky in Pictures and Documents*, 597.

2. Bryan Magee, *The Tristan Chord: Wagner and Philosophy* (New York: Henry Holt, 2002). Numerous articles have been written about this chord, including this book, which uses it as argument to explore the philosophical aspects that made Wagner such an influential composer beyond the musical aspects of this work. A discussion of the *Tristan chord* also appears in Schoenberg, *Theory of Harmony*, 257–67.

3. More information about vagrant chords can be found in Schoenberg's seminal book *Theory of Harmony* (Berkeley: University of California Press, 1983).

Bibliography

Adorno, Theodor W. "Punctuation Marks." Translated by Shierry Weber Nicholsen. *The Antioch Review* 48, no. 3 (1990): 300–305. http://www.jstor.org/stable/4612221.

Albuquerque, Joel. "Suite Sugestiva de Villa-Lobos: paródia, ruido e acaso." Conference paper. *VI Simpósio Internacional de Musicologia da UFRJ*. Rio de Janeiro, 2015. https://www.academia.edu/15125617/Su%C3%ADte_Sugestiva_de_Villa-Lobos_par%C3%B3dia_ru%C3%ADdo_e_acaso_2015_.

Almeida, Renato. *História da Música Brasileira*. Rio de Janeiro: F. Briguiet, 1942.

Almeida, Washington Luiz Sieleman. "Villa-Lobos: Música e Nacionalismo na República Velha." Masters diss., Universidade Federal do Espírito Santo, 2014.

Alvarenga, Oneyda. "Música Folclórica e Música Popular." *Revista Brasileira de Folclore* Ano IX, no. 25 (Sept/Dec. 1969): 219–99. http://docvirt.com/docreader.net/docreader.aspx?bib=RevBrFolcloLP&pasta=&pesq=Oneyda%20Alvarenga.

Alves, Lourdes L. K. A. "A Assimilação ou A Transgressão do Código Linguístico, Cultural e Histórico em Oswald De Andrade." *Línguas e Letras* II, no. 21 (2nd sem. 2010): 127–45.

Amado, Janaína. "Mythic Origins: Caramuru and the Founding of Brazil." Translated by Elizabeth Jackson. *Hispanic American Historical Review 1 (November 2000) 80 (4): 783–811*. doi: https://doi.org/10.1215/00182168-80-4-783.

Amaral, Aracy. "Oswald de Andrade and Brazilian Modernism: An Interdisciplinary Approach to Avant-Garde Visual Arts in the Twenties." In *One Hundred Years of Invention*, edited by K. David Jackson, 155–63. Austin: Abaporu Press, 1992.

Amaral, Aracy. *Tarsila, sua obra e seu tempo*. São Paulo: Edusp, 2010 [1975], 409.

Amaral, Aracy. *Textos do Trópico de Capricórnio: Modernismo, arte moderna e o compromisso com o lugar*. São Paulo: Editora 34, 2006.

Amaral Pereira, Kleide Ferreira do. "Influências Indígenas na Obra de Villa-Lobos." *Revista da Organização de Estudos Culturais em Contextos Internacionais*, no. 22 (1993): 2. http://www.revista.akademie-brasil-europa.org/CM22-04.htm.

Amorim, Marcel Álvaro de. "From Adaptation to Transconstruction: Anthropophagy as Translocal Methodology." *Acta Scientiarum. Language and Culture* 40, no. 2 (July–Dec. 2018). Accessed October 19, 2021. https://link.gale.com/apps/doc/A563457915/AONE?u=anon~7f45533d&sid=googleScholar&xid=23e14098.

Andrade, Marília de. "Oswald e Maria Antonieta—Fragmentos, memória e fantasia." *Remate de males* 6 (Nov. 1986): 67–76. https://doi.org/10.20396/remate.v6i0.8636347.

Andrade, Mário de. *Música, Doce Música*. São Paulo: L. G. Miranda, 1934. The book has been reprinted in 2013 by Editora Nova Fronteira in Rio de Janeiro. https://s9.imslp.org/files/imglnks/usimg/7/71/IMSLP645406-PMLP1035184-1010143416.pdf.

Andrade, Mário de. *Poesias Completas*. Critical edition by Diléa Zanotto Manfio. Belo Horizonte: Villa Rica, 1993.

Andrade, Oswald de. "Anthropophagic Manifesto." Translated by Hélio Oiticica. DanLarsen.art. Accessed October 31, 2021. https://danelarsen.blogspot.com/2015/03/manifesto-antropofago-anthropophagic.html.

Andrade, Oswald de. "O Artista." *Novíssima* II, no. 11 (Aug.–Sept. 1925): 32.

Andrade, Oswald de. *Bois Brésil: poésie et manifeste*. Paris: Éditions de la Différence, 2010.

Andrade, Oswald de. "O Caminho Percorrido." In *Ponta de Lança*, 2nd edition, 93–102. Rio de Janeiro: Civilização Brasileira, 1971.

Andrade, Oswald de. "A Crise da Filosofia Messiânica." In *Do Pau-Brasil à Antropofagia e às Utopias*, 2nd ed., 75–138. Rio de Janeiro: Civilização Brasileira, 1970. https://monoskop.org/images/9/94/Oswald-de-andrade-Obras_Completas-vol6.pdf.

Andrade, Oswald de. *Os dentes do dragão*. São Paulo: Editora Globo, 1990.

Andrade, Oswald de. "L'effort intellecturel du Bresil contemporain." *Revue de L'Amérique Latine* 2, no. 5 (July 1, 1923): 207.

Andrade, Oswald de. *Oswald de Andrade: Literatura Comentada*, selections of texts, notes by Jorge Schwartz. 2nd ed. São Paulo: Nova Cultural, 1988.

Andrade, Oswald de. "O Manifesto Antropófago." In *Vanguarda europeia e modernismo brasileiro: Apresentação e crítica dos principais manifestos vanguardistas*. 3rd ed., edited by Gilberto Mendonça Teles with commentaries by Raquel R. Souza. Petrópolis: Vozes; Brasília: INL, 1976. https://www.ufrgs.br/cdrom/oandrade/oandrade.pdf.

Andrade, Oswald de. "Manifesto of Pau-Brasil Poetry." Translated by Stella M. de Sá Rego. *Latin American Literary Review* 14, No. 27 (Jan.–Jun., 1986), 184–87. http://www.jstor.org/stable/20119419.

Andrade, Oswald de. "A Marcha das Utopias." In *Do Pau-Brasil à Antropofagia e às Utopias: manifestos, teses de concursus e ensaios*. Rio de Janeiro: Civilização Brasileira, 1978.

Andrade, Oswald de. "Mensagem ao antropófago desconhecido (da Fança Antárctica)." *Travessia* 3, no. 5 (1982): 63–64. https://periodicos.ufsc.br/index.php/travessia/article/view/17697/16273.

Andrade, Oswald de. "Meu testamento." In *Testamento de uma geração*. Testimony given to Edgard Cavalheiro, 21–30. Porto Alegre: Livraria do Globo, 1944.

Andrade, Oswald de. "Nova escola literária." *O jornal* (Rio de Janeiro), May 18, 1928.

Andrade, Oswald de. *Pau Brasil*. Paris: Sans Pareil, 1925.

Andrade, Oswald de. *Do Pau-Brasil à Antropofagia e às Utopias: manifestos, teses de concursos e ensaios*. In *Obras Completas*. Vol VI. Rio de Janeiro: Civilização brasileira, 1978.

Andrade, Oswald de. "Poesias reunidas." In *Obras Completas*, v. VII. Rio de Janeiro: Civilização Brasileira, 1974.

Andrade, Oswald. *Poesias Reunidas*. Edited by Jorge Schwartz e Gênese Andrade. São Paulo: Companhia das Letras, 2017.

Andrade, Oswald de. *Ponta de Lança*. Rio de Janeiro: Civilização Brasileira, 1972.

Andrade, Oswald de. [Cunhambebinho, pseud]. "Peret" *Diário de São Paulo* (São Paulo, Brazil), Mar. 17, 1929.

Antokoletz, Elliott. *Twentieth-Century Music*. Englewood Cliffs, N.J.: Prentice-Hall, 1992.

Apollinaire, Guillaume. "Simultanisme-Librettisme." *Les Soirées de Paris*, no. 25 (June 15, 1914): 322–25.

Appleby, David P. *Heitor Villa-Lobos: A Life*. Lanham, Maryland and London: The Scarecrow Press, 2002.

Arcanjo, Loque. *O Ritmo da Mistura e o Compasso da História: O modernismo musical nas Bachianas Brasileiras de Heitor Villa-Lobos*. Rio de Janeiro: E-papers, 2008.

Argüelles, José. *The Transformative Vision*. Boulder: Shambhala, 1975.

Azevedo, Ana Beatriz Sampaio Soares de. "Antropofagia: Palimpsesto Selvagem." Master diss., FFCL-USP, 2012.

Bakhtin, Mikhail Mikhailovitch. *A cultura popular na Idade Média e no Renascimento: o contexto de François Rabelais*. São Paulo: Hucitec, 1999.

Bandeira, Manuel. "Villa-Lobos." *Ariel* 2, no. 13 (October 1924): 475–77.

Barros, C. Paula. *O romance de Villa-Lobos*. Rio de Janeiro: Editora A Noite, 1949.

Bary, Leslie. "Oswald de Andrade's 'Cannibalist Manifesto.'" *Latin American Literary Review* 19, no. 38 (Jul.–Dec. 1991): 35–47. https://writing.upenn.edu/library/Andrade_Cannibalistic_Manifesto.pdf and https://www.jstor.org/stable/20119600.

Bartók, Béla. "The Influence of Peasant Music on Modern Music" (1931). In *Béla Bartók's Essays*. Edited by Benjamin Suchoff. New York: St. Martin Press, 1976.

Basualdo, Carlos. *Tropicália: A Revolution in Brazilian Culture (1967–1972)*. São Paulo: Cosac Naify, 2005.

Béhague, Gerard. *Heitor Villa-Lobos: The Search for Brazil's Musical Soul*. Austin: Institute of Latin American Studies, 1994.

Béhague, Gerard. "Villa-Lobos, Heitor." In *The New Grove Dictionary of Music and Musicians*. Edited by Stanley Sadie and John Tyrrell, v. 26, 613. London: Macmillan, 2001.

Benjamin, George. "How Stravinsky's Rite of Spring has shaped 100 years of music." *The Guardian*, May 19, 2013. https://www.theguardian.com/music/2013/may/29/stravinsky-rite-of-spring.

Bergson, Henri. *A energia espiritual*. Translated by Rosemary Costhek Abílio. São Paulo: Martins Fontes, 2009.

Bergson, Henri. *An Essay on the Meaning of the Comic*. New York: Macmillan, 1914.

Bergson, Henri. *Creative Evolution*. Mineola: Dover Publications, Inc., 2014.

Bernstein, Guilherme. *Sobre Poética e Forma em Villa-Lobos: Primitivismo e Estrutura nos Choros Orquestrais*. Curitiba: Editora Prismas, 2015.

Bosi, Alfredo. "Moderno e Modernista na Literatura Brasileira." In *Céu e Inferno: Ensaios de Crítica Literária e Ideológica*. São Paulo: Livraria Duas Cidades, 1988, 209–26.

Boulez, Pierre. *Notes of an Apprenticeship*. New York: A. A. Knopf, 1968.

Breton, André. *Arcanum 17: With Apertures, Grafted to the End*. Translated by Zack Rogow. United Kingdom: Green Integer, 2004.

Breton, André. *Manifestoes of Surrealism*, Translated by Richard Seaver and Helen R. Lane. Ann Arbor: University of Michigan Press, 1969. https://monoskop.org/images/2/2f/Breton_Andre_Manifestoes_of_Surrealism.pdf.

Brophy, Liam. "Hermann Keyserling, Knight of the Holy Ghost." *The Irish Monthly* 74, no. 879 (1946): 376–83. http://www.jstor.org/stable/20515547.

Brown, Matthew. "Tonality and Form in Debussy's 'Prélude à L'Après-midi d'un faune.'" *Music Theory Spectrum* 15, no. 2 (Autumn, 1993): 127–43.

Bullard, Truman Campbell. "The First Performance of Igor Stravinsky's *Sacre du Printemps*." Ph.D. diss., Eastman School of Music, University of Rochester, 1971, vol. 2.

Buñuel, Luis. "Poetry and Cinema." In *The World of Luis Buñuel: Essays in Criticism*. Edited by Joan Mellen, 105–110. New York: Oxford University Press, 1978.

Burkholder, J. Peter. "The Uses of Existing Music: Musical Borrowing as a Field." *Notes* 50, no. 3 (1994): 851–70, doi:10.2307/898531 (accessed. September 4, 2021).

Bush, Randall. "Heitor Villa-Lobos." *American Music Teacher* 30, no. 4 (1981): 20–21.

Cabral, Renata Campello and Paola Berenstein Jacques. "O Antropófago Oswald de Andrade e a Preservação do Patrimônio: Um Devorador de Mitos?" *Anais do Museu Paulista* 26 (2018), 1–39. http://dx.doi.org/10.1590/1982-02672018v26e32.

Campos, Augusto de. "Revistas re-vistas: Os antropófagos." In *Revista de antropofagia*. São Paulo: Metal Leve, 1975.

Campos, Haroldo de. "Uma Poética de Radicalidade." In *Oswald de Andrade: Obras Completas VII*, 4th edition, 9–64. Rio de Janeiro: Edição Civilização Brasileira, 1974.

Canclini, Néstor García. *Hybrid Cultures: Strategies for Entering and Leaving Modernity*. Translated by Christopher L. Chiappari and Silvia L. López. Minneapolis: University of Minnesota Press, 1995.

Cândido, Antônio. "Digressão Sentimental sobre Oswald de Andrade." In *Vários Escritos*. São Paulo: Livraria Duas Cidades, 1970: 57–88.
Cândido, Antônio. *Literatura e Sociedade*. São Paulo: Cia. Editora Nacional, 1976.
Cândido, Antônio. "Oswald Viajante." In *Vários Escritos*. São Paulo: Livraria Duas Cidades, 1977.
Cândido, Antônio. *Vários Escritos*. São Paulo: Livraria Duas Cidades, 1977.
Cantarino, Carolina and Rodrigo Cunha. Interview with Eduardo Viveiros de Castro. *Com Ciência*, May 10, 2009. https://www.comciencia.br/comciencia/handler.php?section=8&tipo=entrevista&edicao=46.
Cantoni, Angelo. *The Language of Stravinsky*. New York: Georg Olms Verlag, 2014.
Cardoso, Hellen Silva. "Villa-Lobos: Uma 'melodia social.'" *Simbiótica, Ufes* v. ún., no. 1 (June 2012): 183–85.
Carpentier, Alejo. "De lo real maravilloso americano." In *Tientos y Diferencias*, 96–112. Montevideo: Arca, 1967. https://www.literatura.us/alejo/deloreal.html.
Carpentier, Alejo. "Uma Força Musical da América: Heitor Villa-Lobos." In *Villa-Lobos por Alejo Carpentier*. Translated by Emir Sader and J. Jota de Moraes. São Paulo: Imprensa Oficial do Estado, 1991.
Carvalho Oliveira, José de. "Simetria, Invariâncias e Organicidade Escalar, Um Estudo Sobre Padrões e Similaridades Em Villa-Lobos e Debussy." Anais Do III Simpósio Villa-Lobos–USP, 2017: 304-018. https://www.academia.edu/35279267/Simetria_invari%C3%A2ncias_e_organicidade_escalar_um_estudo_sobre_padr%C3%B5es_e_similaridades_em_Villa-Lobos_e_Debussy?email_work_card=view-paper.
Castilho, Pedro de Teixeira and Leo Bryan Lisboa. "O Mau Selvagem: A apropriação do Mito Freudiano de Totem e Tabu por Oswald de Andrade no 'Manifesto Antropófago.'" *Dossiê em tese* 23, no. 1 (2017): 119–32. doi: http://dx.doi.org/10.17851/1982-0739.23.1.119-132.
Castro, Moacir Werneck de. *Mário de Andrade: Exílio no Rio*. Rio de Janeiro: Rocco, 1989.
Castro Rocha, João Cezar de. "Uma teoria de exportação? Ou Antropofagia como visão de mundo." In *Antropofagia hoje? Oswald de Andrade em cena*, Organized by João Carlos Castro Rocha and Jorge Rufinelli. São Paulo: É Realizações, 2011.
Chamie, Mário. "Freud, Oswald de Andrade e Antropofagia." *A Fábrica do Futuro—Residência Criativa do Audiovisual*. Espaço de Aprendizado em Rede. http://sv2.fabricadofuturo.org.br/sitev1/index.php?pag=38&prog=130&id=144.
Chénieux-Gendron, Jacqueline. *Surrealism*. Translated by Vivian Folkenflik. New York: Columbia University Press, 1990.
Chua, Daniel K. L. "Rioting with Stravinsky: A Particular Analysis of the Rite of Spring." *Music Analysis*, 26/i–ii (2007): 59–109. doi: 10.1111/j.1468-2249.2007.00250.x.
Clastres, Pierre. *Arqueologia da violência: Pesquisas de Antropologia Política*, 2nd edition. Translated by Paulo Neves. São Paulo: Cosac Naify, 2011.

Cocco, Giuseppe. *Mundobraz: o devir-mundo do brasil e o devir-brasil do mundo*. Rio de Janeiro: Record, 2009.

Coli, Jorge. *Musica Final: Mário de Andrade e sua coluna jornalística Mundo musical*. Campinas: UNICAMP, 1998.

Contier, Arnaldo Daraya. *Brasil Novo–Música, Nação e Modernidade: Os anos 20 e 30*. N.p.: Edições Verona, 2021.

Corrêa do Lago, Manoel A. *O Círculo Veloso-Guerra e Darius Milhaud no Brasil: Modernismo musical no Rio de Janeiro antes da Semana*. PhD diss., UNIRIO, 2005. http://www.unirio.br/ppgm/arquivos/teses/manoel-lago. Published later as: Corrêa do Lago, Manoel A. *O Círculo Veloso-Guerra e Darius Milhaud no Brasil: Modernismo musical no Rio de Janeiro antes da Semana*. Rio de Janeiro: Reler, 2010.

Corrêa do Lago, Manoel, and Guilherme Bernstein. *Uirapuru: Partitura de estudo comentada*. https://docplayer.com.br/189641987-Heitor-villa-lobos-uirapuru-partitura-de-estudo-comentada-manoel-correa-do-lago-e-guilherme-bernstein.html.

Corrêa do Lago, Manoel, and Guilherme Bernstein. "Do Tédio de Alvorada ao Uirapuru: anotações à partiture comentada." In *Anais do VI Simpósio Villa-Lobos*. São Paulo: ECA – USP (2021), 543–52. https://sites.google.com/usp.br/simposiovilla-lobos/anais-svl/anais-vi-svl-2021.

Corrêa, Murilo Duarte Costa. "O intempestivo e o desterritorializado: Oswald de Andrade e o lugar das ideias no Brasil." *Biblioteca Online de Ciências da Comunicaçao* (2012): 1–18. http://www.bocc.ubi.pt/pag/correa-murilo-o-intempestivo-e-o-desterritorializado.pdf.

Costa, Juliana Ripke da. "Tópicas Afro-Brasileiras Como Tradição Inventada na Música Brasileira do Século XX." Masters diss., Universidade de São Paulo, 2017.

Costa, Oswaldo. "De Antropofagia." *Revista de Antropofagia* 2, no. 9. https://digital.bbm.usp.br/bitstream/bbm/7064/1/45000033273.pdf.

Cott, Jonathan. *Stockhausen; Conversations with the Composer*. New York: Simon & Schuster, 1973.

Craft, Robert. Preface to *A Book about Stravinsky*, by Boris Asaf'ev, iii–xiv. Translated by Richard French. Ann Arbor: UMI Research Press, 1982.

Cross, Jonathan, ed. *The Cambridge Companion to Stravinsky*. New York: Cambridge University Press, 2003.

Cunha, Manuela L. Carneiro da and Eduardo B. Viveiros de Castro. "Vingança E Temporalidade: Os Tupinambás." *Anuário Antropológico* 10, no. 1 (2018): 57–78. https://periodicos.unb.br/index.php/anuarioantropologico/article/view/6354.

Debussy, Claude. *Debussy on Music*. Edited by Francois Lesure and translated by Richard Langham Smith. New York: Knopf, 1977.

Debussy, Claude. *Monsieur Croche et autres écrits*. Edited by Francois Lesure. Paris: Gallimard, 1971.

Deleuze, Gilles. *Nietzsche and Philosophy*. New York: Columbia University Press, 1983.

Delfino, Jean-Paul. *Brasil: a música; panorama des musiques populaires brésiliennes*. Marseille: Ed. Parenthèses, 1998.

Della Torre, Bruna. "Modelos Críticos: Antonio Candido e Roberto Schwarz Leem Oswald de Andrade." *Revista do Instituto de Estudos Brasileiro*, no. 74 (Dec. 2019): 178–96. https://doi.org/10.11606/issn.2316-901X.v0i74p178-196.

Dennison, Stephanie and Lisa Shaw. *Popular Cinema in Brazil: 1930–2001*. Manchester: Manchester University Press, 2004.

Doniger, Wendy. Foreword to the 2004 edition of *Shamanism: Archaic Techniques of Ecstasy*, by Mircea Eliade, xi–xvi. Princeton, NY: Princeton University Press, 2004.

Doolittle, Emily, and Henrik Brumm. "O Canto do Uirapuru: Consonant Intervals and Patterns in the Song of the Musical Wren." *Journal of Interdisciplinary Music Studies* 6, no. 1 (spring 2012): 55–85.

Downes, Olin. "Villa-Lobos Guest at The City Center: Shares Baton With Stokowski—Latter Conducts Orchestra in Beethoven 'Pastoral.'" *New York Times*, February 13, 1945: 21.

Einboden, Jeffrey. "The Genesis of Westliterature: Goethe's West-östlicher Divan and Kerygmatic Pluralism." *Literature & Theology* 19, no. 3 (September 2005): 238–50. doi: 10.1093/litthe/fri029.

Eliade, Mircea, ed. *The Encyclopedia of Religion*, vol. 6. New York: MacMillan, 1987.

Eliade, Mircea. *The Myth of the Eternal Return: Cosmos and History*. New York: Harper, 1959.

Eliot, T. S. *Four Quartets*. Orlando: Houghton Mifflin Harcourt, 2014.

Emerson, Ralph Waldo. "Quotation and Originality." In *Letters and Social Aims*. Boston: Osgood, 1986.

Enciclopedia Italiana di Scienze, Lettere ed Arti iniziata dall'Istituto Giovanni Treccani. S.v."Pulcinella," accessed August 23, 2017. http://www.treccani.it/enciclopedia/pulcinella.

Ewen, David. *American Composers Today: A Biographical and Critical Guide*. New York: H. W. Wilson, 1949.

Fairman, Richard. "Total Immersion: Villa-Lobos, Barbican, London—Review." *Financial Times*, March 10, 2014. https://www.ft.com/content/631b6c3c-a84b-11e3-8ce1-00144feab7de.

Faria, Daniel. "As meditações americanas de Keyserling: Um cosmopolitismo nas incertezas do tempo." *Varia História* 29, no. 51 (2013): 905–23. https://doi.org/10.1590/S0104-87752013000300013.

Ferreira, Rildo da Luz. "O Problema da Intuição Mística Como Instrumento de Investigação Metafísica na Obra de Henri Bergson." *Interações* 15, no. 2 (Nov. 2020): 315–29. https://doi.org/10.5752/P.1983-2478.2020v15n2p315-329.

Fléchet, Anaïs. *Villa-Lobos à Paris: Un écho musical du Brésil*. Paris: Editions L'Harmattan, 2004.

Freitas, Carla Baptista de. "Antropofagia Ritual e Identidade Cultural nas Sociedades Ameríndias: A Representação do 'Outro' na Literatura Brasileira e Portuguesa do Século XIX." Masters diss., Universidade de Lisboa, 2011. https://www.academia.edu/2040594/Resumo.

Frey, John G. "From Dada to Surrealism." *Parnassus* 8 no. 7 (Dec. 1936): 12–15. DOI: 10.1080/15436314.1936.11466615.

Forte, Allen. *The Structure of Atonal Music*. New Haven: Yale University Press, 1973.

Forte, Graziela Naclério. 2014. "O Projeto Nacional dos Modernistas." *Ponta De Lança: Revista Eletrônica de História, Memória & Cultura* 3 no. 4, 27–38. https://seer.ufs.br/index.php/pontadelanca/article/view/3195. Also available at: https://www.academia.edu/7546742/O_Projeto_Nacional_dos_Modernistas?email_work_card=thumbnail.

Foster, Hal. *Compulsive Beauty*. Cambridge: MIT Press, 1993.

Fowles, Bob. "Is This Where I Am," bobfowleslifedrawing1 (blog). http://bobfowleslifedrawing1.blogspot.com/2019/01/is-this-where-i-am-going.html.

França, Eurico Nogueira. *A música no Brasil*. Rio de Janeiro: Ministério da Educação e Saúde, Servico de Documentação, 1953.

Franco, Mauro. "O Passado Manifesto." *Hist. Historiogr.*, no. 24 (Aug. 2017): 179–85. doi: 10.15848/hh.v0i24.1206. https://www.academia.edu/35052727/O_passado_manifesto_Palavras_chave?email_work_card=view-paper.

Freitas, Danilo Mercês and Mayara Ribeiro Guimarães. "A Antropofagia Musical na Poética de Mário de Andrade." *Revista Literatura em Debate* 9, no. 16 (2015): 42–56, http://revistas.fw.uri.br/index.php/literaturaemdebate/article/view/1726/1900.

Freud, Sigmund. *Totem and Taboo: Resemblances between the Psychic Lives of Savages and Neurotics*. London: Routledge, 1919. https://www.gutenberg.org/cache/epub/41214/pg41214-images.html. A more recent edition can be found as translated by A. A. Brill. Mineola: Dover, 1998.

Garcia, Thomas G. "The 'Choro,' the Guitar and Villa-Lobos." *Luso-Brazilian Review* 34, no. 1 (Summer, 1997), 57–66.

Garfield, Seth. "A Nationalist Environment: Indians, Nature, and the Construction of the Xingu National Park in Brazil." *Luso-Brazilian Review* 41, No. 1 (2004): 139–67. https://www.jstor.org/stable/3513749.

Gideon, Siegfried. *Space, Time and Architecture: The Growth of a New Tradition*. Cambridge: Harvard University Press, 1941.

Greenan, Richard. "Traditional Mutants: Tropicália, Nationalism and Authenticity." Masters diss., Cardiff University, 2010.

Greet, Michele. "Devouring Surrealism: Tarcila do Amaral's Abaporu," *Papers of Surrealism* 11 (Spring 2015): 1–39. https://www.research.manchester.ac.uk/portal/files/63517395/surrealism_issue_11.pdf.

Grieco, Donatello. *Roteiro de Villa-Lobos*. Brasília: Fundação Alexandre de Gusmão, 2009.

Grun, Irina Hiebert. "A Recepção da Antropofagia na Arte Brasileira Contemporânea." *Revista Lampejo* 1, no. 6 (Feb. 2014): 24–48. http://revistalampejo.org/edicoes/edicao-6/Volume%2006_Lampejo_12_2014_Oswald/Publica%C3%A7%C3%A3o/01_Oswald/Ensaio2_Irina%20Hilbert_24_a_48.pdf.

Guérios, Paulo R. *Heitor Villa-Lobos: o caminho sinuoso da predestinação*. Curitiba: Self-published, 2nd edition, 2009.

Guérios, Paulo R. "Heitor Villa-Lobos and the Parisian art scene: how to become a Brazilian musician." *Mana* 1 (Oct. 2006): 1–19. http://socialsciences.scielo.org/pdf/s_mana/v1nse/scs_a02.pdf.

Guimarães, Luiz. *Villa-Lobos visto da plateia e na intimidade (1912/1935)*. Rio de Janeiro: Grafica Editora Arte Moderna, 1972.

Gustafson, Ralph. "Villa-Lobos and the Man-Eating Flower: A Memoir." *The Musical Quarterly* 75, no. 1 (1991): 1–11. http://www.jstor.org/stable/742124.

Henderson, Linda Dalrymple. "The Fourth Dimension and Non-Euclidean Geometry in Modern Art: Conclusion." *Leonardo* 17, no. 3 (1984): 205–10. https://doi.org/10.2307/1575193.

Henderson, Linda Dalrymple. *The Fourth Dimension and non-Euclidean Geometry in Modern Art*. Cambridge: MIT Press, 2013.

Hess, Carol A. *Representing the Good Neighbor: Music, Difference, and the Pan American Dream*. New York: Oxford University Press, 2013.

Hill, Peter. *Stravinsky: The Rite of Spring*. Cambridge: Cambridge University Press, 2000.

Hopkins, Pandora. "The Homology of Music and Myth: Views of Lévi-Strauss on Musical Structure." *Ethnomusicolog* 21, no. 2 (1977): 247–61. Accessed April 3, 2020. doi:10.2307/850946.

Hughes, Robert. *The Shock of the New*. New York: Alfred A. Knopf, 1980.

Huscher, Phillip. *Petrushka (1911)*. Chicago Symphony Orchestra program notes. https://cso.org/uploadedFiles/1_Tickets_and_Events/Program_Notes/ProgramNotes_Stravinsky_Petrushka.pdf.

Jackson, Kenneth David. *Cannibal Angels: Transatlantic Modernism and the Brazilian Avant-Garde*. Oxford: Peter Lang, 2021.

Jackson, Kenneth David. "Vanguardist Prose in Oswald de Andrade." Ph.D. Diss. University of Wisconsin-Madison, 1973.

Jackson, Kenneth David. "Three Glad Races: Primitivism and Ethnicity in Brazilian Modernist Literature." *Modernism/modernity* 1, no. 2 (1994): 89-112. doi:10.1353/mod.1994.0030.

Jacques, Paola Berenstein. "Tropicália Brasília: a pureza é um mito." In *Hélio Oiticica: Para Além dos Mitos*. Organized by Giuseppe Cocco and Barbara Szaniecki, 146–61. Rio de Janeiro: R&L Produtores Associados, 2016. https://www.academia.edu/38807287/H%C3%A9lio_oiticica_para_al%C3%A9m_dos_mitos?auto=download or https://blocodofua.com.br/publicacoes/carnaval/12-helio-oiticica-para-alem-dos-mitos/file.

Jardim, Gil. *O Estilo Antropofágico de Heitor Villa-Lobos: Bach e Stravinsky na Obra do Compositor*. São Paulo: Philarmonia Brasileira, 2005.

Jameson, Frederic. *Postmodernism, or the Cultural Logic of Late Capitalism*. Durham: Duke University Press, 1991.

Jáuregui, Carlos A. "Anthropophagy." In *Dictionary of Latin American Cultural Studies*, edited by Robert McKee Irwin and Mónica Szurmuk. Gainesville: University

Press of Florida, 2012, 22–28. https://www.academia.edu/6998258/Antropofagia_Cultural_cannibalism.

Jerke, Angelis. *Musical and Sociological Implications of Villa-Lobos's Prole do Bebê, No. 1*. N.p.: California State University, Long Beach, 2005.

Joseph, Charles M. *Stravinsky's Ballets*. New Haven: Yale University Press, 2011.

Judar, Tânia Veiga. "O Livro-objeto Pau Brasil." Masters diss., PUC-SP, 2016.

Kandel, Eric R. *The Age of Insight: The Quest to Understand the Unconscious in Art, Mind, and Brain, from Vienna 1900 to the Present*. New York: Random House, 2012.

Kartomi, Margaret J. "The Processes and Results of Musical Culture Contact: A Discussion of Terminology and Concepts." *Ethnomusicology* 25, no. 2 (May 1981): 227–49, p. 233 https://www.jstor.org/stable/pdf/851273.pdf.

Kelly, Thomas Forrest. *First Nights: Five Musical Premieres*. New Haven and London: Yale University Press, 2001.

Keyes, Ralph. *The Quote Verifier: Who Said What, Where and When*. New York: St. Martin's Griffin, 2007.

Kiefer, Bruno. *Villa-Lobos e o Modernismo na Música Brasileira*. São Paulo: Movimento, 1981.

Kilgour, Maggie. *From Communion to Cannibalism: An Anatomy of Metaphors of Incorporation*. United States: Princeton University Press, 2014.

Kovács, Steven. *From Enchantment to Rage: The Story of Surrealist Cinema*. Cranbury, N.J.: Associated University Presses, 1980.

Kozel, David. "A Musical Analysis of Mythical Thought in the Work of Claude Lévi-Strauss." *Musicologica Olomucensia* 22 (December 2015): 61–78.

La Fontaine, Jean de. *Fables*. Pittsford: Castle Rock, 2010, Book 2, No. 6, http://www.lesfables.fr/.

Léry, Jean de. *History of a Voyage to the Land of Brazil*. Translated by Janet Whatley. Berkeley: University of California Press, 1992. Also available in its original form as *Histoire d'un voyage faict en la terre du Brésil: autrement dite Amérique* (1585). http://gallica.bnf.fr/ark:/12148/bpt6k54640v.

Lévi-Strauss, Claude. *O pensamento selvagem*. Translated by Tânia Pellegrini. Campinas: Papirus, 1989.

Lévi-Strauss, Claude. *The Raw and the Cooked: Mythologiques, Volume 1*. Translated by John Weightman and Doreen Weightman. Chicago: University of Chicago Press, 1983.

Lévi-Strauss, Claude. *The Savage Mind*. Chicago: University of Chicago Press, 1967.

Lifar, Serge. *Ma Vie*. London: Hutchinson, 1970.

Lima, Luiz Fernando N. de. "Notícia sobre o Primeiro Congresso Internacional Villa-Lobos." *Brasiliana*, no. 12 (Sept. 2002): 2–8.

Lima, Paula Albiero Marconi de. "O Sujeito do Pau-Brasil: São Paulo, Minas Gerais e a Enunciação na Poética Oswaldiana." Masters diss., FFCL-USP, 2015.

Livingston-Isenhour, Tamara Elena and Thomas George Caracas Garcia. *Choro: A Social-History of a Brazilian Popular Music*. Bloomington: Indiana University Press, 2005.

Lopes Graça, Fernando. "Heitor Villa-Lobos." In Vol. 5 of *Presença de Villa-Lobos*, 65–67. Rio de Janeiro: MEC–Museu Villa-Lobos, 1970.

Lopes, Luiz Fernando Vallim: *The transformations of an enchanted bird: Villa-Lobos' Uirapuru and issues of sources, style and reception.* Presentation at "I Congresso Internacional Villa-Lobos." Paris: Institut Finlandais, April 10–13, 2002.

López, Kimberle S. "*Modernismo* and the Ambivalence of the Postcolonial Experience: Cannibalism, Primitivism, and Exoticism in Mário De Andrade's 'Macunaíma.'" *Luso-Brazilian Review* 35, no. 1 (1998): 25–38. http://www.jstor.org/stable/3514120.

Lopez, Telê Porto Ancona. *Macunaíma: A margem e o texto*. São Paulo: HUCITEC, Secretaria de Cultura, Esporte e Turismo, 1974.

Lucie-Smith, Edward. *Latin American Art of the 20th Century*. London: Thames & Hudson, 2004.

Lundy, Craig. "Deleuze's Untimely: Uses and Abuses in the Appropriation of Nietzsche." In *Deleuze and History*, edited by Jeffrey Bell and Claire Colebrook. Edinburgh: Edinburgh University Press, 2009.

Magalhães, Couto de. *O selvagem*. Belo Horizonte: Livraria Itatiaia, USP, 1975.

Magee, Bryan. *The Tristan Chord: Wagner and Philosophy*. New York: Henry Holt, 2002.

Maia, Maria. *Villa-Lobos: Alma Brasileira*. Rio de Janeiro: Contraponto/ Petrobrás, 2000.

Mardrus, L. Delarue. "L'aventure d'un compositeur: musique cannibale." *L'Intransigeant*, Paris, December 13, 1927. http://gallica.bnf.fr/ark:/12148/bpt6k792039k.item.

Mariz, Vasco. *A canção brasileira de câmara*. Rio de Janeiro: Livraria Francisco Alves Editora, 2002.

Mariz, Vasco. *Heitor Villa-Lobos: Life and Work of the Brazilian Composer*. Washington, D.C.: Brazilian American Cultural Institute, 1970.

Mariz, Vasco. *Heitor Villa-Lobos: compositor brasileiro*. Rio de Janeiro: MEC/DAC /Museu Villa-Lobos, 1977.

Martins, Wilson. *O Modernismo (1916–1945)*. São Paulo: Editora Cultrix, 1967.

Mazo, Margarita. "Stravinsky's *Les Noces* and Russian Village Wedding Ritual." *Journal of the American Musicological Society* 43, no. 1 (1990), 99–142.

Mellen, Joan, ed. *The World of Luis Buñuel: Essays in Criticism*. New York: Oxford University Press, 1978.

Melo, Cleisson. "Villa-Lobos: Do Simbólico Ao Semiótico." In *Anais do IV Simpósio Villa-Lobos: Novos Desafios Interpretativos*. São Paulo: ECA – USP (2018), 204–16. https://www.academia.edu/38914988/Villa-Lobos_do_simb%C3%B3lico_ao_semi%C3%B3tico?email_work_card=view-paper.

Menezes Filho, Florivaldo. *Apoteose de Schoenberg*, 2nd edition. São Paulo: Nova Stella, 2002.

Mignone, Francisco. "Villa-Lobos na Música Sinfônica" (Lecture given on October 27, 1966). In *Presença de Villa-Lobos*, 83–93. Rio de Janeiro: MEC, Museu Villa-Lobos, 1969, vol. 3.

Milhaud, Darius. "Brésil." *La Revue Musicale* 1, no.1 (Nov. 1920): 61–62.

Miller, Arthur J. *Einstein, Picasso: Space, Time, and the Beauty That Causes Havoc.* New York: Basic Books, 2001.

Moreira, Gabriel F. "O Elemento Indígena na Obra de Heitor Villa-Lobos: observações musico-analíticas e considerações históricas. Masters diss., UDESC, 2010. https://www.amplificar.mus.br/data/referencias/ver/O-elemento-indigena-na-obra-de-Villa-Lobos—observacoes-musico-analiticas-e-consideracoes-historicas.

Moreira, Gabriel. F. "O Estilo indígena de Villa Lobos (Parte I)." *Per Musi*, Belo Horizonte, no. 27 (2013): 19–38.

Morse, Richard M. "Triangulating Two Cubists: William Carlos Williams and Oswald de Andrade." *Latin American Literary Review* 14, no. 27 (Jan.–Jun. 1986): 175–83. Accessed April 1, 2020. www.jstor.org/stable/20119418.

Nasser, Nívea Abujamra. "Villa-Lobos e A Elaboração de Linguagem e Estilo Característicos." *Thesis* ano V, no. 10 (2008): 48–62.

Nattiez, Jean-Jacques. *The Battle of Chronos and Orpheus: Essays in Applied Musical Semiology.* New York: Oxford University Press, 2004.

Negwer, Manuel. *Villa-Lobos: Der Aufbruch der brasilianischen Musik.* Mainz: Schott Music, 2008.

Netto, Adriano Bitarães. *Antropofagia oswaldiana: um receituário estético científico.* São Paulo: Annablume, 2004.

Neves, José Maria. *Villa-Lobos, o choro e os choros.* São Paulo: Musicália, 1977.

Newman, Rachel. "Primitivism and Identity in Latin America: The Appropriation of Indigenous Cultures in 20th Century Latin American Art." *Art History Honors Papers* 3 (2015). http://digitalcommons.conncoll.edu/arthisthp/3.

Nodari, Alexandre and Maria Carolina de Almeida Amaral. "A questão (indígena) do Manifesto Antropófago." *Revista direito e práxis* 9, no. 4 (2018): 2461–502. doi:10.1590/2179-8966/2018/37974.

Nodari, Alexandre. "A Transformação do Tabu em totem: Notas sobre um(a) formula antropofágica." In *The Forest and the School: How to sit at the dinner table?*, ed. Pedro Neves Marques. Berlim: Archive Books, 2014.

Noheden, Kristoffer. *Surrealism, Cinema, and the Search for a New Myth.* Basingstoke: Palgrave Macmillan, 2017.

Nunes, Benedito. "O Animal e o Primitivo: Os Outros de Nossa Cultura." *Ensaio* 14, supplement (Dec. 2007): 279–90. https://www.scielo.br/j/hcsm/a/G3cP8ZDj47v4RdhhPbRdwWp/?lang=pt&format=pdf.

Nunes, Benedito. "A antropofagia ao alcance de todos." In *A Utopia Antropofágica* by Oswald de Andrade. São Paulo: Globo, 1990, 5–39. https://www.academia.edu/16417381/A_antropofagia_ao_alcance_de_todos_Benedito_Nunes.

Nunes, Benedito. 2004. "Antropofagia e Vanguarda: Acerca do Canibalismo Literário." *Literatura e Sociedade* 9 no.7 (2004): 316–27. https://doi.org/10.11606/issn.2237-1184.v0i7p316-327.

https://monoskop.org/images/a/ae/Oswald_de_Andrade_A_utopia_antropof%C3%A1gica_1990.pdf.

Nunes, Benedito. *Oswald Canibal.* São Paulo: Ed Perspectiva, 1979.

Oliveira, Ana de. "Tropicalia: Ruidos Pulsativos. Geléia Geral." Accessed July 29, 2017. http://tropicalia.com.br/en/ruidos-pulsativos/geleia-geral/antropofagia.

Oliveira, Isis de. "The Structural Metaphors in *Amazonas* by Villa-Lobos and in *Kyrie* by Ligeti." In *Proceedings of the International Conference on Music Semiotics in Memory of Raymond Monelle*. Edited by Nearchos Panos, Vangelis Lympouridis, George Athanasopoulos and Peter Nelson, 233–41. Edinburgh: University of Edinburgh Press, 2013. https://www.academia.edu/2082560/Villa-Lobos_and_nationality_representation_by_means_of_pictorialism_some_thoughts_on_Amazonas.

Oliveira, Jamary. "Black Key versus White Key: A Villa-Lobos Device." In *Latin American Music Review / Revista De Música Latinoamericana* 5, no. 1 (1984): 33–47. doi:10.2307/780111.

Oliveira Pinto, Tiago de. "'Art Is Universal'–On Nationalism and Universality in the Music of Heitor Villa-Lobos." *The World of Music* 29, no. 2 (1987): 104–16.

Oliveira, Willy Corrêa de. *Com Villa-Lobos*. São Paulo: Editora da Universidade de São Paulo, 2009.

Ornelas, Rodrigo. "Oswald de Andrade, leitor de Nietzsche, genealogia, catequese e antropofagia." *Cad. Nietzsche* 41, no. 3 (2020): 220–34. https://doi.org/10.1590/2316-82422020v4103ro.

Østergaard, Edvin. "Composing Einstein: Exploring the Kinship of Art and Science." *Interdisciplinary Science Reviews* 31, no. 3 (July 14, 2006): 261–74.

Paz, Ermelinda A. *Villa-Lobos e a Musica Popular Brasileira: Uma Visão sem Preconceito*. São Paulo: Editora Tipografia Musical, 2019.

Pellecer, François. "Adolphe Piriou (1878–1964)." *Musica et Memoria*, April–May 2004. Accessed August 1, 2017. http://www.musimem.com/piriou.htm.

Peppercorn, Lisa M. *Villa-Lobos: Collected Studies*. Aldershot: Scolar Press, 1992.

Peppercorn, Lisa M. *Villa-Lobos, The Music*. White Plains: Pro/Am Music Resources Inc, 1991.

Peppercorn, Lisa M. *The World of Villa-Lobos in Pictures and Documents*. Aldershot: Scolar Press, 1996.

Pereira, João Batista. "O padre Antonio Vieira: Orador e profeta do V Imperio." Masters diss., Universidade Estadual de Maringá, 2005. http://www.ppe.uem.br/SITE%20PPE%202010/dissertacoes/2005-Joao_Pereira.pdf.

Perpétuo, Irineu Franco. "Biografia analisa legado de Villa-Lobos." *Folha de S. Paulo*, December 16, 2002. Accessed August 3, 2017. https://www1.folha.uol.com.br/fsp/ilustrad/fq2612200211.htm.

Pouzet-Duzer, Virginie. "Dada, Surrealism, Antropofagia: The Consuming Process of the Avant-Gardes." *L'Esprit Créateur* 53, no. 3 (2013): 79–90. https://www.jstor.org/stable/26378854. Accessed April 6, 2020.

Presença de Villa-Lobos. 14 vols. Rio de Janeiro: MEC, Museu Villa-Lobos, 1965–2012.

Pritchard, Jane. "Serge Diaghilev's Ballets Russes—An Itinerary. Part 1: 1909–1921." *Dance Research: The Journal of the Society for Dance Research* 27, no. 1 (2009): 108–98.

Pritchard, Jane, ed. *Diaghilev and the Ballets Russes, 1909–1929: When Art Danced with Music*. London: Victoria and Albert Museum, 2013.

"Pulcinella." *Enciclopedia Italiana di Scienze, Lettere ed Arti iniziata dall'Istituto Giovanni Treccani.* Accessed August 23, 2017. http://www.treccani.it/enciclopedia/pulcinella.

Rachum, Ilan. "Antropofagia Against Verdamarelo." *Latin American Literary Review* 4, no. 8 (Spring 1976), 67–81. http://www.jstor.org/stable/20119009.

Reiss, Françoise. *Nijinsky: A Biography.* New York: Pitman, 1960.

Restrepo, Eduardo. "Antropologia y Colonialidad." *El giro decolonial: reflexiones para una diversidad epistémica más allá del capitalismo global.* Edited by Santiago Castro-Gómez, 289–304. Bogotá: Siglo del Hombre, 2007.

Ribeiro, João Carlos, org. *O Pensamento Vivo de Heitor Villa-Lobos.* São Paulo: Martin Claret, 1987.

Rimbaud, Jean Arthur. "Lettre à Paul Demeny, 15 mai 1871." In *Rimbaud: Oeuvres Complétes.* Edited by André Guyaux, 343–44. Paris: Pléiade, 2009.

Rimbaud, Jean Arthur. *A Season in Hell.* Translated by Delmore Schwartz. Norfolk: New Directions, 1940.

Riom. Charlotte. "Contribuição de Villa-Lobos para a dança cênica: nova historiografia e novos desafios para uma musicologia da dança." In *Anais do VI Simpósio Villa-Lobos.* São Paulo: ECA–USP (2021), 71–94. https://sites.google.com/usp.br/simposiovilla-lobos/anais-svl/anais-vi-svl-2021.

Rodrigues, Lutero. "Villa-Lobos e a "Descoberta do Brasil.'" In *Villa-Lobos, Um Compêndio: novos desafios interpretativos.* Edited by Paulo de Tarso Salles and Norton Dudeque, 179–91. Curitiba: Editora UFPR, 2017.

Rodrigues, Lutero. "Villa-Lobos e o Modernismo da Primeira República." *Revista Música* 19, no. 2 (2019): 244–52. https://doi.org/10.11606/rm.v19i2.165306.

Rodrigues, Lutero. "Villa-Lobos: a temática grega e a música programática." In *Anais do III Simpósio Villa-Lobos: Novos Desafios Interpretativos.* São Paulo: ECA–USP (1917), 135–43. http://www3.eca.usp.br/sites/default/files/form/biblioteca/acervo/producao-academica/002869075.pdf.

Roquette-Pinto, Edgard. *Rondônia. Antropologia. Etnografia.* Rio de Janeiro: Imprensa Nacional, 1917. (Archivos do Museu National, v. XX). The collection was republished as *Rondônia 1912: Gravações Históricas de Roquette-Pinto.* Organized by Edmundo Pereira and Gustavo Pacheco. Rio de Janeiro: Museu Nacional, 2008. http://www.etnolinguistica.org/biblio:roquete-pinto-1912-rondonia.

Ross, Alex. *The Rest is Noise: Listening to the Twentieth Century.* New York: Farrar, Straus and Giroux, 2007.

Rudlin, John. *Commedia dell'Arte: An Actor's Handbook.* New York: Routledge, 1994.

Said, Edward W. *Beginnings: Intention and Method.* New York: Columbia University Press, 1985.

Salles, Paulo de Tarso. "'Tédio de Alvorada'" e 'Uirapuru': um estudo comparativo de duas partituras de Heitor Villa-Lobos." *Brasiliana* (May 2005): 2–9.

Salles, Paulo de Tarso. "Villa-Lobos and National Representation by Means of Pictorialism: Some Thoughts on Amazonas." In *Proceedings of the International Conference on Music Semiotics in Memory of Raymond Monelle.* Edited by Nearchos Panos, Vangelis Lympouridis, George Athanasopoulos and Peter Nelson, 338–45. Edinbourgh: University of Edinbourgh Press, 2013. https://www.academia.edu/2082560/Villa-Lobos_and_nationality_representation_by_means_of_pictorialism_some_thoughts_on_Amazonas.

Salles, Paulo de Tarso and Norton Dudeque, ed. *Villa-Lobos, Um Compêndio: novos desafios interpretativos*. Curitiba: EDUFPR, 2017.

Salles, Paulo de Tarso. *Villa-Lobos: Processos Composicionais*. Campinas: UNICAMP, 2009.

Salles, Paulo de Tarso. "Villa-Lobos: Desafiando a Teoria e Análise." In *Anais do IV Encontro de Musicologia de Ribeirão Preto*, edited by Rodolfo Coelho de Souza, 81–95. Ribeirão Preto: USP-RP, 2012. https://www.academia.edu/2051026/Villa_Lobos_desafiando_a_teoria_e_an%C3%A1lise_Salles_2012_.

Salles, Paulo de Tarso. "Ritual Dance, by Villa-Lobos: A Music Topic in the Tropics." In *Anais do III Simpósio Villa-Lobos: Novos Desafios Interpretativos*. São Paulo: ECA – USP (1917), 66–82.

Salles, Pedro Paulo. "'Nozani-Ná' e As Flautas Secretas dos Homens-Da-Água: Cosmologia e Tradução de Um Canto Paresi." In *Villa-Lobos, Um Compêndio: novos desafios interpretativos*, Edited by Paulo de Tarso Salles and Norton Dudeque, 41–125. Curitiba: EDUFPR, 2017.

Samuel, Claude. *Olivier Messiaen: Music and Color. Conversations with Claude Samuel*. Portland: Amadeus Press, 1986.

Santiago, Silviano. "O Entre-Lugar do Discurso Latino-Americano." In *Uma Literatura nos Trópicos: Ensaios sobre a Dependência Cultural*. São Paulo: Perspectiva, 1978: 11–28.

Santini, Kathleen. "Depois do Surrealismo, Só a Antropofagia." *Atas do IX Encontros de História da Arte: da Percepção à Palavra: luz e cor na História da Arte* 11 (2017): 285–93.

Sartini-Blum, Cinzia. "Incorporating the Exotic: From Futurist Excess to Postmodern Impasse." In *A Place in the Sun. Africa in Italian Colonial Culture from Post-Unification to the Present*, edited by Patrizia Palumbo, 138–162. Berkeley: University of California Press, 2003.

Schic, Anna S. *Villa-Lobos: Souvenirs de l'indien blanc*. Arles: Actes Sud, 1987.

Schoenberg, Arnold. *Theory of Harmony*. Berkeley: University of California Press, 1983.

Schoenberg, Arnold. *Structural Functions of Harmony*. New York: W. W. Norton and Company Inc., 1969.

Schwarz, Roberto. "Nacional por Subtração." In *Que Horas São?* São Paulo: Companhia das Letras, 2nd edition, 2006, 29–48. http://www.afoiceeomartelo.com.br/posfsa/Autores/Schwarz,%20Roberto/Roberto%20Schwarz%20-%20Nacional%20por%20Subtra%E2%80%A1%C3%86o.pdf.

Schweitzer, Vivien. "Chaotic Yet Pensive, Pounding the Keys." *New York Times*, July 24, 2014. Accessed July 29, 2017. https://www.nytimes.com/2014/07/23/arts/music/marc-andre-hamelin-plays-at-the-keyboard-institute.html.

Scigliano, Eric. *Michelangelo's Mountain: The Quest for Perfection in the Marble Quarries of Carrara.* United Kingdom: Atria Books, 2007.

Shaw, Lisa. *Tropical Travels: Brazilian Popular Performance, Transnational Encounters, and the Construction of Race.* United States: University of Texas Press, 2018.

Shaw, Lisa. "'What Does the Baiana Have? Josephine Baker and the Performance of Afro-Brazilian Female Subjectivity on Stage." *Engish Language Notes* 49, no. 1 (March 1, 2011): 91–106.

Shlain, Leonard, *Art and Physics: Parallel Visions in Space, Time, and Light.* New York: Harper Perennial, 2007.

Silva Brito, Mario da. "A revolução modernista." In *A Literatura no Brasil.* Edited by Afrâneo Coutinho, vol. V, 20–37. Rio de Janeiro: Editorial Sul Americana, 1970.

Skidmore, Thomas E. *Brazil: Five Centuries of Change.* New York: Oxford University Press, 2010.

Slonimsky, Nicholas. *Russian and Soviet Music and Composers.* New York: Routledge, 2004.

Smith, Frederick J. *The Experiencing of Musical Sound: A Prelude to a Phenomenology of Music.* New York: Gordon and Breach, 1979.

Solomon-Godeau, Abigail. "Going Native: Paul Gauguin and the Invention of Primitivist Modernism." In *The Expanding Discourse: Feminism and Art History.* Edited by N. Broude and M. Garrard. New York: Harper Collins, 1986.

Sommer, Doris. *Foundational Fictions.* Berkeley and Los Angeles: University of California Press, 1991.

Spivak, Gayatri Chakravorty. "Can the Subaltern Speak?" In *Marxism and the Interpretation of Culture*, edited by Cary Nelson and Lawrence Grossberg, 271–313. Basingstoke: Macmillan, 1988.

Spruce, Richard. *Notes of a Botanist on the Amazon & Andes*, Vol. 1. Edited by Alfred Russel Wallace. London: Macmillan, 1908.

Staden, Hans. *Hans Staden's True History: An Account of Cannibal Captivity in Brazil.* Translated by Neil L. Whitehead and Michael Harbsmeier. Durham: Duke University Press, 2008.

Sterling, Susan Fisher. "Malfatti, Anita." In *The Grove Dictionary of Art Online.* Oxford: Oxford University Press, 2000. https://doi-org.proxy.lib.miamioh.edu/10.1093/gao/9781884446054.article.T2021799.

Sterzi, Eduardo. "Uma Ontologia Política Chamada Antropofagia" Interview by Ricardo Machado. *Revista do instituto Humanitas Usininos* 543, October 21, 2019. http://www.ihuonline.unisinos.br/artigo/7687-uma-ontologia-politica-chamada-antropofagia.

Stockhausen, Karlheinz. "Beyond Global Village Polyphony." In *Towards a Cosmic Music: Texts by Karlheinz Stockhausen.* Translated by Tim Nevil. Shaftesbury: Element, 1989.

Stravinsky, Igor. *An Autobiography.* New York: W. W. Norton, 1998.

Stravinsky, Igor and Robert Craft. *Dialogues and a Diary.* London: Faber and Faber, 1968.

Stravinsky, Vera and Robert Craft. *Stravinsky: In Pictures and Documents*. New York: Simon and Schuster, 1978.
Subirats, Eduardo. *A Penúltima Visão do Paraíso: Ensaios Sobre Memória e Globalização*. São Paulo: Studio Nobel, 2001.
Sztutman, Renato. "The (Re)turn of the Anthropophagites: Reconnecting Oswald de Andrade's Proposal to Amerindian Art-Thought," in *Anthropophagy as Cultural Strategy: the 24th Bienal de São Paulo 1988*, edited. Pablo Lafuente and Lisette Lagnado, 206–20. London: Afterall, 2015.
Tarasti, Eero. *Myth and music: a semiotic approach to the aesthetics of myth in music, especially that of Wagner, Sibelius and Stravinsky*. The Hague: Mouton, 1979.
Tarasti, Eero. *Heitor Villa-Lobos: The Life and Works, 1889–1959*. London: McFarland, 1995.
Taruskin, Richard. "Bartok and Stravinsky: Odd Couple Reunited?" *New York Times*, October 25, 1998. Accessed July 19, 2017.
Taruskin, Richard. *The Danger of Music and Other Anti-Utopian Essays*. Berkeley: University of California Press, 2009.
Taruskin, Richard. "The Rite Revisited." In *Music and Civilization: Essays in Honor of Paul Henry Lang*. Edited by Edmond Strainchamps and Maria Rika Marriates, 183–202. New York and London: WW Norton, 1984.
Taruskin, Richard. *Stravinsky and the Russian Traditions: A Biography of the Works Through Mavra*. Berkeley: University of California Press, 1999.
Thompson, Douglas. "Pound and Brazilian Concretism." *Paideuma* 6, no. 3 (1977): 279–94. http://www.jstor.org/stable/24725725.
Toni, Flávia Camargo. "Mário de Andrade e Villa-Lobos." *Revista do Instituto de Estudos Brasileiros*, no. 27 (December 1987): 43–58. doi.org/10.11606/issn.2316-901X.v0i27p43-58.
Travassos, Elizabeth. *Modernismo e música brasileira*. Rio de Janeiro: Jorge Zahar, 2000.
Vailati, Tecia. "Antropofagia como Mito de Controle." In *Revista TransVersos*. Rio de Janeiro, Vol. 3, No. 3 (Oct.–Mar. 2014/2015): 44–58. ISSN 2179-7528. https://www.e-publicacoes.uerj.br/index.php/transversos/article/view/18558. Accessed: April 6, 2020.
Van der Toorn, Pieter C. *Stravinsky and The Rite of Spring: The Beginnings of a Musical Language*. Berkeley: University of California Press, 1987.
Vargas Netto, Sebastião Leal Fereira. "Antropofagia Cultural: Momento do Pensamento Crítico Latino-Americano." *Revista Eletrônica da ANPHLAC*, no. 17 (Jul/Dec. 2014): 182–303. DOI: https://doi.org/10.46752/anphlac.17.2014.2117.
Vassberg, David E. "Villa-Lobos: Music as a Tool of Nationalism." *Luso-Brazilian Review* 6, no. 2 (Winter, 1969): 55–65.
Veloso, Caetano. *Verdade Tropical*. São Paulo: Companhia das Letras, 1997.
Villa-Lobos: Sua Obra. 2nd edition. Rio de Janeiro: MEC/DAC/ Museu Villa-Lobos, 1972.
Villa-Lobos: Sua Obra. 3rd edition. Rio de Janeiro: Museu Villa-Lobos, 1989.

Vinkler, Beth Joan. "The Anthropophagic Mother/Other: Appropriated Identities in Oswald de Andrade's 'Manifesto Antropófago.'" *Luso-Brazilian Review* 34, no. 1 (Summer 1997): 105–11. https://www.jstor.org/stable/3513808.

Vivacqua, Renato. *Música Popular Brasileira: Histórias de Sua Gente*. Brasília: Editora Thesaurus, 1992.

Viveiros de Castro, Eduardo. *A Inconstância da Alma Selvagem*. São Paulo: Cosac Naify, 2002.

Viveiros de Castro, Eduardo. "O mármore e a murta: sobre a inconstância da alma selvagem." In *A inconstância da alma selvagem*. São Paulo: Cosac & Naify, 2002. The book is available online, where this section corresponds to chapter 3 (125–85): https://ediscipinas.usp.br/pluginfile.php/4100318/mod_resource/content/1/1%20A%20Inconstancia%20da%20Alma%20Selvagem%20-%20Eduardo%20Viveiros%20de%20Castro.pdf.

Viveiros de Castro, Eduardo. *Metafísicas canibais: elementos para uma antropologia pós-estrutural*. São Paulo: Casac Naify, 2015.

Viveiros de Castro, Eduardo. "Temos que criar um outro conceito de criação (2007)." Interview with Pedro Cesarino and Sérgio Cohn. In *Eduardo Viveiros de Castro*, ed. Renato Sztutman, 162–87. Coleção Encontros. Rio de Janeiro: Azougue, 2009.

Volpe, Maria Alice. *Indianismo and Landscape in the Brazilian Age of Progress: Art Music from Carlos Gomes to Villa-Lobos, 1870s–1930s*. Austin: UMI Research Press, 2001.

Volpe, Maria Alice. "Villa-Lobos e o Imaginário Edênico de Uirapuru," *Brasiliana* 29 (Aug. 2009): 31–36.

Volpe, Maria Alice. "O Manuscrito P38.1.1 e a 'tabela prática' de Villa-Lobos." *Revista Brasileira de Música* 24, no. 2 (July–December 2011): 299–309.

Waizbort, Leopoldo. "Villa-Lobos: A Invenção da Identidade Nacional." *Ensaios* (March 1, 2012). Accessed on July 19, 2017. http://osesp.art.br/ensaios.aspx?Ensaio=25.

Waizbort, Leopoldo. "Villa-Lobos e seus Índios." *Presença de Villa-Lobos* 14 (2012): 137–43.

Waizbort, Leopoldo. "Como, Quando e Por Que Villa Desmentiu Benjamin." In *Villa-Lobos, Um Compêndio: novos desafios interpretativos*. Edited by Paulo de Tarso Salles and Norton Dudeque, 17–39. Curitiba: Editora UFPR, 2017.

Watkins, Glenn. *Pyramids at the Louvre*. Cambridge and London: Harvard University Press, 1994.

Watkins, Glenn. *Soundings: Music in the Twentieth Century*. New York: Schirmer, 1989.

Weiss, Allen S. *Perverse Desire and the Ambiguous Icon*. Albany: State University of New York Press, 1994.

Widmer, Ernst. "Bordão e bordadura." Assistant Professor diss., EMAC/UFBA, 1970. *ART Revista da Escola de Música e Artes Cênicas da UFBA*, no. 4 (Jan/Mar, 1982): 9–46.

Wisnik, José Miguel. *O Coro dos Contrários: a música em torno da semana de 22*. São Paulo: Livraria Duas Cidades, 1977.

Wright, Simon. *Villa-Lobos*. Oxford: Oxford University Press, 1992.
Wright, Simon. "Villa-Lobos." *The Musical Times* 133, no. 1792 (1992): 277. doi:10.2307/966063.
Xavier, Ismail. *Allegories of Underdevelopment: Aesthetics and Politics in Modern Brazilian Cinema*. Minnesota: University of Minnesota Press, 1997.
Zanella dos Santos, Daniel. "Narratividade e Tópicas em Uirapuru (1917) de Heitor Villa-Lobos." Masters diss., Universidade do Estado de Santa Catarina, 2015.

Scores

Gershwin, George. *Porgy and Bess*. New York: Gershwin Publishing Corporation, 1935.
Stravinsky, Igor. *The Rite of Spring*. Mineola: Dover, 1989.
Varèse, Edgard. *Amériques*. Revised and edited by Chou Wen-Chung. New York: Colfranc, 1973.
Villa-Lobos, Heitor. *Amazonas.: Poème Indien Brésilien pour Piano*. Paris: Éditions Max Eschig, 1953.
Villa-Lobos, Heitor. *Amazonas: Poème Symphonique*. Paris: Éditions Max Eschig, 1929.
Villa-Lobos, Heitor. *Amazonas: Poema Sinfônico ou Bailado Indígena Brasileiro—sobre um conto indígena de Raul Villa-Lobos*. Rio de Janeiro: Academia Brasileira de Música, 2010.
Villa-Lobos, Heitor. *A Prole do Bebê No. 1*. Rio de Janeiro: Arthur Napoleão, 1918.
Villa-Lobos, Heitor. *Uirapuru*. New York: Associated Music Publishers, 1948.

Index

Page references for figures are italicized.

abstractionism (abstractionist), 38, 198, 206, 222, 227–31, 235n28
African influence, 2, 9, 13, 17, 19–20, 22, 50, 54, 65n47, 211, 241, 268, 277, 279, 282n38, 283n51, 287n101, 307, 311–12, 338n33
Alencar, José de, 295, 299, 306, 319, 325, 341n72; *Iracema*, 306, 341n72; *O Guarani*, 319, 325
Almeida, Guilherme de, 8
Amazonas, xi, 54–5, 59, 88, 97, 100n5, 101n34, 114, 119, 137, 138n23, 139n29, 139n32, 141–203, 209–211, 215, 217–19, 227, 229, 231, 233, 247–48, 252, 261–62, 275, 279; *The Abyss*, 153, 189, *191*, *192*, *193*, *194*, 202n25; *The Amerindian Girl's Mirror*, 167, 173; *Contemplation of the Amazon*, 167, 187, 197; *Dance for the Enchantment of the Forests*, 150, *151*, 176–77, 180, 186, 197; *The Deceptive Mirror*, 185, 187, *188*; *The Discovery*, 185; *Enchantment motif* 156, 175–76, *179*, 182; *Epigraph*, 153–54, 164–67; *The Fight of Desire*, 189, *190*, *191*; *The Girl's Happiness*, *179*, 202n20. See also Theme of the Happiness of the Amerindian Girl; *Jealousy of the God of Winds*, 167, 170, 173, 182, 185; Miremis leitmotif, 139n32, 152–53, *155*, 156, 158, 161n40, 162nn43–44, 164, *165*, *166*, 169, 171–72, 174, 176–77, *179*, 180, 185, 187–88, 190, *192*, 195–97, 200–201; *A Monster Stands Out*, 179, 184; *The Monster's Anxiety*, 185, *186*, 195. See also Theme of the Monster's Anxiety; *The Monster's March*, 179, 182, 189; *The Monster's Region*, 179; *The Prayer of the Amerindian Girl*, 175–76, 197. See also Theme of the Prayer; *The Precipice* 189, *192*, *193*–94; *The Sensual Dance of the Amerindian Girl*, 153, *158*, 179–80.

369

370 ~ Index

See also Theme of the Sensual Dance; Sigh motif, *156*, 161n40, *174*, *176–77*, 190, 192; Theme of the Amerindian Girl, 182, 187, *191*, 192, 195; Theme of the Happiness of the Amerindian Girl, 183; Theme of the Jealousy of the God of the Winds (Jealousy Theme), 182, *183*; Theme of the Monster's Anxiety, 185, *186*, 187, *191*, 195; Theme of the Prayer, *175–76*; Theme of the Sensual Dance, 153, *158*, *179–80*, 181, 183, 229, 345; Theme of the Treason of the God of the Winds, 184. *See also* The Treason of the God of the Winds; The Treason of the God of Winds, 167, 173, *179*; Wrath of the God of Winds, 173–74

Andrade, Mário de, 3, 5, 8, 18, 34n63, 39–44, 56, 60n7, 61n10, 61n12, 61n14, 61n17, 62n19, 143, 151, 159n15, 160n21, 160n23, 161n38, 201n4, 203n26, 231–32, 243, 265, 280n10, 285n75, 286n100, 292, 306; *Clã do Jaboti (The Tortoise Clan)*, 40; *Macunaíma*, 40–41, 44, 306, 337n25; *Pauliceia Desvairada*, 39–40, 243

Andrade, Oswald de, xii, 2–3, 5–8, 9–11, 13–14, 18–19, 22–23, 26–27, 29, 30n10, 30nn12–13, 31n16, 31nn18–20, 31n22, 31n24, 31n26, 32n30, 32nn33–34, 33n40, 34n53, 35n74, 35n82, 39–40, 43–46, 48, 55, 60, 60n5, 61n12, 61n14, 62nn19–20, 62–63nn22–24, 64n45, 67nn68–69, 80, 104, 142, 205, 216–17, 226, 239, 243–44, 246–47, 249, 251–52, 255, 258, 262–64, 266–68, 278, 280n9, 280n12, 281n21, 282n35, 284n65, 284n67, 285n86, 285–86nn88–90, 286n100, 289–93, 297, 302–314, 316–20, 322–31, 333–35, 336nn2–3, 336nn7–10, 337n21, 337n24, 338n28, 338n30, 339n42, 339n45, 339n47, 340nn55–56, 340nn62–64, 341nn66–67, 341n71, 341n77, 341nn79–80; *O Artista (The Artist)*, 45, 62n22; biography, 291–93; "Caraib Revolution," 246, 258, 278, 282n35, 298, 307–8, 311, 317, 334; Manifesto Antropófago (Anthropophagous/Cannibalist Manifesto), 23, 31n26, 44, 216, 243, 260, 278, 289–90, 293–302, 336n3; *Manifesto da Poesia Pau-Brasil* (Brazilwood Manifesto/Manifesto of Brazilwood Poetry), 5–6, 39, 226, 243, 262, 285n88, 286n89, 292, 312n13; *Pau-Brasil*, 6–7, 30n14, 31n16, 40, 44–45, 264, 266, 285–86nn89–90; *Serafim Ponte Grande*, 22, 35n82

anthropophagy/anthropophagic, xii–xiii, xivn1, 1–5, 7–11, 13–29, 30nn10–11, 31n19, 32n38, 34n57, 35n75, 35n80, 35n84, 35n87, 38–44, 46–9, 56–58, 60n5, 61n13, 63n26, 80, 89, 104, 113, 122, 139n32, 144, 196, 207–08, 211, 216, 219, 233, 241–51, 254, 256–61, 263–64, 277–80, 283n47, 284n61, 286n100 289–92, 297, 299–306, 313–19, 321–22, 324–29, 331–36, 336nn2, 336n8, 338n29, 340n59, 340nn63–64, 341n68, 341n70, 341n72; anthropophagic aesthetic, 1–36; anthropophagic assimilation, 89, 113, 139n32, 208, 249, 279; *Anthropophagic Manifesto (Cannibalist Manifesto). See* Andrade, Oswald, *Manifesto*

Antropófago: anthropophagic movement, 5, 18–26, 39–40, 43, 49, 246, 250, 290, 303n3, 306n8, 313n16, 318n21, 319n24, 325n39, 340n63. *See also* cultural cannibalism

appropriation(s), 13, 21, 26–9, 38–9, 58, 155, 219, 246, 249, 253, 266, 284n66, 315
Aranha, Graça, 4, 30n9
atonalism (atonality), 137, 229, 231
Augurs chord, 202n18, 230–31, 343

Bach, Johann Sebastian, 47, 58, 64n37, 90, 99n3
Baker, Josephine, 83n21, 252–53, *254*, 255, 276, 283nn52–53
Bakhtin, Mikhail, 249–50, 292nn32–33
Ballets Russes, xi, 50, *51–2*, 53, 57, 59, 65n50, 81, 88
Bandeira, Manuel, 8, 33n43, 103, 264, 274, 287n103, 287n107
Barroso, Ary, 164, 201n3, 283n48
Bartók, Béla, 37–38, 46–47, 49, 53, 64n33, 65n48, 66n56, 152, 166, 199, 203n28, 214, 232, 237n73, 242, 345
Beethoven, Ludwig van, ix, 29, 47, 164, *191*, 232, 344
Belle Époque, 160n24, 206, 234n3, 264
Berg, Alban, *131*, 140nn42–3, 166
Bergson, Henri, 143, 159n18, 212–13, 235n29, 236n49, 319, 326, 341n65
Berlioz, Hector, 151, 269; Symphony Fantastique, 269
Bopp, Raul, 22, 306
Brahms, Johannes, ix, *111*
Brazilian Modernism (Brazilian Modernists), 2–9, 13–14, 17, 20–21, 27, 30n10, 32n28, 32n30, 34n63, 37–40, 43, 63n27, 70, 112, 211, 242, 264, 277, 279, 302
Breton, André, 5, 9, 18, 243–46, 248, 255, 263, 271, 278, 280n5, 280n8, 281n17, 281n19, 284n55, 287nn111–12; First Manifesto of Surrealism, 5, 243–44, 255, 263, 280n5, 280n8, 281n17, 284n55; Second Manifesto of Surrealism,

244–45, 262, 280n5, 280n8, 281n17, 281n19, 284n55

Cabral, Pedro Álvares, 239–40, 293
Campos, Augusto de, 23, 26, 289, 336n2, 341n68
Campos, Haroldo de, 23, 26, 31n23, 33n44, 205, 266, 341n68
Cândido, Antônio, 13, 18–19, 30n13, 33n41, 34n58, 60n5, 62n19, 292, 336n2
Canide Ioune Sabath (*Yellow Bird*), *123*, 139n32, 162n44
carnival marches and pop songs: *Caramuru* (Antonio Nássara and Sá Roris, composers), 103–4, 137n2; *Chiquita Bacana* (João de Barro, composer), 252–53; *Dama das Camélias* (*Lady of the Camellias*, João de Barro and Alcyr Pires Vermelho, composers), 163–64; *Eva* (*Eve*, Haroldo Lobo and Milton de Oliveira, composers), 205; *História do Brasil* (*History of Brazil*, Lamartine Babo, composer), 239, 240, 340n60; *Indio Quer Apito* (*The Amerindian Wants a Whistle*, Haroldo Lobo and Milton de Oliveira, composers), 141; *Índio do Xingu* (*The Xingu's Amerindian*, Klécius Caldas and Rutinaldo, composers), 141–42; *Máscara Negra* (*Black Mask*, Zé Keti and Pereira Mato, composers), 69, 78; *Papai Adão* (*Father Adam*, Klécius Caldas and Armando Cavalcanti, composers), 205; *Pele Vermelha* (Haroldo Lobo and Milton de Oliveira, composers), 163; *Pierrot Apaixonado* (*Pierrot in Love*, Noel Rosa and Heitor dos Prazeres, composers), 78; *Todo Dia Era Dia de Indio* (*Everyday was Amerindian's*

Day, Jorge Ben Jor, composer), 142; *Uirapuru* (Murilo e Jacobina Latini, composer), 85–86; *Yes, nós temos bananas* (*Yes, we have bananas*, João de Barro, composer), 253, 283n48
Cendrars, Blaise, 45, 226, 252, 270, 285n89, 287n104, 292
Chalup, René, 264, 270–71, 287n103
Chaplin, Charlie, 228, 270–71
Chirico, Giorgio de, 143, *245*, 257, 260
choros, 45–46, 50, 55, 65nn47–8, 66n58, 100n12, 103, 122, 159n14, 201n4, 203n26, 203n32, 242, *273*, 280, 281n24, 282n40, 287n106
"Ciranda, Ciradinha" ("Circle Little Circle"), *75–76*, 80, 82n15, 83n19
Claudel, Paul, 52, 65n52
Cocteau, Jean, 16, 33n49, 44, 252
collage, 24, 38–39, 60n4, 222, 226, 243, 250, 268
Columbus, Christopher, 240, 272, 293, 309, 318, 336n11
commedia dell'arte, 69–71, 77, 80, 82n9
complementary rhythm, 107–8, *181*, 183, *189*, 192, 343
Correa, Zé Celso Martinez, 26
cubism (cubist), 1–3, 32n32, 206, 220–26, 233, 235n48, 241, 257, 261, 268, 271
Cultural Cannibalism (Cultural Anthropophagy), xii, 2, 9–15, 17–19, 23, 26, 28–29, 31n26, 45–46, 56–57, 59, 80, 242, 254, 261, 270, 289, 291–92

Dada(-ism/-ist), 1, 3, 91, 206, 241–45, 250, 260–61, 265, 277, 281n15, 281n26, 282n31, 286n93
Dalí, Salvador, 244, 250, 252, 257, 264, 282n42
Danças Características Africanas, 55
Debussy, Claude, 54, 58, 70, *127*, 128, 132, 137, 137n10, 140n50, 166, 200, 201, 203n34, 208, 214, 230; *Children's Corner Suite*, 214; *Prelude to the Afternoon of a Faun*, 54, 137n10, 200; *Syrinx*, 137n10
Deleuze, Giles, 49, 258, 284n66, 339n49
Diaghilev, Serge, 50, 52–53, 57, 65n50, 71, 88, 100nn11–12, 277
Di Cavalcanti, Emiliano, 3, 8, 39
Duchamp, Marcel, 91, *225*, 226–27, 264, 281n26

Einstein, Albert, 212–13, 220, 222, 227, *228*, 229, 235n31, 236n49, 236nn61–62
Eliade, Mircea, 199–200, 203n29, 203n31, 218, 261, 285n82, 319; "eternal return," 11, 199–200, 203n29, 218, 285n82, 261 319–20, 336, 339n49
expressionism (-ist), 1, 3, 29, *188*, 206, 241–42, 267, 269

fauvism, 1, 206, 241–42
feminism (feminist), 292, 336n8
Fibonacci, xii, *115*, 244
first Weberian archetype, *165*, 166, 201n7, 344. See also Tristan chord
folklore, xii, 15, 20, 43, 46–47, 49–50, 56–57, 63n28, 64n37, 66n56, 99n5, 208, 211–12, 255, 278, 287n106, 322
folk music, xii, 44, 47, 49–50, 56, 74, 83n19, 199, 211, 214. See also Carnival marches and pop songs; "Ciranda, Ciradinha;" "Viva o Zé Pereira"
Freud, Sigmund, 9, 23, 207, 217, 242, 244–45, 249, 257, 262, 269, 278, 291, 294, 297–98, 301–4, 308, 316, 322, 327–38, 330, 333, 335, 338n28, 339nn44–45, 341n80; *Totem and Taboo*, 217, 245, 316, 328, 333, 339nn44–45, 341n80; *The Uncanny*, 269

futurism (futurist), 2–3, 9, 13, 29, 30n4, 114, 206, 211, 224–27, 235n27, 243, 260–61, 285n78, 291
Futurist Manifesto, 2, 30n4

Gershwin, George, 117, 119
Gil, Gilberto, 24–25
golden mean (golden section), 94, 101n30, 120, 124, 139n29, 139n34, 158, 162n48, 180, 184, 192, 202n17, 202nn19–20, 202n25, 344, 345
Gomes, Carlos, 61n18, 99n4, 240, 285n80, 319; Il Guarany, 240, 319
Green-Yellow Movement. See Verdeamarelismo
Group of Five, 5, 30nn10–11, 40
Grupo da Anta, (Tapir Group) 4, 7
Guattari, Félix, 49, 258. See also Deleuze, Giles

hierophany, 199–201, 218, 258
Houston, Elsie, 247

impressionism (-ist), 1, 29, 43, 54, 113–14, 119, 125, 135–36, 138n20, 173, 175–77, 206, 208, 231, 241–42
inversion, 10, 94, 117, 156, 165, 176, 179, 185, 187–88, 201, 229, 250, 260, 273, 305, 307–8

Keyserling, Hermann von, 249, 257, 294, 298, 308, 310–11, 318, 322, 338nn30–31

Léger, Ferdinand, 264, 271
leitmotif, 89, 92, 100n19, 112, 115–16, 132, 136, 139n32, 152–53, 155–56, 158, 161n35, 161n40, 162nn43–44, 164–66, 169, 171–72, 174, 176–77, 180, 185, 187–88, 190, 192, 195–97, 200–1, 261
Lenda do Caboclo, 55

Lévi-Strauss, Claude, 23, 26, 137n13, 248, 256, 260, 278, 281–82nn28–29, 284n59, 285n73, 312–13, 316, 319, 338n37, 339n43; La Pensée Sauvage (The Savage Mind; O pensamento selvagem), 26, 256, 284n59, 312–13, 316, 338n37, 339n43; The Raw and the Cooked, 260, 281n28, 285n73
Lifar, Serge, 59, 81, 88, 100nn11–12

Magritte, Rene, 198, 231, 257
Malfatti, Anita, 2–3, 5, 30n5
Marinetti, Filippo Tomasso, 2, 31n24, 243, 285n78
Martelo, 103
Marx, Karl, 23, 302, 321, 335. See also Marxism
Marxism (Marxist), 8, 34n65, 216, 242, 244, 257, 284n58, 291, 302, 308, 310
Milhaud, Darius, 22, 52, 65n51, 66nn53–54, 70, 266, 273
Mindinha (Arminda Neves D'Almeida), 63n24
Miranda, Carmen, 25, 254, 255, 276, 283n48, 283n53
Modern Art Week of 1922, 3–5, 15, 24, 30nn9–10, 39, 44, 282n34, 330
Montaigne, Michel de, 216, 243, 249, 257, 294, 298, 308–9, 325, 335, 338n29
Myremis, 54, 88, 142, 144, 146, 153, 159nn7–8, 160n23, 160n28, 162n43

Naufrágio dos Kleônicos (Shipwreck of Kleonicos), 54, 88, 101n29, 159n7
Nazareth, Ernesto, 273; Apanhei-te Cavaquinho, 273
neoclassic (-al/-ism/-ist/), 1, 29, 82n5, 159n14, 241–42
Nietzsche, Fredrich (Nietzschean), 11, 23, 258, 284n66, 314, 319, 320, 322, 335, 339n42, 339n49, 341n81

noble savage, 17, 20, 104, 112, 138n16, 240, 310, 319, 325
Noigandres, 23, 237n70, 341n68
Nozani-ná, 122, 140n49

Oiticica, Hélio, 24–25, 61n13, 290, 336n3, 337; *Tropicália*, 24, 61n13

Péret, Benjamin, 247, 281n21
Petrushka, 71, 73, 77, 78, 81, 82n6. See also Stravinsky, Igor, *Petrushka*
Petrushka chord, 74, 230
Picasso, Pablo, 14, 67n73, 214, 215, 220, 221, 222–23, 224, 235n31, 236n49, 236nn61–62, 241, 252; *Les Demoiselles D'Avignon*, 215; *Girl with a Mandolin*, 221; *Woman in Hat and Fur Collar*, 224
Picchia, Menotti del, 4–5, 7–8, 30n11, 63n27
pictorial (-ism), 116, 134–37, 168–69, 173, 182, 197, 231, 275
Pierrot, 69, 77–78, 79, 83n21, 263, 266–67. See also Petrushka; Polichinelo
Pignatari, Décio, 23, 341n68
polarization, 91, 95, 96, 109, 110, 162n49, 166, 180–81, 186, 229, 233, 345; polarization by exclusion, 96, 162n49, 180–81, 229, 345
Polichinelo, xi, 54, 59, 69–84, 181, 214, 219, 233, 263
Polichinelo chord, 131, 140n41, 202n24, 230, 345
Polichinelo/Pulcinella, 71, 72, 73, 78, 82nn4–6, 82n9. See also Petrushka; Pierrot
Pound, Ezra, 1
primitivism (-ist), 1–2, 5–7, 13–18, 20, 22, 30n12, 31n25, 33n40, 33n45, 33n50, 50, 55, 83n21, 112, 116, 119, 136, 142, 148, 157, 176, 201, 203n32, 211–12, 214–19, 227, 233, 241–49, 251, 258–59, 261–62, 277, 285n75, 291, 304, 309, 312, 317, 320, 325, 335
Prole do Bebe Suite No. 1 (*The Baby's Family*), 54, 59, 70, 73, 80, 82n3, 82n6, 214. See also Polichinelo

quartus paeon motif, 122–23, 139n3

Ravel (Ravelian), 54, 65n48, 70
recapitulation, 107, 117–19, 126, 153, 154, 158, 180, 182, 185–89, 195, 200–1, 267, 274, 334; harmonic recapitulation, 117–18; textural recapitulation, 153; thematic recapitulation, 107, 118–19, 126; timbristic recapitulation, 186; tonal recapitulation, 153
Revista de Antropofagia, 7–8, 23, 26, 32n38, 41, 43–44, 281n21, 289–90, 297, 302, 322, 335, 336n2, 340n63
Ricardo, Cassiano, 4, 7, 8, 45
Rimbaud, Arthur, 1, 30n1, 291; *Une Saison en Enfer* (*A Season in Hell*), 291
Rimsky-Korsakov, Nikolay, 50, 57, 89, 137–38nn14–15, 161n35
Rodin, Auguste, 11
Roosevelt-Rondon Expedition, 49–50, 135, 137n10, 140n49, 237n69
Roquette-Pinto, Edgard, 49–50, 65n49, 122, 137n10, 140n48, 237n69
Rossini, Gioachino, 264, 265; *William Tell Overture*, 264, 265
Rousseau, Jacques, 243, 249, 257, 291, 294, 298, 308, 310
Rubinstein, Arthur, 65n51, 66n54, 70–71, 80–81
Rudepoema (Savage Poem), 80–81

Salgado, Plinio, 4, 7–8
Satie, Erik, 44, 54, 252
Schoenberg, Arnold, 65, 73, 78, 147, 152, 165, 166, 201n8, 229, 230–32,

234n4, 236n62, 237n73, 263, 266, 269, 277, 347, 347nn2–3; *Gurre-Lieder*, 147; *Pierrot Lunaire*, 78, 228, 266–67
Schubert, Franz, 275; *Erlkönig*, 275
semitone sliding, 106, 137n7, 138n24, 346
serialism, 229
Shipwreck of Kleonikos. See Naufárgio dos Kleônikos
Sibelius, 37, 208
sonata (form), 89, 97, 111, 182, 200, 212, 223, 233
sound band, 73, 74–75, 227, 346
sound block, 227, 261, 346
sound stain, 137n6, 192, 227, 229, 231, 346
Sousa, John Philip, 276; *Stars and Stripes Forever*, 276
Stravinsky, Igor, xi, 16, 33n50, 37–38, 44, 46–48, 50, 52–54, 57–60, 64n32, 64nn35–36, 64n39, 65n48, 65n50, 66n54, 66n56, 67n70, 67n73, 70–71, 73–75, 77–78, 80–81, 82n5, 82nn7–8, 82n10, 82n13, 83n23, 88–89, 91, 92, 94, 99n3, 100n19, 101n23, 107, 109, 112–13, 136, 137–38nn14–15, 138n18, 140n50, 144–52, 160n20, 160nn25–26, 161n33, 161n35, 188–89, 198–99, 201, 202n18, 203n28, 208, 210–12, 215, 219, 222–23, 226–27, 229–32, 234n8, 235n39, 236nn50–52, 236n57, 236n60, 236n64, 236n66, 237n73, 241–42, 262–63, 277, 343, 347n1; *Firebird*, xi, 52–53, 57, 65n50, 71, 85–101, 112, 134, 138n15, 143; *Le Sacre du Printemps (Rite of Spring)*, xi, 16, 22, 33n50, 38, 47, 52–54, 57, 81, 91–92, 101n26, 107, 109, 118, 138n18, 141–44, 145, 146–47, 148–50, 151, 160n25, 166, 167, 177, 179, 181, 188–89, 194, 198–200, 202n18, 208, 210, 215, 218, 222–23, 226–28, 230–31, 234n8, 235n 39, 236n51, 236n57, 236n60, 242, 261–62, 343, 345; *Petrushka*, xi, 52, 57, 71, 73, 74, 75, 77, 78, 80, 81, 82n10, 234n8
structural metaphor, 116, 170, 185, 196–97, 201n10, 202n12, 219, 223, 226, 231, 346
Suite Popular Brasileira, 55
Suite Sugestiva, 247, 263–74, 275, 276, 277, 279, 286n90, 287n108, 292
surrealism (surrealist), xiii, 1–5, 9, 11, 17–8, 29, 32n36, 49, 80, 83n22, 91, 99n4, 114, 124, 136, 198, 206, 209, 217, 233, 236n53, 239–87, 291, 294–95, 298–99, 308, 310, 319–20, 329, 333, 335
symmetry, 92–94, 97, 107, 114, 117, 119, 132, 139n29, 169, 179, 186, 189, 229; mirror symmetry, 92–93, 114

Tarsila do Amaral, x, 5, 8, 11, 12, 30n10, 31n19, 39, 44–5, 55, 63n24, 242, 246–47, 249, 252, 281n23, 281n25, 283n47, 286n90, 286n100, 287n104, 290, 292; *Abaporu*, x, 11, 12, 242, 246, 281nn22–23, 290
Tédio de Alvorada (Weariness at Dawn), 54, 88–89, 91, 94, 100nn14–15, 101n29, 104, 118, 123, 137n10, 140n46, 142, 144, 146, 159n7, 159n14, 160n20, 160n24, 161n28
texture, 70, 73, 92, 109, 113–14, 120, 129, 131, 134, 136–37, 139n37, 152–53, 169–70, 173–76, 178, 182–87, 189–93, 197–99, 209, 212, 223, 226–27, 233, 261–62, 344–46; texture, background, 173, 175, 185–86, 187, 189–190, 192, 223, 344; texture, foreground, 173, 185–86, 191, 223, 344

tone painting, 168, 174, 196–97, 274, 374
tone poem, 54, 86, 196–97
transculturation, 26–9, 35n80, 38
Tristan chord, 105, *106*, 117, 126, 132, *134*, 137n7, 138n24, 140n41, 165–66, 229–30, 344, 347, 347n2
tritone, 74–75, 92, 94–97, 105–6, 109, *110*, 112, 118, *121*, *125*, 127, 130, 152, 166, 172–74, *178*, *182*, 192, 344
Tropicália (Tropicalism/tropicalist), 23–6, 31n27, 33n42, 35n73, 61nn13, 254, 290
Tupi (Tupi-Guarani/Tupiniquim/Tupinambá), 5–8, 11, 13, 25, 31n28, 32n37, 34n69, 39, 85–86, 103, 141, 163, 240, 258–59, 281n22, 293, 297, 303, 307–9, 315, 320, 322, 326, 330–31, 334, 338n29, 339n40

Uirapuru, xi, 54–5, 59, 81, 85, 86, 87–89, *90*, 91, *92–97*, 98–101, 103–4, *105–8*, 109, *110–11*, 112, *113–15*, 116, *117–28*, 129, *130–34*, 135–40, 142–44, 146, 150, 152, 159n14, 160n20, 160n24, 161n28, 161n36, 163, 166, 196, 201, 202n11, 202n19, 202n23, 208–09, 211, 217, 219, 222, 227, 230–31, 233, 234n6, 240, 247–48, 252, 261–62, 270, 279, 281n26, 285n76, 285n83, 346; Celebration Theme, *121*, *123*, 124; Handsome Indian Theme, 121, *122–23*, 124, *134*, 136; Theme of the Indian Huntress, 95, *117*, *120*, *134*, 136; Theme of the Jungle, 89, *94–7*, 106, 109, 112, 117–19, *120*, 126, 134–35, 139n28, 139n38; Theme of the Ugly Indian, 95, *110*, 112, 129, *130*, *134*, 135; Theme of the Uirapuru, 89, *90*,
91, *92–3*, 94, 97, 101n28, *106*, 107, *108*, 109, 112, *113–15*, 116, 118, *119*, 123, 126, 130, *134*, 135, 202n11

vagrant chords (vagrant harmonies), 126, *134*, 165–66, 233, 347, 347n3
Varèse, Edgard, 65n48, 147, 149, *150*, *157*, 210, 247, 252
Vargas, Getúlio, xiii, 22, 163, 232, 242, 280, 283n48
Veloso, Caetano, 25–26, 35n71, 61n14
Verdeamarelismo (The Green-Yellow Movement), 4–5, 7–9, 30n11, 45. See also Grupo da Anta (the Tapir Group)
Villa-Lobos, Lucília (nee Guimarães), 53, 59, 66n53
Villegaignon, Nicolas Durand de, 309, 325, 338n29
violinophone, x, 128, *129–30*, 135–36, 144, 147, 149–50, 153, 160n21, 161n31, 175, 177–78, *186*
"Viva o Zé Pereira" ("Long Live Zé Pereira"), 76, 77, 83n19. See also Zé Pereira

Wagner, Richard (Wagnerian), 6, 54, 58, 89, 105, *106*, 120, 127–28, 132, *133*, 136–37, 137n7, 138n26, 144, 147, 149, 161n35, 165–66, 201, 208, 230, 262, 285n85, 347, 347n2; Tristan and Isolde, 106, 120, 132, *133*, 138n26, 285n85, 347
Weariness at Dawn. See Tédio de Alvorada

Xingu, 141–42, 158n2

Zé Pereira, 76, 80, 83n17. See also "Viva o Zé Pereira"

About the Author

Ricardo Averbach is director of orchestral studies at Miami University and past president of the College Orchestra Directors Association. Originally from Brazil, after graduating in engineering at the Universidade de São Paulo, he received his degree in conducting at the National Academy of Music of Bulgaria and his doctoral degree at the University of Michigan. Averbach conducts regularly in South and North America, Europe and Asia, having performed as guest conductor in over fifteen countries. His discography includes several world premiere recordings. As a scholar, he has published a number of articles in peer-reviewed publications and the critical edition of *Villa-Lobos's The Insects Martyrdom* with the Theodore Presser Company. He lives with his family in Oxford, Ohio.

www.ingramcontent.com/pod-product-compliance
Lightning Source LLC
Chambersburg PA
CBHW051250300426
44114CB00011B/970